KU-530-163

Starting at Home

CARING AND SOCIAL POLICY

Nel Noddings

University of California Press   Berkeley   Los Angeles   London

ID No: 10000389

Dewey No: 361.610973 (Res. Locen)

Date Acq:

University of California Press
Berkeley and Los Angeles, California

University of California Press, Ltd.
London, England

© 2002 by The Regents of the University of California

The excerpt from Marianne Moore's "Silence," copyright © 1935 by
Marianne Moore, copyright renewed © 1963 by Marianne Moore and
T. S. Eliot, is reprinted with the permission of Scribner, a division
of Simon & Schuster, Inc.

Library of Congress Cataloging-in-Publication Data

Noddings, Nel.
   Starting at home: caring and social policy / Nel Noddings.
     p.   cm.
   Includes bibliographical references and index.
   ISBN 0-520-22556-2 (alk. paper).—ISBN 0-520-23026-4 (pbk. :
alk. paper)
   1. Altruism. 2. Caring. 3. Home—Social
aspects. 4. Moral education. 5. Social policy—Moral and
ethical aspects. 6. United States—Social policy—Moral and
ethical aspects. I. Title.

HM1146.N64 2002
171'.8—dc21   2001027682

Manufactured in the United States of America
10 09 08 07 06 05 04 03
10 9 8 7 6 5 4 3 2 1

The paper used in this publication is both acid-free and totally
chlorine-free (TCF). It meets the minimum requirements of ANSI/
NISO Z39.48-1992 (R 1997) (*Permanence of Paper*).

EDHCC

10000339

Restricted

Loan

07
10
5

This book is due for return on or before the last date shown below.

9/10/07.

2/4

2/10/08

16.

23/10/08

CONTENTS

ACKNOWLEDGMENTS

I wish it were possible to thank all of those who have contributed over many years to the form and content of this book—all the writers, teach ers, students, and colleagues who have influenced my thinking. Although I can't name everyone, thank you.

Special thanks go to Larry Blum, who read large portions of the manuscripts and gave valuable advice, Eva Feder Kittay for sound advice on several examples, Virginia Held for helpful comments on rights and needs, Michael Slote for inspiring discussions on care as virtue versus care as relation, the New York Society for Women in Philosophy for responses to an early version of the chapter on needs, the Philosophy of Education Society for sponsoring the exchange between Slote and me, an anonymous reviewer who responded with "admiration and outrage" to a draft of several chapters, Paul Smeyers for his recognition of care's wider applications, and to my colleague Steve Thornton for all the thoughtful discussions during long walks on the boardwalk.

I also owe hearty thanks to Gina Lee for so much help with the word processing and to Rocky Schwarz for directing that operation so ably.

Of course, both love and thanks go to my husband, Jim, and our children and grandchildren for respecting my work time and workplace (with all its clutter).

It has been delightful, too, to work again with Naomi Schneider and the University of California Press. I am grateful for your trust and support.

INTRODUCTION: STARTING AT HOME

In the last two decades, much has been written about caring as an approach to moral life and about care theory as a contribution to ethics.[1] Feminist writers (both women and men) have been strong advocates of caring, tracing its central ideas to women's relational experience and arguing that women and men alike might enjoy richer lives if they shared the tasks and the joys of caring.

The approach I take here reverses a long philosophical tradition. The custom, since Plato, has been to describe an ideal or best state and then to discuss the role of homes and families as supporters of that state. What might we learn if, instead, we start with a description of best homes and then move outward to the larger society? The question is intriguing in itself, but answering it should effectively address an objection that has sometimes been raised against care theory—namely, that it is a fine "domestic" theory but has little to contribute to policy making at the societal level.

Caring, as a moral orientation, is neither domain nor gender specific, but taking this position does not compel us to deny that the *origins* of care may be domain specific—that they lie in the small group setting that we have come to call "home" and, probably, in parental love. If this is true—if, that is, our sense of caring and being cared for starts at home—then it is reasonable to examine this beginning seriously, to study it philosophically.[2] We can then ask about the social policy implications of care theory and the development of care in individual lives. I believe that school as well as home should be central in any adequate discussion of moral life and social policy. Starting at home does not suggest that we must remain there. Theories, like children, can grow up and move into the public world.

I begin the book by describing care at the theoretical level. The first three chapters provide a phenomenological analysis of care and suggest how care theory might prevent certain harms and meet some particular needs that have proved difficult to address from other theoretical perspectives. Although both men and women are often guided by an ethic of care, I focus on the connection between care and women's experience. I argue that "natural" caring—a form of caring that does not require an ethical effort to motivate it (although it may require considerable physical and mental effort in responding to needs)—is developmentally prior to and preferable to "ethical" caring. Ethical caring, when it must be summoned, is properly aimed at establishing or restoring natural caring. Because at least two parties are involved in every caring encounter and both contribute actively to the relation, the most useful theoretical description remains open to situational and personal variations. Yet the resulting semitheory can be useful in guiding social policy.

One might reasonably ask why another social or political theory is needed, so the argument turns next to a critique of important current theories. These theories, especially liberalism, contain serious defects, and these defects are most obvious at the level of social policy making. Liberalism, communitarianism, critical theory, and variants of these three philosophies have contributed generously to social thought, and I make no attempt to criticize them in their totality. My intent is to show exactly what weaknesses need to be corrected and to identify the specific defects that care theory might profitably address.

An important point in this discussion is the tension between freedom and equality that has characterized liberal thought in the twentieth century. The work of Isaiah Berlin is particularly useful, especially his wise advice that we face up to the unpleasant fact that not all highly valued human goods can be realized at once in a given community.[3] Berlin advised that when we must sacrifice a bit of one value to achieve another, we should, at the least, honestly admit what we have done. I suggest that, despite classical liberalism's fears of paternalism, a caring society must sometimes intervene in the lives of adults to prevent them from harming themselves.

With the exception of John Dewey and, more recently, Amy Gutmann, liberal theorists have had surprisingly little to say about educa-

tion. In contemporary U.S. society voters who consider themselves liberals are typically interested in schools and the problems of schooling.
Liberal philosophers, however, at least in their theorizing, are often si-
lent on issues of schooling, and when they do speak their comments are
somewhat naïve—as though issues of child rearing and education are
somehow only peripherally related to social policy.[4] I think, like Dewey,
that education is not just a category of social policy; rather, it must be
at the very heart of an adequate social theory.

The debate between justice and care must also be addressed. This
debate is closely related to questions on "caring-about" (caring about
people who are at a distance from us in terms of social status, culture,
physical distance, or time—that is, the future).[5] Caring-about supplies
an important motive for justice and generates much of its content. It is
necessary, then, to discuss the relation between caring-about and "caring-for" (direct, face-to-face caring). When we cannot care directly for
others but wish that we could—when, that is, we sincerely care about
the well-being of others we rely on principles of justice that approximate (or enable others to undertake) the actions we would perform if
we could be bodily present. After establishing that relation and the close
connection between caring-about and justice, I describe the interplay of
care and justice in a way that should inform social policy.

The outcome of the analysis of current theories will be recognition
that we need a description of the self that starts with neither a mature,
rational choice maker nor an abstractly described member of specific
groups. We need, instead, a thoroughly relational description. A careful
examination of the relational self can reveal the importance of encounter
in developing selves. Children of nomads in the Sahara have encounters
that are very different from those experienced by children in the suburban United States, but children in poverty-ridden parts of New York
or Chicago have encounters that are different from those experienced
by children in Scarsdale and Winnetka. It will hardly do to describe these
very different selves as modern selves, postmodern selves, western selves,
cosmopolitan selves, or any collective term that might be applied to
them. As encounters are added to the relation we call a "self," questions
arise about the nature of encounters and who controls them. How much
control should a society exert over the encounters of its citizens? On
another, more existential, level, how much control does the growing self
have over its own encounters, particularly its reflective encounters—its
encounters with the objects of thought, memories, affective responses,
and visions of its past and future?

. . .

The first five chapters of the book provide background material for the constructive efforts of part II. I lay out in part I a picture of the moral orientation — caring — that will guide this work, and I discuss why it is needed and what it may accomplish. In part II, I analyze how good people develop in the best homes.

I am aware that the expressions "good people" and "the best homes" will raise alarms in many readers. I will not offer one, final definition of what it means to be a good person, nor will I paint a picture of one ideal home, but I will select one ideal to which I will refer repeatedly as "best." In a sort of internal dialogue I will raise questions about the visions of good people, which vary, and the workings of ideal homes. I will ask, for example, whether there is anything that all people learn in ideal homes, and I will respond that, among other things, there is at least one guide to moral practice: never inflict unnecessary pain. The variability in using this guide centers on interpretation of the word *unnecessary*. We will see, also, that there is a universal characteristic of ideal homes. In every ideal home is someone who does the work of attentive love; he or she responds to needs with a dependable "I am here."

In some cases it will be clear that, for some purposes, I favor one ideal over others. For example, when I discuss the sources of moral justification offered in ideal homes, I will favor one that subjects others to logical criticism but allows them to stand without condemnation. Its superiority consists in exactly this, that it encourages us to care for one another in a way that liberals would describe in terms of tolerance or respect. Care theory, however, recognizes that even when we cannot always give respect, we can continue to care. In some cases I will give several reasons for preferring one ideal formulation to another and leave it to readers to decide on the strength of the arguments. In other cases I will argue that some practices are instrumentally more sound than are others in a liberal-democratic society.

When theorizing about social policy begins from the perspective of home, we explore what kind of encounters shape the growing self and enhance the continuing growth of mature selves. The infant organism encounters bodies, both animate and inanimate. It begins to locate its incipient self in a place and, as its own self develops, it becomes aware of encountering other selves. In all three of these large arenas of encounter the emerging self acquires a sense of what it means to be a good person.

I ask how far we can extend the attitude of caring that is characteristic of the best homes into the larger social domain. The best homes, I argue, rarely use coercion, but when they do, the purpose may be to prevent members from doing harm to themselves, not merely to prevent harm to others. Similarly, the best homes seldom invoke the concept of negative desert (one who does something bad deserves something bad in return).

The products of ideal homes are persons whose traits and behaviors are captured as principles and exemplars in moral philosophies, although it may be reasonable to interpret moral principles as more nearly descriptive than prescriptive. Philosophers as different as Dewey and Aristotle have pointed out that a moral prescription means little to one who has not already lived it or experienced it in close connection with other selves. Recognition of this fact does not entail the assumption that people bear no responsibility for their acts (although we must ask *how* much they do bear), nor does it suggest that any real home can so faithfully meet the criteria of ideal homes that good persons are thereby guaranteed. But we can, perhaps, do better than we have done so far.

One of the most important guidelines that will emerge from part II is that no policy or rule should be established that makes it impossible for agents to respond positively to those over whom they have some charge or control. I am not saying that we must always and everywhere respond positively to expressed needs, although I will suggest that we should try to come as close as we can given conditions, resources, merits, and the needs of others. The import of the guideline is that rules and policies should not make it *impossible* for responsible agents to vary their responses in ways that might benefit their charges.

How far can we apply these ideas in social policy? Both public and private domains figure in the development of an adequate social theory. It is generally recognized that "justice-thinking" arises in the public domain and develops most fully in the highly educated. The caring orientation arises at home and seems to flourish in those who (even when well educated) remain responsible for the direct care of others. A social or political theory that begins at home has different components than does one that starts with the larger community or state. The middle part of this book attempts to identify such components.

When we start our theorizing with images of fully functioning, rational adults in public life, it is easy to suppose that freedom and equality are paramount goods. They are important, to be sure, but when we start at home we see that something like "fulfillment" is even more important. Good parents want their children to achieve some form of success or fulfillment as whole human beings. As we develop our thinking from the inside out (so to speak), questions will arise about the larger community's role in contributing to this fulfillment. It is a tricky business to avoid the abuses associated with "positive" views of freedom (in which one is free to become what he or she *should* become). I argue that the fear of paternalism and other specters of the positive view often leave us paralyzed.

If what is learned at home is consonant with care theory as I outline it, we may then ask whether the attitudes and responses characteristic in the best homes can somehow be extended into public policy making. This is the focus of part III. Care cannot act alone. Indeed, in a society such as ours it cannot act alone even at home, since the manifestations of care in the home are, at least, properly influenced by the progress of justice in the larger society. Notice, however, that from the perspective taken here, justice itself is dependent on caring-about, and caring-about is in turn dependent on caring-for. By using the idea of an expanded moral domain to guide our thinking, it should be possible to discuss problems of social policy in some depth.

Where does this take us? As we move into part III, where we apply what has been learned at home to several current social problems, I criticize social policies that make it impossible for agents to respond positively. In the chapter on homes and homelessness I argue that the caring professions should be guided by flexible policies that will allow practitioners to respond adequately to the needs of very different clients. Similarly, in the chapter on deviance I argue that rigidly prescribed punitive approaches should yield to methods that make greater use of positive incentives. I also suggest that any corrective practice that does more harm than the behavior it is aimed at correcting should be abandoned. No good home would continue to employ methods that increase suffering and antisocial behavior in the hope that they would—against all the available evidence—force a prescribed, "better," pattern of behavior. In the wider social domain that suggests an end to the disastrous war on drugs.

In the last chapter I use the widely recognized fact that the best homes are centers of education to recommend that the school curriculum should include serious preparation for home life as well as professional and civic life. This aspect of education has never been fully developed. Where education for home life has appeared at all in serious form, it has been reserved for women, and its prescription as a form of education for women was designed as much to exclude them from the standard curriculum as to prepare them for their roles as wives and mothers. Moreover, not all women have received even this form of education. Today both women and men need to be better informed and more adequately prepared to establish and maintain a home. The education that starts at home is one that affects the lives of children for years to come, and there may be nothing more powerful that a society can do to advance the well-being of its people (both male and female) than to strengthen their commitment and competence as homemakers.

Finally, I should say something about the dual reasons for the title, "Starting at Home." The words point to my intention to start social theorizing at home, with the infant and its first encounters. But I also want to emphasize the central importance of improving life in everyday homes and the possible role social policy might play in this improvement. Hence, the last chapter is offered as a set of social policy recommendations on educating for home life.

Part One

CARE THEORY

CHAPTER 1

Caring

Most people agree that the world would be a better place if we all cared more for one another, but despite that initial agreement we find it hard to say exactly what we mean by *caring*. The objective of this chapter is to lay out a basic phenomenological analysis of caring—an investigation of how caring is experienced—that will provide a starting point for elaboration and critique and, eventually, a description that can guide individual moral life and social policy. Throughout the discussion we will be guided by two basic questions: How can we avoid harming ourselves and one another? How can we care better for one another?

First I must defend the contention that care is basic in human life and not something to be regarded as an added attraction—that indeed all people want to be cared for. Of course, a few people will insist that they do not want care. They may respond gruffly to recommendations on caring with comments such as "I don't want care; I want respect!" or "I don't want anyone caring for me; I want to be left alone. Just don't bother me." Comments like these reveal an understanding of *caring* as something intrusive, something fussy, something for children and dependents. One may respond to Mr. Gruff, however, by pointing out that he does indeed want a certain kind of response from others, and those others who meet this need sensitively may well be said to care for him. The fact that people describe caring very differently is a good reason for not starting its analysis by listing its particular manifestations. Any specific example may be rejected by as many as those who accept it.

Even a fairly abstract description of what we aim at in caring may induce the reaction "not for me." For example, Milton Mayeroff begins his discussion of caring by writing, "To care for another person, in the most significant sense, is to help him grow and actualize himself."[1] This definition is very appealing to teachers, counselors, therapists, and parents, and it will be useful when particular situations are discussed. But notice that it begins with a focus on the carer, the one who is doing the caring. Here caring is defined in terms of someone, the carer, who will help another grow. We might want to pause and ask: is this what the cared-for wants or needs at this moment? Immediately we see two problems. The first involves *where* a description of caring should begin. Should we begin with the carer as moral agent, or with the cared-for? Or should we perhaps begin, as the pragmatists might, with the situation?

The second question—is caring a virtue, a demonstration of moral excellence?—is closely bound up in the first. Indeed, answering it may force an answer to the first. If caring is a virtue, we are drawn to the start suggested by Mayeroff's description. If, however, we regard caring as a desirable attribute of relations, then we may prefer to start with the cared-for, his or her needs, and how the carer responds to those needs. Some sense of personal identity is required to speak of caring as a virtue. Who is this person to whom the virtue is attributed? What sort of creature is a "person"? I do not reject entirely the notion of caring as virtue, but I want to defer these questions for a bit.

Let's begin instead with relation in the form of encounter. Two people meet, and one or both have specific needs. Perhaps it is just a friendly encounter—no obvious needs, no requests to be met. Even in this situation there are hidden needs, and the conversants may become aware of them if a comment is troublesome. For example, I may become aware of my own need for privacy, or recognition, or respect, or polite language if my partner seems pushy, ignorant of my work, or rude in her choice of words. In the sense that we want certain of our needs to be met, we all want to be cared for.

Some years ago, in discussion with an anthropologist on my campus, I advanced the idea that caring might be an empirical universal—that is, that it could be found everywhere. The anthropologist had his doubts about this but countered with a possibility that now seems right to me. What appears everywhere, he said, is the desire to be cared for. As I noted above, this desire may take different forms, and the desire itself may be so deeply submerged in layers of success and autonomy that a person will be unaware of it and so deny it. Despite this, humans clearly never outgrow the need for care. The need merely takes on new forms.

A Phenomenology of Care

In developing a phenomenology of care, I do not undertake a formal phenomenological analysis as prescribed by Edmund Husserl. I accept the careful criticisms that have been directed at that enterprise by Jean-Paul Sartre and Jacques Derrida, among others.[2] There is no way to rid ourselves of every vestige of the empirical to get at a transcendental or pure consciousness; further, such a goal may not even be desirable. Even if it were possible, a formal analysis of the Husserlian kind would not further my project. I am interested not in ultimate structures of consciousness; I seek a broad, nearly universal description of "what we are like" when we engage in caring encounters. I am interested in what characterizes consciousness in such relations, but I do not claim to have found an essence or attempt to describe an ultimate structure; nor do I depend on a sense of consciousness as supremely constitutive of reality. Rather, the attributes or characteristics I discuss are temporal, elusive, subject to distraction, and partly constituted by the behavior of the partners in caring.

For purposes of managing the discussion, I describe an encounter in which one party is the carer and the other is the cared-for. Positions may subsequently change, but for now I will call the carer *A* and the cared-for *B*. What characterizes A's consciousness as she responds to B? To achieve a sense of what goes on between A and B we need to look at many situations in which people have "found themselves caring."[3] Readers are invited to engage in this process also. Perhaps the first thing we discover about ourselves as carers in caring encounters is that we are receptive; we are attentive in a special way.

Some people describe themselves as *empathic* when they care, but I want to be careful with that word. Although it is derived from the Greek word for affection, passion, or feeling, it is peculiarly western and masculine in its English usage. It is said to mean "the projection of one's own personality into the personality of another in order to understand him better; intellectual identification of oneself with another."[4] The attentiveness of caring is more receptive than projective, and it is not primarily intellectual, although it has an intellectual dimension. The notion of empathy as projection and as intellectual is part of the framework that I want to reverse. Caring is not controlled entirely by the carer—it is a mode of shared control.

A second definition of *empathy* is directed at objects, but it reveals an attitude toward people as well: "the projection of one's own personality into an object, with the attribution to the object of one's own emotions, responses, etc.; also called the *pathetic fallacy*."[5] When a person projects himself or herself into another person, as one does with objects in the pathetic fallacy, and attributes his or her own feelings to the other, the process is again one of control, of universalization. On one level we might assess such moves as generous; they attribute to others the same pains, feelings, and passions that we undergo. Indeed, much of the common western folk-ethic is built on such an idea: do unto others as you would have them do unto you. In the present analysis, however, I will reject this approach. In caring encounters I receive the other person and feel what he or she is feeling even if I am quite sure intellectually that I would not myself feel that way in the given situation. It may be that *empathy,* which is a fairly new word, was introduced by thinkers who found *sympathy* too soft and wanted a cognitively more respectable word. But *sympathy*—"feeling with"—more nearly captures the affective state of attention in caring. Even the definition in physics seems more useful: "a relation of harmony between bodies of such a nature that vibrations in one cause sympathetic vibrations in the other."[6] In the analysis of caring, however, we must note that directionality is from cared-for to carer. The cared-for need not feel what the carer feels, although in mutual relations the flow may, of course, go both ways. The important point here is that in some special way the cared-for is primary; he or she is the site of initial "vibrations."[7]

Moral philosophers have not said much about attention (or "engrossment," as I have called it), and only rarely has the receptive aspect of attention been emphasized. Simone Weil is an outstanding exception. She starts her discussion this way: "In the first legend of the Grail, it is said that the Grail . . . belongs to the first comer who asks the guardian of the vessel, a king three-quarters paralyzed by the most painful wound, 'What are you going through?'" This question acts as a foundation for moral life. It signals the openness of the questioner. Weil continues. "The love of our neighbor in all its fullness simply means being able to say to him: What are you going through? It is a recognition that the sufferer exists, not only as a unit in a collection, or a specimen from the social category labeled 'unfortunate,' but as a man, exactly like us."[8]

Here, in a typical existentialist move, Weil refuses to subsume the individual in the system. She says that we must not start with a collection and "specimens"; rather, we must meet the individual. She also makes a move that I will challenge later (in discussion of a relational self): she regards the sufferer "as a man, exactly like us." We may want to avoid this universalization. We may want to regard the other person as unavoidably different—not ever "exactly like us." For the present, however, we are concerned with her account of attention. She writes: "This way of looking is first of all attentive. The soul empties itself of all its own contents in order to receive the being it is looking at, just as he is, in all his truth. Only he who is capable of attention can do this."[9]

Reception, not projection, marks the attention described by Weil. The reception is not totally passive. A soul (or self) empties itself, asks a question, or signals a readiness to receive, but the state that develops is thoroughly relational. When I attend in this way I become, in an important sense, a duality. I see through two pairs of eyes, hear with two sets of ears, feel the pain of the other self in addition to my own. My initial self is vulnerable, and it will be changed by this encounter. Knowing this, I may resist giving my attention. Indeed, probably no real encounter could represent a state of "pure attention." It is always a fragile condition subject to distraction or rejection. (It is important to note that what I receive from the other person does not always arouse a harmonious vibration of sympathy. After an initial stab of pain or an involuntary laugh, I may feel revulsion. It may not be easy or even possible to make this encounter into one of caring. I will return to this large problem.)

We can learn more about the attention characteristic of caring by following Weil's discussion a bit further. Her analysis of attention is carried out in the context of the "right use of school studies" in developing a love of God and fellow human beings. Weil believed that the study of geometry, for example, could increase students' capacity for attention and that an increased capacity for attention, directed appropriately, would increase their power of prayer. In turn, a greater connection to God should produce a stronger link to human beings. Through their enhanced attention to God, students should be better able to ask another person, "What are you going through?"

I think Weil was wrong on this, and wrong in two ways. First, there is no convincing evidence that people capable of attention to, say, mathematics are more attentive to God than they would have been without that capacity. Second, attention to God only sometimes produces the effect Weil hoped for. Some people do become saintlike in their relations with other human beings, but others turn inward and concentrate entirely on the connection to God; still others do horrible things to their sister-men in the name of God. The sort of transfer Weil expected is not likely to occur. Thus the strength of Weil's argument really rests on "the right use" of school studies, and it is conceivable that a use can be found that might enhance the moral sense of students. I doubt, however, that the desired effect can be obtained by increasing the capacity for attention through the study of geometry. If people are to learn how to attend to living others, they must have appropriate opportunities and guidance in attending directly to living others.

The claim here is not that the *form* of attention necessarily differs with its object. Creative artists, scientists, and mathematicians have reported a receptivity very like the one I attribute to the consciousness of carers. The object "seizes" them, "speaks" to them, "reveals itself" to them. The structure of consciousness may be the same, but just as the capacity for such attention in mathematics does not transfer to a like capacity in, say, sculpture, it does not transfer to other consciousnesses either. Indeed, a well-developed capacity for attention in an intellectual field may even set up resistance to receiving the another human. Having the capacity for receptivity in any field makes one at least implicitly aware of its power, of what may follow. Too often people have chosen to accept William Butler Yeats's beautifully expressed resignation: "The intellect of man is forced to choose / Perfection of the life, or of the work." We will want to question this also.

The language used by Weil, on first sight, seems compatible with care theory as I will develop it here, but there is an even deeper difficulty that separates Weil's view from mine. In chapter 6, as the discussion of home and early life develops, we will see that despite her often concrete language Weil does not concentrate on the well-being and response of individual human beings for their own sake but, rather, on something "impersonal" in each. I will reject this move to religious abstraction, but I defer the argument until later.

The attention characteristic of caring has been described by Gabriel Marcel as "disposability (*disponibilité*), the readiness to bestow and spend oneself and make oneself available, and its contrary, indisposability."[10] One who is indisposable does not attend, is not "there" even when physically present. As Marcel puts it, "When I am with someone who is indisposable, I am conscious of being with someone for whom I do not exist; I am thrown back on myself."[11] Martin Buber has also described the receptivity characteristic of an encounter. In an I-Thou encounter the other person is neither an object of study nor data to be assimilated to one's active cognitive structures: "He is no longer He or She, limited by other Hes and Shes, a dot in the world grid of space and time, nor a condition that can be experienced and described, a loose bundle of named qualities. Neighborless and seamless, he is Thou and fills the firmament."[12]

The cared-for, so encountered, does not of course "fill the firmament" forever. The moment of nearly pure relation passes; one must think what to do. Buber acknowledges this. We cannot live entirely in the I-Thou mode, but the tragedy is, Buber warns, that we *can* live entirely in the I-It world; we can fail completely at the tasks of attention and receptivity. Indeed, Buber described such an incident in his own life. A young man came to him ostensibly to discuss ordinary matters, and Buber responded to him at that level. Somewhat preoccupied, Buber failed to detect that the young man was contemplating suicide and had come to him not for chitchat or everyday information but for help in making a decision. It might not have been possible for Buber to prevent the suicide that occurred, but he blamed himself for a failure of attention.[13] All of us experience such failures of attention, usually in less consequential matters, but some people seem never to develop the capacity for attention. Self-absorbed—sometimes brilliant, sometimes dull—such people go through life "indisposable."

Attention—receptive attention—is an essential characteristic of the caring encounter. The carer, A, receives what-is-there in B. But clearly more than attention is required. A must respond in some way. If B is trying to accomplish something he may want A's help, or perhaps—as is often the case with children—B is simply calling out, "Watch me, watch me!" Thus, in addition to the attention that characterizes A's consciousness in caring, there is also a feature we might call *motivational displacement*. A's motive energy begins to flow toward B and his projects. Consider a typical example. Ms. A, a math teacher, stands beside student B as he struggles to solve an equation. Ms. A can almost feel the pencil in her own hand. She anticipates what B will write, and she pushes mentally toward the next step, making marks and erasures mentally. Her moves are directed by his. She may intervene occasionally but only to keep his plan alive, not to substitute her own. She introduces her own plan of attack only if his own plan fails entirely and he asks, "What should I do?"

Motivational displacement follows on the heels of attention if A is sympathetic to B's plight. If B is in pain, A will want to relieve that pain.

If B needs to talk, A will listen. If B is perplexed, A will offer what she can to bring clarity to B's thinking. Many things can block the flow of motivational displacement. A may receive accurately what B is thinking and feeling and be so repelled by it that helping in his "project" is unthinkable. The caring encounter is not necessarily dead when this happens, but something akin to a Kantian effort is required to transform the encounter into one that will permit the continuation of attention. Perhaps a new project will then arise, and A's motive energy will again flow freely. Occasionally, it will be necessary to obstruct B's plans—to dissuade him if possible and, if not, to actively oppose him. Even in such cases, when the moment of danger is past, A will make an effort to restore a caring relation if B wants or needs it. The newly constructed relation may, of course, be severely constrained by the foregoing conflict.

Sometimes something in A, not in B's project or attitude, resists motivational displacement. Like Buber, A may be preoccupied and fail at attention. Even if attention occurs, A may resist the transition to motivational displacement. She may think, "Uh-oh. I can see where this is leading. I don't have time for this" (or "I can't handle this," or "Why me?" or "Not again!"). We are aware when this happens that the encounter is no longer a fully caring encounter. It may be restored by continued conversation and compromise, and many caring encounters are satisfied by something less than what the cared-for initially had in mind. It is not necessary, possible, or ethically desirable for A to say yes to every request B makes.

In a caring encounter A's consciousness is characterized by attention and motivational displacement, but this characterization tells us nothing about what A will actually do or should do. The implication that some sort of positive response is required by the internal state itself is clear. Before discussing this in detail we need to fill out the phenomenological picture by considering B's consciousness.

B is a party in the caring relation, and as Buber insisted, "relation is reciprocity."[14] By this Buber did not mean that B must take his or her turn as carer. In many mature relations we will want to insist on such mutuality, but there are many situations where mutuality is not possible: between parent and young child, between teacher and student, between physician and patient. All of these are necessarily asymmetric, and yet there is reciprocity. The cared-for contributes something essential.

Besides being the site of initial "vibrations," the cared-for responds in a way that shows that A's efforts at caring have been received. B's consciousness is characterized by the recognition or realization of care, and "I am cared for" would be the appropriate verbalization of B's state of consciousness. Again, B's state of consciousness doesn't tell us exactly what B will do or should do. It merely suggests some form of response that will be detectable by A. Reception of A's caring by B completes the relation. It allows us to say that the relation or encounter is one of caring.

In summary, we have the following situation: (A, B) is a caring relation (or encounter) if and only if

   i. A cares for B—that is, A's consciousness is characterized by attention and motivational displacement—and

  ii. A performs some act in accordance with i), and

 iii. B recognizes that A cares for B.

If the encounter is part of a continuing relationship or series of encounters, B's responses become part of what A receives in the next episode. These responses are essential both to the completion of a particular episode and to the health of future encounters. They are the means by which A monitors her efforts, and they provide the intrinsic reward of caring. Without such responses, parents, teachers, counselors, and doctors suffer disillusionment, fatigue, and eventually burnout.

Construing caring as an attribute of a relation draws our attention to both parties in a situation. The virtue sense of caring is still significant. We do, after all, say such things as, "He is a caring person," "They are a caring family," "Nurses are more caring than doctors." When we understand the relational sense, however, the virtue sense takes on new meaning. Indeed, the virtue seems to be embedded in (i) of our definition. We might say that a caring person is one who fairly regularly establishes caring relations and, when appropriate, maintains them over time. This is very different from starting with a carer's intention ("I care") and assessing how faithfully the carer carries out the intention according to his or her own ideal view. In a relational view we have to ask about the effects on the cared-for, and the carer's actions are mediated not only by the initial needs of the cared-for but also by the observable effects of whatever the carer does. Monitoring effects becomes especially important as episodes of care are strung together over time.

The Goal of Care, and Caring over Time

Earlier I put off discussion of the object or goal of care so that a common description of caring at the level of consciousness could be developed.

I mentioned Mayeroff's definition of what it means to care for another person: "to help him grow and actualize himself." We have seen that a brief caring encounter need not involve such a grand objective. In long-term relationships, however (even in the one-year relationship between teacher and student), growth is often the object of caring. From whose perspective should we define growth? Can growth be a stable and/or unitary goal?

In describing maternal thinking (a mode of thinking and feeling that certainly involves caring), Sara Ruddick writes of three great maternal interests: preserving the life of the child, promoting his or her growth, and shaping an acceptable child.[15] These interests arise, Ruddick says, from the demands made by the child itself. At birth the child is completely helpless except for its summoning cry and response at nursing. Someone must preserve its life. As it grows physically, it is engaged more and more in attempts to master its environment; this effort, guided wisely, manifests growth. Further, the child continually seeks a circle of acceptance, and wise parents try to shape the child for acceptability in the circles they regard as healthy. At any given time, in any episode, caring may be directed at one or a combination of these interests.

The objective of care shifts with the situation and also with the recipient. Two students in the same class are, roughly, in the same situation, but they may need very different forms of care from their teacher. This is a point that can hardly be overemphasized. Every human situation is unique by virtue of differences in the participants. Science and philosophy have concentrated on generalization and universalization, and this concentration has been accompanied by an almost exclusive emphasis on method in science and the agent-as-method in ethics. Even in virtue ethics, where at least the agent is not a mere vehicle of methodical logic, too much attention is perhaps given to the person who embodies virtues. In the approach under development here, attention goes first to the recipient of care and to the relation between carer and cared-for.

Preservation, growth, and acceptability are not fixed as ideals in either the carer or the society to which the carer belongs, although of course both will have effects on the shape of caring. Following our phenomenological description, caring will always depend on the connection between carer and cared-for. It is easy to forget this, and so the world is filled with claims to care and accusations that the professed carers do not care ("nobody cares") and even that they exploit the recipients of their pseudo-care. It is essential, then, to maintain the distinction between care as a virtue and care as an attribute of relation. It is entirely possible for an individual, exercising a host of recognized virtues, to care sincerely (in the virtue sense) and yet not connect with the recipient of care. This failure—which has been documented in virtuous figures from parents to prophets—is usually blamed on recalcitrant learners or followers. Under such thinking children who do not accept the care of their parents deserve the mishaps that follow, and the children of Israel deserved to be bitten by fiery serpents, slain by their leaders, and swallowed by the earth. There is a nucleus of wisdom in these views, but the relational approach will give a greater scope to the analysis of situations and urge continuous reflection on what we do and how we use our words.

Every encounter in a relationship over time can be described phenomenologically in the terms already discussed. However, there are new features. When we care over time, traces of previous encounters remain in memory and often affect new encounters. Further, we think about those for whom we care. Some of us pray, some worry, some dream, some plan, some do all of these. Indeed, separation often increases and deepens care. Parents who couldn't wait to get away for an evening without their children find themselves talking about the kids over their candle-lit dinner. Part of every vacation is given over to finding suitable gifts for those left behind, and carers often return from journeys with new ideas for making their caring more effective. If these plans are the result of an epiphany of sorts—"now I see what she needs!"—or of deep reflection on the relationship, they may be successful, but if they are plans generated from the carer's own needs and abstract thinking, they may lead to new disappointments.

Like *caring* itself, the words we regularly use in discussing long-term relationships need relational analysis. In parenting we need to consider what it means to *plan* for the future of one's children. Parents often save for their children's college education, but what if the children don't want to go to college? What if their aptitudes and interests lie elsewhere? Similarly, plans are often made for the elderly as though a particular old person were "a unit in a collection." Social policy, perhaps inescapably, works with collections and social categories, but there may be ways to transform such thinking, and these will be considered in later chapters.

Caring-About

So far the discussion has focused on caring-for—the face-to-face occasions in which one person, as carer, cares directly for another, the cared-for. There are many circumstances, however, in which we care about others even though we cannot care directly for them; that is, we are somehow touched by their plight and want to do something to improve it. In *Caring* I distinguished caring-for from caring-about:

I have brushed aside "caring about" and, I believe, properly so. It is too easy. I can "care about" the starving children of Cambodia, send five dollars to hunger relief, and feel somewhat satisfied. I do not even know if my money went for food, or guns, or a new Cadillac for some politician. This is a poor second-cousin to caring. "Caring about" always involves a certain benign neglect. One is attentive just so far. One assents with just so much enthusiasm. One acknowledges. One affirms. One contributes five dollars and goes on to other things.[16]

The basic distinction between caring-for and caring-about remains important (although the particular language does not matter), but I think now that caring-about deserves much more attention. Indeed, caring-about may provide the link between caring and justice. Chronologically, we learn first what it means to be cared for. Then, gradually, we learn both to care for and, by extension, to care about others. This caring-about is almost certainly the foundation for our sense of justice. Susan Okin has argued strongly that John Rawls's theory of justice contains at its heart "a voice of responsibility, care, and concern for others."[17] Rawls himself acknowledges that citizens under political liberalism need capacities for both a sense of justice and an individual conception of the good. The perspective taken here is that caring supplies the basic good in which the sense of justice is grounded.

Caring-about moves us from the face-to-face world into the wider public realm. If we have been well cared for and have learned to care for a few intimate others, we move into the public world with fellow-feeling for others. We are moved by compassion for their suffering, we regret it when they do not experience the fruits of care, and we feel outrage when they are exploited. Often we wish that we could care directly, but because that is impossible, we express our care in charitable gifts, in the social groups we support, and in our voting. These are not insignificant ways of responding, and they are ways that can be encouraged in schools.

Caring-about does have inherent flaws. It can, as I said, be "too easy." Even when conscientiously engaged it can become self-righteous and politically correct. It can encourage dependence on abstractions and schemes that are consistent at the theoretical level but unworkable in practice. Perhaps worst, it can elevate itself above caring-for and distort what might be called the natural order of caring.

Let's examine each of these flaws. The tendency toward self-righteousness and political correctness is built into caring-about. Charles Dickens gave us vivid portraits of do-gooders who proclaimed their caring loudly but failed to care for those in their immediate circles. Mrs. Jellyby and other insufferable Dickens characters not only failed to care for those near them, they did not even care enough about the avowed objects of their care to consider the actual effects of their charities.[18] When we consider pathologies of care more deeply, we will see that a risk similar to this inheres in caring-for, too. It is only partly blocked by emphasizing the relational sense of caring over the virtue sense.

The tendency toward abstraction is illustrated in much political and social theory, and it is one reason that so many feminists are wary of theory.[19] The temptation to create grand schemes and universal narratives is hard to resist once we move into the public realm. Individuals become elements in a collection, and principles govern what might better be guided by caring responses. Those who create the theories begin to serve them by defending, revising, and extending them. Others get caught up in debates over them, and those needing care may be all but forgotten. Theorizing may also be translated into caring about great causes. At this global level, theory does not flee from action, but it may become a form of terror in the world. It proclaims an ideology, and individual cared-fors may become mere symbols.

When the tendency to theorize is celebrated, caring-about may brush aside caring-for as too immediate, personal, parochial, or emotional to be widely effective. A personal story may help to illustrate my point here. Some years ago, when my husband and I had added to our family by adopting Asian American children, a colleague commended us, but then remarked, "But, of course, adoption is not the answer." He wanted a solution at the grand level, one that would "take care" of all parentless children. I responded with some irritation, "Well, it's the answer for these kids." Now, on reflection, I think we were both partly right. There is no adequate substitute for caring-for (direct caring)—of this I am convinced—but intelligent, conscientious caring-about can suggest ways to extend caring-for to many more recipients.

The key, central to care theory, is this: caring-about (or, perhaps, a sense of justice) must be seen as instrumental in establishing the conditions under which caring-for can flourish. Although the preferred form of caring is caring-for, caring-about can help in establishing, maintaining, and enhancing it. Those who care about others in the justice sense must keep in mind that the objective is to ensure that caring actually occurs. Caring-about is empty if it does not culminate in caring relations.

Those who work in the Kantian tradition are inclined to elevate justice (or caring-about) above caring-for. They often fear the emotion or affect that is central to caring-for. Okin notes that the "Kantian connection" so pronounced in Rawls's work makes it difficult for him "to acknowledge any role for empathy or benevolence in the formulation of his principles of justice."[20] Despite this, Rawls does acknowledge a moral sense that cannot be derived wholly from the rational in his distinction between "rational" and "reasonable."[21] His reasonable person regards other persons in a way that cannot be traced to rational self-interest alone. It seems, however, that Rawls thinks that this moral sense can be traced to a form of Kantian moral sense that is devoid of feeling. In contrast to the Kantian position, David Hume insisted that the final sentence on morality, "that which renders morality an active virtue" is feeling: "This final sentence depends on some internal sense or feeling, which nature has made universal in the whole species. For what else can have an influence of this nature?"[22] Care theory takes a Humean position on motivation and inverts Kantian priorities. Caring-for is the natural, desired state; caring-about, emotionally derived from caring-for by either extension or rebellion (to be discussed a bit later), must serve caring-for to achieve its own objectives.

Learning to Care and Be Cared For

The preceding discussion about the priority of caring-for over caring-about suggests an emphasis on what Hume called cultivation of the moral sentiments. Education in both home and school cannot be content with developing rationality and cognitive skills. If caring-for is basic in moral life, then an education that develops this capacity is essential.

Learning to be cared for is the first step in moral education. Rawls makes something like this a law of psychological development: "First law: given that family institutions are just, and that the parents love the child and manifestly express their love by caring for his good, then the child, recognizing their evident love of him, comes to love them." His second and third laws claim that when a person's capacity for fellow feeling has been established, as in the first law, he or she will (in a just society) develop "ties of friendly feeling and trust toward others" and will accordingly uphold the just arrangements of which he and his loved ones are the beneficiaries.[23] His entire discussion of moral education is presented in the interests of stability. Once a just, well-ordered society has been established, citizens must maintain it, and Rawls's three laws of psychological development are offered in this interest.

From a care perspective, Rawls's account fails on several counts. First, and most important, what role do moral sentiments and natural attitudes (we may include care here) play in establishing the well-ordered society? If a just society can be reached by purely rational or, more accurately, reasonable means, why are ties of affection and the like needed to maintain it? Second, such laws simply do not exist. As we discuss caring in more and more depth, we will see that although there are strong tendencies, there are no laws. Caring itself is subject to pathologies, and these are not always clear to us even as they are occurring. Third, family institutions have been manifestly unjust for centuries, and yet many parents and children have loved one another and many children have learned to care. Fourth, although one can agree with Rawls that loving parents express their love of the child by "caring for his good," this statement is much too cryptic. What is a child's good? How does one care for it? If the child does not recognize the parents' caring, what can be done?

To survive a child needs at least minimal physical care. To grow, to become an acceptable person, a child needs more. Urie Bronfenbrenner says, "In order to develop, a child needs the enduring, irrational involvement of one or more adults in care and joint activity with the child. . . . Somebody has to be crazy about that kid."[24] The emphasis here is on a passionate love that enjoys the child. A parent who is "crazy about that kid" likes to spend time with the child. There is companionship and joy in joint activity. Such a parent does not use purposive-rational planning to eke out an occasional hour of "quality time." Most moments spent together are pleasurable for both parent and child.

In this kind of setting, where parent and child work together, play together, and talk to each other, a child learns all sorts of things incidentally. Casaubon, the narrator of Umberto Eco's *Foucault's Pendulum,* remarks: "I believe that what we become depends on what our fathers teach us at odd moments, when they aren't trying to teach us. We are formed by little scraps of wisdom."[25] Philip Jackson makes a similar point in discussing how we are formed by teachers.[26] Yet in so many of our encounters with children, both as parents and teachers, we are guided by purposive-rational thinking: we plan, strategize, instruct, correct, monitor, and control. There is something deeply wrong in all this and, paradoxically, when we see that something is wrong, we are inclined to use the same procedures more rigorously. We find it hard to give up the tendency to use prescriptive technologies. Our reaction is similar to that of the stubborn defender of Enlightenment reason: when things go wrong, use more reason. He might better say, "Let's use a different kind of reason," or "Let's use reason to reflect on the reason we've been using," or even, "Let's go have a drink together and put all this aside for a while." In education, as in parenting, the key may be relation, not control.

Buber made relationship the very heart of education. He wrote that every child longs for the world "to become present" to him or her through communion: "The child lying with half-closed eyes, waiting with tense soul for its mother to speak to it—the mystery of its will is not directed towards enjoying (or dominating) a person, or towards doing something of its own accord; but towards experiencing communion in the face of the lonely night, which spreads beyond the window and threatens to invade."[27] Buber's point is that someone must be ready to respond to the child's longing. That person need not be perfect. Moreover, caring over time need not be—in fact, never is—an unbroken series of caring encounters, but it must be marked by a basic constancy. The adult must convey a message to the child: "I am here for you."

When parents cannot or will not convey this message, other adults must do so. The most likely candidates are teachers. Even in the lives of children with caring parents, teachers serve as additional models of caring adults—that is, adults who can regularly enter relations that are properly called *caring*. The message "I am here for you" signals a willingness to listen, to help, to defend, and to guide. It is, as Buber noted, the foundation for the most vital relationships: "Trust, trust in the world, because this human being exists—that is the most inward achievement of the relation in education. Because this human being exists, meaninglessness, however hard pressed you are by it, cannot be the real truth. Because this human being exists, in the darkness the light lies hidden, in fear salvation, and in the callousness of one's fellow-man the great love."[28]

Child rearing and education are central to care theory because caring-for precedes caring-about and because learning to be cared for precedes both. Human beings are not "cast into the world"; we are born into it, and we are guided into social life. A realistic social theory has to consider how caring persons can be raised and educated in an imperfect world. Such a theory is necessarily both melioristic and open. It is melioristic insofar as it gives sound guidance for social improvement, and it is open because, to be effective, it must leave much to the arena of human interaction and judgment. It cannot prescribe exactly what should be done in every situation, and it leaves itself open to continual correction.

The Centrality of Women's Traditions

Because care theory starts at home, women's experience is an important source for identifying key concepts. Most political philosophy has started with the associations of adult males: How should people interact? Who should govern? By what laws will they live? If homes and families are considered, their role in contributing to the larger community is paramount.

Here the emphasis is reversed. Our most treasured human capacities are nurtured in families or homelike groups. Charles Taylor has expressed doubt that these capacities can be developed entirely within families. Their development, he says, depends on an entire civilization.[29] Now, of course, families and civilizations interact; I would not argue to the contrary. But it is by no means clear that only one form of society will allow the development of these capacities. Moreover, despite the overall success and glories of a given civilization, many of its members will fail to develop the admired capacities, and this failure can often be traced to family life. We could argue, and some philosophers have so argued, that dependence on the family for the intellectual and moral growth of citizens is a mistake. What we need, from this perspective, is a more perfect state that can ensure the appropriate growth of all its citizens. Dreaming up such a state is a task for utopians.

Taylor does not make such an argument, but he does move perhaps too quickly beyond the family to the society in which the family is situated. He wants to argue, against philosophical individualists, that one's recognition that a civilization has produced the capacities on which rights are based commits one to the sustenance of that civilization. This may be so, but it is not obvious. What seems to follow logically is that a parent owes to her children the conditions and resources that produced the treasured capacities in the parent. It is reasonable to suggest from that start that a person who truly values these capacities may want to nurture them in others as well, but this is not a purely logical conclusion.

One has to care about others. The variety of desires expressed and outcomes achieved in intimate circles tends to keep open the possibility that the civilization must be changed, not merely maintained.

Currently available empirical evidence shows that women are generally more liberal than men on social issues, particularly on support for the disadvantaged and on children's issues.[30] The suffragists of the nineteenth century predicted that this would be true, but they based their argument on the belief that women have a natural moral superiority. I do not argue for women's moral superiority or for some "natural" attribute in women that makes them more compassionate. I argue, not from essentialism (which, for me, remains an open question but not a useful one), but from experience. The basic argument is that people who are directly responsible for the care of others (if they themselves have been adequately cared for) will likely develop a moral orientation that is well described as an *ethic of care*.

It is not only that women have actually done most of the care-giving work for centuries; the expectation that they should do so has in itself had important effects. This expectation can be found in historical documents, biography, and fiction. It is well illustrated in a subplot in a novel by P. D. James, *A Taste for Death*. Two of Dalgliesh's detectives, Massingham (male) and Miskin (female), face problems with elderly relatives—he with his father, she with her grandmother. Massingham, while living in his father's house, nevertheless avoids contact with the lonely old man whenever he can. Miskin, who desperately wants her freedom, decides during a police emergency not only to take her grandmother in but also to try to resolve the emotional problems between them. When the grandmother is mugged and needs her, she has to take a day off in the middle of a politically important murder investigation. Massingham, although sympathetic, says:

> "It's not going to be convenient."
> She said fiercely: "Of course it's not bloody convenient. You don't have to tell me. When would it ever be?"
> Walking beside him down the corridor . . . she suddenly asked:
> "What would happen if your father fell ill?"
> "I hadn't thought. I suppose my sister would fly home from Rome."
> Of course, she thought. Who else?[31]

The expectation that women will do direct care when it is necessary remains strong.[32] Where it has given way, the newer expectation is not that men will accept equal responsibility (although, of course, they sometimes do) but that the public will or should somehow provide care so that occupational work will not be interrupted. Many of us agree that such support should be provided. Yet, in countries where public care giving is much more generously supported than it is in the United States, complaints still arise about the lack of human caring—warmth, personal concern—in the care taking.[33] Thus the problem cannot be entirely defined in terms of public responsibility. People long to be cared for by those who have a personal interest in them.

It is women who, traditionally, have provided this care. It makes sense to study this experience empirically as well as philosophically. How can we describe what is learned when one is cared for and how can we describe what is learned when one cares for others? What broad categories appear in all of these situations? What personal and cultural variations appear in each category? What pathologies arise? Can we predict which implementations of caring or being cared for will lead most reliably to caring-about without losing the caring that should be its point? The task is both descriptive and normative, and the trick will be to know when we have passed from one to the other.

From Natural Caring to Ethical Theory

The preferred way of relating to one another morally can be called *natural caring*. By "natural" I mean a form of caring that arises more or less spontaneously out of affection or inclination. In natural caring the phenomenological features described earlier do not require a special ethical effort; they arise directly in response to the needs of the cared-for. No mediating ethical-logical deliberation is required. That is not to say, of course, that no effort is needed in deciding on and carrying out a physical response. The effort expended in the "act" part of caring may range from minimal to heroic, but receptivity and motivational displacement occur in direct response to the cared-for. I mean nothing more by "natural" than this. In particular, I do *not* mean to suggest that the capacity for natural caring does not need cultivation. On the contrary, I will argue that it needs continuous and sensitive cultivation. Natural caring is the sort of caring usually identified with care in intimate circles—in parenting and friendship. It is also seen frequently in neighborly interactions and in emergencies involving strangers. For example, we spontaneously respond to neighborly greetings, requests for directions, and requests for help from injured strangers. In all such cases we receive "what is there" in the other person and want to respond positively.

In contrast, there are times, even in the closest human relations, when the feeling associated with natural caring—"I must"—does not arise spontaneously. Then, if we value ourselves as carers, we summon ethical caring—a dutiful form of caring that resembles a Kantian ethical attitude. On such occasions we respond as carers because we want to uphold our ideal of ourselves as carers. We overcome our own resistance by asking ourselves, "How would I respond if I really cared? If I were at my best as a carer, what would I do?"[34] Although this move is often necessary, it is very risky because the recipient of our care frequently detects our ambivalence and may resent our acting from duty.

Care theory reverses Kantian priorities. By placing natural caring above ethical caring, we suggest that ethical caring is instrumental in establishing or restoring natural caring. Indeed, it is often the case that as we draw upon ethical caring the blockage to natural caring is removed, and the relation once again becomes one of natural caring. A person not only needs experience in caring to do this, she or he also needs to have made a commitment to be a caring person. In another significant departure from Kantian theory, care theorists do not turn to logic for a categorical imperative; rather, they turn to an ideal of character. This turn to character does not imply that care theory is itself a form of virtue theory; again, it elevates natural caring above the caring that requires an effort of character. It should not be surprising that care theory bears some resemblance to Kantian and virtue theories because both have contributed enormously to metaethical thought.

At bottom, however, care theory is consequentialist (but not utilitarian). It asks after the effects on recipients of our care. It demands to know whether relations of care have in fact been established, maintained, or enhanced, and by extension it counsels us to consider effects on the whole web or network of care. If we have established a caring relation with one person at the cost of weakening a larger web of care, can we be said to have cared? This is a topic I will address in the next chapter, and it is important both theoretically and practically. As we examine pathologies of care, we will encounter the logical limits of theory.

Several critics have suggested that care theory, despite my disclaimers, is based on principle. One might, for example, suggest as a basic principle: always act so as to establish, maintain, or enhance caring relations. A carer, however, does not refer to this principle when she responds to a person who addresses her. The "principle" is *descriptive,* not prescriptive. The behavior of carers is well described by this principle, but their motivation arises either spontaneously (in natural caring) or through deliberate reflection on an ideal of caring that has become part of their character. Thus, although the characteristic "I must" sounds Kantian, its source is either spontaneous inclination or the "caring self" that has been under construction for a lifetime. In this, caring is very close to virtue ethics.

Another Kantian (or at least, Rawlsian) reversal is suggested by the foregoing discussion. Rawls has described the need for "reflective equilibration"—a process by which ethical agents check their concrete judgments against the principles enunciated in the basic ethical theory.[35] According to Rawls, reflective equilibrium guards against our making judgments out of personal interest or emotional entanglement, while it also invites reflection on (and perhaps revision of) theoretical principles. The emphasis in Rawls is clearly on the former. In contrast, care theory puts greater emphasis on the continual examination and growth of an individual's ethical ideal. The ethical ideal gives stability to our judgments and helps us to avoid capricious behavior, but the needs of others provide the primary material for our response and continually stretch the ethical ideal.

In this chapter we have outlined a basic description of caring relations and of the contributions made by carers and cared-fors. We have also discussed the importance of "caring about" and how it is linked to the more fundamental concept of "caring for." Learning to care about depends on learning to care for, and that in turn depends on oneself having been cared for. We have launched a project that reverses traditional philosophical procedure. Instead of starting with an ideal state or republic, we will start with an ideal home and move outward—learning first what it means to be cared for, then to care for intimate others, and finally to care about those we cannot care for directly.

When we care, we intend to offer some positive form of response. Often our aim is to prevent harm, and we have to be concerned not only with harms that threaten from outside but also with those harms people may do to themselves. Moreover, our efforts to care may miscarry, and we have to consider the possibility that there are pathologies of care. We turn to the topic of harm next.

CHAPTER 2

Harm and Care

When we care, we want to respond positively to the needs of another, and a primary need is protection from harm. If harm is threatened by something on the outside—by another person, a natural disaster, or an illness—most social theories suggest some form of protection. Liberalism, as we will see, allows a society to intervene if one person threatens to harm another, but it abstains from intervention when a person's behavior threatens harm to himself (except in the extreme case of suicide). In contrast, care theory is deeply concerned with self-inflicted harms and, indeed, even seeks a way to promote the growth of others. It is also concerned with harms permitted by or inflicted by law and with those sometimes inflicted in the name of care. A question arises whether carers can intervene positively in the lives of adults without falling into paternalism.

Harm is generally regarded as a physical or material hurt, and it is usually (but not always) associated with the concept of "moral wrong." If one suffers a *harm,* it is often the case that one has been somehow morally wronged. Thus, if a physician jabs a needle into my arm to prevent me from getting tetanus, I have not been harmed; however, if he or she does this merely to inflict pain, I certainly have been harmed— I have been wronged. From the perspective of traditional ethics it is possible to be wronged without being harmed. Someone might, for example, lie to me without causing me real harm; it can be said, however, that I have been wronged. The basis for this claim is the idea that persons are owed respect, and lying to them violates that respect. This raises the issue of what we mean by "person" and, since this is not an entirely coherent concept, I will not depend on it. If another expresses hurt because of a lie, I have to admit a clear (if only temporary) failure of care. It is also possible that I can be harmed (physically hurt, as in war) without being wronged. In this case the act of harm is held to be morally justifiable. Although the distinction between harm and wrong has been important in some ethical traditions, I want to avoid it, at least for a while, and concentrate on harm.

John Stuart Mill, in his classic *On Liberty,* wrote, "The only purpose for which power can be rightly exercised over any member of a civilized society against his will is to prevent harm to others."[1] Mill's statement has been challenged by people who think that a society should exercise power in molding its citizens — that is, in preventing them from doing harm even to themselves[2] — and my argument on social policy will move cautiously in this direction. Even those who agree with Mill have engaged in heated debate over what it means to harm someone.

In later chapters we will talk about harms induced by failures to care: violence done by people who have not been cared for themselves, and the miseries people inflict on intimate others because they have not learned how to care. In this chapter I describe a limited range of harms, in particular those that are legally or morally allowed and those that are done in the name of caring itself, and explore the connection between harm and obligation. Because this exploration begins with the human desire to be cared for (rather than to be free or to be happy or to belong, all of which can be derived from a more basic desire), we will emphasize the perspective of the one who claims harm, needs help, or in some way solicits our care.

Legally Protected Forms of Harm

In the United States law concentrates primarily on the prevention of physical and material harm. Although it constrains us from inflicting demonstrable harms on one another, it has great difficulty in addressing harms that are not easily demonstrated, such as psychological injuries unaccompanied by physical or material change. Courts do recognize "mental anguish," but usually that anguish is inferred from the state of physical damage and the recognition of what any reasonable person would go through under such circumstances. Mental anguish by itself (for example, the continuous verbal abuse that some children endure —

often without recognizing that they have been wronged) remains untouched by law, and I do not argue that law should attempt to control such wrongs directly. Education and social policy, however, can help limit this type of harm.

Besides being unable to identify and cope with most psychological harms, U.S. law, unlike most European law, imposes no positive duties on its citizens. We are forbidden by law to harm one another, but we are not legally obligated to help someone who is in danger. Indeed, "the law has persistently refused to impose on a stranger the moral obligation of common humanity, to go to the aid of another human being who is in danger, even if the other is in danger of losing his life."[3]

Mary Ann Glendon recounts several cases and cites a "long line of decisions" that have consistently exonerated people accused of failing to aid others in distress. "In a well-known case, the operators of a boat-rental service sat on the shore of a lake on the Fourth of July and watched as an inebriated customer slowly lost his grip on his overturned canoe and drowned. A unanimous Massachusetts Supreme Judicial Court confirmed that the defendants were not obliged to heed the drowning man's screams for help."[4] Other cases have exempted adults from any responsibility to rescue young children from obvious danger even when the saving act would not have put the rescuers in any danger at all and would cause them little inconvenience. The only exception to the principle of "no duty to rescue" involves people who have prior legal responsibility for the victim—parents, designated guardians, and the like. Strangers have no duty to rescue, and as Glendon wryly notes, we are almost all strangers to one another under the law.

Most of us find these incidents at least disquieting, and we are inclined to judge the watchers-from-the-shore to be morally culpable even if the law exonerates them. We feel that in the name of common humanity one should respond to cries for help, warn people of impending danger, or restrain a toddler who is about to run into a busy street. Our natural reaction underscores a point made by John Caputo about obligation: obligation happens.[5] Normal people who have been well cared for themselves will respond to those who cry out for care. From the perspective taken here, something is wrong with people who do not. If law cannot (or should not) intervene, education might be able to produce people who are more morally sensitive. Unfortunately we as a society are more concerned with low mathematical achievement than with failure to aid other human beings in pain or danger.

Debate about responsibility addresses not only the response of individuals but also that of governments, as Glendon notes:

A variant of this no-duty principle recently achieved constitutional status when the Supreme Court announced that the Constitution imposes no obligation on government or on government employees to assist distressed individuals — "even when such aid may be necessary to secure life, liberty or property interests of which the government itself may not deprive the individual."[6]

Virginia Held refers to the picture of individuals reflected by the no-duty-to-rescue principle as the "Robinson Crusoe image" — every man independent and self-sufficient. She points out that this is inaccurate as a general description of society and argues that government has a responsibility to encourage care.

The arguments for government to provide positive enactments to those in need are at least as strong as those for government to protect us against interference. We ought to acknowledge that our fellow citizens and our fellow inhabitants of the globe have moral rights to the food, shelter, and medical care that are the necessary conditions of living and growing. When the resources exist for honoring such rights there are few excuses for not doing so, through governmental implementation where appropriate.[7]

Notice that Held casts her argument in terms of "moral rights" and that she recognizes "few excuses" for not honoring such rights. What is the source of these rights? Although I agree with Held wholeheartedly that we should respond positively to need, I would not locate our obligation in rights, unless by "right" we mean a conventional response to need — a response some particular community has institutionalized. A right so defined could be overturned, revised, or replaced. The notion of universal rights, natural rights, or God-given rights seems a fiction, as Alasdair MacIntyre notes:

There are no such rights, and belief in them is one with belief in witches and in unicorns. The best reason for asserting so bluntly that there are not such rights is indeed of precisely the same type as the best reason which we possess for asserting that there are no unicorns: every attempt to give good reasons for believing that there *are* such rights has failed.[8]

Rejecting the idea of natural rights — rights as either God-given or somehow inherent in human beings — does not compel us to reject the idea of rights or use of the word. It would be foolish (and ungrateful, in a way) to brush aside the social progress that liberalism has promoted under the banner of rights. I argue that rights arise as a recognition of the obligation to respond to needs. They capture our social or political consensus on this obligation, and they are anchored in the kind of people we are, the traditions into which we have been born and educated, the virtues we have cultivated, and our capacity to respond to the pains and needs of others. Agreeing with MacIntyre about the origin and/or existence of rights necessitates a careful analysis of community and intelligent heteronomy. If we are not compelled as rational autonomous beings to respond to preexisting rights (rights that can be logically discovered), then the origin of this widespread feeling of obligation must lie elsewhere. As we will see, the notion of community will not by itself solve our problem either.

Let's set aside for the moment the important question of why people fail to respond and all the issues involved in teaching people to care. We need to explore the nature of harm more fully. A question that has been asked since the days of Socrates is this: is it permissible to harm those who harm or threaten to harm us? Socrates, in a discussion with Polemarchus, suggests that a just man ought not to injure anyone, that injury will produce a deterioration "in that which is the proper virtue of man"—justice itself.[9] But, then, is punishment for illegal acts an injury? Is killing in warfare unjust? As just persons, we normally tell the truth and regard lies as injuries of a sort. Should we, therefore, tell the truth to our enemies? I think Socrates's approach quickly leads us astray. Either the just person cannot function in the world as it exists or justice must be defined in such a way that all sorts of injuries are permitted in its name. How else might we proceed? I want to offer a few stories now to trigger thoughts about a possible alternative.

George Orwell related an experience as a member of an execution party during his days as a colonial policeman in Burma that deeply affected his attitude toward capital punishment. As the party started across the prison yard, a dog came bounding out to greet the men. Before it could be captured, it leaped on the prisoner (whose hands were tightly tied) and tried to lick his face. After the dog was restrained, the march continued. The prisoner walked steadily, but at one point, despite the men who gripped him by each shoulder, he stepped slightly aside to avoid a puddle on the path.

It is curious, but till that moment I had never realized what it means to destroy a healthy, conscious man. When I saw the prisoner step aside to avoid the puddle I saw the mystery, the unspeakable wrongness, of cutting short a life when it is in full tide. This man was not dying, he was alive just as we are alive. All the organs of his body were working—bowels digesting food, skin renewing itself, nails growing, tissues forming—all toiling away in solemn foolery. His nails would be growing when he stood on the drop, when he was falling through the air with a tenth of a second to live. His eyes saw the yellow gravel and the gray walls, and his brain still remembered, foresaw, reasoned—reasoned even about puddles. He and we were a party of men walking together, seeing, hearing, feeling, understanding the same world; and in two minutes, with a sudden snap, one of us would be gone—one mind less, one world less.[10]

The unexpected intrusion of the ordinary into a solemn event triggered for Orwell the feeling of "unspeakable wrongness." Yet, when it was over they all felt an "enormous relief ": "One felt an impulse to sing, to break into a run, to snigger. All at once everyone began chattering gaily."[11] Notice that the relief and nervous chattering in no way suggest that the execution party approved of what they had done. Notice, too, that widespread revulsion to capital punishment does not imply that we must logically go all the way with Socrates. At times we may indeed have to inflict injuries or harms on others who are dangerous or recalcitrant, and our task is deciding how to constrain what we do so that the entire web of care is preserved as nearly as possible. It will not do either to define away "injury" by confining it to the innocent or to say that the guilty merit the pain we inflict on them. As Socrates suggested, "just" people feel themselves diminished when they inflict harm.

What if Orwell and the other members of the execution party had voiced their revulsion? What if they had said, "This stinks!" and abandoned the assignment? The very thought is incredible; that is, we cannot find credible the notion that men would abandon that which they had accepted as duty just because of a momentary moral doubt. What is so powerful here? Education? Threat of punishment? Fear of looking foolish? Almost certainly it was not, in this case, a sense of justice, and perhaps it is rarely such a sense that makes it possible for people to ignore a cry (implicit or explicit) that flies from one human being to another: "Help me!"

I am not going to argue against capital punishment here (I do so in chapter 11), nor am I going to analyze the various justifications that have been offered for its use. I want to stay close to the events themselves and ask what it is that makes it possible for human beings to participate in such acts. We are trying to understand *why* we inflict harms and fail to care. Surely the traditions to which communitarians would recall us are, at least partly, responsible. A member of an official execution party does not throw down his badge and gun and exclaim, "This stinks!" We will see, in a later discussion of good homes and schools, that children in these settings gradually learn how they (and all of us) are disciplined by the customs and rituals of the cultures in which they live. They learn that much of social life is scripted. The tighter the script, the surer we can be that the acts so prescribed may not be naturally attractive.

Consider another form of legal killing—war. Michael Walzer presents five different accounts of soldiers who found themselves unable to shoot when an enemy soldier suddenly turned into "just a man"—a man taking a bath, smoking a cigarette, admiring a balmy spring day. Here again is Orwell, who tells of his experience in the Spanish Civil War.

At this moment, a man, presumably carrying a message to an officer, jumped out of the trench and ran along the top of the parapet in full view. He was half-dressed and was holding up his trousers with both hands as he ran. I refrained from shooting him. It is true that I am a poor shot and unlikely to hit a running man at a hundred yards. . . . Still, I did not shoot partly because of that detail about the trousers. I had come here to shoot at "Fascists"; but a man who is holding up his trousers isn't a "Fascist," he is visibly a fellow-creature, similar to yourself, and you don't feel like shooting him.[12]

Walzer immediately remarks that Orwell's comment, "you don't feel like shooting him," is not a moral one and that he (Walzer) is trying to sort out morally permissible acts of civil war from those that are not justifiable. But it is precisely attempts of this sort—to justify various acts of injury and neglect—that lead some postmodern philosophers to give up on ethics. The alternative, and we have barely hinted at it thus far, is to say with Caputo, "Obligation happens, the obligation of me to you and of both of us to the other. It is all around us, on every side, constantly tugging at our sleeves, calling upon us for a response."[13]

To which "tugs at the sleeve" should we respond? If it is enough for Orwell to say, "you don't feel like shooting him," is it enough for another man to react to a horrible act by killing the perpetrator and then confessing "you feel like shooting him"? What tugs at our sleeve most strongly at these moments—particularly at the sleeves of academics—is the manicured hand of justification. Let's resist that tug a bit longer.

We have heard two stories suggesting that many of us find it hard to commit even legalized acts of injury and brutality when ordinary events intrude. When someone appears suddenly as "just like us," we find it hard to do him or her an injury. Was Weil right after all, when she said that we must look at the unfortunate as individuals "exactly like us"? This really won't do for several reasons. First, the Other is *not* exactly like us, and we do an injury of sorts by assuming that she is. Second, when we find out that the Other is actually different, we may object to or even hate the difference. And third, when we hate the difference, we may well hate the Other. Orwell wanted to shoot fascists, not men. It came as a revelation of sorts to see a fascist holding up his pants. Thus we cannot depend entirely on the intrusion of ordinary events to keep us from harming one another, and the fiction that others are "exactly like us" is easily destroyed by both events and political language.

What we have learned from these stories is that people are socialized into contradictory patterns. On the one hand, decent, loving people do not want to injure other human beings; on the other, the same decent people are led to believe that honor or acceptability requires behavior that would otherwise be repugnant. By making a man into a fascist or a condemned criminal, we make it right or at least acceptable to kill him. Despite this, for thoughtful men like Orwell, it still can't be right to kill a man who is holding up his trousers (at least, "you don't feel like it") or who has enough dignity to step around a puddle. To patient readers who want to jump right in now and shout, "But these acts often *are* justifiable! You can't avoid that," I will respond gently: just wait a bit. The fact that we can be so torn by contradictory forces suggests that alternatives may exist—and that is where we must leave things for the moment.

Pathologies of Care

In the previous section we saw that citizens (in the United States) are not required by law to care for one another—not even to save a life when the saving act requires little or no risk. We saw also that powerful forms of socialization make it seem right to harm others when something they have done—or even something they stand for—is abhorrent to us. Now we will see that much ordinary harm or injury is inflicted in the name of care itself.

Self-righteous, dogmatic, rigid, and cruel forms of "care" have been popular topics in fiction. One of the most repugnant (and convincing) accounts appears in Samuel Butler's *The Way of All Flesh*. The story is told by Ernest's godfather, who observes the trials Ernest undergoes at the hands of his "loving" clergyman father, Theobald. He pauses in his storytelling to give this sarcastic advice to parents "who wish to live a quiet life":

Tell your children that they are very naughty—much naughtier than most children. Point to the young people of some acquaintances as models of perfection and impress your own children with a deep sense of their own inferiority. You carry so many more guns than they do that they cannot fight you. This is called moral influence, and it will enable you to bounce them as much as you please. Tell them how singularly indulgent you are; insist on the incalculable benefits you conferred upon them, firstly in bringing them into the world at all, but more particularly in bringing them into it as your own children rather than anyone else's. Say that you have their highest interests at stake whenever you are out of temper and wish to make yourself unpleasant. Harp much upon these highest interests.[14]

Ernest's father never failed to impress his son with his fatherly goodness and his son's wickedness: "When Ernest was in his second year, Theobald, as I have already said, began to teach him to read. He began to whip him two days later."[15] Later, in a time of crisis, Ernest's godfather thought

of the long and savage cruelty with which he [Ernest] had been treated in childhood—cruelty none the less real for having been due to ignorance and stupidity rather than to deliberate malice; of the atmosphere of lying and self-laudatory hallucination in which he had been brought up; of the readiness the boy had shown to love anyone that would be good enough to let him, and of how affection for his parents only died in him because it had been killed anew . . . each time that it had tried to spring.[16]

Ernest was, in some ways, fortunate. He learned to admit that he disliked his parents and to sever his connections with them. Although he suffered all through his youth and made mistakes that are comical to readers (but horribly real to Ernest), he was not faced with the opportunity to convert his own suffering into cruelty to others. Indeed, he was saved from becoming a clergyman by a near tragedy that turned his life around. Cruelty was not passed from him to a new generation.

If we compare Ernest's story to those recounted by the psychologist Alice Miller, we see two major differences.[17] The members of the Nazi high command studied by Miller—all of whom had rigid upbringings like Ernest's—never came to the realization that they had been treated cruelly as children. This is the first difference. These officers continued to believe that their childhood sufferings really were for "their own good." Miller contends that these people never developed real selves, and it did not (perhaps could not) occur to them that authority could be questioned. Pain suffered without acknowledgment becomes like a commodity; it is stored up and passed on without reflection. The second difference is that Ernest was saved from the opportunity to inflict pain.

I am not arguing here that the Nazi officials "couldn't help themselves" or that Ernest might not have resisted inflicting pain even if he had had the opportunity. I am interested, rather, in how we can educate children so that they can tell genuine caring from pernicious fakery and how we can reconstruct our institutions so as to reduce opportunities to do harm and increase the possibility of positive human response. In particular I am interested in how we can reduce the homesickness described by Butler—that is, a sickness of the soul induced by a failure of care at home.

Using the framework I laid out in chapter 1, it is easy to refute the claims of Ernest's parents to care. Because Ernest saw and acknowledged that he was not cared for, the relation cannot be labeled a caring one. What if he had insisted—as Theobald did, of the relation between himself and his father, George—that the relation was indeed one of caring? I think we have to assess such a situation as a pathology of care; that is, the relation seems to satisfy the phenomenological criteria, but the result is clearly undesirable.

This observation suggests that we cannot reasonably leave the description of caring at the purely phenomenological level. We want some sort of positive result for the cared-for, perhaps growth, as Mayeroff suggests, or happiness and reasonable comfort, as Butler suggests, or at least freedom from unnecessary suffering. It is necessary to ask what guides us as we try to separate genuine caring from fake caring and also from caring that has deplorable results. The temptation in philosophical work is to make the original criteria stick by further elaboration and deeper analysis, and indeed such efforts are part of the fun and excitement of doing philosophy. If, however, we want our work to have practical effects, we have to turn away from work that carries us too deeply into abstraction. But, with such cautions in mind, we should not prematurely turn away from theorizing either.

In Ernest's case it is clear that our theoretical criteria allow us to say that the father-son relation was not one of caring. The case of Theobald and George is harder because both insisted that caring was present. On what grounds, then, can an outsider say that it was not? Attention was certainly present; in fact, it was intrusive and overweening. We might try to argue that such attention is not the receptive sort described by Weil since it does not ask, "What are you going through?" But this is not clear. Both fathers—Theobald and George before him—saw much of what their sons were thinking and feeling, but they used this insight to hurt and control. Well, then, surely there was a failure of motivational displacement. Neither father let his energy flow toward the projects of his son. This analysis seems right, but it doesn't solve our problem. First, the fathers would have argued that their sons should not have considered the projects and pursuits they actually entertained. For their own sakes, the sons had to be steered in another direction. Second, if we insist that the failure occurred exactly here—in failing to support their sons' projects—we invite a bigger problem. As carers, must we support the projects of the cared-for regardless of the worth of the projects?

The answer to this is, obviously, no. We will not support our sons in projects that will hurt others. Our basic criteria will serve us here as we redirect our attention to others in the network and explain how support of a particular project will lead to a failure of care with others. When we say no to someone, does this represent a lapse of care? Often it does not. First, there are many reasons why we might have to say no to a given project, and much depends on how the "no" is delivered and received. Consideration of the mode of delivery reminds us that the projects we are discussing here are almost always secondary to the single greatest project or need: to be cared for. If a negative answer is given in a loving and reasonable way, that major need may well be met. If the cared-for understands and is willing to change his project, caring can be maintained.

There may be a period—brief or long—in which the cared-for rejects our claim to care and insists, "You just don't care!" These are very difficult periods in which the one who wants to care must exercise skill and patience. From the virtue perspective caring is perhaps at its height at this point; from the relational perspective it has lapsed, and I think it is best to face this. When such incidents occur regularly over long periods of time, carers should reflect deeply on their attitudes and actions. The pain and disappointment of the cared-for should induce a commitment to change. This never happened to Ernest's parents, and his incipient love was "killed anew, again and again and again."

Where do we stand in our present analysis? We can say with assurance that the relation between Ernest and his parents was not one of caring, but it would have been hard to make this assessment from a virtue perspective. When Theobald died—quietly, with no suffering, in a vigorous old age—the general verdict was positive: "He was not only liked, he was beloved by all who had anything to do with him"; "a . . . perfectly just and righteously dealing man"; "We shall miss him sadly." Only his three children "joined insincerely in the tribute of applause."[18] They knew (at least intuitively) the difference between caring for another and caring only for oneself and one's reputation.

The case of Theobald and his father, George, represents a genuine case of pathological caring. If we were working from a Sartrean existentialist perspective, we would have to lay heavy blame on Theobald for allowing this to happen. He recognized fleetingly what his father was doing to him, but he not only accepted it, he followed his father as a model. Sartre would call this "bad faith" of the most obvious sort.

From the care perspective, however, we are not so interested in a judgment as we are in what might have prevented such a perversion of care. Orwell, in describing his experiences at a reputable British public school, notes that children *believe* adults.[19] Even when he was whipped for stumbling in his Latin translations, Orwell did not think to question the headmaster's tactics. Physical abuse was regularly used, and it seemed to be effective. Small boys learned Latin, English grammar, and the dates of historical events. Referring to the headmaster and his wife, Orwell writes, "I hated Bingo and Sim, with a sort of shamefaced, remorseful hatred, but it did not occur to me to doubt their judgment."[20] Having been caned once for bedwetting and again—and harder—for confiding that the first "didn't hurt," young George learned the "abiding lesson" of his boyhood: "I was in a world where it was *not possible* for me to be good. . . . Life was more terrible, and I was more wicked, than I had imagined."[21] Accounts such as these underscore a point I will develop as we discuss an approach to social response that begins in home and school life. Children (and eventually adults) need to live in a world where it is possible to be good, and they need to learn what it means to be cared for.

We still have not solved the major problem that faces us. On what grounds do we reject another's project? When the cared-for wants to do something that will likely hurt someone else, we need only invoke the criteria already at hand to show that other caring relations would collapse if we supported the project. Suppose the proposed project would not hurt others. Are we justified in rejecting it on other grounds? There are many reasons why we might not help in a given project—lack of resources or priorities of time among them—but we can usually maintain caring relations by addressing the underlying need to be cared for; that is, we can respond with sympathy to the cared-for's enthusiasm for a project even if we cannot help with it.

There are occasions, however, especially with young people, when we think it would be better for the cared-for if he or she did not do *this* but something else. Here we tread close to the pathology already identified. In chapter 12 I discuss this problem at the level of social theory.

Should government merely protect its citizens from violations of their liberties, or should it provide positive guidance toward some well-formulated ideal? At what point does freedom become license, and at what point does guidance become coercion? In the first case we may find a society in which "nobody cares"; in the second we may create a society marked by a different pathology—self-righteous avowals of care, claims to virtue, rules enforced ostensibly for citizens' own good, and, in general, blindness to the real suffering of actual people. I think it is fair to say that in all human interactions today, from parenting to those involving the federal government, we suffer more from lack of care than from coercion. Nevertheless, the pendulum is swinging, and it is important for those of us who advocate care and guidance to show that we are aware of pathological forms of care and also to make recommendations that will avoid or control these pathologies.

Before moving on to another pathology of care, one more aspect of Ernest's story should be explored. Ernest, much to the chagrin of his godfather, married a former servant and had two children. His wife, Ellen, turned out to be an alcoholic and—lucky for him—she also turned out to be a bigamist. His marriage was no marriage at all. With Ellen out of the picture, Ernest found a loving foster home for his children and allowed them to grow up free and loved in a working-class environment. When his son decided to become a "bargeman" like his foster father, Ernest responded by buying a steamer for the boy and his foster father. Ernest apparently broke the cycle of control, bitterness, and hatred that had characterized his own upbringing, although the burden of getting it right fell on other shoulders.

Ernest's hands-off solution was, of course, compatible with Butler's views on marriage and parenting. Other solutions were surely possible. Ernest could have hired a nanny and kept the children with him; he could have found an enlightened school where his son might have prospered. For our purposes, the point is that we probably can't decide once and for all whether freedom should be construed as freedom from interference or as freedom to become what one *should* be. Even dedicated liberals who subscribe wholeheartedly to the first with respect to government, behave for all the world as though they accept the second when it comes to their own children. This problem will occupy us continually as we move from the home setting into the larger public domain.

Another pathology of care occurs in some long-term relationships that fail to develop mutuality in caring. Again, although the phenomenological criteria for caring encounters often seem to be satisfied in these relations, something is wrong. Typically a woman does far more than her share of caring, and her husband or partner simply accepts care as his due. Because this situation has a long history—one in which the lack of mutuality was held to be justified by a patriarchal society—some of today's feminists worry that an ethic of care will maintain the traditional exploitation of women.[22] I have never argued that an ethic of care is only for women. I have argued that it arises more naturally from the sort of experience traditionally provided for women than from that provided for men. This is an argument for changing the experience of both so that something like a universal caregiver model is offered for all.

Philosophically, looking at the lack of mutuality, we are again faced with the problem of either accepting a pathology or trying to show, under the description already laid out, that such exploitative relationships are "not really caring." I think we might do a fairly convincing job of showing that women involved in such relationships often have to work harder and harder to produce the response carers need to continue effective caring. We could construct a logical argument along these lines. But why do this? Our eventual description of caring would be so refined that fewer and fewer real cases could be found to fit it. Moreover, empirical evidence of exploitative relationships is plentiful, and we would do better to address this fact head-on and ask how caring can be maintained and exploitation reduced. As we explore the possibilities, we must keep in mind that there are no guarantees that caring can be maintained without the possibility of pathologies creeping in. We are not attempting to construct an unassailable logical structure; we are, rather, looking for a way of being in the world that will reduce harm and increase care.

There are several powerful answers to the charge that caring is a "dangerous ethic."[23] First, care theorists must emphasize moral education—that is, education for caring. Care is an ethical orientation for everyone, not just women. Males and females have been subjected to powerful patterns of gender socialization for centuries. These patterns are changing, but many societal features still put women at a disadvantage. Consider, for example, the notoriety of the Susan Smith case. Smith confessed to killing her two young children. Whether she did so in an aborted suicide attempt or as part of a deliberate plot to free herself for a new romance we will never know. Over the months of the investigation and trial many cases of parental murder were reported—almost all of them committed by fathers. One case, reported in a single paragraph on an inside page, involved a father who beheaded his young son by the side of the road. Another involved a father who asphyxiated his two

young children (about the ages of Smith's children) after being forced
to pay child support. Cases such as these are reported every week and
usually create only a local stir—nothing like the national dismay caused
by Smith's crime. Why? Because *mothers* do not kill or harm their children. Such an act seems unthinkable to most people. Why is it not
unthinkable, then, for a father?

The ethic of care aims for a transformation of mind and spirit that
would indeed make it as unthinkable for a man to kill his child as it now
is for a woman to do so. The danger is that, as we hear more and more
stories about women harming their children, we will no longer find it
"unthinkable" for either parent to kill a child. Instead of abandoning an
ethic of care because of its danger to women, I would prefer to extend
it to men as a way to reduce the danger to everyone. Accomplishing this
will be hard work, and it will not be achieved by the usual forms of
political action, although some political action will certainly be necessary.

Many feminists deplore the fact that women still bear a dispropor-
tionate share of responsibility for raising children and maintaining a
home even though they work full time outside. To say that this is unfair,
that it is a violation of justice, does not get us very far. Indeed, if this
line of argument is pushed far enough the ethic of care might deteriorate
to a form of Kantianism in which care would be a grim duty, and those
who wished to avoid the duty could construct elaborate rationales for
their escape. We can decry the unfairness of allowing women to continue
to provide most of the care giving, but, if the result of a more equitable
distribution of tasks is two grim and grudging "caregivers," what have
we gained?

Care must be made attractive. It must be emphasized that a life of
care is not necessarily a life of "cares and burdens" but, rather, one of
joy and fulfillment. It may require occasional sacrifices (what ethic does
not?), but it does not require self-abnegation. The education and socialization of all children should include many stories of men and
women who have led deeply satisfying lives in caring relationships, and
feminists eager for political action should be pressing for massive
changes in education.

I offer an analogy that may be useful. In today's schools educators
are trying hard to increase the participation of young women in mathematics and science. The rationale is that women have been deprived of
opportunities for high-paying jobs by their lack of preparation in these
subjects. It seems to worry a just society when young women lag behind
young men in skills valued by that society. Unfortunately it does not

seem to worry that same society at all that young men lag behind young women in preparation for elementary education, nursing, early childhood education, or full-time parenting. These occupations, traditionally female, are not highly valued. The male standard of evaluation is taken for granted. The question now arises whether we should simply accept this or try to change the standard of evaluation. My claim, which is supported by arguments in succeeding chapters, is that we must work to change the standard of evaluation if we seriously want to reduce harm and increase care.[24] We can claim, rightly and enthusiastically, that men have long been deprived of many of the joys that accompany everyday caring. In many cases they have not been encouraged to develop the skills and attitudes that make life deeply satisfying.

Another objection to an ethic of care is that it is prone to parochialism.[25] Examination of this objection may or may not lead to an identifiable pathology. It is certainly true that one can find caring in the inner circle to be so rewarding that she or he happily withdraws from the concerns of care in the public domain. We may not be able to resolve whether women have done this in the past because they lived an ethic of care or because they were virtually powerless to effect reforms in the public domain. Clearly many women have confined their care to home and local arenas, but many others, whose language suggests at least an implicit ethic of care, have been leaders of social reform. We might list Jane Addams, Pearl Buck, Elizabeth Cady Stanton, Dorothea Dix, Florence Nightingale, Sara Josephine Baker, Jeannette Rankin, Frances Kelley, Luisa Capetillo, Anna Julia Cooper, and Dorothy Day.

Consider the case of Anna Julia Cooper. Although she was very active in both professional and public spheres, at age 56 she adopted her brothers' orphaned grandchildren, five children aged six months to twelve years.[26] Robin Berson remarks:

While she seemed to cope admirably with five children and their needs, Cooper's own needs suffered; with five new dependents, she was unable to meet Columbia's one-year residency requirement for the Ph.D. degree. Totally unwilling to accept defeat, Cooper managed to transfer her Columbia credits to the Sorbonne, where another several summers' research enabled her to complete her dissertation.[27]

Cooper was the fourth black American woman to receive a Ph.D. Her life of dedication to oppressed groups, to the children in her inner circle, and to personal fulfillment shows that a life of caring need be neither deprived nor severely restricted. Caring directly for one's family (however that is defined) does not preclude some form of caring in public life, but the two forms are different, and we will analyze the difference in some detail later.[28]

It seems to me that two questionable notions operate in the judgment that an ethic of care induces parochialism. The first suggests that women's attention to the inner circle prevents effective action in the public domain. There are so many counter-examples in the biographies of women (some noted above) that this notion can be declared false and discarded. It is not the ethic of care but a lack of political power that has kept women from greater public involvement. Indeed, I would argue that the ethic of care has given many women the incredible energy and dedication required to overcome enormous obstacles to public activity.

The second notion is harder to dismiss. Those involved in direct care for even a few people know that there are limits to what one carer can do. I said in an earlier work, and I reaffirm it here, that we cannot care for everyone, if by "we" the speaker refers to some finite group. To suppose that we can or that we ought to is a lovely but wild dream. The best we can do is to care directly for those who address us—those we actually encounter (notice that this includes strangers)—and indirectly for others by working to establish social conditions in which care can flourish. To suppose that these tasks are identical is the great liberal error. We do not care, in the direct sense, through welfare grants, coercive schooling, or military action. We have to work toward a world in which "it is possible to be good"—one in which carers are enabled to care without sacrificing their own lives and in which caring goes beyond politically correct rhetoric. Recognizing the necessity of such work is the reason for rehabilitating *caring about* and giving it the place it deserves.

Is there any sense in which the broad charge of parochialism represents a genuine pathology of care? One other possibility must be explored. When great symbolic differences create enemies, we are likely to stand with "our own." An ethic of care faces this honestly. There is no need to create elaborate justifications that we will continue to maintain for fifty years or even for centuries in the face of evidence that contradicts them. Although there are certainly cases where "our" side is clearly right in any adequate ethical framework, in most cases we stand with our own because they *are* our own. Here is Orwell again:

As I write, highly civilized human beings are flying overhead, trying to kill me. They do not feel any enmity against me as an individual, nor I against them. They are "only doing their duty," as the saying goes. Most of them, I have no doubt, are kindhearted law-abiding men who would never dream of committing murder in private life. On the other hand, if one of them succeeds in blowing me to pieces with a well-placed bomb, he will never sleep any the worse for it. He is serving his country, which has the power to absolve him from evil.[29]

The ethic of care refuses to absolve us from this evil. If we cannot find it in our conscience to refuse to destroy another person simply because he or she wears a label (recall Orwell's difficulty in discerning the fascist in the man holding up his trousers), then we must at least acknowledge the tragedy and reject elaborate schemes of justification. Second, we must work even harder for a world in which "highly civilized . . . kindhearted . . . men" do not commit legal murder — a world in which it is possible to be good. An ethic of care does not *justify* standing with one's own; it recognizes that most of us will do this, and it seeks to promote conditions under which this basic psychological orientation will not be called forth to the detriment of others. Thus, the undeniable fact that almost all of us side with our own in times of real threat is not a pathology of care. It is a fact of life to be reckoned with, and ethical theories must take it into account. The pathology lies in the ideologies that would have us believe we are justified in harming others even when nonviolent alternatives exist for defending ourselves.

Encounter and Obligation

So far, in this chapter and the previous one, we have discussed several encounters and responses, or failures to respond: the watchers-on-the-shore who callously let a man drown, a small boy struggling to learn Latin with the help of physical punishment, detective Miskin's simultaneous disgust at society's expectations and personal acceptance of responsibility for her grandmother, Ernest's efforts to love his unlovable parents, and Cooper's generous adoption of five children when her career was still developing. In each case we have seen that when the possibility of obligation arises, some accept the obligation ("obligation happens") while others — often in the service of some predetermined ethical principles — reject or distort the obligation. Even those who take a phenomenological (or descriptive) approach to ethics may differ strongly on the source or locus of the moral values that should guide us.

The differences are well captured by Edith Wyschogrod:

Phenomenological efforts to resolve the problem of generality in connection with moral problems have begun from two diverse starting points. The first, a tack taken by Max Scheler, Nicolai Hartmann, and others, assumes that values are instantiated in the world and have properties that are open to intuitive grasp. Values are singled out as having independent being and as accessible without having an actual locus in things. The second approach begins with the embodied existent's actual encounters with other persons and finds an empirical locus for these transactions. Martin Buber, Gabriel Marcel, and Emmanuel Levinas turn to the experience of the Other to develop an account of social existence in which interactions with others disclose a sphere of responsibility prior to propositional language or moral action.[30]

From this second perspective the weight and depth of need call forth obligation before any decision is made on exactly what to do. We accept responsibility for the Other and are accountable to the Other, not to a set of *a priori* rules. "Absolutely present, in his face, the Other—without any metaphor—faces me."[31] In encounter, obligation happens. But one needs practice in responding with care to what arises in encounters.

Diane Koos Gentry tells the true story of Gladys Milton, a black nurse and midwife in the Florida panhandle. As we read the story of Ms. Milton—how she raised and educated a large family, the hours she puts in nursing and delivering babies, the time she devotes to her church, the incredible dedication of her "spare" time to volunteer work—we know we are in the presence of a remarkable woman. Whatever it is to be moral, Gladys is it: "Her days off are often jammed with volunteer work, taking blood pressures or visiting shut-ins. 'I like to do things for people. It's my friends who make me tick, always have. I love people and I care what they think of me. I'd feel awful if someone didn't like me.'"[32]

By the standards of traditional ethics, Gladys might be found lacking in autonomy. In Kohlberg's developmental scheme she might be assessed as stuck in stage 3—the "good boy—nice girl" stage. She wants people to think well of her, and she guides her own action by the response of others to what she says or does. This mode of response could be unprincipled or even self-seeking, but the story of Gladys's life makes it clear that she is neither. She would not "do anything" to get people to like her. Rather, she puts the needs of others first and judges the efficacy of her response by the way people react to her efforts. Her life illustrates the holistic nature of morality; we know how to judge her statement by *her life,* not by referring it to a set of principles or the description of moral states, or even by her own problematic statement: "I'd feel awful if someone didn't like me." It is clear from her life that

she uses something like a favorable response from the cared-for to evaluate her own efforts to care. Looking at the life of Gladys Milton, we
have to acknowledge both a contribution and a deficiency in Kohlberg's
description of stage 3. He makes a clear contribution in pointing to the
potential weaknesses in wanting to be liked and approved of, but he
misses the potential growth inherent in stage 3 (or, better, in an other-
oriented attitude). The great advance offered by Carol Gilligan is the
possibility of moral development that moves toward an increased capacity to respond as carers rather than toward abstract principles and
ultimately a principle of justice.[33]

Gladys's life and the lives of many others provide examples of what
it means to accept obligation—to live a life of response. The great difficulty from a traditional perspective is that we find it hard to generalize
from Gladys's life. Must we *all* do what Gladys does? Of course not.
The lesson goes much deeper and involves personal capacities, the nature
of regular encounters in a particular life, and the complexity of one's
own web of caring. Indeed, we might well argue that the traditional
emphasis on universalizability has provided a way of escaping—not of
meeting—obligation. What cannot be done by all of us cannot be demanded of any of us. Saintly lives illustrate possibilities; they show us
ways in which obligation occurs and can be met. We cannot expect that
everyone will or should respond as Gladys does, but by watching her,
we may learn new possibilities for our own lives. As Wyschogrod notes,
"the saintly body acts as a signifier, as a carnal general that condenses
and channels meaning, a signifier that expresses extremes of love, compassion, and generosity. In their disclosure of what is morally possible,
saintly bodies 'fill' the discursive plane of ethics."[34]

We examine such lives to see what is possible, but we must go beyond
the heroic and the saintly to ask what conditions might make it possible
for most of us to respond with care to others. What must we learn and
how best can we learn it? Male and female encounters have typically
been very different and so have the expectations for what comes out of
these encounters. Can we, perhaps, transform the world into a more
compassionate and joy-filled place by deliberately providing different
experiences and working toward a new valuation of formerly devalued
activities? To accomplish such a transformation will require bold and
forward-looking thought.

In this chapter we discussed forms of harm that are protected by the
law. In the United States not-caring is protected by precedents that
support "no duty to rescue," and the practice of capital punishment

endorses actual harm. In virtually all nations the harm done in "legal" activities such as punishment of criminals and war is protected, even encouraged. We asked what supports our inclinations to harm and to fail to care and how such failures can be understood.

We also examined pathologies of care and found two that can hardly be disputed. A relation that seems to an outside party to be perverse and mutually damaging may be judged *caring* by its members. The remedy for this seems to be enlightened education on what it means to care; people have to learn what it means to be cared for. This remedy raises a host of culturally sensitive issues. The second pathology is found in the lack of mutuality in mature relationships. Again, both parties may assess the relationship as one of caring, but the view from outside suggests that one party is badly exploited and the other badly spoiled. Moral education seems the logical remedy for this problem, but both the assessment and the remedy may be culture-specific.

One candidate for pathology was rejected. Caring in itself does not induce parochialism or a withdrawal to the inner circles of care. Lack of power and hopelessness are the more likely roots of this phenomenon. Women who have had some social power have often used an ethic of care with positive effects in both domestic and public life. They use caring-about to ensure the establishment of relations in which caring-for can occur.

Finally, the connection between encounter and obligation was explored. In agreement with other dialogical approaches, I suggested that "obligation happens" to those who are sensitive to the needs that are revealed in encounter. By "obligation" we mean an inner sense of "I must" that is induced by the expressed or perceived needs of another person. I have not yet said clearly what I mean by "needs," and I turn to that question next.

CHAPTER 3

Needs

We have seen that an ethic of care seeks to prevent or alleviate harms to others and to oneself. An ethic of care also seeks, more broadly, to identify and respond to needs. In the dominant current social theories, harms to others are prevented through the enforcement of rights. This move is often made without considering or even mentioning needs. An ethic of care does not reject the concept of rights, but it logically construes rights as originating in and anchored in needs. I will start this chapter with a brief discussion of how rights might arise from needs and then proceed to an analysis of ways in which we might identify and classify needs. At the end of the chapter we will see that existing political and social theories have flaws that prevent them from addressing needs adequately.

Rights from Needs

Before launching an argument for a needs-based concept of rights, I should remind readers that care theorists do not agree on every feature of an ethic of care. In particular, some may see the concept of rights as independent of needs. In the version of care ethics presented here I try to show that rights do arise from needs. If I am right on this, it makes sense to turn to the primary concept in developing both care theory and a social policy guided by it. To illustrate the genesis of a right, I will start with an everyday situation and try to show how its initial claim might be justified. In what follows I will speak of Ms. A's *need,* although readers may object that her "need" is really a mere "want." A bit later, I will discuss the distinction between wants and needs. Here is an ordinary household story:

Ms. A is at her wit's end with the noise in her house. Finally, getting everyone's attention, she says, "Mommy has a right to some peace and quiet!" How is this "right" justified (if it is)? Supposing that the group addressed contains at least one person old enough to understand Ms. A's claim, the argument may be laid out as follows:

1. There is a situation, a set of conditions, that gives rise to a need.

2. The need is communicated in clear terms.

3. At least someone in the group of hearers interprets the statement of need accurately and sympathetically. The reaction is "I can see that." (Nancy Fraser's discussion of needs interpretation is useful here.)[1]

4. Having acknowledged the legitimacy of the need, the group now examines its own role in producing the noise and its (potential) power to reduce it. The response is "We can do that."

5. The need is formally granted as a right; that is, the group of hearers recognizes the legitimacy of the need and its own power to meet the need: "We *should* meet this need."

This homely example is instructive both in what it reveals and in the objections it raises. First, one may properly object that we do not usually grant a right to an individual except as a member of some group that has already acquired a right. To secure a *right* to peace and quiet, Ms. A would have to organize a movement in the public arena. One could argue, however, that the process described at the household level can be generalized to the political domain.

A critic might now exclaim that this is ludicrous. The language of rights should not even be used in a case such as this. I can half concede that, philosophically speaking, Ms. A should not have used the word *right* to describe her desire (or need, if we grant her that) for peace and quiet. However, it is not implausible that Ms. A *would* actually use such language, and this is a point that reinforces my decision not to start the development of social theory with rights. Our language today, in liberal democracies, is saturated with talk of rights. We should dig beneath this talk for the wants, desires, interests, and needs that gave rise to it.

The critic who complains that the situation is not an appropriate arena for a discussion of rights can be answered with a deeper, more direct answer. He or she would be correct to point out that rights are granted to publicly recognized groups and that, indeed, these groups usually play the role of Ms. A; that is, they express the need, and they are both recognized and organized. When a group has the power to press its demands in the public arena, it often acquires the right it seeks. The right may then be extended to other similar groups and, in some cases, to all human beings.

Now we must ask about those people who are not so well organized. What of the isolated people such as housewives, who are not publicly recognized as a group? What of those, such as children, who are rationally immature? Must their needs wait until the rights already granted to some other group are extended to them—sometimes in a convoluted logic that distorts the real need? This observation, I think, gives us a strong reason to start with wants and needs and turn to rights only when wants and needs are better understood. This in no way diminishes the importance of rights that are already established.

The process I've described holds up across a wide variety of cases. Reviewing the steps from want or desire to recognized need and then to right, we see that negotiation is required to reach agreement on a need; it is (or may be) required again in determining whether the group addressed is the one that should respond. Even when a need is legitimated, the question of administration remains. In the case considered here the oldest child may not be able to control the younger ones, a willing adult may not have the requisite skills, or the need may be only partly met because participants disagree on the level of noise that should bother a reasonable person. The degree of both need and satisfaction may be debated, but if a need has risen to the level of a right, the one who claims the right feels justified in demanding that it not be denied.

Needs historically rise to the level of rights through the steps already described. A group expresses a need as a demand for a right. The audience that is addressed listens and has the power to act (or acknowledges that the demanding group has the power to seize what it wants), and it grants the right, sometimes after a bloody struggle. Admittedly, the demand often uses universal language ("All men are created equal"), but the intent is not always universal. Extension of the right to all persons may be a slow process.

The example I have given only hints at how we might justify the large negative rights—rights that guarantee freedom from intervention—that we cherish in a liberal society, but I argue that roughly the same process is followed. Why, for example, do we need free speech? The process of legitimizing such a need follows a historical pattern very like the one I have described for a simple household problem. It is not surprising to learn that even a doctrine such as the divine right of kings arose from a felt need. Because a group had been threatening the power of the monarch in France, Louis XIV's bishop, Jacques-Bénigne Bossuet, elaborated the doctrine of royal absolutism known as the divine right theory. A similar claim to royal rights was made in England by the Stuarts. The genesis of rights can, thus, be traced to a felt need; to proceed, the process requires sufficient power in either those claiming the right or in those responding to the demand.

The fact that rights grow out of needs does not suggest that they should be equated with needs or, for that matter, with power or interest. Once a need has been sanctified as a right, all those who fall into that particular class of rights-bearers "have the right" whether or not they feel a need or evince an interest. Rights protect needs, interests, and powers regardless of whether specific individuals claim them and even, in some cases, if they deny them.

The main point for our present purpose is that, without rejecting the language of rights, we need not and perhaps should not start with the concept of persons as rights-bearers. We can start instead with humans as organisms needing care. That makes the caring relation (between carer and cared-for) basic. Notice, however, that we have no proud or even respectable word for "one who needs." "Needy" is not a label that any of us can embrace with the pride that accompanies "rights-bearer." Yet if we understand the caring relation more deeply, if we understand the noncontractual nature of reciprocity in caring, we may give more generously to those who need and accept with better grace our own need for care.

Starting with needs, then, is a cautious strategy. Rights proliferate rapidly,[2] but needs are usually examined more carefully because, I suppose, they often connote positive obligation. Critics may object strenuously here. "Rights proliferate!" they might exclaim. Needs are far more notorious in this respect. There is no end to them, and we are hard put to distinguish genuine needs, to tell needs from wants, or even to find an acceptable method of identifying them. Spare me complaints about the proliferation of rights! The point is well taken. However, it is clearly rights-talk that gets attention in the public domain. Because we have been reluctant to admit needs-talk into public discussion (in part, perhaps, because of its historical association with Marxism), needs remain in a shadowy, semiprivate domain.

What (beyond fear of Marxism) accounts for our reluctance to tackle needs philosophically? When we acknowledge a need, we may be called upon to do something, to give up something, or to respond sympathetically and effectively to someone, whereas acknowledgment of a right often means leaving people alone, not interfering. It may not be surprising that so much of feminist political theory is explicitly or implicitly needs-based.[3] It calls attention to our human condition as beings who have needs and urges discussion of our needs in the public arena, not only in private settings. Rights-talk has almost always been conducted in the public domain, and its focus has been on the relation between individual and formal government. Even today there are rights construed in such a way that certain practices (limits on speech, for example) are not allowed in government-sponsored institutions but continue in force in private institutions. The conduct of personal life and "private" interactions has fallen under the negative protection of rights, but needs-talk is far less respectable. The sharp separation of public and private has made a public response to needs regarded as private very difficult. In chapter 14 we will see, for example, that it has been almost impossible for public schools to teach anything substantial about homemaking and child rearing because such material has been associated with private life. Despite the slogan advanced by feminists—"the personal is political"—we have not moved very far in exploring the implications of this slogan for education.

The Identification of Needs

Because care as a social theory is based on needs, we have to identify the needs that various social groups should meet, and this is a notoriously difficult task. Much of this will be deferred for the discussion of what is identified, satisfied, and learned at home. Here we are concerned primarily with approaches that do not quite work and the reasons we need a different one.

There is little difficulty in identifying biological needs, although they are certainly modified by factors such as age, gender, and culture. All human beings need food, water, shelter, and protection from harm. Biological needs are, we might say, expressed biologically.

Other needs arise from wants. For example, a child may want a pet, a hug, undivided attention, or a particular item of clothing. Still other needs are inferred as needs of the child by thoughtful caregivers; the need for schooling is such a need. Needs that arise from wants are expressed needs too, but these are often expressed in words as wants and desires. When do we acknowledge wants and desires as needs? We might use criteria such as these: the want is fairly stable over a considerable period of time and/or it is intense; the want is demonstrably connected to some desirable end, or, at least, to one that is not harmful, and the end is impossible or difficult to meet without the object wanted; the want is in the power (within the means) of those addressed to grant it; and the one wanting is willing and able to contribute to the satisfaction of the want. When these criteria are met, most groups will acknowledge an expressed need.

In contrast, inferred needs are not initially expressed by the one in need. Few children express a need for schooling, but once exposed to it, they may express a need for further schooling. Of course, the opposite may happen. Children may express a stable ("can't wait") desire to go to school and, after exposure, decide they want nothing more to do with schools. In such unhappy cases the need remains an inferred need. Again, children do not often express a need to care for others, but adults infer the need for them to learn how to care. As they acquire such learning, the need may become an expressed need—one that seems to have been there all along.

A consideration of "basic needs," or what David Braybrooke calls "course-of-life" needs, is the usual starting point for social theories when they consider needs at all.[4] Basic needs include, at the least, physical or biological needs, safety or security needs, and certain social needs. Such needs are clearly universal at some level, but a theorist may make any of several mistakes in moving quickly from an identification of basic needs in general terms to possible plans for meeting the needs. Although basic needs are stable over time, they are not stable in the short run. At a given moment, someone may need shelter or companionship, not food. Particularly obtuse parents, for example, often shove a bottle in the baby's mouth every time it cries; wiser parents try harder to identify the present need. Mistakes of this sort are made at every level, even the international. Some years ago, after a devastating earthquake in Afghanistan, wealthy nations flooded the area with food and clothing. As it happened, building materials, not food or clothing, were sorely needed. These examples (and many more might easily be given) suggest that carers need to know something about the individuals or groups to whom they are responding. They need information about internal conditions—the sufferings, longings, and fears of those who need care—as well as external conditions.

Well-intentioned social policies designed to provide for basic needs sometimes fail or work less well than we wish precisely because we assume that needs are stable when they are not. Clearly, people need food to survive, but if another need—say, drugs or recreation—intervenes, a needy person may forego food in its favor. If, for example, the society has decided on food stamps as a means to relieve hunger, it may find itself in the position of providing currency for the purchase of other wants. Food stamps are more negotiable than food itself. The concern from the perspective of an ethic of care is not only fraud and the illegal use of food stamps (although such behavior is a concern) but also, more important, the failure to meet legitimate needs. By choosing a social policy that invites corruption, we may fail to meet the real physical needs of both the stamp holder and his or her family. Further, engaging in illegal practices may make it harder for a person to satisfy healthy social needs and those needs associated with self-esteem. One could argue also, as Sissela Bok has on lying,[5] that certain practices harm both the perpetrator and the community by lowering trust and what might be called moral vitality. Preventing such behavior, however, requires a level of attention to individuals that may diminish their autonomy. In general, giving adequate attention to the identification and satisfaction of needs raises the risk of paternalism. This worry will be discussed at some length, and it will be clear that there are times when we cannot find a needs-based solution that is free of problems more worrisome that those we had set out to solve. That may be the case with food stamps.

Not only do theorists often assume the stability and uniformity of basic needs, just as often they move too quickly to calculate how resources may best be distributed to meet legitimate needs. This is a second common mistake. Although much interesting and important work has been done in making these calculations, the thinker who "starts at home" finds many of the assumptions and standard moves disquieting.[6] For example, does it seem right to ignore degrees of satisfaction as many of these models do? We saw that the degree of both need and satisfaction was debatable in our initial case. We might also ask whether there are situations that really are Pareto-optimal. Such situations are said to be those in which no one's condition could be made better without worsening someone else's. Such a situation seems a theoretical fiction since we would almost never accept it as real in the context of home or small community. Instead, we would enlarge the set of variables to be considered, tinker with boundary conditions, consider compensatory provisions—some immediate and others long-range.

We need to ask several questions in such situations: How much better for X? How much worse for Y? And in what ways? What will the relative positions be after our tinkering? How long will the benefit (or harm) last? Family members often accept a minor or brief disadvantage to better the lot of one member—sometimes even to satisfy an idiosyncratic desire. They also strive to increase their material resources, and they attempt to provide nonmaterial compensation for material sacrifices. It is not just that highly mathematicized schemes are inevitably artificial (which does not mean that they are not useful), but they tend to fix our attention on their own gamelike quality. We become absorbed in the intricacies of the game instead of the plight of real people.

A third common misstep is to arrange needs in hierarchical form.[7] The identification of basic needs should not imply that other needs cannot exist at the same time. A person can need both recognition and love while he or she needs food and shelter. Alison Jaggar points out that

people want and need far more than physical survival. . . . But I do think that our common biological constitution provides part of the groundwork for determining objective criteria of human need. No adequate philosophical theory of human need can ignore the facts of human biology. . . . Far from being irrelevant to political philosophy, these facts must form its starting point.[8]

When we feed hungry people, we are responding to a basic biological need. When, at the same time, we engage in friendly conversation with them, we are responding to a basic social need. It is a mistake to assume that people must first satisfy the need for food or shelter before they can feel a need for affiliation and even self-actualization.

As we attempt to identify basic needs, then, we should not overlook biological needs, but neither should we stop with them. Joan Tronto points out that "what it means to meet basic needs adequately obviously depends upon cultural, technological, and historical circumstances."[9] I agree totally. The needs that are expressed will be influenced by cultural factors, and the response available will depend on available resources. What is regarded as an adequate effort in any given situation depends on both what is needed and what can be given. This underscores the concern I expressed earlier about ignoring the degree of satisfaction. An adequate theory may rightly be more nearly complete for a particular time and place than for universal application. Even so, I will argue, it will be *properly* incomplete in the sense that it will leave room for individual and small group judgment and action.

Tronto then heads in a direction that I resist.

Since caring rests upon the satisfaction of needs for care, the problem of determining which needs should be met shows that the care ethic is not individualistic, but must be set in the broader moral context. Obviously a theory of justice is necessary to discern among more or less urgent needs.[10]

I think this may put the cart before the horse. I agree fully that we must look at the broader context, not just the "moral" context. Confining our inspection to the present moral context may indeed prejudice our analysis. Although I am ready to agree that we may need a theory of justice, I do not think that it can be developed adequately without first developing a social theory of care. This project will, of course, require attending to how relevant cultures now construe justice, but I do not want to be entirely constrained by such views at the outset.

The last common mistake that theorists make springs from their failure to attend to cultural influences — the "cultural, technological, and historical circumstances" to which Tronto draws attention — on wants and needs. Wants and needs proliferate in complex societies and, further, they are manipulated consciously for profit and unconsciously through the various media. What responsibility does a society have for recognizing and meeting wants that it has aroused? For example, should such a society, through its government, make some effort to control the manipulation of desire? I will leave this question open for now, but we should note that the word *encounter* is once again significant. The bombardment of stimuli in an affluent society creates a multitude of opportunities for encounter, but there is more than one way of completing an encounter. In particular, we will be concerned with encounters that are merely reactive and with those that are reflective. Does government, through its system of education, have a responsibility to promote reflective encounters? If so, how can it do so?

An Alternative Approach

Is it feasible to build an adequate social theory by starting with what occurs in ideal homes? The concept of an ideal home (not *the* ideal home) will serve several purposes. First, it will provide a theoretical framework in which to identify universal categories — categories that must be addressed by anyone speaking of homes. Second, it will give us a device for filling out the categories in a way that should be instrumentally sound; that is, I argue that some forms of an ideal home are better suited to certain goals and are more likely to meet certain needs than are other forms. Here I will just sketch the possibilities as a preview of sorts.

Suppose we start with Ruddick's maternal interests, as identified in chapter 1.[11] A maternal figure (female or male) must respond to three great demands (or needs) of the child: preservation, growth, and acceptability. These needs are both practical and universal, but their explication—their filling out—involves us in personal, cultural, and practical complexities. How are these needs to be described? How are various expressions of them to be interpreted? And how far will they take us? On this last question, our concern is how far to extend our recognition of these needs; that is, over what range of human beings should these needs be recognized? If they properly apply only to children, we have to ask at what age or stage we will no longer accept responsibility for another's growth or acceptability, and we have to ask also about new needs that arise—needs that cannot be captured by the three already identified.

Consider, for example, a need that is often expressed late in life. Ms. A notes that her young children have never expressed a need to be useful, although they often "want to help." A more generalized, stable desire to be useful is something she hopes to instill in her children. In contrast, her elderly mother (who lives with Ms. A) says over and over again that she "needs to be useful." The old woman cannot see well, her hearing is bad, and she can do little that requires physical effort because of advanced osteoporosis. Ms. A studies the conditions: her family likes fresh vegetables and fruits, and her mother needs to feel useful. Therefore Ms. A puts her to work shelling peas and lima beans, snipping the tails off string beans, peeling apples, and the like.

We see in this simple scenario that even an expressed need, accepted as legitimate, must be interpreted and administered in context. We see also that the need expressed by Ms. A's mother might be described as an extension of the acceptability need. In childhood the need for acceptance is clear and internal, but the need for acceptability is external; parents infer that children have such a need. In later life, when people have internalized the criteria for acceptability, they often express a genuine need to be not only accepted, but acceptable in some significant way. Every society depends on this process of converting inferred needs to expressed needs. It is a major part of socialization, but it also induces mixed evaluations. We applaud some conversions and deplore others. We explore ways to control the process, and we then worry about the process of control. We properly want to put limits on government's efforts to control our identification and pursuit of wants and needs, but we recognize the importance of exercising considerable control in the lives of children. Their needs for preservation, growth, and acceptability make demands on us, and our efforts to identify and meet their needs create further wants and a whole set of inferred needs that require control and even coercion.

Whatever we eventually uncover, it is clear from the start that if we recognize these three needs (or something like them), we are committed for at least a time to what Berlin has called a positive concept of liberty.[12] Under such a concept we are concerned not merely with providing liberty so that people can pursue their own legitimate goods but, even more, with establishing structures and customs that will facilitate their becoming what they *should* become. When we are dealing with children, we expect to intervene regularly not only to prevent harm to others but also to shape the character and personality of the child. Dare we move in this direction with adults? Under what circumstances?

Starting at home, with children, we identify biological needs as essential for preservation. To preserve the life of the child we must provide food, clothing, shelter, and safety. Our particular culture adds further biological needs that have been identified, tested, and widely accepted: immunizations, regular check-ups, dental care, diets to control allergies, and the like. We see that some of these needs or demands start out as wants or desires, are then interpreted and assessed, and eventually become recognized needs. Others start out as inferred needs; that is, technological or medical advances make certain desirable procedures widely available, and the society infers that all of its people need these services. In some cases those who are coerced to undergo the procedures may be initially resistant; this happened with immunizations, for example. In other cases the obvious desirability of a service or procedure creates a want that is quickly acknowledged as a need.

Some needs are inferred in the sense that they do not arise as expressions from the needy. When a child is hungry and cries, that is a direct expression of need (although, of course, the cry can be misinterpreted), and the universality of the need is easy to detect by observation. The "need for immunization" does not arise quite so directly. Three elements work together to produce a public assessment that children need to be immunized: something in the child—susceptibility to disease; something in the environment—an organism that causes disease; and something in the cultural resources—a vaccine. Similarly, the need for education beyond the rudiments of survival is largely an inferred need, one established by those in positions of responsibility for those who are said to have the need. Again, when members of a society recognize the value of the inferred need, it may become an expressed need and, as such, may far exceed the original need in its scope.

The interaction of expressed needs and inferred needs operates at many levels. Parents may have an expressed need for books and intellectual conversation. Initially their children may not express such a need, but the parents (acting from their own satisfaction at having such needs met) infer a similar need in the children. Often, through repeated invitations and perhaps limited coercion, the children will internalize such a need, and it will become an expressed need of their own. Studying, discussing, and evaluating this process—what might be called the socialization of needs—are important tasks for education both at home and in school.

Now, in a sense, one might argue that all needs are inferred since even a cry must be interpreted, but the terms *expressed* and *inferred* still capture an important distinction. An expressed need is internal: it arises in the cared-for either consciously or behaviorally. If an inference is made, it is made directly from observation or sensory reception of the cared-for. In contrast, an inferred need proceeds from the carer's framework. It may include meticulous consideration of the cared-for's condition, available resources, and cultural demands in which carer and cared-for are immersed, but it does not arise directly as a want or desire in the cared-for. Thus the need for immunization is an inferred need since it arises in response to a set of external conditions. We might say that it has dual origins because the internal needs of the child must be considered, but the dominant aspect is external.

Needs associated with growth, such as the one for education, also exhibit dual origins. Any normal child wants to do certain things for himself, and we recognize the universality of such wants. We even say he *needs* to feed himself, climb the stairs, manage his own toileting, and the like. Beyond such basic needs associated with growth are many that are inferred by examination of a particular culture and our own place in that culture. We have a picture in our minds of how the child should grow, and we infer certain needs from that picture and from the child himself. These inferred needs are always worrisome. If the child has not expressed a want or desire, on what grounds do we pronounce a need? Usually we speak of the child's "interests." We do this regularly and most of us would argue that we *must* do it, but the practice often makes us uneasy because we are establishing needs for another. When we behave this way with adults, we might be accused of paternalism, which would horrify us. Still, I will argue that there are circumstances in which we must take the risk.

The process of legitimating an inferred need differs from the one by which expressed needs are legitimated. Suppose that Ms. A has an adolescent son, Ben. Ben has taken two years of college preparatory mathematics but balks at the thought of a third year. Ms. A points out that Elite U., which has been the tacit college choice for Ben, requires a third year. Ms. A also notes that she has the resources to send Ben to Elite U. Further, Elite U. is more or less the standard choice for families like Ben's. Ben needs to take a third year of math if he wants to be admitted to Elite U. We can sketch the steps in negotiating this need as follows:

1. Someone in a position of responsibility or authority (in this case, Ms. A) assesses the external conditions (Elite U. requires three years of college prep math) and the available resources.

2. From this evaluation, a need is inferred. Ben *needs* a third year of math (or, it is in Ben's interest that he take a third year of math).

3. Negotiation takes place. The next steps depend on the outcome of negotiation.

4a. The cared-for (Ben) may convince the carer that the prospect of a third year of math is too horrible to entertain seriously. He may even persuade his mother that, given his present interests and demonstrated capacities, Elite U. is not the best place for him. The need is rejected as irrelevant; that is, it remains the case that any student aspiring to Elite U. needs a third year of math, but Ben—having rejected Elite U.—does not.

4b. The cared-for may reluctantly accept the need as argued by Ms. A. In doing so he may elicit promises of assistance and support—for example, tutoring help, understanding, and sympathy—if he cannot earn As, and the like. The need is accepted.

We see from this everyday example that the process of establishing needs for particular persons is complex. Interpretation and negotiation are required with expressed and inferred needs alike. Carers do not simply impose such needs in the way that rightly worries opponents of positive liberty, but neither do they simply accept the initial refusal of the cared-for. They fear that rejecting a need as irrelevant may be equivalent to inflicting an actual harm, and they want to prevent those "in need" from harming themselves. They initiate a dialogue that should result in a decision that is acceptable (or nearly acceptable) to both parties. In chapter 12, in another context, we will pursue the possibilities set out in 4a more deeply. For example, Ms. A. may not simply accept Ben's argument against a third year of math but may press for an alternative plan that seems reasonable to both. Both Ben and Ms. A. are interested in promoting Ben's growth.

It is even more obvious that we as adults infer needs in the area of acceptability. To be sure, the child expresses a need for affection and for approval, but adults decide when praise or censure should be given. Some form of affiliation has to be regarded as a basic need, for we now know that the need is so fundamental that failure to meet it may result in the child's failure to grow or even in the child's death. Thus most of us believe that affection at some level must not be withheld; it is a basic need, not a personal preference or blind desire. Affiliative interests include some whose satisfaction may appropriately be regarded as dependent on desert. The child sometimes *deserves* to have wants along these lines satisfied, and the same child sometimes does not deserve this satisfaction. The great difficulty here (discussed at length in chapter 9) is to decide which wants or expressed needs should be satisfied with no consideration of desert and which should be contingent on the child's meeting certain criteria of acceptability.

An ideal home (a theoretical entity) has near-perfect ways of negotiating these issues. Needs judged as basic are met unconditionally and are never deliberately withheld. Fervent wants are heard, interpreted, modified, approved contingently (often on grounds of desert), and satisfied. Inferred needs are articulated, heard by the cared-for, perhaps resisted, perhaps again modified, accepted, assisted, and met. The process of identifying and satisfying needs is thus a highly complex process.

In a first attempt at identifying basic needs at a universal level, then, we agree that biological needs (survival, security, and affection) must be included. We may speak of these as a need for preservation, but we see also that there are basic needs associated with growth and acceptability. Some of these may emerge in forms familiar to us in liberal ideology—the need not to be physically restrained, for example, or basic ego needs such as self-esteem—but others may not be so easily captured in that framework. It would seem, for example, that all of us need to have at least some of our nonbasic wants met, and I would include this as a basic need. It would be a poor life indeed if we never enjoyed the satisfaction of a want that is not itself a basic need. Should any particular such wants be met? On what grounds should we establish priorities among them? What limits should be established?

I have alluded to the likelihood that some needs—proclaimed as rights in liberal ideology—will arise as we undertake the task of identifying and responding to needs "starting at home." It is not an oversight to omit them here. What I want to do is to start with the human biological organism who, in continually expanding encounters and relations, becomes a person. Starting this way, we avoid an a priori conferral of rights that may constrain us so tightly that we cannot intervene to prevent people from harming themselves or to provide for needs that the cared-for has not expressed. Admittedly, such a project demands exquisite sensitivity to cultural differences and power relations, resistance to the temptation to act self-righteously in "helping" others, and recognition of the ever-present possibility that one may do more harm than good. The worry is captured eloquently by Berlin. He writes of those who would coerce others toward ways they would accept if they were not "blind or ignorant or corrupt":

This renders it easy for me to conceive of myself as coercing others for their own sake, in their, not my, interest. I am then claiming that I know what they truly need better than they know it themselves. . . . I may declare that they are actually aiming at what in their benighted state they consciously resist. . . . Once I take this view, I am in a position to ignore the actual wishes of men or societies, to bully, oppress, torture them in the name . . . of their "real" selves.[13]

Although this worry cannot be ignored, we have already discussed pathologies of care and have taken a strong stand against coercion. We must use coercion at times—and not just to prevent harm to others—but every proposed act of coercion raises a question and calls for the consideration of alternatives. We must find a way to avoid coercion where we can and yet not fall into a paralysis that allows a deplorable waste of human potential. This double need requires an approach to social policy different from the traditional schemes that have started with public life and rational entities somehow cast full-grown into the world of discourse and debate.

Although I do not claim her endorsement for my particular project, Held describes the goal well. She speaks of a morality that might be superior to existing ones.

It would be a morality based on caring and concern for actual human others, and it would have to recognize the limitations of both egoism and perfect justice. If we turn to the social and political theories that would be compatible with such a view of morality, we see that they would have to be very different not only from the patriarchal models of precontractual conceptions but also from the contractual models that so dominate current thinking. Contractual relations would not be ruled out, but they would cease to seem paradigmatic of human relations.[14]

In this chapter I have suggested that needs may be classified into two categories: expressed needs (those arising in the cared-for) and inferred needs (those arising externally). I have also—in a rough, preliminary way—described the processes by which those needs are legitimated. Both processes are complex and require further elaboration. I have also acknowledged that an ethic of care does not have to reject the concept of rights. Because we believe that rights arise out of needs, however, we must move slowly. Ideologies or theories that leap quickly beyond needs or, just as quickly, tie needs too tightly to desert ignore matters that properly belong at the center of an adequate social theory.

We move into the next chapter with a fairly clear idea of what it means to care and the risks we take when we do so. The next task is to see just what must be corrected in existing social and political theories in order to use a morality of care effectively. We know that we want a social policy that will reduce harms not only to others but also to those directed at the self. As we develop such an approach, we must remain aware of the harms that can be done in the name of caring, and this awareness has to be sharpened as we consider ways in which to meet inferred needs.

CHAPTER 4

Why Liberalism Is Inadequate

So far we have seen that we need a social philosophy that will guide us, not prescribe for us. We have noted that such a philosophy or theory is properly incomplete; it leaves space for local deliberation and judgment. In this sense social policy guided by an ethic of care has something in common with Aristotle's phronesis,[1] but it also differs sharply in several important respects. It is not so dependent on individual character because we are concentrating on a relational definition of caring and, indeed, a relational definition of self. If *relation* is basic to an ethic of care, then *encounter* becomes crucially important, since a relation is filled out in encounter. A central problem for the social theory developed here is the control and enrichment of encounter. When we reject a severely hierarchical ordering of the community, we have to find a way to manage encounter through shared authority.

We have also seen that an adequate social theory must be able to address harms to the self as well as to others, and it must address a full range of harms, not just physical and property harms. I'll say more here about this problem and the dilemmas it presents for liberalism. Finally, in the previous chapter, we began a discussion of needs and classified them as *expressed* and *inferred*. It is the latter category that raises a special problem for liberalism, but it is fair to say that liberals generally avoid the concept of needs.

No attempt will be made here to launch a comprehensive attack on liberalism. Library shelves are already groaning under such critiques. Further, there is so much in liberalism that any reasonable person should want to retain that one must be careful to suggest alternatives that do not ignore or destroy its vital contributions.[2] After a brief discussion of recent critiques, my own will fall roughly into three areas. First, liberalism makes a faulty start when it bases its tenets on the mature, rational being; second, its emphasis on freedom creates major dilemmas in how to relate to beings who are not (or are thought not to be) fully rational; and, third, its emphasis on equality, combined with its highly selective definition of self, gives rise to social policies that treat equality as sameness.

Critiques of Liberalism

Criticism of liberalism is often the opening salvo of communitarian treatises. There are several types of liberalism, but all of them emphasize liberty or freedom. Classic liberalism, which traces its roots to John Locke, focuses on life, liberty, and property, and it construes the main role of government as ensuring nonintervention in the lives of its citizens as they pursue their legitimate goals.[3] Under this form of liberalism, citizens have mainly negative rights and obligations. They have the right not to be unduly restricted and a corresponding obligation not to infringe the similar rights of others. Another form of liberalism, a heritage in part from Jean-Jacques Rousseau, puts greater emphasis on equality.[4] Throughout the twentieth century a great tension has existed within liberalism between emphases on liberty and equality. In American liberalism the focus on equality has become almost synonymous with the liberal attitude; in European liberalism emphasis is more likely to be on freedom, and liberal parties often stand in opposition to workers' or labor parties. In a broad sense today's American liberals and most conservatives both belong to the liberal tradition—one group representing equality and a large role for government in achieving and maintaining it and the other emphasizing freedom and a relatively small, noninterventionary role for government.

A growing body of critical thought charges that liberalism and its two great ethical systems—Kantianism and utilitarianism—overemphasize the autonomy of individuals (although some in the Kantian tradition object that utilitarianism does not promote autonomy but curtails it), perpetuate a myth of the presocial individual, adhere to an arrogant universalism, neglect the central role of community, and contribute to a society dominated by a bureaucratic and therapeutic mentality. Such charges come from communitarians, postmodern thinkers, and feminists, among others. It is only fair to say that the charges were also made forcefully by fascist philosophers earlier in the twentieth century.[5] All I want to do here is identify those criticisms that may be addressed by an alternative relational theory.

One of the most important criticisms leveled at liberalism is that its view of the person is faulty (this criticism is addressed more fully in chapter 5). Not only is too much emphasis placed on autonomy (as in Kantian ethics), but much liberal machinery depends on a rational decision-maker who bears little resemblance to real persons. For example, in the influential work of Rawls, a heuristic device is employed in which imaginary citizens are placed in the "original position," behind a veil of ignorance, where they are to decide on the principles and rules by which they will be governed.[6] Entering the original position requires persons to put aside their real identities and retain only their rational capacities and general information about their society. Situated as they are, behind a veil of ignorance, they literally do not know who they are, to what traditions they belong, what their social status or physical condition might be, or even what their personalities are like (for example, whether they are risk-takers or more cautious types). In this position, Rawls said, people would be most likely to choose rules that would be fair to all.

Communitarian critics charge that a person in the original position is not really a person at all.[7] Persons, they insist, are cultural entities, unavoidably products of the cultural traditions that nourish them.[8] It is a great mistake, these writers contend, to suppose that there can be (even in the imagination) genuine persons who are devoid of projects, allegiances, loves, and personalities. Even as a heuristic, then, the veil of ignorance misleads us; it causes us to overlook the aspects of personhood that actually influence our political and social decisions. I argue below that starting with the mature, rational human being is a wrong start in itself, but the communitarian view is little better for it also skips too quickly over childhood and home to locate the source of selfhood in broad cultures.

The argument between liberals and communitarians is often cast as one about the priority of the good and the right. Liberals emphasize the right—procedures and rules that should leave all individuals free to pursue their own individual and group goods. Communitarians emphasize the good and insist that a vision of what is good and what is valued precedes the establishment of rules and even concepts of justice. Thus, for communitarians, concepts of justice are themselves products of traditions and may differ across cultures.[9]

Emphasis on formal rules and rights tends to elevate *gesellschaft* (formal institutions) over *gemeinschaft* (informal community). Communitarians charge that such emphasis aggravates the twentieth century dilemma—the domination of bureaucratic procedures together with a therapeutic mentality that tries to adjust people to a society bereft of traditions and a common vision of the good. Taylor and MacIntyre criticize the instrumental (or bureaucratic) attitude and the narrow pursuit of self-expression and self-fulfillment (aspects of the therapeutic outlook). Taylor describes both and their relation to liberal procedural ethics.

The primacy of self-fulfillment, particularly in its therapeutic variants, generates the notion that the only associations one can identify with are those formed voluntarily and which foster self-fulfillment, such as the "lifestyle enclaves" in which people of similar interests or situation cluster—e.g. the retirement suburbs in the south, or revocable romantic relationships. Beyond these associations lies the domain of strategic relations, where instrumental considerations are paramount. The therapeutic outlook seems to conceive community on the model of associations like Parents without Partners, a body which is highly useful for its members while they are in a given predicament, but to which there is no call to feel any allegiance once one is no longer in need. The ethic generated beyond self-fulfillment is precisely that of procedural fairness, which plays a big role in the instrumentalist outlook.[10]

Here Taylor reminds us that groups of people gathered voluntarily together for one common purpose or interest are not necessarily a community. Upon what tradition do they call? What allegiances hold beyond the immediate purposes? In the present context of our concern about care and harm, we would want to ask also how far care is extended to members of such a "community" and what safeguards are established to prevent harm to outsiders.

One of the most objectionable features of liberalism, according to postmodern critiques, is its assumptions on universality. Because rationality—the exercise of reason—is taken as the basic distinguishing feature of persons, the one that confers upon us both agency and an innate right to respect, liberal philosophers often suppose that one mind, used well, can legislate for the whole world. For example, Jeremy Bentham, an early utilitarian, allegedly remarked that he could legislate for all of India, and presumably for the whole world, from the privacy of his study. The insistence on universalizability and the power of rational thought to "get it right" for everyone is central to the liberal tradition. Indeed, in describing deliberation in the original position, Rawls admitted that only one thoroughly rational thinker is really necessary because all other such thinkers would have to agree.

At first glance it seems that communitarianism, with its great respect for various traditions, is in a stronger position to respond to postmodern objections to "grand narratives" and the "totalizing" moves characteristic of liberalism. Communitarianism has its own forms of totalization, however, and these may be even more dangerous than those of liberalism. Further, adherents of universalism are not unaware of the problems in liberal ethics, and many have modified their views accordingly. Jürgen Habermas offered this description in an interview:

What then does universalism mean? Relativizing one's own form of existence to the legitimate claims of other forms of life, according equal rights to aliens and others with all their idiosyncrasies and unintelligibility, not sticking doggedly to the universalization of one's own identity, not marginalizing that which deviates from one's own identity, allowing the sphere of tolerance to become ceaselessly larger than it is today—all this is what moral universalism means today.[11]

Postmodern thinkers nevertheless easily spot significant vestiges of the grand narrative in Habermas's universalism: the high value placed on rational argumentation, an assumed "we" committed to relativizing their own beliefs and according rights (defined by whom?) to strangers, and "not marginalizing," which surely suggests a center occupied by entities willing to remove margins.[12] It is reasonable to ask whether communitarianism can do any better against the postmodern attack than liberalism can. I have raised questions in my own criticism about the wisdom of according the same rights to all regardless of whether the candidate for rights has the capacity required for responsible exercise of those rights. I will say more about this in the next section.

Finally, we must consider the communitarian claim that liberalism neglects community. We have already seen that community and traditions are neglected at the theoretical roots of liberalism. The myth of the presocial individual conveys the belief that autonomous rational agents can detach themselves from their cultural heritage, personal loves, and individual projects and decide matters of fairness and justice. Dewey, in an unusual episode of agreement with Walter Lippmann, wrote:

At the basis of the scheme lies what Lippmann has well called the idea of the "omnicompetent" individual: competent to frame policies, to judge their results; competent to know in all situations demanding political action what is for his own good. . . . [It] held that ideas and knowledge were functions of a mind or consciousness which originated in individuals by means of isolated contact with objects. But in fact, knowledge is a function of association and communication; it depends upon tradition, upon tools and methods socially transmitted, developed, and sanctioned.[13]

It is not only at its roots that liberalism neglects community. Its great emphasis on individual rights and negative responsibilities also tends to eclipse the everyday demands of community. Glendon charges that "rights talk" has led to a loss of discourse on responsibility. Unlike people in some European nations, citizens of the United States have few, if any, positive duties. As we noted in chapter 2, under legal precedents that claim "no duty to rescue," we do not have to save a drowning child unless we bear a special responsibility for that child (that is, it is our own child or one left explicitly in our care). The emphasis on negative duties has eroded not only a sense of responsibility for one another but even our understanding of human sociality.

Neglect of the social dimension of personhood has made it extremely difficult for us to develop an adequate conceptual apparatus for taking into account the sorts of groups within which human character, competence, and capacity for citizenship are formed. In a society where the seedbeds of civic virtue—families, neighborhood, religious associations, and other communities—can no longer be taken for granted, this is no trifling matter.[14]

Today, western society is suffering considerable malaise, and liberalism is under attack for its apparent neglect of values. In addition, as liberalism tries to defend itself against charges of individualism and to show that it values community, it has encountered new dilemmas. A question has been raised, for example, as to whether a liberal state can extend to groups the kind of rights it grants individuals. The dilemmas arising in contemporary education are illustrative.

Consider the 1987 case *Mozert v. Hawkins,* in which a group of Christian fundamentalist families brought suit against a school board for undermining their religious views in a required reading program.[15] I'll discuss here just one component of the complaint. One of the stories in the required reader depicts a boy cooking while his sister reads to him. The Mozert parents complained that this reversal of gender roles contradicts biblical teaching and that exposing their children to such views threatens the group's free exercise of religion. They did not insist that the reading program be abandoned, but only that their own children be excused from it. Now, putting aside the nightmare of control that a multiplicity of such cases might induce, how should a liberal state respond?

If we were to follow the recommendations of William Galston, who claims that "liberalism is about the protection of diversity, not the valorization of choice,"[16] we would be caught on the horns of the dilemma. Galston says that a liberal state must educate for tolerance. "The state may establish educational guidelines pursuant to this compelling interest. What it may not do is prescribe curricula or pedagogic practices that require or strongly invite students to become skeptical or critical of their own ways of life."[17]

It is not clear where Galston should stand in the Mozert case. He could argue that the Mozert parents should be allowed to withdraw their children from the offending reading program on the grounds that their (forced) participation challenges parental beliefs and thus weakens liberal commitment to diversity. He could also argue that, in the name of tolerance, all children should be exposed to a variety of ways of life. This stand would be consistent with his recognition that tolerance requires at least minimal awareness of other customs and beliefs, but the argument for (and from) tolerance just doesn't work. To begin, one could argue that the object of lessons such as the reading lesson described is not tolerance; it is to provide information and inspiration to promote equality of women. It is part of a liberal social agenda that *does* threaten some ways of life. Further, as we shall see in a bit, it is not clear who needs the lesson in tolerance.

If we were serious about maintaining even anti-liberal forms of religious diversity, we would be tempted to grant the request of the Mozert families. Then the schools could (should?) follow a pattern that has become familiar over the last few decades, one of removing from the curriculum everything regarded as offensive to various groups that base their complaints on religious, ethnic, racial, or gender grounds. The dilemma is clear. Even a minimal, political liberal state has a social agenda. One prime aspect of today's agenda is to promote gender equality. If we allow children to avoid lessons that frankly depict and deliberately advocate gender equality, how can we ensure that girls will be aware of their rights in a liberal society? Is not at least this much required of civic education in a liberal society? And if this is required, as one part of a liberal social agenda, what other matters must also be included?

Galston avoids the hard question of what to do about the particular gender problem by emphasizing tolerance. On this reading, which seems to be the one he prefers, the state has a right to "expose" children to other ways of life in order to promote tolerance. The request of the Mozert families, then, would be denied as antithetical to the tolerance goal. Gender equality is not just another way of life, however; it is part of a positive social agenda. As such, its promotion cannot avoid inviting students from Mozert-like groups "to become skeptical or critical of their own ways of life."

The dilemma deepens when we consider the following. Suppose that, in opposition to Mozert, a group of humanist families sues the board along these lines: "If you do *not* teach our children to be skeptical, to think critically, and to question, you are undermining *our* basic philosophical beliefs. We believe, with Socrates, that the unexamined life is not worth living, etc. True, you are not telling our children that they may not question and reflect, but you do not invite or encourage them to do so. We see such encouragement as the main point of education, and education so defined is fundamental to our humanist belief system. Further, political liberalism, as advocated by Rawls and others, is supposed to extend the principle of tolerance to philosophical ideals as well as religious views.[18] Ours is a well-recognized philosophical view. Indeed, we might claim it as *the* view underlying the most current forms of liberalism."

Now what does the board do? Surely both sets of parents are right in the sense that they perceive the threats accurately. On the one hand, a Deweyan-liberal education undermines fundamentalist practice at its very roots. On the other, education without critical thinking does not even qualify as education to humanist parents and thus unfairly burdens their system of belief.

One response to these dilemmas—and I think it has to be entertained thoughtfully and in depth, although I deplore it—is to frankly recognize the fact that there are many publics in this nation, not just one, and to consider abandoning the system we are used to calling "public education." Another response for liberals is to "realize the relative validity of [our] convictions and yet stand for them unflinchingly."[19] Such a stand would compel us to embrace a comprehensive liberalism and face the question squarely of just what that involves. Ultimately, it might mean moving beyond liberalism. Still another response, one to be elaborated later, is thoroughly relational. It would recognize that exposure to other ways of life runs in several directions. Indeed, liberal educators and policymakers may be in greater need of lessons in tolerance than the fundamentalists whose ideas they scorn. From a relational perspective, the problem that should have top priority is the maintenance of nonviolent relations.

The ideas of fundamentalists baffle me, too, but their need for care in the form of recognition and neighborly affection does not. What happened in the wake of the Mozert case (near destruction of a community) might have been avoided by relational thinking.[20] Suppose we acknowledge three important facts: first, that we live in a liberal democracy; second, that most of us prefer to retain the liberties of choice granted us in such a society; and third, that liberalism must have a social agenda. In regard to a social agenda, an effective liberalism must acknowledge that its very procedures imply substance. For example, if there is to be free access to some good for *all*, then there must be free access for women. If citizens must give legitimacy freely to a continuance of liberal democracy, they must be educated for critical thinking. Otherwise they could not raise critical questions about the system of governance, and their consent could not be considered free. From a liberal perspective, then, the school must teach women's rights, and it must teach critical thinking.

Without denying these three facts, can relational thinking modify the liberal stand and contribute to the maintenance of community? I think it can. Consider this scenario. Suppose the school principal has a real dialogue with the worried mother, call her Ms. B. The principal listens. She disagrees with Ms. B, but she acknowledges the genuineness and depth of her convictions. She says, in effect, "Okay. We'll allow you and other mothers to come in and teach your children reading from the older text. But you have to understand that these situations will arise again and again. We *do* believe in equality for women, and that belief is bound to emerge in other contexts. However, we want your children to remain with us, so let's try your plan and see how it goes."

An adequate social policy allows this sort of local dialogue and compromise. A primary aim of theory should be to guide the development of social policy that can respond to the needs of people who disagree at the local level. But where do we start in our thinking? An important criticism of liberalism is that it has chosen a starting point that creates dilemmas that may be resolvable only if we start differently.

The Wrong Start

Basing a social theory on the thoughts and actions of mature rational beings who make choices to satisfy their wants neglects the reality of human life. When life begins it is best described initially in terms of needs, not wants. As children grow, they develop wants, and these are influenced somewhat by genetic predisposition but mainly by encounter. Children's wants are shaped by a great variety of agencies, only some of which have their best interests in mind. In the best homes children learn that some wants cannot be met and that some should not be pursued. Fully formed human beings exercise more than consistency in testing their wants, and they do not always weigh their wants against the reasonable wants of others. Often decisions are made on the basis of loving concern for a particular other or for the relation in which they find themselves.

The idea of a rational life plan as it is discussed by Rawls puts too narrow a focus on life. This is a place where we have to be careful. Most of us agree with Rawls that it is desirable to be in some control of our own lives. We want to plan, and we do not want our plans to be disrupted by avoidable lacks or unjustified demands. These plans, however, are probably not best described as "life" plans. Life is too complex, too contingency-filled, too emotional to be described as *a* plan. A plan suggests an end, a design, a set of chosen means and, thus, concentrates too narrowly on technique and instrumentality. It seems more nearly accurate to describe life as "composed" rather than planned.[21]

It will not do either to reject talk of life plans and resort to Martin Heidegger's language of "thrown-ness"—the idea that humans are "thrown" or "cast" into the world. With this language, too, we head in a direction that is alien to the vast majority of human beings. The notion captures something important, of course, in reminding us of contingency, temporality, and possibility, but it is a wrong start. It ignores birth, helplessness, and the real need for a physical home in favor of wandering in the world and finding a home in thinking.

Gaston Bachelard describes the house as a human being's first world: "Before he is 'cast into the world,' as claimed by certain hasty metaphysics, man is laid in the cradle of the house. . . . A concrete metaphysics cannot neglect this fact . . . since this fact is a value. . . . Being is already a value."[22] Bachelard goes on to say, "Life begins well, it begins enclosed, protected, all warm in the bosom of the house,"[23] but he can't mean this literally. Some lives are not so sheltered. His pronouncement is poetic—pointing to a reality that exists in real memory for some and imaginative memory for others; it is in itself a statement of value. Life *should* start this way, and he is right that the house—the first physical home—appears again and again in the psyche as a longing, if not as an actual memory. Bachelard's complaint that a metaphysics that starts with being "cast into the world" is one that "passes over the preliminaries" is well taken.

Bachelard's fact, or value, regarding how life starts has a parallel in the work of Weil. She, too, makes a statement that is almost certainly false factually but sounds exactly right as a value.

At the bottom of the heart of every human being, from earliest infancy until the tomb, there is something that goes on indomitably expecting, in the teeth of all experience of crimes committed, suffered, and witnessed, that good and not evil will be done to him. It is this above all that is sacred in every human being.[24]

This expectation is not indomitable. It can be destroyed, and its very contingency makes it sacred. The sacred, however it is defined, requires both identification and preservation. The expectation of good is exactly what a good home preserves. Life that is, at the outset, "enclosed, protected, all warm" is the way life should be, and such a beginning helps to introduce and to maintain the sacred in human life.

It is understandable, if fundamentally wrong, that liberalism has settled on wanting and rationality as the basic characteristics of human life. Liberalism did not enter political thought by itself. It was accompanied by nationalism and capitalism, and it would be foolish not to recognize the modern nation-state as an enterprise. Since the state is caught up in a desire for its own power (or, some would say, even for its own profit) and because its authority largely depends on its financial success, it is easy (but not logically necessary) to attribute the same motive and indication of success to individuals in liberal societies. Again, it is a wrong start. Human beings, whether or not they have souls, are spiritual beings—beings characterized by something soul-like: loves that transcend personal interest, whims that defy the narrowly rational, a sense of wonder that exceeds obvious possibilities, and a capacity for play.

A better start for developing a social theory is with relation and encounter. Encounter is the fount of experience, and not all encounters are planned. Some *are* planned and initiated by mature, rational agents. Some are planned and controlled by others; this is especially true for children. Still others are fortuitous—some contributing to happiness, some to misery, some so trivial that no real experience arises from them. Others are initiated foolishly. An adequate social policy has to consider how best to guide encounters. In what situations does a society leave its citizens completely free to offer, choose, or just bumble into encounters? When and over whom does society exercise control? When does society refuse to control but frankly decide to persuade? It is hard even to ask these questions when theorizing begins with the mature rational human being—someone who is assumed to be capable of assessing his own set of wants for consistency and reasonableness.

The problem of societal control is, of course, as old as Socrates. Few of us would accept the Socratic-Platonic solution of state control, but many of us wish it were possible to intervene cautiously in cases of homelessness, mental illness, drug addiction, compulsive gambling, and other harms to the self. To decide, as a liberal society does, that everyone comes under the harm principle at a certain age is to make a double mistake. First, it too often neglects the expressed needs of minors while accepting too easily the inferred needs established by those in authority. Second, it accords rights universally over the "mature" group without regard to the capacities on which those rights rest. Coercion is used too freely—unjustifiably, I will argue—with one group (the young), and it is not used with another even when the need is demonstrably clear. I should hasten to say that if I were faced with the choice between the coercion and censorship of the Platonic state and the hands-off attitude of the current liberal state, I would choose the latter. There is much to be treasured in our liberal heritage, but freedom is not the only good to be cherished. The project here is to construct a social policy that will not reject the freedom of liberalism but will modify it in ways that acknowledge varying capacities for particular freedoms.

Dilemmas of Freedom

Freedom is not always defined in terms of the rational autonomy favored by liberalism. In chapter 3 I mentioned Berlin's worries about what he called "positive" freedom. His distinction between negative freedom (the sort traditionally associated with liberalism) and positive freedom is worth further discussion.

The first of these political senses of freedom or liberty . . . which I shall call the "negative" sense, is involved in the answer to the question "What is the area within which the subject—a person or group of persons—is or should be left to do or be what he is able to do or be, without interference by other persons?" The second, which I shall call the positive sense, is involved in the answer to the question, "What, or who, is the source of control or interference that can determine someone to do, or be, this rather than that?"[25]

Berlin notes that the questions are very different and that they have diverged greatly in their development. The first, the negative view, puts emphasis on individual autonomy; the second, the positive view, emphasizes what might be called intelligent heteronomy. Many people who hold religious worldviews favor the second. They believe that all right-thinking persons should be under the guidance of God, and some believe that this translates into accepting the rules and pronouncements of a particular religious institution. In the current political climate those who take the positive view often posit the idea of character as central to political life. Those who govern us (whose governance we accept and trust) should be people of sound character, and good government should encourage citizens to develop good character. Freedom, in this sense, is not freedom to be or do what one pleases. It is freedom to be or to do what one should be or do.

A major problem for liberalism is that it puts such weight on the negative sense that it risks losing sight of its own prescription for the positive. On rereading Mill one sees everywhere reference to both intellectual and moral virtues: perception, judgment, discriminative feeling, mental activity, firmness, self-control, originality, passionate love of virtue.[26] He says that adult human beings who allow the world to control them have "no need of any other faculty than the ape-like one of imitation."[27] Thus there is more than one way to live, and the way of critical, reflective intelligence is not only a choice, it must be cultivated; it represents a positive view par excellence. It is strange, then, that liberalism so often speaks as though the characteristics on which it depends for its legitimacy belong to human nature itself. Mill clearly knew that the being he described was relatively rare, and he deplored the contemporary condition of education. Yet he gave only parenthetical acknowledgment to this knowledge when he defended his harm principle. Admitting that society has a right to intervene when one person's behavior threatens another's interests, he insisted that

there is no room for entertaining any such question when a person's conduct affects the interests of no persons besides himself, or needs not affect them unless they like (all the persons concerned being of full age, and the ordinary amount of understanding). In all such cases there should be perfect freedom, legal and social, to do the action and stand the consequences.[28]

There are questions on both ends of the dilemma suggested here. What exactly should we expect by way of an "ordinary amount of understanding"? Why should reasonable choices, choices that both arise from and contribute to originality, be withheld from those not yet "of full age"? Liberals have often tried to avoid the first question entirely by showing that the most egregious personal acts of individuals *do* affect the interests of others and therefore fall under the harm principle. They less often face up to the import of the question, which is, namely, a full and frank description of the positive view and what it means for the cultivation of liberal citizens. Liberalism is here caught in a genuine dilemma (perhaps irresolvable). On the one hand, the production of citizens capable of freely granting legitimacy to a liberal democracy requires an education guided by a positive liberal view. On the other, recognition of a comprehensive or positive view violates the central notions of liberal political neutrality and the inherent rationality of mature human beings.

The first part of the problem has become increasingly important in recent years. Political scientists and sociologists have become aware that liberalism and democracy are not synonymous. Beyond the reality of socialist democracies that, leaving aside differences in economic policies, may or may not be liberal in other social policies is the reality of illiberal governments that have been placed in power by free and fair—democratic—elections.[29] The basic liberties cherished in liberal democracies are often violated in these states. One possible explanation for this common occurrence is that the establishment and maintenance of a *liberal* democracy depends on a tradition of open public discourse—much like that discourse described by Mill.[30] Recognizing this deepens the dilemma. The neutral, liberal, procedural state takes on a mythical quality.

Dewey, almost alone among early-twentieth-century political philosophers, saw the problems inherent in the second question, the one of how much choice to allow the young. Insisting on the need for an education compatible with life in a liberal democracy, he incurred the wrath of those opposed to a secular humanist worldview.[31] More surprising, he aroused the anger of many who should have appreciated his careful attention to community and the contributions of tradition. Dewey, insisting on a definition of democracy as a "mode of associated living,"[32] anticipated much of the current debate between liberals and communitarians. More important, from the perspective of this book, he recognized the vital importance of public schooling in providing the conditions necessary for democratic life. The anger and misunderstanding that his work induced should have served as a warning of the storms to come.

A Deweyan education, one emphasizing critical inquiry and a continual search for evidence, might indeed tend to undermine many illiberal belief systems, but, balanced by an equally committed search for "the great community," it need not have a destructive effect. Modified by processes suggested by an ethic of care, such an education might contribute to stability, civility, and personal growth. Unmodified, an education aimed at autonomy, critical thinking, and individual liberty clearly represents a threat to fundamentalist groups and others who hold these aims to be sinful.

The problem of relations between a liberal state and illiberal subgroups within it is widespread, and the issues that arise within schools are just one set of such problems. The dilemmas become more twisted when we consider another legacy of liberalism—the split between the public and private. Because so much of liberal philosophy was developed around the notion of a mature, rational individual in a time when only propertied, white males were regarded as meeting the criterion, it was predictable that home and family would be regarded as private in the sense that a man should be able to govern his home without outside interference. As liberalism, to its great credit, began to recognize the implications of its central definition—that women, people of color, and unpropertied persons also qualify as rational—a struggle began to find a way to extend to all people the rights previously assigned to a dominant few. But the legacy of separation remains, and today many groups that might be regarded as illiberal are among the strongest supporters of a sharp separation between public and private life.

The difficulties that this separation raises for education are multiple. Should parents be free to educate their children as they see fit so long as they do provide some form of education?[33] If a state grants such freedom to parents (once only the father), what can be said of the rights and needs of children? Freedom for the parent may mean a form of bondage for the children. The problem becomes even more complicated when we consider how important home and family are to school success. Study after study has shown that a prime determinant of school success is a home in which education is valued either explicitly or implicitly in the educational status of its adult members. Knowing this, many of us would like to transform the school curriculum into one that treats home and interpersonal relations as equal in importance to the subjects traditionally associated with success in the public world.

Resistance to such a move is vigorous and widespread, and it has a tangle of roots. The basic curriculum now in schools was designed by males for male life—occupational success and political participation. The "curriculum" for home life was handled at home by women, who had little hope of participating meaningfully in the kind of life typical for men.[34] Almost certainly, then, gender bias is one root of the resistance. It is now far more acceptable for a woman to be like a man and to study what men have studied than for a man to be like a woman and to study topics, tasks, and problems traditionally associated with women.

Another root of the resistance is more directly a legacy of liberalism. Liberalism's intimate connection to an economics of freedom leads to educational policies that emphasize preparation for the world of economic activity. Success is defined in terms of economic success, and equality in terms of equal opportunity. Concern for economic freedom has become so dominant that many parents resist the attempts of schools to introduce service learning, cooperative learning, and attention to studio art, music, and the performing arts. Thus a move to include the study of homes and home life in an intellectually rich and serious way is resisted on several grounds: such studies do not prepare children for economic freedom, they violate the freedom of parents to control the education of their children for private life, and, depending on their content and the methods used to teach them, they may well undermine the free exercise of religion. To argue effectively for an education that includes adequate preparation for domestic life and for forms of success not directly linked to the economic, we need a social theory that starts differently, is broader in its concerns, and attends more forthrightly to needs.

I want to say just a bit more about what is at stake here. Hannah Arendt and many others have written about the loss of "the public" realm.[35] Arendt, looking at the French, cast her lament in a way that is especially interesting now.

Modern enchantment with "small things," though preached by early twentieth-century poetry in almost all European tongues, has found its classical representation in the petit bonheur of the French people. Since the decay of their once great and glorious public realm, the French have become masters in their art of being happy among "small things," within the space of their own four walls, between chest and bed, table and chair, dog and cat and flowerpot, extending to these things a care and tenderness which, in a world where rapid industrialization constantly kills off the things of yesterday to produce today's objects, may even appear to be the world's last, purely humane corner. This enlargement of the private . . . does not make it public . . . , but, on the contrary, means only that the public realm has almost completely receded.[36]

In today's climate the "private" realm is shrinking, too. The domestic realm—surely an appropriately large part of the private realm—is swiftly becoming an arena of stress and turmoil, and recent studies have suggested that both men and women often turn to the workplace as an escape from the home. As the domestic realm (where children of necessity reside and where the elderly *might* reside) recedes, what is left? As money-making becomes central, the pressures of work are relieved largely by a retreat to spectacle in the form of sports, television, and sensationalist publications.[37] The private now flees from the domestic. If we find this unacceptable, something must be done to restore both a vigorous public realm and a healthy, creative domestic realm. Schools today, in blind complicity with economic forces, push harder and harder for goals tied to financial success and neglect a rounded education that would foster a full life of participation in public and domestic domains.

In summary, a fundamental paradox of freedom arises from liberalism's central notion—the negative rights of a mature rational being. Concentrating on the negative freedom (freedom from intervention) of individuals, liberalism has disguised its own impressive positive view.[38] Its claims to neutrality have angered many opponents who see clearly that affairs conducted under the guidance of liberal social policies, education in particular, cannot be defended by claims to neutrality. Further, liberalism's reluctance to explore thoroughly the capacities on which mature rights depend has led to neglect of the needs of many who do not possess the requisite capacities. This neglect is often defended as a preservation of the victim's freedom and rights. It has also led, somewhat perversely, to coercion of the young and neglect of their expressed needs.

Liberalism, in defending the separation of public and private domains, is caught in the dilemma of whether to grant families the right to control the education of their children. Allowing such control clearly puts some children at risk and, besides depriving them of opportunities that a fair liberal state has pledged to keep open, may even dull their capacities to exercise the kind of judgment required to sustain a liberal state.

Finally, the close association of political and economic liberalism has led to a narrow view of adult life as a life focused on economic and occupational goals. As this view has gained a stronger and stronger hold in education, academic achievement has become increasingly defended as an avenue to personal and national economic success. Nowhere is this view more prominent than in current debates on equality and equity.

Dilemmas of Equality

Human beings cherish many goods, and it is not possible to promote all of them simultaneously. This is another of Berlin's wise observations.[39] We may have to sacrifice some of one great value to realize another. What we should *not* do, Berlin advises, is pretend that by emphasizing one we have somehow magically increased the one that has actually been sacrificed. Thus he notes that we might well sacrifice some of our freedom to achieve equality, but we should not pretend that, in doing so, we have somehow increased freedom. That is a separate and supremely important question. When he wrote on this clash of goods, Berlin almost certainly had in mind the Soviet Communist experiment. A sacrifice of some freedom is surely acceptable to democratic thinkers if equality can be achieved and if that equality produces greater freedom for those whose status is raised. If no greater freedom for those lower in status is forthcoming, then there is an absolute loss of freedom, and we should face this honestly.

In this century liberals have been torn between the defense of freedom and the pursuit of equality. As the liberal consensus shifted toward equality, some conservatives claimed (with some historical justification) that they were in fact the only true liberals remaining. If, however, we put aside the question of which great good—freedom or equality—should prevail in this time, we see that other important questions remain. What do we mean by equality? Is its meaning stable across all domains of human activity? Is a reduction in the "general welfare" to be welcomed if it results in equality without inducing misery? In responding to this last question, we may decide that one principle really cannot apply to all domains. For example, many of us might consent to a reduction in the wealth of the richest members of society if that reduction clearly raised a substantial number of people out of poverty without plunging any others into misery. This consent might not be forthcoming were we to seek equality in educational achievement by ignoring the development of our most talented or by withdrawing resources from them. We might rightly worry about the effects not only on the talented but also on the society that would benefit from their talents.

The kind of equality insisted upon by liberal theorists is "moral equality." By this theorists do not mean to suggest that all people are equally good morally. Rather, they mean that every person has moral worth in a just society and that, in such a society, the distribution of goods will not depend on some hierarchy of moral good, nor will it entail strict equality. "Equality before the law" seems to be the ideal, and this seems for the most part to be desirable. To what degree is it practically coherent? An ironic joke that has circulated for some time culminates in the judgment that a rich man and a poor man are equally forbidden to sleep under a bridge.

The problem runs deep. Suppose Mr. Sade and I are both guilty of torturing children. Surely we deserve the same punishment. Is this much clear? Well, not until we consider whether this is the first (or third or n^{th}) occasion for both of us, and not until we consider the extent of the torture, its results, and so on. Then we may proceed in our hypothetical legal thinking. But there is a flaw in the whole notion. Look again at the sentence "Suppose that Mr. Sade and I are both guilty. . . ." There is no possibility that I (or most other persons) could do such a thing. We are all capable of many evils and, although it is important that we understand the depth of our possible depravities, most of us are not capable of torturing children. Mr. Sade and I are very different selves, and the idea that we have "equal moral worth" is questionable. If we interpret "equal moral worth" to mean simply that we will be treated equally before the law for a given transgression, we find ourselves in a position very like the one of forbidding both rich man and poor man to sleep under a bridge. To give "equal moral worth" a practical meaning, we have to pledge ourselves as a society to raising and educating all children so that selves like Mr. Sade are not produced.

The principle of equality before the law has to be one of punishing crimes equally, but even this is not that simple. If it really is the case that many "selves" could not possibly commit some of the crimes under consideration, is it "impartial" to prescribe equal punishment for all who commit that crime? Here again we see that a definition of "self" in terms of mature rationality is inadequate, especially if we simply suppose that everyone not certifiably mad comes into possession of this capacity at a given age. In the next chapter I give much attention to the idea of a relational self, a self under continuous construction.

It may be that, at least at present, our society cannot do better through its legal system than to prescribe equal punishment for equal crimes. Many legal theorists are trying to find ways to make the actual application of punishment more just. In this effort they come up against another dilemma of equality. Although, because of their assumed equality in rationality, lawbreakers are held equally responsible for their acts, everyone knows that those who can afford highly competent legal defense are less likely to be convicted and, when they are, they are more likely to get lighter sentences. This is a widely recognized problem of justice, and I am not suggesting that efforts to apply laws justly should be abandoned. Nor am I following Clarence Darrow in claiming that no one is really responsible for his or her acts because all acts are conditioned.[40] What I will suggest is that with a better understanding of the notion of self we may be able to recommend stronger roles for various agencies (other than law) to prevent the development of selves that regularly hurt themselves and others. The idea of equality is not of much use here because selves are not interchangeable.

Let's suppose that the idea of equal moral worth is addressed more convincingly to basic needs and liberties. If it is wrong for our society to let me starve, it is equally wrong to let you starve. Is this intuitively agreeable conclusion best described in terms of moral equality or could it be described better in terms of reciprocal caring? It should matter to us that someone is suffering, and this mattering does not depend on some moral equality inherent in persons. Indeed, the very idea is inverted. It is precisely because a significant number of us have learned to care about the suffering of others that we posit some form of moral equality.

None of this implies that the basic insights of justice should be abandoned or that we should not hold certain rights inviolable. My argument is that we should remember that rights have arisen from acknowledged needs and wants. These differ across times, circumstances, and persons, and there are times when we must return to rudimentary events in order to respond adequately as carers.

The temptation to interpret equality as sameness pervades social policy. In education, equality construed as sameness is creating havoc. It is beyond the scope of this chapter to discuss fully all of the problems in this area, but a few have to be mentioned here. Reformers all over the country are pressing for equity in school funding. It does seem right that schools in regions with similar costs of living should receive roughly the same funding. When this case is pressed, however, opponents often claim that the problem "isn't money" or that "money won't help." Most of these opponents would object strenuously if, even though money supposedly isn't the issue, funding for their own schools were threatened. The inequalities of funding have in fact produced what Jonathan Kozol has vividly described as "savage inequalities,"[41] and a liberal democracy should be ashamed to allow these inequalities to persist.

However, the opponents of more money for failing schools do have a point when they say "money won't do it," and this is why we are faced with a dilemma. Poor children in drug-infested neighborhoods with crumbling housing probably need *more* money for their education than rich children do. Money, however, is not the only problem. Some home environments, in everything from the food supplied to intellectual stimulation, are more conducive to school success than others. We know this, and yet we do little in schools to prepare students for the domestic roles that will mean so much to their future children. Further, unless schools are closely linked to other social agencies so that all work together in establishing comprehensive environments for children, many children will still be involved in unhealthy activities. Schools are not easily separated from their settings. What goes on outside of schools affects what happens inside them and vice-versa.

The final dilemma I want to consider here is the approach to equality that prescribes the same curriculum for all children regardless of their backgrounds, plans, or interests.[42] Now that this curriculum for all has been combined with high-stakes testing in many places, we stand on the brink of social disaster. In the next decade, unless the standards are relaxed, many children will fail to get high school diplomas, and if a long history of reacting in exactly this way (reducing standards to avoid unacceptable levels of failure) repeats itself, we will have wasted years of effort and sacrificed many young lives in a wrong-headed approach to equality. Children are not interchangeable parts. They are not equally capable physically, intellectually, or emotionally, and they have wonderfully different gifts and interests. Beyond certain vital skills, children need different courses of study to flourish. This is a major topic for later discussion. Instead of establishing high and uniform standards for all children, we should be working toward differentiated curricula that would encourage children to work toward high standards in areas of their own legitimate interest.

In closing this chapter I want to emphasize the paradoxical nature of liberalism's legacy. In emphasizing the liberties that we cherish, it has handicapped us in responding to obvious needs. We are reluctant to intervene in the lives of adults who are, by liberal premise, rational, but who may be, by commonsense evaluation, not entirely rational. This legacy has left us baffled about the status of children, and we sometimes use questionable coercion in the name of equality. It has maintained the split between public and private realms in order to support important freedoms, but in doing so it has made it very difficult for some to exercise these freedoms. Finally, it has perpetuated an odd view of the self. When the self is described as "unencumbered," as a rational choice mechanism, communitarians are right to say that this is not a real self. We encounter a much richer, positive view of what constitutes a liberal self when liberalism is analyzed more carefully. Because this view has so often been suppressed, we fail to question whether it is even implicitly adequate, whether the sort of preparation for its development that we prescribe in education is compatible with its ideal, or how it might be amended. We are left with a vital, basic question: what is a self?

CHAPTER 5

A Relational Self

We now have some sense of the ways in which traditional social theories fail us—in particular, how an emphasis on the prevention of harm to others may reduce the concern for care and how an emphasis on community may allow and even encourage harm to those outside well-defined circles of care. We earlier noted that care itself has its pathologies. In this chapter we will consider the self and how it should be described. We will see here that neither the liberal view nor the communitarian view is really adequate and that there are difficulties in postmodern views as well, although I will draw heavily on some of these. After this critique I'll develop a relational view that should prove more satisfactory for developing an adequate social policy.

Questionable Views of the Self

Philosophers have long been interested in the nature of the self and problems of identity. It is beyond the scope of this work to discuss all of the views and problems that have occupied philosophers, theologians, neuroscientists, and psychologists. We do need to consider a few prominent views, however, because they are central to the ethical and social problems with which we are concerned.

The first view to consider is the one associated with liberal theory, which was alluded to in chapter 4. Here the Enlightenment self is described in a variety of ways, but it is always characterized by autonomy (an essential freedom), equality, rationality, and unity. All of these characteristics can be challenged. Perhaps selves have only limited autonomy, are equal in only tenuously established ways, and are guided by a rationality (or something bigger than rationality) that goes well beyond making "self"-interested or even disinterested choices. Perhaps they do not achieve unity (if they achieve it at all) by constructing a rational life plan.

This liberal view contains practical as well as theoretical difficulties. At the practical level one can see that the self described has little relation to actual people living actual lives. Rawls says that "the nature of the self as a free and equal moral person is the same for all."[1] The conception of the right is supposed to guarantee this, but this in fact is not the case. No rules of justice can guarantee that various encounters and the affects generated in them will not induce obligations that are regarded as supererogatory by the theory but obligatory by those undergoing a particular experience. No theoretical commitments can burst the bonds of ethos entirely—unless the ethos is precisely one in which theoretical commitments hold a high place. And many actual people—recognized as rational—are as attracted to various forms of evil as they are to right and to good.

Rawls writes repeatedly of a "rational plan of life" that, under a system of justice as fairness, all people are to be allowed to pursue. But who can do this? Historically, who has come close to doing this? The answer is almost a cliché: western, white, well-educated males. This cliché-like answer is important. If only one sort of person has been able to describe his life or "self" this way, we can take two different attitudes toward that fact. We can take Rawls's generous attitude—that, in fairness, everyone should now have that opportunity—or we can question the desirability of the idea itself. We may freely admit that we seek many of the objectives sought by Rawls: elimination of the worst features of poverty, oppression, domination, and so on. Maybe, however, we can start from a more basic, realistic conception of human selves. Perhaps, as I suggested earlier, we should challenge the notion of life as a rational plan.

Segments of almost every life may be described in terms of a rational plan, of course, but few lives can be described this way as totalities. It is obvious that many women, even privileged women, have led their lives very differently. Mary Catherine Bateson makes this point in the introduction to her study of five artistic women.

The recognition that many people lead lives of creative makeshift and improvisation surely has implications for how the next generation is educated.

. . . Once you begin to see these lives of multiple commitments and multiple beginnings as an emerging pattern rather than an aberration, it takes no more than a second look to discover the models for that reinvention on every side, to look for the followers of visions that are not fixed but that evolve from day to day.[2]

One could argue that Rawls does not intend the expression "rational life plan" to exclude lives of creative makeshift, that in fact the expression is shorthand to refer to constellations of shifting ends that are rationally considered and that should not be blocked by individual or systematic interference. Only Rawls himself can say exactly what he means to include, but his language throughout *A Theory of Justice* suggests the sort of life lived by men who could more or less decide the trajectory of their lives over long periods of time. Indeed, his intellectual predecessor, Immanuel Kant, exemplified just such a life—quiet, orderly, stable. He did not have to move when a spouse's work required it or cease work when children became ill or work at menial jobs when a position was lost. None of this detracts from his monumental achievements. Noting that, as the poet Heinrich Heine said of him, Kant did not really "have a life" merely suggests that elaborate, abstract social schemes and recommendations may arise more directly from particular kinds of life than their creators realize.

We see in unified, semicomplete theories the aporias postmodern writers are so fond of finding—great gaps in which unspoken possibilities may be brought to the surface. For example, is it reasonable to claim that people in the original position—behind the veil of ignorance—will really choose the rules of justice Rawls lays out? And will they do it out of enlightened self-interest, weighing the possibility that they may turn out to be one of the disadvantaged? Susan Okin has argued, rightly I think, that Rawls's theory logically requires that people in the original position care about others as well as themselves. I think it does, but I'm not sure Okin is right when she says that it *must* be interpreted this way.

I have argued that Rawls's theory of justice is most coherently interpreted as a moral structure founded on the equal concern of persons for each other as for themselves, a theory in which empathy with and care for others, as well as awareness of their differences, are crucial components.[3]

Rawls's own language suggests that he would like to avoid discussion of care and concern as much as possible. His quest is clearly more like that of Kant, who wanted a set of procedures that would effectively provide justice for all regardless of whether the citizenry is peopled by "angels or devils."[4] Rawls recognizes that certain "cooperative virtues" such as justice and fairness, fidelity and trust, and integrity and impartiality are necessary in a just society, but for individual human beings these virtues are derived from a rational assessment that institutions characterized by and supportive of the cooperative virtues must be maintained by all.

There is something attractive about this. Recall Orwell's sad comment that, as a child, he lived in a world in which it was impossible for him to be good. I, too, will seek a social policy that makes goodness possible, but I do not think it can be found without a much deeper examination of interpersonal virtues. Acknowledging that people in the original position are both rational and moral begs for a full discussion of what it means to be moral and, unless the analysis includes a broad vision of what it means to be rational, objections can be raised to the great emphasis put on rationality.

If the liberal view of the self, abstracted as finely as it is in Rawls's formulation, is unsatisfactory, the fuller view offered in communitarian literature also raises problems. Here it is acknowledged that selves are more than rational beings. They are formed by the times, culture, and situations in which they live. Taylor, for example, takes a relational view:

I am a self only in relation to certain interlocutors: in one way in relation to those conversation partners who were essential to my achieving self-definition; in another in relation to those who are now crucial to my continuing grasp of languages of self-understanding—and, of course, these classes may overlap. A self exists only within what I call "webs of interlocution."[5]

I will argue that, rich as this view is, it is still too poor. The self is formed not only in communication but also in encounter with objects and events that induce affects; moreover, the developing self can be reflexive—it can encounter itself and pose questions for itself. It can be knocked out of its habitual ways by a chance occurrence, remarks that come from outside the usual web of interlocution, or a dramatic challenge to its current plans. Further, it is not completed until death, and sometimes not even then. Relational views that center on culture or refer to "socialized individuality" are common and may appear in liberal writing as well as communitarian,[6] but we have to probe more deeply to find out what we are dealing with. In liberal theory, talk of socialized individuality is little more than a recognition of empirical reality. Liberals become liberals through a process of socialization as well as choice, but the self of liberal *theory* is primarily a principled rationality. Other qualities are set aside for purposes of developing theory.

MacIntyre deplores both the role-taking self espoused by Erving Goffman (empty, he says, save as a "peg" on which to hang roles) and the totally open self espoused by Sartre, one that must be built from scratch through individual choice. MacIntyre contrasts these views with premodern, traditional ones in which selves were acknowledged to be embedded in associations. He writes of such a self:

I am brother, cousin and grandson, member of this household, that village, this tribe. These are not characteristics that belong to human beings accidentally, to be stripped away in order to discover "the real me." They are part of my substance, defining partially at least and sometimes wholly my obligations and my duties. Individuals inherit a particular space within an interlocking set of social relationships; lacking that space, they are nobody, or at best a stranger or an outcast.[7]

MacIntyre of course recognizes that people today have many more associations than people did in premodern times and are not so dependent on one tribe or group to develop an identity, but his basic description still seems right. One is not a *self* when stripped of all these associations.

The descriptions offered by MacIntyre and Taylor are as yet too abstract. We learn a great deal from their analyses of premodern and modern selves, but we are still dealing with idea-like selves. Something has been left out. When MacIntyre says that these characteristics do not "belong to human beings accidentally," we have to agree at a high level of abstraction: all people, real selves, are selves in virtue of their relationships. But the particular kinds of relationship *are* in large part accidental, and we need to explore this feature of human relatedness. A self cannot be described in terms of mere rationality or choice, but neither can it be wholly described in terms of its time and culture. I am not just a modern or postmodern self, one of a set, all of whom are shaped in general by relationships. I have been shaped by particular relationships and by my attitudes toward them.

Another problem arises when the narrative nature of the self is emphasized.[8] In one sense, of course, a life may be interpreted as a story, and the story of every self so told involves to some degree the stories of whatever traditions the person has been part of. Two difficulties present themselves. One is that relatively inarticulate selves are assimilated to dominant traditions, and important differences are thus lost. Another is that such a description may put too much emphasis on the authorship of the self. These sound like contradictory objections, but I believe they both involve problems of extremes. At one extreme, a self is entirely lost in something like the "Protestant tradition" or the "modern self"; at the other, partners in the relational self are assimilated to the author, and unity is sought in a centered entity.

Both liberals and communitarians refer to a "unity of self." For the former, unity is said to be provided by the conception of right; for the latter, it is dependent on a conception of the good—on a tradition. Rawls, for example, identifies the unity of self with a rational life plan, and his theory of justice with its emphasis on the right is supposed to guarantee that all members of the just society will be free to construct and pursue their own legitimate goods. Communitarians, in contrast, locate unity in commitment to the traditions, relationships, and webs of interlocution through which every individual is shaped. Recall MacIntyre's claim that, without these relationships, a person is "nobody."

Perhaps the self at its best is not a unity, at least not a unity in the sense traditionally described. When we raise questions about central (almost beloved) concepts such as "unity," we are not necessarily advocating their supposed opposites. Rather, as Heidegger argued so eloquently, to think "against values therefore does not mean to beat the drum for the valuelessness and nullity of beings"; for example, arguing against "humanism" does not imply that one advocates inhumanity.[9] To argue against the unity of self is, at least initially, to ask what this has meant in the past and whether its meanings have been implicated in the harm we do and in our failure to care.

Another way of looking at the self starts right out by denying its unity. Sometimes such views posit a composite self, one made up of personlike parts.[10] Unity is lost at the level of *the* self but is found again in the parts. The notion is not bizarre. We know from studies of colonial and postcolonial experience that many lives have exhibited the qualities described in theories of the composite self. Deeply embedded in this approach, however, is the persistent longing for unity. The hope seems to be for some event or vision that will unify the parts. When that unity comes, it is often at the expense of parts of the self hardly recognized or of other selves. Like mutually distrustful members of a community, parts of the self can unite when threatened by an external enemy. Similarly, distinct parts of a self may war for dominance, and the integrity achieved by assimilation may be extolled while the differences lost are not mourned.

The self can be described as "diverse" without splitting it into little, individually homogeneous selves. Such a view accepts a multiplicity of goals, values, and competing desires. Even here, however, writers tend to emphasize autonomy and unity. Diana Meyers, for example, warns that autonomy is lost "when the fulfillment of opposed desires cannot be assigned to separate spheres or alternating occasions or when competing desires cannot be satisfied to an acceptable degree."[11] Before settling on a reconciliation to maintain autonomy or fulfillment, we must probe more deeply to see whether we want to cling to these notions. To what degree is autonomy possible or even desirable? Should we tolerate fragmentation in the short run, as Meyers suggests, so long as such tolerance enriches our lives and points toward eventual unity? Or must we, as several postmodern thinkers have suggested, simply face the reality of fragmentation and of our positions as spectators and bit players in a series of spectacles?[12] Can we admit that reality without approving of it?

Contemporary discussion of diversity within the self is heavily influenced by concern for diversity in communities and the search for ways to sustain such communities. It is important work, but perhaps we should move more slowly and spend more time on the relational self before tackling political issues. Treating the self as metaphorically equivalent to a community begs the questions that arise in connection with community. So let us set aside for now the concept of multiplicity, compositeness, and diversity. What else might we mean by a relational self?

Relational Selves: A First Approach

Many philosophers today agree that the self is a relation, not a substance,[13] but they often move directly to either confine that relation to encounters with human beings, or to the immediate categorization of kinds of relation, for example, Buber's I-Thou characterized by reciprocity or Emmanuel Levinas's I-Other characterized by irreducible difference. I want to move more slowly and first take the notion of relation at its most general and mathematical level.

Suppose we begin by describing the self at a given moment *as* a relation—that is, as a set of encounters of the sort:

$$A_t = \{(A_1, B), (A_2, C), (A_3, D), \ldots (A_4, e), (A_5, f) \ldots \}$$

where A represents various descriptions of the self prior to time t, capital letters (B, C, etc.) stand for other human beings, and small letters (e, f, etc.) stand for objects, ideas, and other nonhuman beings. The rule by which pairs are entered is simple but vague: 1) the self at the moment of encounter is always one element, but it need not be the first element; and 2) there must be some affect or meaning for A in the encounter. At this stage I will not attempt to specify the level of affect or try to disentangle affect and meaning. I just want to eliminate the multitude of casual elbow-brushings that mean nothing to us as individual encounters. Walking down Seventh Avenue in New York, for example, I may brush against or "see" hundreds of individuals, but the individual encounters are largely affect-free or meaningless. I may feel something about "crowds" and "cities" and, indeed, encounters of this kind at both physical and mental levels may be entered; they become part of the growing self.

Perhaps even this start, meant only as a heuristic, is too hasty. Selves are not born. It would be more accurate to start with the human organism and note that this organism is the entity that encounters people, objects, its own parts, and so on. A rudimentary self develops as the organism reacts to encounters, is satisfied or distressed by them, and can begin to anticipate satisfaction or distress. A rudimentary self, in skeletal form, might be symbolized as

$$S_R = \{(O_1, W_1), (W_2, O_2), (W_3, O_3) \ldots \}$$

in which the O_i represent the organism at various times and W_i represent the objects of encounter. But no *self* develops if these pairs represent mere "bumps" or collisions. The organism must be affected by them and an elementary form of meaning must be present. Thus we might describe a first string of mere encounters and a second layer of affects—raw feels—accompanying them. As the pairs representing encounters and affects become ordered, a self begins to emerge. When an infant anticipates that his cry will produce mother, relief, and satisfaction, a self is forming. (This is why many of us believe that a child's earliest cries should be answered promptly and consistently.)

With only a string of encounters and a layer of affects, the self is rudimentary indeed. It would be hard to distinguish a human self from other "higher" biological forms. As we examine the encounters themselves, however, we see that they involve language. Human parents talk to their infants and shape early babblings into communicative utterances. Thus the encounters in a human infant's life are different from those of other animals in that 1) they involve organisms that have markedly different natural features, and 2) the caregivers of human infants are already selves. Both criteria are necessary. Children raised (in legend and rarely in fact) by nonhuman nurturers do not develop selves, and nonhuman animals raised by humans do not develop selves, although they may exhibit signs of personality. One could even grant a notion of rudimentary self in many animals — encounter, affect, anticipation, initiative in encounter, and displays of satisfaction or distress may all be present.

Still another layer must be present if we are to speak of real selves. This is a layer of evaluation that rates the affects of the first layer. (Some philosophers call these ratings second-order evaluations.) As a self, in contrast to other animals, I not only evaluate encounters as satisfying or distressing, but I evaluate my own affects. I think whether I should feel the way I do about various encounters. Past encounters become the objects of new encounters. The self at previous moments becomes another object of encounter, affect, and evaluation. I approve of certain ways of being in the world and reject others. Further, some are approved or rejected unreflectively (without this second layer of evaluation, on the basis of mere feels), some become habitual (evaluated once and for all), and others are objects of continual scrutiny. This highly complex relation, the self, will continue to add encounter-pairs in which one element is its present self or its associated organism, others in which self and organism constitute the pair, and still others in which self and past or future self (imagined) compose the pair.

In this elementary and highly abstract start I have asserted that the self *is* a relation, that it is dynamic, in continual flux, and that it is a center of affect and meaning. We could now concentrate on this abstract scheme and try to perfect a notational system. We have capital letters for people and small letters for everything else. But should we not differentiate among concrete objects, places, ideas, collectives, and so on? Such a scheme quickly outlives its usefulness, but let's remember that a self contains encounters with things of the sort listed. Indeed, if we had a master computer to identify and call up various clusters, we could confirm the dominance of certain kinds of subrelations in, for example, the poet, the mathematician, the sports lover, the seamstress, the master chef.[14]

It is obvious, however, that we can say only just so much from looking at the pairs that make up the relation. We need to know about the affects and meanings attached to the entries. Here we need something like Sartre's "for-itself," a consciousness — one without content — that can be directed at itself. I say "something like" Sartre's reflective consciousness because I do not want to follow Sartre in his separation of body and consciousness, facticity and freedom, being and nothingness. What we need instead is an awareness that directs thought, an awareness that is very much part of the human organism. Sartre's great contribution, it seems to me, is his description of reflective consciousness directed at its own workings and the part this consciousness plays in constructing a self. We do not need to posit total freedom for this consciousness, and indeed such a move causes great difficulties when we enter the domain of ethics. Further, we need not regard the apparent lack of content of that consciousness as fixed or impermeable. We might better regard it as directed and colored by moods, atmosphere, genetic inclinations, and the nature of objects it focuses upon. It takes on content, empties itself, and renews itself.

We must pause here to ask two important questions: Who or what acts in the world—an organism, a person, or a self? How are these terms related? We certainly talk about "selves" meeting and interacting, and I will not avoid such language in the chapters that follow. Perhaps it is best, however, to think of a *person,* the indissociable combination of organism and self, as the entity that acts. The organism is both mind and body; we posit no split between the two. It might be useful to think of the self as a sort of script by which the organism directs and interprets its encounters. Thinking of the self this way allows us to explain how it is that selves can continue to be augmented even after the organism dies. Biographers, friends, and relatives who discuss a particular self add countless pairs to the relation that is the self. Looking at the self this way reminds us that the organism is not the sole "author" of the script-like self; other selves contribute to its construction. In what follows I will often use *self* and *person* interchangeably. Both self and person will be said to act, but the distinction should be kept in mind.

In encounter, consciousness is colored by both feeling and cognition. On close examination we surely uncover several layers of evaluation, as already noted. At the first level, certain encounters are assessed as pleasurable or painful; at the next, such pains and pleasures are evaluated more normatively as encounters to be sought or avoided; at still another, the affect itself may become an object of reflection, and A may reflectively encounter herself with respect to the affect. Consider, for example, an encounter that triggers strong feelings of pity. A has, presumably, experienced pity in other circumstances, but this incident induces a train of reflective thought. Symbolically, the chain might look like this:

$$(A_1, B) \longrightarrow (A_1, \alpha) \longrightarrow (A_1, A_\alpha)$$

A has encountered a person B and has felt affect α, identified as pity. A now encounters or thinks about α—what arouses it, whether it is good or bad and in what senses, and what its effects are. Then A may begin to think about herself with respect to this affect, A_α.

Technically, each A in the chain should have a different subscript, but, again, I do not want to get bogged down in perfecting a notational system. I want, rather, to discover what this kind of exercise will suggest for further exploration. Clearly, feelings can be the objects of thought, and oneself can also be an object of thought. If our supercomputer were to reveal a self with no reflexive pairs, we would surely raise questions about the person's character and/or personality.

If we were able to perform this kind of analysis on Heidegger, for example, would we find a lack of reflexive pairs? Looking at his philosophy, we might agree with Theodor Adorno, who said that his philosophy "is fascist right down to its innermost components,"[15] but other philosophers disagree. Looking at his self in the way suggested by our relational scheme, we might instead find significance in Arendt's comment to Karl Jaspers about Heidegger: "What you call impurity I would call lack of character—but in the sense that he literally has none and certainly not a particularly bad one."[16] Persons who lack character may be unreflective selves or they may be selves whose reflection is rarely directed at themselves or aroused by encounters with particular others. Heidegger may have been so obsessed with the idea of Being that he became detached from the beings who might have induced such reflection.

What else might be triggered by thinking of the self in this way? Some judgments can be made on a quantitative basis. If we find many pairs (A, m), where m represents, say, mathematics and A is an adult, we can be fairly sure that A is attracted to mathematics. We might then want to examine A's self for balance. Are there encounters with persons and other living things? Has the life been sacrificed to the work? (What do we mean when we make such a distinction?) We might be inspired to do comparative studies. Examining mathematically inclined selves, we might find other common interests, for example, music or poetry. We might examine such selves across cultures or across times and compare premodern with modern mathematicians, or Asian with European.

The quantity of encounters tells us something about the centrality of persons, ideas, and things in A's life, but quantity cannot tell us all we'd like to know. We may want to know something about the quality of the encounters. In studies like that of Jacques Hadamard we learn something about the working habits of mathematicians and their typical attitudes and casts of mind.[17] Thus, like novelists and biographers, we might extract a particular encounter and attempt to describe it in considerable depth. In doing this we would clearly have to connect the particular encounter with earlier and future encounters and, perhaps, with related stories from other lives. The abstract scheme with which we started is a graphic reminder of the complexity of selves. How do we select the encounters that are related? Which relations make the best story? Who is in the best position to tell the story? These questions cannot be answered in a definite way. Even the self in question may—properly—describe herself differently at different times.

The multiple possibilities are mind-boggling and suggest a reason why biographies vary so much and why new biographies of persons described many times continue to interest us. If to the enormous number of possibilities in the subject's life we add those of the biographer's, and imagine how these influence selection, we can be sure that biographical work is endless. Sociologists might extract sequences involving selves and various institutions: how do selves (of a particular kind—defined by, say, socioeconomic status) encounter social agencies, police, medicine, or industry? Anthropologists might examine selves (culturally defined) with respect to various cultural practices or artifacts. Psychologists might examine sequences of encounters with objects of learning. Psychoanalysts might dig out encounters that the organism has forgotten.

We might be interested instead in particular kinds of relation. In chapter 1 I defined caring as a relation (A, B) in which the first member of the pair, A, is designated as the carer and the second member, B, as the cared-for. A's caring is characterized by receptive attention and motivational displacement; B's contribution is some form of recognition or response. If A and B meet these criteria, the relation can rightly be called caring. But what exactly does A do? And how does B respond? How does caring manifest itself across times, cultures, individuals, a multitude of contexts?

No one of these approaches can describe a self fully. A self cannot be captured in terms of its time, culture, profession, or roles. If we are interested in the development of caring persons, we need to know about the particular encounters that support or undermine caring, the kinds of encounters that induce people to harm others, and the patterns that mark sensitivity and insensitivity. The selves described by liberal theory and by current communitarians are, in some ways, "dangerous" selves because they concentrate too narrowly on the individual or the cultural group that many today use as a single source of identification. Loosed on the world, they do a form of psychological violence, and reflected inwardly, they limit the self unnecessarily.

So far I have used a mathematical notation to define a relational self, but my objective is not to establish an airtight mathematical definition. Rather, my objective in starting this way is to show how complex and difficult the search for a self really is. We can see immediately how different selves are and how irreducible that difference is. Indeed, a given self A_t, is different from the self A_{t-1} identified with the "same" physical body at an earlier moment. When A at time t tries to describe her earlier self—say, in adolescence—the description involves a selection from the pairs available at time t, and it may be augmented by thoughts of the future. We might ask what (or who) does this selecting? Doesn't the process of selection imply a self of the traditional sort? That move does not seem necessary. The relational entity encounters a person, idea, or thing; the relation "has" a body with a brain that can think. Memories pop out. Sometimes the memories selected represent the way things actually happened; sometimes they appear as they were revised by later encounters; sometimes they are constructed from bits of fantasy right on the spot. A brain, influenced by the self (past encounters) and the present situation, does the selecting.

Is A_t best described as this enormously complex relation? How could we possibly recognize other selves or predict their behavior? Of course, all selves are dependent on bodies, and we usually identify one another by face, but bodies change, and we may fail to recognize someone we haven't seen in a long time. The voice or some other physical attribute may help in identification, but the source we usually depend on is common memories—parts of another self that coincide with or trigger parts of our own. If none of these emerges, we say that the other is no longer the self we remembered.

Habitual and "True" Selves

Common subsets of encounters provide a major source of recognition, but there is also something we might call the "habitual self." This subset of each self is largely a product of its everyday culture. Certain kinds of encounter are so frequent that they become rule-bound. When I meet a neighbor, Joe, on the sidewalk at seven o'clock and say, "Good morning," I would be astonished and a bit troubled if Joe responded, "The battle of Actium was fought in 31 B.C." This response is not culturally predicted. Thus, of course, communitarians are right to insist that our culture or webs of interlocution are important sources of our selves. If we concentrate exclusively on these sources, however, we engage in cultural anthropology, and we may forget to consider other aspects (or parts) of selves.

The mention of cultural anthropology advises a reconsideration of our initial scheme. We realize that a set of encounters cannot describe the self fully. We need to know something about the setting of those encounters and their content. Is the content consonant with the setting? What are the cultural expectations for such an encounter? Does the self accept these expectations without reflection, or do the next encounters reveal a change of focus? What quirks of personality and character affect the responses we observe?

Consider again the encounter with Joe. Although I would not expect the response about Actium (unless, say, we had been talking about Roman history on the previous night), I might not be surprised by other comments. Joe may be habitually grumpy, and "What's good about it?" may be typical of him, or he may be taciturn and give only a nod to my greeting. Again, he may be a friendly sort who will follow a greeting with genuine expressions of concern for my well-being. Or, if he and I share the same occupational interests, we may fall into conversation about these. A certain range of responses is typical of Joe, and if something outside this range is uttered, I may leave the encounter thinking, "Joe is not himself today."

Thus, in addition to cultural practices that prescribe how we should behave in particular circumstances, the idiosyncratic features in our encounters contribute to the development of our selves. We are different selves, and only some of our encounters are traceable to culture. Recall Orwell's reaction to the events at the execution in which he participated. An execution is a highly scripted affair precisely because the authoritative agency does not want idiosyncratic responses to emerge. Every step is prescribed. Each person plays a narrowly prescribed role. The judge who pronounced the sentence is typically not one of the execution party. The person who pulls the lever or throws the switch does only that and is usually screened from the prisoner. The guards march beside. The chaplain prays. The observers watch. Even the prisoner is expected to behave in a solemn, compliant fashion. When unexpected events occur, the script is ruptured, and alternative scripts burst into consciousness. For Orwell, when the dog came bounding among them, the execution party became "a group of men." They might have been heading toward a picnic, a day's fishing, or a cricket match. In any of those situations a canine greeting would be entirely acceptable. In *this* situation, however, it induced shock, and who knows what else? In Orwell it prompted reflection; in others it may have triggered mere annoyance, hatred of animals, or even deeper hatred for the prisoner. Rarely—in fact almost never—does such an event induce immediate rebellion. The habitual, script-following self is dominant.

This discussion raises an interesting point of debate. Many writers, among them some philosophers, speak of something they call a "true" or "authentic" self. Oddly, this true self is often identified as a self that rarely emerges, one buried deep inside that requires a heroic effort to reach. Meyers, for example, uses several "exhibits" to start her analysis of autonomy and authenticity.[18] One is that of Nora in Henrik Ibsen's *A Doll's House,* who starts on the road to a true self by deciding to leave Torvald. Clearly Nora is not exhibiting her habitual self when she decides to ignore what people think or what her children will undergo as a result of her leaving. Is Nora turning toward or away from a true self? What makes a choice more or less representative of that true self? We might invoke an entirely different example. In Carol Shields's *The Stone Diaries,* Mrs. Flett, who started life as the motherless Daisy Goodwill, becomes successively Mrs. Flett, Mrs. Green-Thumb (when she writes a gardening column for a local newspaper), and Grandma Flett. Has she any "true" identity?[19] Has she sacrificed her true identity when she subdues her occasional inclinations to rudeness or is her reputation for being "unfailingly gracious" a main mark of her true self?

At the extremes, cases like Nora's and Mrs. Flett's illustrate the tensions between the two prominent positions we've been discussing. In the one, autonomy is prized and closely identified with authenticity, a true self. In the other, a willed faithfulness to one's position and responsibilities is favored and considered more reflective of a true self. What is missing in both is a fuller account of other subsets of selves and what effects the actions of the "true" self have on these other subsets. Some other subsets of the relational self, while distinctly and irreducibly different from the self under examination, are inextricably part of that self. A wound to one of these others is a wound to the relation and hence to the self. The true self, if such a thing exists, cannot be found deep within its psychic self (construed as separate from other selves and things), nor can it be described in general cultural terms.

We continue to find gaps and complications in the definition with which we started, but all of these are enlightening. In defining the self as a relation, we've seen the need to recognize a habitual self and to explore the settings in which encounters occur. But perhaps we have made a mistake in defining the self as a set of affects or meaning-laden encounters. At least we need to say more about the affects that admit an encounter to the relation we are calling a self. In everyday language, a self made up of encounters characterized by pain, fear, shame, and hatred will be different from one characterized by pleasure, love, acceptance, and compassion. It may be useful to examine these affects more closely.

Consider some of the cases mentioned earlier. In *The Way of All Flesh* we learn that Ernest was beaten by his father, Theobald, in a well-intentioned effort to teach the child to read. The affects connected to these pedagogical encounters were mixed. Ernest experienced pain, humiliation, and guilt. He wanted to love his parents, but that love was killed again and again. Because his godfather helped to validate his suffering, he was able finally to put a rational valuation on his experience. His parents were unable to convince him then that all the daily cruelties were really kindnesses in disguise. What happens to children who are not allowed even to express their pain?

Miller, in her retrospective psychological study of members of the Nazi high command, concluded that *all* of the men she studied failed entirely to develop selves.[20] It was not simply a failure of autonomy, Miller argued, but rather that these men had never developed selves at all. What could be meant by such a claim? Using the scheme with which we started, we would have to argue that selves are formed inevitably. I am hesitant to say that a *distorted* self is formed, because that suggests that there is something we might call an undistorted or true self. It seems more accurate to say that a cruel and unfeeling self was developed. If such a self is a distortion, then we have to face the fact that we hold a norm for selves, and that this norm excludes the kind of cruelties exhibited by the Nazi leaders. We do *not* mean that a self will necessarily develop in a humane way if it is allowed to "grow naturally." A norm, in this sense, is something we must work to achieve.

Still, it is worth analyzing what happened to the men studied by Miller. They were brought up rigidly, moralistically. When beaten or humiliated, the initial affect had to be pain. What happened next? Miller says that they were not permitted to express their pain, that instead they were forced to evaluate the pain as somehow necessary—"for their own good." In a sense, then, most encounters were entered with false evaluations; genuine affects were suppressed and false ones registered. It would be hard to avoid the conclusion that, in their later deeds of cruelty, these men were indeed expressing something like true selves—the selves that had been under construction since infancy.

What shall we say of Orwell and Ernest? They, too, were subjected to rigid, moralistic upbringings. Ernest, a semifictional hero, was aided by a kind godfather. What saved Orwell? He and his classmates were physically abused so that they would learn Latin. Some of his classmates, like Miller's subjects, came to approve of the cruelty visited on them. They recognized the efficacy of the treatment (they *did* learn Latin) and no doubt passed the treatment on to their own children and students. How did Orwell escape? The most honest answer, of course, is that we do not know.[21] How did he acquire the reflective character of mind that enabled him to hate his oppressors even though he could not question their judgment? Why was he sensitive to the cruelties largely accepted by his peers?

Educators who struggle with these questions cannot hope to find absolute answers. We can conclude with some confidence that the constant presence of a loving and honest adult will help a child to make honest entries in the growing relation that is the self. We might also tentatively conclude that reflection is a powerful tool in self-building and that education should encourage it. It is, indeed, easier to recommend Orwell as an exemplar than to figure out how he became the self we encounter in his essays.

We need to say more about the questionable notion of a true self. Philosophers who retain the idea usually do so because they want to protect autonomy. Setting autonomy aside for the moment, let's see if we can make any sense of a "true self." What characterizes a true self? If we answer that it is one that does what it really wants to do, listeners may rightly ask why we do not call this an "autonomous self," and they may warn us against circularity in our eventual defense of autonomy. Further, how can one ever be sure that she is doing what she really wants to do? One can be contented and happy with one's occupational and personal life and still wonder whether another form of life might be even truer to "herself." It seems more reasonable to use explicit language and to say, "I love what I'm doing, but I wonder what life would have been like if I'd become a psychiatrist?" or "I made a good decision ten years ago." Reference to a true self is not helpful in this context.

Many people think of a true self as the self that *ought* to be. The true self is thus identified with an ideal self, and I do not want to discard the notion of an ideal self. Most thoughtful people have a conception of an ideal self—a self they would like to become, and parents and educators want to encourage both a defensible ideal and the effort required to reach it. It is confusing and misleading to call the ideal self a "true self." The ideal, by its very nature *as ideal,* is not a present reality; it is not guaranteed, and it does not lie beneath the surface as bedrock that can be reached by digging away the top layers. Further, the ideal self always and necessarily has a moral aspect. Like the present self, it is relational. I should pause here and say that, in one sense, the ideal self is a reality. It is that subset of the self regarded as best. In ethical caring we consult this ideal and try to live up to it, but we recognize that the ideal remains under construction and that it is not always easily accessible.

A true self cannot be described as simply autonomous; it cannot reasonably be *the* self that could be, since we have no way of knowing the opportunities missed or the satisfactions that might have been; and it cannot without redundancy be identified with an ideal self. Perhaps the best candidate for a true self is a public manifestation that matches inner feelings and expressions. Thus, perhaps, we see Mary's true self when she expresses what she really feels, when she has not adopted a *persona* for public exhibition. But this won't do either. Grandma Flett in *The Stone Diaries* was "unfailingly gracious," yet we hear bits of internal dialogue that suggest impatience and even dislike. Was her true self the gracious part or the impatient part?

We do speak meaningfully (if misleadingly) of a true self in this sense of genuineness. If Jack loses his temper under pressure, we may say, "Now we've seen the real Jack. His true self came out in that argument." Bill may rise heroically in a demanding situation and, paradoxically, we say the same thing: "His true self came out." It may be that as both observing and introspective selves we just do not want to accept the whole self as a true self. In part, our reaction is against the habitual self. We know (hope, fantasize) that there is more to our selves than these habitual selves, and yet we may carefully guard against situations likely to call forth another subset of the self because we are not sure what that nonhabitual self will be like. It is easier to stick with the script and delude ourselves that we possess unity or integrity.

It seems reasonable to discard the notion of a true self. Every search for it ends either in contradiction or in some notion for which we already have a satisfactory name. The self as described here is a relation, an enormously complex relation in which we can locate a substantial subset I have called the habitual self and a smaller subset that might be called the present ideal self. Many other subsets are present in this self, and they may be called forth in a variety of combinations.

Encounter is clearly paramount in the construction of self. There is still a subject associated with the relational self—it is that subset in which the organism or present self is the first element—but this subject is neither a fully constituting nor a fully constituted self. I do not create the world; neither am I totally constructed by it. Indeed, I cannot know exactly how much or how far I constructed the world I live in. I shape some things, and I am shaped by not only these things but also others over which I have no control. I am a spectator in a wild and explosively beautiful world, and I can become a *mere* spectator—one who moves restlessly from one spectacle to another.[22] To what degree can I decide what to do or to be?

Autonomy

Philosophical interest in autonomy has several sources, but the two most important are probably the epistemological and the practical.[23] In trying to figure out how human beings could have some control over their lives in a physical and causal world, philosophers have wrestled with the problem of free will and freedom in general. Kant posited a "transcendental subject," an essentially free self, that is capable of autonomous will. Through the correct use of reason, this subject can discover what is right and, with a good will, choose the right because it is right.[24] This transcendental subject or self, Kant held, is prior to the ends sought by the physical or empirical self, and this priority in turn establishes the priority of right over good. Autonomy for Kant is not the everyday freedom most of us think about when autonomy is mentioned; rather, it is our inborn freedom to embrace and follow the moral law discoverable within us.

Discussions of autonomy are riddled with paradoxes, and one arises immediately with the Kantian conception. In what sense are we *free* if reason used rightly binds us all to exactly the same conception of what is morally right? When Kant introduced his notion of autonomous will, the freedom offered was heady indeed; it meant freedom (in morals at least) from the authority of church and state. A new and wonderful inner freedom was proclaimed. It seems clear, however, that the locus of authority was not shifted to an empirical, individual self but to a stern and abstract self. Indeed, if all that were involved here were free and well-considered choice, then we might predict evil selves as well as moral selves.[25] The autonomous will cannot possibly furnish a foundation for morals unless, coupled with reason, it consistently wills the good. How is this good to be established when the will is cut off from the real world? Many of Kant's followers have tried to remedy this great fault, but the gap between moral and empirical self remains.

Today most discussions of autonomy focus on decision making. An autonomous person, it is said, makes up his or her own mind to do what he or she really wants to do. Must the decision be a morally good one if it is really autonomous? Can we genuinely desire what we know to be evil? Are moral autonomy and personal autonomy two distinctly different things? These are some of the questions in which philosophers have become mired.

Paradoxes arise even at the everyday level. Consider Marcel Proust's M. Verdurin: "He never formed an opinion on any subject until she [his wife] had formed hers, it being his special function to carry out her wishes and those of the 'faithful' generally, which he did with boundless ingenuity."[26] M. Verdurin seems to have been happily engaged (even creatively engaged) in doing and believing what his wife had decided. Can one decide autonomously to be heteronomous? Most philosophers answer this positively, noting that "autonomous" people join religious orders and accept the dictates of authorities within them. But then it cannot be autonomy itself that we respect but, rather, the posited *capacity* for autonomy that is, apparently, retained in such situations.

Another member of the Verdurin coterie, Dr. Cottard, presents a somewhat clearer picture. He consistently waits to hear the opinions of others because he wants to conform and be accepted. He has a more significant problem than his heteronomy. He has great difficulty understanding what others mean. In the language of care, he lacks a receptive competence and, although he is desperate for acceptance, he cannot tell the literal from the figurative or a joke from a serious comment. He is thus pathetically isolated in his heteronomy. We might do better to abandon the language of autonomy and heteronomy here entirely and describe Dr. Cottard as inordinately dependent on the opinions of others, as intellectually dishonest, as emotionally insecure, as pathetically eager for acceptance.

In the discussion of autonomy I do not want to lose track of my main purpose, which is to explore the questions of why people (however selves are defined) fail to care adequately for other people and why they so often harm both themselves and others. The discussion of autonomy is not meant, then, as either a defense or a rejection of autonomy. The object is to figure out how much control we have over the formation of our selves. As the discussion proceeds, some doubts will be raised about the usefulness of autonomy as a concept. In most situations a more explicit, transparent concept is preferable and, from the relational perspective, the very distinction between autonomy and heteronomy becomes almost unnecessary. We may begin to wonder why autonomy has been so important to western philosophers, but another set of examples may help us to understand its importance.

Virtually everyone defends an everyday sense of autonomy. No one wants to be beaten, blackmailed, or otherwise forced into doing something. We want to make our own decisions and be free of obvious coercion. Even at this everyday level, however, paradoxes arise, as we have seen. Consider the following example. I have been simultaneously a homemaker and a professional woman. For about four years I was exclusively a homemaker; for another four years I was a dean. There is no question which occupation is more prestigious in our society, but in which was I more autonomous in the ordinary sense? As a homemaker I could plan my days freely. Of course, there were tasks that had to be done, but I scheduled them to suit myself. There were interruptions (crying babies, skinned knees, uninvited salespersons, and so on), but I was able to build response time into my daily schedule. What is more, I loved the people who were the main source of demand on my time, and I wanted to respond to their needs. I often had fun doing so. As a dean much of my time was scheduled by others. I was told that I "had to be" in a particular place at a particular time, that a certain group expected me to greet them at another time, that so-and-so had to see me this very afternoon, and so on. Further, I disliked many of these tasks. Much of the day was devoted to jobs I really did not want to do. In the everyday sense of autonomy, I was more autonomous as a homemaker than as a dean.

Yet, if I had to choose one or the other *exclusively,* I would probably choose being a dean. Why? I suppose the choice would be governed by the fact that deaning is closer to the academic work I really want to do than is homemaking. This observation suggests some support for connecting autonomy to the power of carrying out a rational life plan, but it is not at all clear that a given plan has itself been freely chosen, or that some other plan might not be preferred if the chooser were better informed, or that one might not do just as well with a life of "creative makeshift." Indeed, I have already suggested that the notion of a rational life plan is highly artificial. We compose our lives. It is only the availability of comparative experiences that makes the expression of preference possible, and it is not at all clear that *autonomy* has much to do with the choice. We are swayed by the exigencies of the moment, and we rationalize a plan in retrospect.

Philosophers have discussed autonomy in several ways. Their main objective has been to defend autonomy against socialization—that is, to show that selves are not simply products of socialization but have some control over what they do and even their own creation. Meyers has summarized three main ways in which it has been said that persons achieve autonomy: reflection on socialization, continual examination of the self for coherence, and conscious commitment to the features of self that one identifies and evaluates as good.[27] Each approach purports to find a way to transcend socialization, and each has some usefulness; indeed, reflection on socialization will play a central role in our discussion of what is promoted in the best homes.

As we reflect on encounters and the affects that accompany them, we surely gain (or seem to gain) some control over our lives. The presence of reflective pairs in a given self is in itself a sign of some control. How do we become reflective selves, and how do we extend the range of reflection without inviting paralysis? Further, given the focus of this investigation, we have to ask whether reflection is always morally good. What happens after an episode of reflection? Are the relevant relations strengthened? The connection to autonomy is tenuous, and one wonders whether it might not be reasonable to examine reflection in its own right. Can valuable reflection be heteronomous?

As we develop the notion of a relational self, we see that the distinction between autonomy and heteronomy becomes increasingly blurred. If selves are relations as described in the previous section, it is unclear how autonomy and intelligent heteronomy differ. We are influenced by others, and encounters with these others actually provide the building blocks of the self under construction. We would, of course, prefer not to be "led around by the nose," and reflection may contribute to our capacity to resist such manipulation, but we also need to know when to accept advice and guidance. More important, from the care perspective we *must allow* ourselves to be affected by the needs and predicaments of others. Moral philosophy has tried to prescribe our responses so clearly that "right thinking" should tell us what to do under particular circumstances; here moral autonomy is defined as our dutiful choice of the right response for the right reason. Not only is this view of autonomy questionable, it is not clear how reflection contributes to it. Indeed, reflection on this view of autonomy and on our own lives has led many of us to reject traditional ethics.

What seems to survive this examination is not autonomy but the importance of reflection. When we discuss relational virtues, we will have to analyze reflection much more deeply. We also see the germ of another problem in using reflection as a criterion of autonomy. As we acquire self-knowledge through reflection, we have to evaluate what we have learned. This means that we may have to make a distinction between moral and personal autonomy. I'll return to this problem in the discussion of the third approach to autonomy.

What of coherence as a criterion for autonomy? Again, there seems to be something valuable about the notion of coherence with respect to selves. Many well-educated people study their beliefs and actions and try to root out inconsistencies and contradictions. Are we more self-directed as we increase coherence in our selves? From a relational perspective this conclusion is doubtful. Any sufficiently rich life is likely to be littered with inconsistencies. Walt Whitman put it this way:

> Do I contradict myself?
> Very well then I contradict myself;
> I am large, I contain multitudes.[28]

There are many subsets in every self that might plausibly be activated in different circumstances. In the moral aspects of our encounters, as Caputo puts it, "Obligation happens." It tugs at our sleeve with varying degrees of success. I may respond to a plea generously at one time, indifferently at another, angrily at still another. It has been a great philosophical project to seek and destroy these inconsistencies — to prescribe how we must respond and under what conditions. It may be, however, that as relational selves we learn more from our ambivalence and inconsistencies than we do from the continual pursuit of coherence. When I respond generously, that response becomes part of my self and represents a real possibility for future encounters. Similarly, when I respond angrily (to a similar plea), I may learn something about the conditions I need to respond graciously, whether I value such a response, and what I can do to control the conditions that encourage the response I value. I may also experience both wonder and guilt as a result of my responses. Meyers says that "recurrent regrets signal failed autonomy,"[29] but one could as easily argue that recurrent regrets signal enhanced sensitivity, unusual demands (greater opportunities), and increased knowledge of the opportunities. When I know from experience how I *can* respond to the needs of others, I may undergo guilt and regret more often than I would if I had settled for a lesser, more coherent self.

Again, an argument against coherence as a criterion of autonomy should not be taken as advocacy for incoherence at the level of argument. Most thoughtful people examine their beliefs from time to time and try to eliminate obvious contradictions. Often we do this by moving to a higher level of abstraction. For example, Ms. A may reject the notion of a personal god who answers prayer and yet feel the need occasionally to communicate with such an entity. She might, like Dewey, redefine "god" as the active relation between the real and the ideal,[30] or she might rationalize her behavior as part of the immortal conversation—a means of talking to great minds and personalities. If the behavior persists, must Ms. A reconcile her beliefs and behaviors by such a higher rationalization or confess theism? Why can't she accept the ambiguity and embrace the mystery? The acceptance of ambiguity and mystery could be a powerful relational move, one that might increase her appreciation for both believers and unbelievers. Further, this willingness to leave some things unsettled may be important in learning both to care and to refrain from doing harm. Thus, although people properly strive to remove gross contradictions from their belief systems, when inconsistencies seem to be embedded in life itself we might do well to develop an openness and humility that refuses the demand for complete coherence. Or is such an attitude itself a form of coherence?

In summary, coherence does not seem to be a defining characteristic of autonomy. A self-directed person may reject coherence at some level without accepting or failing to notice inconsistencies in his or her arguments. Indeed, at some level, argument may have to yield to poetry and poetics. Clearly, a person who follows others blindly or makes contradictory statements without reflection lacks both coherence and independence of mind, but this does not imply that the presence of those two qualities makes a person autonomous. The drive for coherence may be a product of socialization, and independence of mind is sometimes hard to distinguish from whimsicality or lack of discipline. Independence of mind, like reflection, will need closer examination. The discussion of coherence has not given us any reason to retain the high valuation traditionally placed on autonomy.

The third approach to defending autonomy against socialization suggests that persons can transcend socialization by identifying with their own traits and attributes. From this perspective one becomes autonomous by studying, evaluating, and making a commitment to certain of one's own desires and characteristics. Those desires and characteristics valued highly are affirmed and incorporated into an authentic self. This approach involves self-knowledge and self-appraisal. Both are worth-while activities, but, if the self is a relation, they cannot be conducted merely by processes of introspection and rational analysis. They must involve sensitivity to and consultation with others. Further, evaluation of one's desires involves a norm or ideal against which the desires are measured. Does evaluation necessarily separate the worthy from the un-worthy? What sort of evaluation can accomplish this?

The problems that arise in this approach sometimes force us to make a distinction between moral autonomy and personal autonomy, but this distinction suggests a radical separation I have already denied. If "I" am a relation, my personal autonomy and my moral autonomy (if such autonomies exist) cannot be so separated. If I choose to "incorporate my devils," as Friedrich Nietzsche advised, all those I encounter will be affected by that incorporation and their responses will necessitate a harder embrace of those devils or a revision in my commitment. There is no clear, complete way to separate my orientation to self and to other.

Further, if we begin to distinguish domains of autonomy, where do we stop? For example, can we reasonably speak of mathematical auton-omy? Some years ago, while I was tutoring some teenagers in mathe-matics, I noticed several apparent learning styles. Some students would dig right in and try to figure out what to do. Others would pause and explicitly ask, "What did the teacher say about this?" These students would not make a move until they could "remember" what the teacher had said about problems of the sort under consideration. I have put *remember* in scare quotes because the memory recited to me was often inaccurate. Inaccurate or not, it guided what the student did next.

There is a sense, then, in which it is reasonable to say that some students are mathematically heteronomous—they do what the teacher tells them to do—but are any students mathematically autonomous? Even Isaac Newton said that if he saw farther than others it was because he stood on the shoulders of giants. If we are somehow guided by the mathematics itself rather than by our teachers, are we thereby autono-mous? Talking this way doesn't seem to solve any problem. We would do better to describe more explicitly what students are doing.

Socialization plays a very large role in our lives. A child born into the Bantus or the Yanomami is unlikely to create and solve problems in Euclidean geometry or aspire to conduct a great western orchestra. Even children born into a society whose traditions include both geometry and great orchestras may take very different attitudes toward these features of their culture. Our problem, as parents and teachers, is not to make our children autonomous (since, first, there is a built-in contradiction in such an effort and, second, the term has very little meaning in a relational view), but to supervise their encounters, help them think about their encounters, and evaluate those experiences honestly. Surely reflection on one's socialization and accepting or rejecting parts of it for good reasons are important things to learn. They are, perhaps, more important (and certainly more useful) than the concept of autonomy that has subsumed them.

I want to pursue the mathematical example a bit further because we may learn something more generally useful from it. Although we cannot give an airtight definition of mathematical autonomy—and I have been arguing that we should probably abandon the language of autonomy—we can plausibly describe the behavior of students who regularly replay their teacher's words, of students who respond with active mathematical thinking, and of those who respond haphazardly to whatever clues they can detect. It might also be useful to help students better understand their own behavior. Do they know that their behavior can be described as suggested above? Do they know that they are not the first or only people to respond this way? Do they want to change? Is change possible? Is it necessary?

These are deep and significant questions. Too often in education we establish as a goal for all students a way of response that is congenial for only a few. Further, instead of fostering self-understanding, we simply try to find strategies that will foster growth toward the behavior *we* have evaluated as desirable. As we saw in chapters 3 and 4, this is one of the great dilemmas of education under liberalism. We feel the paradoxical need to force children to "become autonomous." If we were seriously concerned about the development of autonomy, however, we would not behave in this way; even if we set autonomy aside, the benefits of self-understanding, evaluation of one's desires and interests, and practice at decision making seem unquestionable. When we concern ourselves with learning to care and to refrain from harm rather than merely learning mathematics, the case becomes even more cogent.

The self is a relation. It is constructed in encounters with other selves and with objects and events in the world. It is neither the constituting subject that uses others as objects of its own representation nor a fully constituted subject capable only of subjective feeling. It has attributes, and it has a substantial continuity. There are reasons to doubt whether unity is one of its properties, however, and the notion of an autonomous self is riddled with difficulties. If we want to avoid the difficulties encountered in both liberalism and communitarianism, we need to explore more fully how this relational self develops and what norms we want to establish for it.

We started this chapter with a heuristic device — a mathematical description of the relational self as a set of ordered pairs continually growing as a result of encounters and the affects associated with them. The device itself quickly lost its usefulness, but it helped us to appreciate the enormous complexity of the concept "self." We then suggested thinking of the self as a sort of co-constructed script that directs and interprets the activities of the organism. Together, the organism and this scriptlike self constitute a person. In looking at the self this way, we deny two philosophical extremes — one that insists upon the essential freedom of the self to construct itself and another that sees the self as entirely shaped by the environment.

I described the "habitual" self as that subset of the relation (or that part of the script) that is regularly activated. I rejected the concept of a "true" self as muddled and misleading, and I defined an "ideal" self as that highly valued subset of the self that can be called upon in times of ethical decision making. Finally, I raised questions about the usefulness of concepts such as autonomy, unity, and coherence, and suggested that, of all the concepts associated with self, reflection is probably the most important and useful.

The next task is to describe the development of strong, healthy persons — inclusive selves containing attractive, competent habitual selves, ideal selves capable of sustaining caring relations, and reflective selves capable of directing the continued growth of the person. This task starts in homes, and we turn now to an exploration of the development of strong selves in ideal homes.

Part Two

OUR SELVES AND OTHER SELVES

Interlude

The Original Condition: Dependency and Home

The relational self begins its development *in utero*. It is, at the extremes, either loved, wanted, and protected, or ignored, unwanted, and, perhaps, abused. In intermediate cases, of which there may be very many, the pre-self is wanted and loved, but the mother is ignorant of what the growing fetus encounters in the womb and how these encounters might be controlled.[1] The organism, not just the self, is formed in rudimentary encounter. The mother's care of herself, some elements of which are beyond her control, contributes to the healthy development of the child. In times of great hardship even conscientious mothers may, through no fault of their own, produce children who cannot survive or who, if they do survive, suffer retardation or other forms of bodily deformation. When we move to social policy, it is obvious that the very first consideration should be the health of wanted fetuses and the mothers who will bear and care for them. Clearly, in every culture, it is in everyone's best interest to produce healthy children and to maintain the health of their caregivers.

The original condition of every human being is utter dependency. Romulus and Remus notwithstanding, real babies are totally at the mercy of human caregivers. These caregivers supply nourishment in the form of food, love, and direction. In Ruddick's terms, maternal thinkers (whether women or men) are concerned with preserving the life of the child, promoting its growth, and shaping it toward acceptability in some cultural context. These three great maternal interests often come into conflict and, across cultures, priorities can differ dramatically. In some cultures children who cannot "grow" are discarded; in others, such children are treasured and protected. In western culture the attitude varies not only by era but, even today, from family to family. What is meant by "growth" and "acceptability" also varies widely. In every culture, however, in situations where parents take their responsibility seriously, these three great interests are relevant.

The next five chapters are organized around the encounters of the brand new and developing self in its original dwelling: home. A home is not always a happy place and, indeed, it is sometimes a place of misery and fear, but, happy or unhappy, it is the new being's initial dwelling place. If it is healthy, it is the place where the work of attentive love is done, as Ruddick notes:

At the heart of a mother's arrangements is a "home." A home may consist of several families, of all the women and children of a community, of one mother in one room with several children, of a male and female parent and their children, of two or more men or women together, who may or may not be lovers. Whatever its particular structure, a home is the headquarters for a mother's organizing and a child's growing. Home is where children are supposed to return when their world turns heartless, where they center themselves in the world they are discovering.[2]

Like Ruddick, I do not want to limit the discussion of home to a setting for nuclear families, nor do I want the focus to be on what today's politicians call "family values." Instead, I want to ask what children inevitably encounter at home and what kinds of experience shape the developing relational self. Eventually, of course, I am interested in how the home and its values can be extended into the world. At present, political theory—when it shows any interest at all in private life—is focused on the application of public norms to private life; that is, it is concerned with justice in the home and family. In contrast, I am concerned with care, a relation characteristic of the best homes, in public life. Theodore Zeldin captures part of this:

There are a few schools in the West which try to teach children to understand other people by making them play the role of another, which in effect is an invitation to widen one's idea of what a home is. If home is where one feels comfortable and understood, but still retains one's privacy and mystery, if it is where one both takes care of others and is taken care of, while also having the right to be left alone, and if it is one of the great personal and collective works of art that all humans spend their lives attempting to raise up and to keep from falling down, then the art of creating homes, as distinct from building houses, still has a long way to go, and still remains within the province of magic. Instinct or imitation are not enough to make a home.[3]

Zeldin takes homemaking seriously, and so do I. There is no scheme of government that will work as well for devils as for angels, and there is no community of human angels upon which we can model a public utopia. What we need is an educational scheme and, eventually, a public policy that creates the best people possible through the best possible conditions and yet stays open to the possibility that these people will create still better conditions and still better people. What sort of nurturance should be provided in the best homes? How and where can a society compensate for the widespread lack of such provision?

I need to say something about the words *best* and *ideal*. Occasionally I will use "ideal" to describe a home guided by a particular philosophy or worldview. In this sense there can be more than one ideal, and we may contrast ideals. "Best" will refer to the ideal generated by care theory. At times it will have a universal connotation. The best homes everywhere maintain relations of care and trust, do something to control encounters, provide protection, promote growth, and shape their members in the direction of acceptability. At other times "best" will be judged instrumentally; that is, some homes are best for the development of characteristics and practices that are facilitative in liberal democracies. In the latter case I do not mean to suggest that homes in other cultures are absolutely deficient. Rather, my claim is that some practices yield better results than do others in western liberal democracies. I argue that, in well-intentioned efforts to respect all cultures, our society often deprives children (and their families) of the knowledge they need to succeed in such societies.

The notion that the best home stands as a model for public charity and benevolence is an old idea. Feminists and romantics in the nineteenth century often wrote about the redemptive qualities of good mothering and the salutary effects of these qualities exercised in the public arena. Feminists argued strongly that the moral qualities of women would make a positive difference in public life if women were allowed to vote.[4] The argument was used, also, to promote educational opportunities for women. Today hardly anyone would claim moral superiority for women, but there is some recognition that the projects traditionally associated with women are valuable and should be somehow extended into the larger social domain. At the same time, thoughtful women have experienced frustration in trying to emulate their fore-mothers in times characterized by all sorts of complexity. As early as the 1950s Anne Morrow Lindbergh captured the dilemma of traditional women in a postmodern world.

The inter-relatedness of the world links us constantly with more people than our hearts can hold. Or rather—for I believe the heart is infinite—modern communication loads us with more problems than the human frame can carry. It is good, I think, for our hearts, our minds, our imaginations to be stretched; but body, nerve, endurance and life-span are not as elastic. My life cannot implement in action the demands of all the people to whom my heart responds. . . . Our grandmothers, and even—with some scrambling—our mothers, lived in a circle small enough to let them implement in action most of the impulses of their hearts and minds. We were brought up in a tradition that has now become impossible, for we have extended our circle throughout space and time.[5]

The demands are indeed too many for an individual to satisfy, but it may be a mistake to assume that large impersonal institutions can do an adequate job in the individual's stead. Even when their basic physical needs are met, people often feel uncared for in institutional situations. A better solution is to spread caring, like literacy, over the whole pop-ulation. To do this, we need to study how caring develops, and we need to study both caring as a virtue (caring-as-virtue) and caring as a relation (caring-as-relation). We need to ask certain questions: What are the attributes of carers—people who reliably respond to cries for care? What are the conditions under which caring relations best develop?

A child's first encounters are with bodies—animate and inanimate objects. An infant is an organism that interacts in limited ways with its environment. Early interactions will gradually transform the organism into a growing self, but much happens to the child between the infant-organism state and the stage of full, rational selfhood. Feminists in al-most every discipline have insisted on the centrality and respectability of bodies. Human beings, even fully mature adults, are neither detached rationalities nor mere collections of responses to environmental stimuli. They are inspirited, thinking bodies, and it is their bodies that launch the development of selves through a multitude of complex encounters.

The growing organism also encounters places—places for eating, resting, playing, hiding, thinking, and seeking companionship. The home is our first universe, as Bachelard said. What is home like? What sounds, sights, smells, tastes, touches, or memories does it provide? How does its setting influence the growing self? Philosophers are beginning, at last, to attend to place. Edward Casey notes that many of the words with which philosophers have long been concerned—*politics, ethics, society, community*—have roots in words that signify or imply place. Yet "place," despite auspicious directions in contemporary thought, is rarely named as such, and it is even more rarely discussed seriously. Place is still concealed; it is "still veiled," as Heidegger says specifically of space.[6] Because we start our analysis at home, we must consider place seriously.

In addition to bodies and places, children encounter other selves and, through these other selves, ideas and the social environment we call culture. The selves encountered have themselves been shaped by and have contributed to the shaping of bodies and places. The structure of our discussion is not perfect: one cannot separate bodies, places, and selves so neatly without considerable artificiality. Despite this, the structure serves a developmental purpose, and it will help us to recover concepts and aspects of moral life that are too often ignored. Indeed, children themselves are ignored far too often in philosophy. Bernhard Schlink identifies this in *The Reader,* when the narrator's father, a philosopher, tries to respond to his son's troubled attempt to convey the problem with which he is struggling.

When he answered, he went all the way back to beginnings. He instructed me about the individual, about freedom and dignity, about the human being as subject and the fact that one may not turn him into an object. "Don't you remember how furious you would get as a little boy when Mama knew better what was good for you? Even how far one can act like this with children is a real problem. It is a philosophical problem, but philosophy does not concern itself with children. It leaves them to pedagogy, where they're not in very good hands. Philosophy has forgotten about children." He smiled at me. "Forgotten them forever, not just sometimes, the way I forget about you."[7]

Because we start at home, we cannot forget about children. The discussion begins with bodies—the entities of first encounter. The reader should keep in mind that I do not separate mind, body, and spirit; all belong to the organism *in toto*. Only the self is something different, attached to and dependent upon the organism during its life, but capable of a sort of immortality as a relation that can be endlessly analyzed, dissected, and repeatedly reconstituted.

CHAPTER 6

Bodies

At birth a body recently encapsulated in another body emerges to encounter a world of sensory experience. It has had encounters in the womb, but none of them has been visual. Now there are sights, sounds are no longer muffled by surrounding fluids, "feels" vary from silky to rough. Air moves over the skin and is sucked into newly functioning lungs; food is taken into the mouth and is tasted. Little by little the new body learns to control its own functions and, eventually, it accepts controls forced on it by parents as part of its self-control. It learns that there are sensory delights—some encouraged, some shared, some forbidden or hedged about with rules. It learns something about movement in space and encounters with other bodies. It experiences pain, and eventually it learns the reality of death. It learns how to behave in a well-established variety of settings; indeed, in many social situations the part of the body that we call mind seems not to be engaged at all—certainly not in any critical role. All of these encounters contribute to the developing relational self.

First Encounters

The world's religions have often denigrated the body, regarding it primarily as a container for an immortal soul. Christianity has contributed to this contempt for bodies, and women's insistence on the centrality and essential goodness of bodies has often led to their continuing devaluation as thinkers and moral agents. Pearl Buck has described in poignant language the conflict between her father, a fundamentalist Presbyterian missionary in China, and her mother, a woman who sought all her life for some sign that the religion she served had some bodily reality. Her father, Absalom ("Andrew" in Buck's biography, *Fighting Angel*), had little interest in home and family and worried more about the spiritual health of his wife than about her physical and emotional well-being. The death of children brought Andrew and Carie, her mother, into open conflict. When a parishioner's child died, Andrew was quick to say, "Doubtless it was the Lord's will and the child is safe in heaven." Carie agonized for the bereaved mother and responded, "Oh, and do you think this fills the mother's heart and arms?"[1] Not until the very end of her life did Carie dare to feel justified in speaking so. Like many other women through all of religious history, she accused herself of weakness of faith and lack of understanding.

Even while blaming herself for spiritual failing, Carie often spoke her heart. Buck writes:

Once I heard someone say of another's dead child, "The body is nothing now, when the soul is gone." But Carie said simply, "Is the body nothing? I loved my children's bodies. I could never bear to see them laid into earth. I made their bodies and cared for them and washed them and clothed them and tended them. They were precious bodies."[2]

In the lifelong conflict between Carie and Andrew we see the basic positions of two very different ideal homes. In one the body is cared for primarily as the earthly home of an eternal soul; in the other the body is precious in itself as the essential organic manifestation of a relational self. Children in both homes are protected, nourished, and disciplined. Both homes will likely avoid the infliction of unnecessary pain, but they may disagree on what it means for pain to be unnecessary. In the second home pain will not be inflicted on the body for the sake of the soul but only for the health of the body itself.

This chapter looks first at birth and dependency and the contributions of dependents to the caring relation. Then it considers issues of control, sensual pleasure, other bodies, and pain. In all of these sections attention will be centered on the bodily human organism, but we cannot forget that the body is the organ of encounter and that, through its encounters, a self is developing.

Birth and Dependency

Bodies are indeed precious. They provide the initial bond between mother and child. Once an inseparable unity, at birth the child and mother become visibly separate entities. Touch—fleshly connection— is paramount after this separation, as Adrienne Rich points out:

From the beginning the mother caring for her child is involved in a continually changing dialogue, crystallized in such moments as when, hearing her child's cry, she feels milk rush into her breasts; when, as the child first suckles, the uterus begins contracting and returning to normal size, and when later, the child's mouth, caressing the nipple, creates waves of sensuality in the womb where it once lay; or when, smelling the breast even in sleep, the child starts to root and grope for the nipple.[3]

Even for mothers (or fathers) who bottle-feed their infants, there is an overwhelming bodily connection. Holding the child as it nurses, inhaling its newborn fragrance, gazing at its physical perfection, mothers and fathers are moved by something that cannot be entirely captured in words. It is bodily response. Both child and parent are involved in this bodily response, and perhaps a reminder is needed here. One need not be a parent to be affected by what happens in homes. Most of what is developed here is from the perspective of the child. *Every* person started life at home, however various homes might be.

The first days and weeks of care giving should establish a caring relation. Note that I have said "should." What follows is, perhaps, debatable and thus must be marked as a "filling out" that is subject to dialogue. Because the child and its response are essential to a caring relation, that response must be elicited and treasured from the very first. For example, Ms. A and her husband agreed that every new baby's cry should be answered as quickly and positively as possible. Psychologists once had the effrontery to tell parents that such immediate attention would "reinforce" the child's crying and result in a spoiled child. This, of course, is nonsense—the result of a theory applied in total contradiction to the living evidence. With all of their infants, Ms. A or her husband always responded immediately, at first with their actual presence and, a bit later, with their voices: "Mommy's here, darling. Go back to sleep." That usually worked, and when it did not, they responded again with their physical presence. From the perspective of care theory, this early exchange of summons and response is fundamental. Rich puts it this way: "The child gains her first sense of her own existence from the mother's responsive gestures and expressions. It's as if, in the mother's eyes, her smile, her stroking touch, the child first reads the message: *You are there!*[4]

You are there! This is the child's inner reaction to the parent's response, "I am here." That constant response, "I am here," is the foundation of a relation of care and trust. It might function as both the introduction and the conclusion of this chapter. Projected onto the social scene it represents the assurance that every community should offer its members in time of need. It is worth noting that "I am here" uttered by a parent to a child represents an inversion of the biblical response offered by Moses and the prophets in answer to God: "Here I am." The "here I am" of the prophets was uttered in obedience to a higher power. "I am here," said by a parent to a child, is an offering of love that flows downward from those with greater power to those with less. In this respect care theory inverts Aristotle's priorities as well. Greater love is owed to the weak, immature, and helpless, not to the powerful, and a sign of mature psychology is the capacity to give care and love.

You are there. Experienced by the child, this is the beginning of a life of healthy interdependence, not one of lonely autonomy. Loneliness is terrifying at the start of life and at many times later in life. Direct experience of another's aloneness sometimes reminds us in a visceral way of our own psychic pains—some long forgotten or deliberately repressed. In *The Stone Diaries,* Shields describes the scene of a tragic birth. (The child of this birth will become Mrs. Flett, mentioned in chapter 5.) An itinerant Jewish peddler discovers a woman who had recently given birth. She is lying dead on her kitchen floor. After summoning help, the peddler stands with the doctor and a neighbor observing the dead woman, who was clearly beyond their help from the start. With the doctor's arm about his shoulder, the Jew feels for the first time in many years that he *belongs,* if briefly, to this small group joined in compassion. Then his eye falls on the child.

The child was still alive and breathing . . . everyone was hovering around the dead woman. But there on the kitchen table was a baby wrapped in a sheet. Its lips were moving, trembling, which was how he knew it was alive. . . . [H]e felt perfectly the infant's loneliness of an extreme and incurable variety, the sort of loneliness he himself had suffered since leaving home at eighteen.[5]

For this baby, mother was not there. It is precisely this existential loneliness that homes are designed to prevent. The person lying in a doorway or huddled on a steam grate for warmth has lost a great deal more than shelter. Abram Gozhdë Skutari, the Jewish peddler in Stone's story, understood this. The doctor's arm about him and the shared tears reminded him both of his own loneliness and the vast emptiness in so many human lives.

[T]hat child's sadness never left him. He swore he'd never seen a creature so alone in the world. He lived a long life and made a million dollars and loved his wife and was a decent father to his sons. But he grieved about that baby all his days, the curse that hung over it, its terrible anguish.[6]

We do not know, of course, whether a newborn puffing out its lips and groping in vain for its mother suffers "anguish." In the absence of direct evidence, we hope not. It is too horrible to think of "terrible anguish" in every child abandoned on a hillside in famine-stricken China or stuffed into a garbage can in affluent America, but Abram's reaction is, perhaps, the one we want to cultivate. This terrible aloneness at the beginning of life (or in any period of dependency) must be prevented.

The total physical dependence of infancy is sometimes repeated in old age. Even when the dependency is only partial, it can be hard for a formerly active, "independent," person to accept. Buck's father, for example, never stopped working, but in his old age he finally needed his family.

Sometimes at twilight he would seem timorous of being alone, as though he remembered the old ghost stories he had heard as a child. He wanted the lights early, and he wanted to hear human voices, to have people about him. Carie's daughter stayed near then, and spoke cheerfully of small things, and sat by him with everyday sewing in her hands, and encouraged the children to run in and out. He was comforted by such small ways, and warmed, though he never knew how to share in the life of home or children. But he sat and watched and the look of fear went out of his eyes and after a while he could go up to bed.[7]

In old age the body may revert to its infant ways. In Doris Lessing's *Diaries of Jane Somers,* Maudie, whom Jane befriends, experiences her body weakening. Sometimes her bowels give way, and often Jane—who never dreamed she could perform such a task—washes her. Maudie hates this dependency, but she welcomes her new friend. Like Andrew, Maudie fears silence and needs the sounds of life around her. And somewhere, if not in her upbringing or prior experience, then perhaps in vicarious experience, Jane—the elegant fashion editor—has learned to care for a body in need. In the hospital, fighting off inevitable death, Maudie needs help in the battle.

"Lift me up, lift me up," says Maudie, and I pick up this little bag of bones and set it upright, and smooth back her wispy hair, and say, "Enough for a minute, Maudie, I must sit down."[8]

Jane's body was also feeling the struggle. So, too, were the nursing sisters, whose spirits and touch remained gentle even when their backs and legs ached. For Jane, through these trying days, her own greatest comfort was the bodily comfort of lying in a perfumed bath for an hour or so.

The young child learns gradually about the body. Its functions must be controlled, but what attitude will be taken toward its nakedness, its waste products, its odd noises, its blood shed in small injuries, its tears, spit, and vomit? How shall these encounters be evaluated? What will the child learn of other bodies? Will he or she some day be able to clean up after bodies without revulsion and with continuing tenderness? This would seem to be a major task of education, if not at home, then somewhere. As the child's response is treasured, so it is hoped that the grown self will have learned to cherish a full range of bodily responses: a smile returned, a hand held, a face turned appreciatively to the sun, a sigh of satisfaction over a cup of soup, a delighted chuckle over some nonsense on television, a polite thank-you uttered or facially expressed.

Nothing in the above discussion should be interpreted to mean that bodily functions are never repulsive; many bodily effusions are smelly and disagreeable. Indeed, that obvious fact was used by some saints to glorify the mortification of their own bodies as they cleaned vomit or excrement with their tongues.[9] What is to be sought, however, is not some perverse glory but the health and comfort of both one's own body and the bodies of others. One who attends to the bodily needs of another concentrates on the response that is elicited by feeding, cleaning, and comforting, not on her own goodness.

Care of human bodies has long been the duty of women. Does it make a difference in the way women look at the world? Does it help to explain the gender gap that exists in today's political views? It is unlikely that any one set of experiences can explain a complex phenomenon, but just as we now offer girls opportunities to play with blocks and trucks and to engage in competitive sports just in case these activities have something to do with mathematical development, it seems reasonable to suggest that both males and females learn to care directly for human bodies just in case these activities have something to do with the development of mature empathy. It is not always pleasant work, as Ruddick notes:

As the philosophers warned, to welcome female or male bodies requires welcoming incontinence, irregularity, discharge, pain, decay, and finally, death. But these are part of bodily life and cannot be relegated to the female. Aches, flushes, and multiple failures of function and sense afflict both male and female human bodies. The conception of the normal body as a controlled and steady (and therefore male) instrument of human will is a fantasy not even realized among healthy men.[10]

It is clear that no human body is just a home for reason and that denigration of the body contributes little to the purification of soul. It is not only a healthy attitude toward their own bodies that we should want for our children; a loving respect for other bodies must be developed.

The human infant is almost wholly body. A self develops as the dependent body encounters other bodies—their feel, sight, sound, taste, and smell. Such encounters are inevitable and universal, but their interpretation is not. Caregivers help the child to evaluate these encounters, to recognize pleasure and pain *as* pleasure and pain, to expect reasons for necessary pain and consolation for suffering. Right from the start the response of the cared-for is central to the caregiver's decisions and attitudes. Weil argues that this response must be divided into two levels: a "superficial" one that is concerned with one's personal rights and needs, and a deeper one that is inextricably tied to an impersonal good. It is the latter, she says, that is sacred.

At the bottom of the heart of every human being, from earliest infancy until the tomb, there is something that goes on indomitably expecting, in the teeth of all experience of crimes committed, suffered and witnessed, that good and not evil will be done to him. It is this above all that is sacred in every human being.[11]

From the care perspective Weil is right in what she identifies as sacred. It is indeed this capacity for response to care that is sacred. But I think she is wrong to suppose that this capacity is indomitable. Indeed, one might argue that its fragility is part of its sacredness. It is precisely *because* the expectation of good is fragile that we must be so careful to preserve it. Now and then we encounter people who, through great courage and optimism, retain this expectation in the teeth of adversity. Just as often, we meet those — William James's sick or melancholy souls — who expect evil, and we see that their expectations are, as James touchingly affirmed, more realistic than the sunny expectations of their optimistic peers.[12] In most of us, however, the expectation of good, if initially aroused in early childhood, is lost somewhere in the world and rekindled and lost again in cycles. In practice it is tempered by actual events and real encounters, but this practical result does not alter Weil's claim that the expectation is sacred.

Where I part company with Weil is on the abstract location of the expectation and the similarly abstract home of the sacred. This difference illustrates again the difference between two ideal homes — one that might be called soul-centered, the other body-self–centered. Interestingly, both may embrace a deep and vigorous sense of the sacred, but for the second the sacred is found in everyday life. For me, the sacred expectation must be in each concrete individual, not in something abstracted from all human beings. For Weil, the thing being killed by cruelty and carelessness is not so much the hope and love in one human being (as in Ernest's case) but, rather, Hope and Love as sacred qualities belonging somehow to the whole class of humans. It is easy to overlook this emphasis in Weil when we read certain passages that seem to express devotion to the concrete, particular Other. It cannot be overlooked in a passage such as this:

There are also many cries of personal protests, but they are unimportant; you may provoke as many of them as you wish without violating anything sacred. . . . So far from its being his person, what is sacred in a human being is the impersonal in him. . . . Everything which is impersonal in man is sacred, and nothing else.[13]

This is not Buck's mother, Carie, speaking. Indeed, it is reminiscent of the attitude that challenged Carie's warm nature all her life. It does not reflect maternal thinking — a deep concern for *this* child in *this* situation and in future situations that may be affected by *this* moment. One of the lessons learned at home (or in church or in school, but not in a church guided by abstract theologies or in schools organized by abstract disciplines) is that every encounter between actual embodied beings matters. The particular response of the particular Other is what is sacred. This response is sacred not because it omits the profane, absurd, cruel, or mistaken, but because it provides us with the material by which we judge our own acts and their effects. Used properly, it helps us to establish or maintain relations of care. It is sacred, also, because it is the whole point of what we call our rationality. Without the other's ears, to whom would we talk?[14] How would we learn to correct our conceptualizations? Without the other's gaze, touch, and smile, how would we live?

Both carer and cared-for develop as human selves through interactions in which the response is treasured. The young child learns that she is valued and has some control over her own fate; she can summon the one who-is-there. The caregiver learns to appreciate a full range of human response. And in old age, when the body again becomes dependent, connection with one who understands can make the difference between relative security and terror.

Control

As the child grows interactions become more complex. The body grows, interacts, and must learn to control itself. The body—of which mind, emotion, and spirit are all parts—will be taught habits of cleanliness, attitudes toward the physical body and its functions, tastes in food, the modulation of voice, the appropriate movement of energetic limbs, the management of bodily skills that emerge naturally in maturation, and a host of other things. The particularities taught will differ from culture to culture and, to some degree, from family to family, but in all cases the body will be taught to control itself. This teaching can be done lovingly and gently or with the righteous cruelty experienced by Ernest in *The Way of All Flesh*.[15]

What is at stake in this early teaching and learning? Freud traced many of the world's neuroses to forgotten or repressed early experiences. Miller argues persuasively, if retrospectively, that some of the greatest horrors committed by adults are caused by faulty methods of child rearing. Many people fail even to recognize the possibility of alternatives to their own coercive upbringing, and others hold a religiously based belief in the need to punish the child's body for the sake of its soul. In homes that do not recognize such separations every hurt inflicted has somehow to be justified, not in abstract law but in the response of the cared-for to offers of consolation.

The need to justify any pain inflicted and to offer consolation rises directly out of the requirements of caring. A caring *relation* requires a response from the cared-for that recognizes the efforts of the carer as caring. Thus Weil was unqualifiedly right when she said that one must always try to respond in a satisfactory way when another asks, "Why am I being hurt?" It is not sufficient from the care perspective, however, to recognize only hurts dealt to the impersonal, as Weil suggested in the earlier passage. Indeed, sensitive child-caregivers struggle to satisfy that cry even when it seems entirely unjustified. The caregiver must persist in firm, gentle, and responsive conversation until either the pain is relieved or the cared-for understands or, at least, accepts on faith the necessity of the pain.

Control, in the hands of maternal thinkers, is aimed at transfer. Such caregivers want to reduce their own overt control and pass it to the child, and their control of the child is accompanied by attentive love. This approach contrasts sharply with that of certain fathers that Ruddick describes.

Fathers have legal control over important aspects of their children's lives and moral authority to judge their choices, though they have neither developed the gifts nor borne the burdens of maternal work. . . . The point about—or against—Fathers is that their authority is not earned by care and undermines the maternal authority that is so earned.[16]

Ruddick is not arguing that all men, or even all fathers, are bad men. Rather, "Fathers" (with a capital *F*) designates a class of people who wield authority without doing the work of attentive love. In public policy such exercise of authority merits the label "paternalism." This definition of paternalism will help us to avoid some of the objectionable features of coercion when that coercion is exercised reluctantly for the good of those who are harming or neglecting themselves. It won't do, of course, to avoid charges of coercion by calling it something else, but the coercion used in attentive love really is different. It is open to negotiation, it pays attention to expressed needs even as it presses for inferred needs, and it weighs harms and goods and stands ready to back off if harms threaten to overwhelm goods. Attentive love is direct-contact work, and it is the function of public policy to establish the conditions under which it can flourish.

The amount of control exercised by a caring parent fluctuates with the child's perceived progress as judged from two perspectives. From one perspective, the aim is the child's independence; that is, the goal is to help the child toward competence and mastery of its environment. Most caregivers are eager to yield the tasks of personal care—feeding, hygiene, bathroom functions, dressing—to the child as he or she is able to accept responsibility for them. From another complementary perspective, the caregiver wants to raise a child who will be intelligently heteronomous and sensitive to both the needs of others and his or her own continuing dependence.

The emphasis on autonomy in the last two centuries is perhaps understandable. When Kant freed moral agents from the control of church and state, and science demanded the free formulation and test of hypotheses, freedom to control one's own life seemed to be a logical next step. Kant did not free the empirical self, of course, and science dictated control by method, not by individual. The individual autonomy praised by nineteenth-century political theorists was something new. Beginning in the last century it has, in some forms, become a perversion of the earlier Kantian notion, one that identifies autonomy with the power to do what one wants to do without regard for what one ought to do. Good parents are more concerned with promoting the sort of internal control that Kant identified with autonomy; they want their children to monitor their own conduct and behave, without coercion, in ways acceptable to them (the parents). Because it is an enormous responsibility to direct the lives of others into ways from which "they will not depart," parents must continually inspect, reflect upon, and revise their own practices and attitudes.

I make a deliberate choice here that will affect the perspective taken on social policy. One could argue that parents (and public authorities) should recognize and abide by a community's clear and stable rules, and that it is these rules that should be internalized by the young. In contrast, my approach is much closer to Deweyan pragmatism: rules must be well conceived for their present purposes, and they are always hypotheses of a sort. Further, acceptance or rejection of such hypotheses depends heavily on the response of those controlled by the rules. Carers want to promote healthy, happy growth, not mere conformity, and not only the kind of growth that leads to material success.

A responsible society needs an attitude that will allow it to exercise sensitive control. I argue, for example, that people should not be allowed to sleep on the street (even if they claim this as a right), but that the relevant public must respond to complaints that shelters are not safe, hygienic, or consonant with the promotion of human dignity. We ought not to be deterred by charges of "paternalism" unless we are indeed guilty of exercising control without attentive love, and I must emphasize again—not for the last time, because it is so important—that attentive love is not the sort avowed by Ernest's parents or Dickens's Mrs. Jellyby in *Bleak House*. In contrast to self-righteous love, attentive love listens, it is moved, it responds, and it monitors its own action in light of the response of the cared for.

Parents are not alone in disciplining bodies. Parents are themselves disciplined by the community, by the whole culture. It really is bodies that are so disciplined. By this I do not mean to introduce a separation of mind and body; both are integral parts of the organism that encounters the world and thereby develops a self. There are, however, encounters that are primarily cognitive and others that are mainly physical. When I refer to the body here, I point to activities that have a low cognitive content. Our bodies are disciplined to behave in certain ways, and although we act consciously and even voluntarily in many of the situations I will describe, we rarely reflect on what we are doing. Consider the following scenarios.

1. The congregation sits quietly and listens to a preacher who makes astonishing claims that would surely be questioned in another setting. He may even charge the group with sins few of them have committed or urge them to support causes that many reject. No one says, "That's plain silly!" No one says aloud, "I reject that."

2. A large audience listens to a musical performance in an open auditorium. There is plenty of space and grassy lawn just outside the open doors. The performers play a rondo, and the body wants to dance. But no one does. Everyone sits quietly, perhaps tapping a foot softly. At the end, there is applause. Clapping hands is an appropriate bodily response; dancing is not.

3. Revisit the execution party described earlier by Orwell. Despite the repugnance bordering on revulsion felt by many participants, each one plods along, filling the role assigned to him. The body is so well disciplined in this case and the event so well scripted that the mind can do little but raise excuses and manufacture rationalizations: "If I don't do this, I'll be punished. If I don't do this, someone else will. If I don't do this, I'll look silly."

4. Children sit in orderly rows taking tests. It is May, and the outdoor world is beautiful. As Thomas Hardy wrote, the May month is flapping its glad green leaves. The tests go on for a solid week, day after dull day. No one says aloud, "The heck with this." No one leaves.

In all of these cases, and we could offer many more, bodies are so well disciplined that overt rebellion is all but unthinkable. Michel Foucault has described modern disciplinary methods in terms of power and "political anatomy." This political anatomy produces a "soul" that inhabits each person, and (in an ironic inversion) this soul becomes the prison of the body.[17] The soul described by Foucault is not, of course, the individual immortal soul, once thought to be trapped in a fragile, mortal body. Foucault's soul is a mighty, diffuse, and inescapable soul that holds all of us in its sticky grasp. Foucault is careful to remind us, however, that the power diffused through this soul is not all bad; it is not something to be overcome—even if it could be. Rather, it is something to be understood.

When we understand how we are affected by cultural and political power, we are in a better position to assess its effects. We cannot eliminate the power itself, but we can evaluate some of the activities it ritualizes, and then we can take one of several steps: we can endorse the activity on reasonable grounds, we can separate ourselves from it (as many have from religious institutions), we can work politically to eliminate this particular activity (as many of us are working to eliminate capital punishment), we can deplore it and allow those who suffer from it to express their unhappiness. This last seems a wishy-washy response, but it is more powerful than it appears on the surface. Parents and teachers who deplore the current emphasis on school examinations can at least allow students to express their unhappiness. They can offer consolation for a pain they cannot remove. This is better than constructing elaborate and phony rationalizations for psychological suffering that is almost certainly unnecessary. At the same time, teachers and parents can work openly to control the practice and reduce the suffering.

Good homes want to produce acceptable children—we would be hypocrites to deny this—but the best homes want children to understand why certain practices and attitudes are deemed acceptable. These homes do not inflict pain to achieve acceptability, and they offer consolation for pain inflicted by institutions that are part of the realm of acceptability. Among the many things children must learn to control are feelings, and among the feelings that must be controlled are those involving sensual pleasure. Possibly no aspect of human development has been handled so badly by so many for so long.

Sensual Pleasure

Home is the place legitimized in western tradition for sexual relations between married couples. Even under widely recognized sanctity, sexual

relations have often been robbed of sensual pleasure by religious stric-
tures, customs, and ignorance. It was not unusual in the nineteenth
century, for example, for young women to believe that "nice women"
did not enjoy sex and only gave way to it as a duty. It was not unusual,
either, for otherwise respectable men to seek sexual pleasure outside
marriage to supplement the dutiful engagements within wedlock.

Whatever twentieth-century people have actually experienced in marriage, it is clear that few have found it easy to discuss sexual pleasure
with their children. Early on, children are taught that certain parts of
their bodies are "private"—not to be shown or touched in public. Sometimes (*often* in past generations) this rule has been extended to one
against masturbation, and all sorts of dreadful admonitions have been
recorded. Boys were warned about going mad from indulging in the
practice. Mothers were advised to tuck their young children in at night
with their hands outside the covers to prevent illicit exploration and the
sensual pleasure likely to result from such exploration. Much of the
teaching on sexuality has itself been bodily in its mode—a hand with-
drawn, perhaps with a slap; a shake of the head ("no-no") accompanied
by a frown; a haughty drawing up of the shoulders and looking down
the nose, suggesting we are above all that; stern words of warning,
delivered by tone and without explanation.

One wonders how a civilization at once so sex-soaked and so afraid
of sensual pleasure emerged. Of course, rules governing sexual activity
have had beneficial as well as harmful effects. They have operated to
limit sexually transmitted diseases, protect children, ensure the lawful
inheritance of property, and contribute to general stability. But why
should pleasure itself be associated with wickedness? Augustine, one
may recall, counseled that the marital act—even when accompanied by
pleasure—was saved from wickedness if the couple moderated their
pleasure and thought of procreation. We are all affected by this long
tradition of shame and secrecy—so much so that we hardly know how
to react when confronted with an entirely different attitude.

In Jill Paton Walsh's novel, *Knowledge of Angels,* the stranger-hero
Palinor teaches two young people how to make love. Having enjoyed
sex with the young woman, Dolca, Palinor orders her young lover, Joffre (who has discovered them in bed) to undress.

Joffre obeyed. He stood beside the bed with his teeth chattering in his head.
Palinor said to Dolca, "Sweethearts or not, you can refuse if you like." She
shook her head. "Lie down with her," he said to Joffre. Then, reaching over
her, he took Joffre's wrist between his fingers, dipped the boy's hand in the
oil jar, and laid it in place. As though the boy's fingers were the keys of an

instrument, he played them with his own. "Like your lute," he said to the boy softly. Then, as she began to cry, "Now!"[18]

Palinor proceeds to teach Dolca and Joffre how to achieve sexual pleasure. It is not an exaggeration to say that, throughout most of western history, a man like Palinor would be regarded as far worse than the reprehensible Fagin, who taught poor boys how to steal. To compound the sin, Palinor engages in homosexual activity with Joffre. The scene is shocking, not because it is in any way sensationalized but, rather, because it seems so natural as Walsh tells the story. The vast majority of us (I include myself here) cannot even imagine a mode of education that would permit such instruction. Yet, if we are reasonable, we have to ask how we got ourselves into a condition in which it is impossible to instruct the young in a way that will both enhance their pleasure and increase their consideration for one another. If we object to Palinor's hands-on instruction, can we at least consider verbal instruction that might lyricize sexual pleasure and separate it unequivocally from violence?

Recently I heard a story that seems to illustrate a reasonable attitude in these highly ambiguous times. At a three-generational gathering, a teenage boy living in the host household initiated sexual activity with his seven- or eight-year-old niece. The act was not, as we say, consummated, and the little girl immediately reported it to her parents and grandmother. The boy went into hiding. It may be important to know that the boy was adopted and that the mother of the little girl was a biological child of the parents who were hosting the event. Both parents and grandparents took the attitude that no real harm was done. The boy obviously did not intend to harm his niece. The family was as concerned about the missing boy as about the girl's reactions. Both kids recognized that the activity was not acceptable, and, when the boy was located, a brief discussion confirmed his remorse and his understanding of the unacceptability of his act. There was never a repetition of such behavior. Both children are now grown up, and family relations have remained warm.

The story could have had a very different ending. Boys have suffered condemnation and ostracism for lesser offenses. Girls have been traumatized more by the judgments following such events than by the events themselves. These parents, without endorsing the behavior, made it clear that such behavior was both natural and unwise. It was not to be repeated, but it was not considered hellish. There would be no permanent scars.

Sexual pleasure is only one of the forms of sensual pleasure that are often forbidden, curtailed, or neglected in homes. Sensual pleasure blends
into the sensuous. All of the senses can be alive with pleasure. Infants
know that eating brings sensual pleasure as well as the satisfaction of
hunger. Later, a kitchen filled with delightful aromas brings olfactory
pleasure. Perfumed baths, silky clothing, soft colors, curtains moving
gently in a breeze, birds singing, a cat purring, a mother's lullaby, a perfectly set table—all can induce bodily pleasure. Indeed, it might be argued that sensory pleasure is the starting place for aesthetic appreciation.

It may well be that the deplorable level to which modern taste has
fallen can be as easily blamed on our puritan heritage as on some postmodern, nihilistic abandon. If we wash ourselves and clean our living
spaces only for hygienic reasons, why not sit about in clean undershirts
and gobble our food from paper plates—showing our pleasure and our
rebellion simultaneously by allowing great gobs of juice to run down
our chins and splash on our plates? One popular television ad depicts
just such a scene. How to react to such scenes is part of what children
learn in homes. Is the behavior disgusting because proper people do not
behave like slobs? Is it funny? Is it something to be imitated? Is it a sign
of pleasure that has so far eluded us? Or is it simply unattractive? Taste,
without arrogance or deceit, is learned (or not) at home.

Some would carry the discussion of taste not only into aesthetics but
even into morals and political philosophy,[19] but I do not think that
aesthetics can provide a dependable ground for ethical life. Experiencing
aesthetic disgust because a doomed prisoner's mask bursts into flame
when the executioner turns on the electric chair may send sensitive observers looking for a less upsetting mode of execution. A *moral* response
must be concerned with the horror of any act that deliberately and systematically prevents human beings from responding to the cry of one
who says, "Help me."

The cultivation of taste can perhaps open one's mind to the interests
of others. Zeldin describes such a program in connection with food:
"The French schoolchildren whose syllabus now includes systematic lessons in the art of tasting are the pioneers of an important revolution.
An open mind about food, and about the taste of foreigners, inevitably
modifies one's attitudes to one's neighbors."[20] I doubt that such modification is either inevitable or necessarily positive, but it stands as a possibility. More important, such a program is a recognition that the training of taste and pleasure is valuable in its own right. If we believe that
taste and pleasure are connected and important, we are sustained by a
kind of faith as we educate our children. There are no guarantees in this

work and no standardized tests that we can use to measure our progress. We proceed on the faith that judiciously chosen encounters and the affects they induce are paramount, and so we expose our children to those things we take to be good, and we share our own delights, reservations, reflections, and griefs in the hope that our example will trigger deeper and more genuine affect in them. Nevertheless, when we understand how enormously complex the relational self is, we tremble at the possibilities.

As children get their first lessons in beauty and the delight that it induces, they also get a sense of priorities. Is the ritual of a lovely table and aesthetically pleasing meal for company only? Is it a duty fulfilled grimly by a mother who demands appropriate appreciation? Is it an obsession that can never be relaxed? Or is it clear that this ritual serves the mutual pleasure of all those who live in or visit this house? In the accumulation of such encounters, children learn something of balance. The best home is neither a sterile picture of loveliness designed for photographers nor a place devoid of beauty but, rather, an environment in which beauty serves the delight of its inhabitants.

Like so many other topics that are essential to an undertaking of the present kind, volumes could be (and have been) written on the aesthetics of place. In most cases I have to be satisfied with just enough to hint at the principles of social policymaking that will follow. In this case, however, the topic is so central to the project that we will return to it in the next chapter, which is devoted to shelter and place. In addition, I will return to the topic of bodily pleasure in the chapter on other selves. There we will consider whether approbation of bodily pleasure necessarily requires an acceptance of hedonism.

Encounters with Other Bodies

Other bodies are among the objects most often encountered in human life. Other selves are the chief concern of ethics and moral theory, and the interactions of selves and groups of selves are central to political and social philosophy. Chapters 8, 9, and 10 will be devoted to a discussion of other selves. Here, the discussion will be confined to bodily encounters.

As a way of life, caring puts a great emphasis on bodies. Bodies must be nurtured, and the spirit dependent on them is the locus of a suffering that goes beyond physical pain. Very young children can be taught to sympathize with pain and need. For example, ordinary hunger is familiar to children: they can understand at an early age that other stomachs rumble with hunger and that caring human beings respond to this obvious need. Jim Lee, in his Chinese cookbook, tells this story:

When I was a boy in China, many did not even have rice to eat. I will never forget the wandering beggars (usually entire families) who stopped in our village and went from house to house to beg for a handful of rice on which to live for one more day.

Because my father was able to send us money from America, where he was working in a laundry, we were among the more affluent families in the village. We kept two earthen crocks of rice [one for the family, one for beggars]. . . . As the youngest in the household, I was given the privilege of giving out the usual handful of raw rice to each member of a beggar family. This was the custom in our village, and it was a practical one. Not only did a child learn compassion and gratitude for his own good fortune, but his hands were small.[21]

Thus a child might learn the virtues of both charity and frugality. In the encounters described by Lee the small child was taught to respond to bodily need. The beggars at the door could not be thought of as other selves because they were unknown and the child could not yet think in such terms, but the encounters certainly contributed to a developing relational self. The unfortunate beggars at the door and the two crocks of rice became central figures in the place known to this small boy.

New bodies have first to locate themselves in space. Indeed, all bodies have to do this when either their usual place changes or they move to a significantly different place.[22] But orientation with respect to place is somewhat different from location in space. Infant bodies, accustomed to the confines of liquid and soft tissues, are thrust suddenly into a world where arms and legs may be extended fully without touching anything. Some cultures protect infants from the shock of too much space and emptiness by swaddling them and keeping them close to an adult body. Other cultures, valuing (perhaps unconsciously) freedom and generous personal space, allow infants to kick and reach out freely. Sometimes these infants are frightened by their own movements and exhibit a "startle" reaction very like one that occurs when support is removed and the body falls.[23] Whether these early responses are properly called emotions or precursors of emotion, sensitive parents protect infants from falling (even safely) and loud noises. Some babies eventually enjoy the thrill of being tossed in the air and caught, but enjoyment of such a game may depend on the trust that has been established between adult and child.

Learning where one's body ends and the external world begins is another task. Locating an object visually, reaching, and grasping are practiced and learned.[24] The body must learn also to draw an object toward itself at just the right speed to avoid painful bumps. Eventually toddlers learn that the existence of objects does not depend on their being in exactly one place. Objects may move or be moved and occupy different places. Some objects, live objects, move on their own; others are stationary unless moved by another object. Orientation in space depends on the reliable behavior of objects. When inanimate objects move (as in spaceship conditions) or seem to move (as in vertigo or in hallucinations), one's disorientation can be extreme.

When people have oriented themselves from childhood to certain geographical features, the shock of moving to another locality may be difficult to overcome. Casey describes the plight of the Navajo who were relocated to separate them from the Hopi:

The results of the relocation (a notion for which the Navajo say there is no word in their language) have been disastrous. A quarter of those relocated have died, including an unusually high number from suicide. Alcoholism, depression, and acute disorientation are rampant. . . . What is striking in the Navajo tragedy . . . is the explicit acknowledgment by relocated people themselves that the loss of the land was the *primary* loss . . . to take away the land is to take away life.[25]

Other bodies, both animate and inanimate, orient us in space and time. For the Navajo accustomed to seeing a particular mountain *just there,* colored *just so* in morning or evening, moving to a place where that mountain is no longer *there* induced a grief as great—sometimes greater—than that of losing a loved one. Loved ones *do* die, however much we resist the thought. Mountains do not move, and identity can be lost when it is so tied to a feature that has hitherto been permanent. Similarly, it is understandable that a solitary old person may grieve more over the loss of a pet than over the death of a seldom seen, perhaps once close relative. The pet has become part of the place that represents an extension of the body; it has filled moments of everyday activity, and life without it is not the life to which one has become oriented.

The child learns about the fragility of bodies. Live objects can be hurt; inanimate ones can be broken. In good homes children are taught early to avoid inflicting pain. "Don't hurt the kitty! See, pet the kitty this way." Admonitions not to pinch, not to bite, not to clamber carelessly over other bodies are part of most children's early socialization. Adults differ, however, on whether pain should be used as an instrument to teach children not to hurt others. From the perspective taken in this book, such use is an enormous mistake. We should want children to avoid the unnecessary infliction of pain because they have learned to share the pain of others and be distressed by it, not because they fear retributive pain to themselves. With respect to pain, a care orientation is more fundamental and more permanently important than a justice orientation is. A sense of fairness will also be cultivated in good homes, but it is not fairness that should prevent the infliction of pain. Indeed, an approach to pain predicated on fairness suggests that pain is sometimes deserved, and I want to avoid this result. I'll say more about the long, deeply harmful tradition that connects pain and desert in the next section and in chapter 9.

In all homes, everywhere, children encounter other bodies. In the best homes, as I will argue, children learn to treat other bodies with care. Reciprocal affection is a basic source of dependable pleasure. Live bodies, including those of pets, give great pleasure and show their appreciation for sensitive handling. Objects also often yield reciprocity of sorts; they show themselves best in certain locations, they shine with proper polish, and they glow with a patina of age. We will return to the subject of place and its objects in chapter 7.

Pain and Death

The body is not only a center of everyday need and pleasure; it is also the locus of pain and suffering. A reasonable orientation to the problems of human life must recognize the pervasiveness of pain in the struggle to live. Ernest Becker comments:

Existence, for all organismic life, is a constant struggle to feed—a struggle to incorporate other organisms they can fit into their mouths and press down their gullets without choking. Seen in these stark terms, life on this planet is a gory spectacle, a science-fiction nightmare in which digestive tracts fitted with teeth at one end are tearing at whatever flesh they can reach, and at the other end are piling up with fuming waste excrement as they move along in search of more flesh.[26]

One might brush aside animal terror and pain, as Augustine and many other thinkers did, but even with such pain set aside, the quantity of human pain in the world is huge. Philosophers and theologians have tried all sorts of strategies to avoid the horror of pervasive pain. C. S. Lewis, for example, said that we can't logically add pain x in me to pain x in you to get a total pain of 2x.[27] His basic point is that no one person is asked to bear the sum total of human pain and that we should focus on the balance of pain and pleasure in any given life. This seems reasonable until we see the extremes of pain inflicted on some individuals. Then we need something more than the notion that "into each life a little rain must fall." One of the worst responses to this reality is the one Lewis gave to his wife's suffering with cancer. He held that such suffering is somehow *necessary:*

But is it credible that such extremities of torture should be necessary for us? Well, take your choice. The tortures occur. If they are unnecessary, then there is no God or a bad one. If there is a good God, then these tortures are necessary. For no even moderately good Being could possibly inflict or permit them if they weren't.[28]

This attitude leads to an analysis that starts with the assumption that the pain we suffer and observe is somehow deserved, or at least necessary for soul-building; it is legislated by the Creator. In contrast, one who begins theorizing from the home outward could never make this mistake. Such a view can be seriously entertained only when some theory centered on another world or a collective beyond the immediate suffering intervenes. Of course, it may happen that a particular individual, courageous by nature and determined to grow, actually constructs a better self from his or her own suffering. I do not deny this, nor do I deny the clear fact that suffering through the loss of a loved one sometimes produces wonderfully constructive results. These things happen and should be acknowledged. Their occurrence in no way implies that the suffering that triggered them is necessary.

When we start with the original condition, we see no necessity for the death of Mercy Stone Goodwill (mother of the lonely infant who will become Grandma Flett), the deaths of four of Carie's beautiful and much-loved children, the hanging of a man who had sufficient sensibility to step around a puddle on his way to the gallows, the awful suffering of Lewis's wife, Joy, or the terminal suffering of Maudie, who begged Jana again and again, "Lift me up, lift me up." These are not necessities, they are merely universal happenings—all either avoidable or, at least, reducible. Social policy anchored in the best natural attitudes of home life will reject any justification for the infliction of pain that does not demonstrate convincingly that either the pain is necessary for the physical well-being of the victim (for example, vaccinations, dental work, some operations), or the pain is inflicted reluctantly to prevent even greater pain or harm to others (for example, the severe wounding of an attacker).

Religion has too often glorified pain and suffering, and the nondeserving who suffer have sometimes been led to believe that they have been chosen for their ordeal. They are not wicked and have not earned the pain; rather, it is said, they are blessed—somehow exalted by it. This is held to be true for martyrs, for example. Much suffering has been attributed also to sin. From this perspective sinners deserve their pain and suffering. Augustine said it clearly:

If there were misery before there were sins, then it might be right to say that the order and government of the universe were at fault. Again, if there were sins and no consequent misery, that order is equally dishonored by lack of equity. But since there is happiness for those who do not sin, the universe is perfect; and it is no less perfect because there is misery for sinners.[29]

Augustine's statement is patent nonsense unless souls are thought to be eternal. Obviously, the wicked often thrive on earth, and the innocent often suffer. Therefore followers of Augustine have to believe that a fair reckoning will take place in the hereafter. Even this promise has been blemished by the notion that unbelievers should be cast into the fires along with the wicked. The philosopher-mathematician G. W. Leibniz told roughly the same story much later; he accepted as a necessity that multitudes of souls should suffer eternal damnation to maintain a harmonious balance of sin and retributive suffering.[30]

Perhaps the most important proposition in this book is this: *pain should not be regarded as deserved.* Physical pain and desert should be separated, and in many of the best homes they are. Parents in these homes do not punish their children physically, and they do not link physical pain to acts that "deserve it." This does not mean that no physical pain is ever inflicted or that it is not recognized that we sometimes bring pain on ourselves. I must try to explain this seemingly contradictory statement.

A few months ago a visiting grandchild—just a toddler—grabbed my face and, pinching hard, refused to let go. It was very painful, and I slapped her hand to liberate my bruised face. She cried. I did not tell her that she was a bad girl and deserved the slap. I told her the exact truth—that when people are hurt, they often hurt back to defend themselves and that I was sorry for her pain, and that she should be sorry for mine. When she gets a little older, I will explain to her that even loving adults sometimes run out of patience and use physical force—a swat on the bottom, a rougher than usual grasp on an arm or a shoulder. Good parents feel bad about such incidents, but few of us are perfect, and they occur. Children understand this; they too lose patience and commit acts disapproved by their better selves. Thus, it is commonsensical to recognize that we do quite often bring things on ourselves; we share some responsibility with one we have pushed too far. This is not to say that we deserve the resulting pain. By her or his own admission, the one inflicting pain would have responded differently if she or he had been physically or emotionally able to do so.

Pain demands relief and consolation. When we have inflicted pain, we should undergo a commensurate emotional suffering, and that suffering is properly relieved by appropriate restitution to the victim. It should not be relieved by some religious exercise. Is this to say that the suffering of guilt is deserved? I think this is true—we often do earn the guilt we feel. One of the greatest lessons to be learned in the best homes is how to manage guilt: how to accept it when it is earned, how to relieve it through restitution, how to reflect on the incidents that give rise to it, how to help others relieve theirs and maintain relations of care and trust. This is another topic to which I will return in chapters 12 and 13.

Children must also learn that bodies die, but, again, they should not be taught to associate death with desert. It is far better to believe that "every man's death diminishes me." Recall Orwell's remark in chapter 2 on the "unspeakable wrongness of cutting a life short when it is in full tide." Children should be taught that this applies to enemies, criminals, and fools as well as to the innocent. It may happen that one is called upon to kill in self-defense or in genuine defense of one's home or country, and I am not arguing for total pacifism. I am arguing for the acknowledgment of tragedy and the continuing quest for a better way.

Bodies are precious. In homes children learn how to manage their own bodies and how to respond to the other bodies they encounter. They learn various attitudes toward bodily needs and sensations. In some homes bodily pleasure is forbidden or rigidly controlled; in others it is celebrated but dedicated to mutuality—to a deep commitment to the pleasure of others as well as oneself. I strongly endorse the latter and have suggested that the cultivation of sensuous pleasure is a foundation for aesthetic appreciation.

• • •

In this chapter we have examined two topics that are central to my whole project. The first is the matter of control. Adults control children, but the control of a caring adult is always aimed at the partial liberation of the child. It is aimed at independence of a sort, but I do not want to call this independence "autonomy," for I have said that this concept is too confused to be of much use to us in either child rearing or public policy. This control is aimed at helping children master their own bodily functions, impulses, and attitudes. It is hoped that children will always be intelligently persuadable, that they will in fact remember and reflect upon the encounters that invite them toward their better selves. Of great importance in the discussion of control is the insistence that control be exercised with deliberation and sensitivity. Control must not be relinquished in the face of demands for various inchoate rights when it is obvious that the well-being of those controlled is not enhanced by such giving over, but it must always be aimed at its own withdrawal. In social policy, as in homes, control must be accompanied by attentive love as nearly as that attribute of family life can be practiced.

The second topic is the highly controversial idea that physical pain should be dissociated from desert. Clearly, this is not something taught in all homes. It is offered, and will be more thoroughly argued for later, as something that *should be* taught in homes. It is from such homes that we can extrapolate to sound social policies.

The infant body that will become a self through encounter after encounter is always situated, located in a place. Some of its most important encounters are with the places in which it is situated. We turn to that set of encounters next.

CHAPTER 7

Places, Homes, and Objects

Other bodies, other selves, are encountered in places, and the place associated with the original condition—utter dependency—is home. Most people think of home as a place that provides food and shelter. A home must, of course, give shelter from rain and cold, but it must also provide a refuge from danger, humiliation, worldly stress, and the struggle for recognition. At home, sheltered, we can be ourselves. A home, ideally, is both a place in which to reside and a place from which to venture forth. Casey describes "two ways to dwell"—residing and wandering.[1] A child who is well sheltered, one who has a healthy home, can wander forth and, as Heidegger put it, dwell in the world.

In exploring what is encountered in homes, we must look at houses (the physical embodiment of homes), spatial arrangements, and objects. We must also consider what lies beyond the house—the yard or city street, town or village, and region. When the heart longs for home, it sometimes longs for particular objects in a remembered arrangement, and sometimes it longs for the sights, sounds, and smells of a beloved region. In this chapter we begin with that love of place and move next to the connection between place and self or identity. Then we consider the house as a physical place, together with its objects; in well-studied encounters with objects, children learn a form of cherishing. Putting great emphasis on the love of homes and home-places, I have to consider whether that love can entrap us in provincialism. Finally, we start the journey outward, toward dwelling in the world.

Love of Place

Robert Browning sings the love of geographical place: "O, to be in England/Now that April's there."[2] Other poets bring us up close, not only to a beloved country or region but also to home itself. Thomas Hood writes:

> I remember, I remember
> The house where I was born,
> The little window where the sun
> Came peeping in at morn;
> He never came a wink too soon,
> Nor brought too long a day,
> But now, I often wish the night
> Had borne my breath away![3]

Hood's poem is filled with longing for a place, its sights, and the innocence and anticipation associated with childhood. Unlike the knowledge of angels, that of human beings is bright in the morning and fades at evening.

Places figure more prominently in fiction, autobiography, and poetry than in philosophy. Hardy's Wessex, Robert Frost's New England, Willa Cather's Nebraska, Proust's Combray, Wendell Berry's Kentucky, and Henry David Thoreau's Walden Pond are all familiar to us through literature. The passionate appreciation of place does not seem to induce warlike patriotism—it takes political ideas to do that—but it may lead to the defense of questionable practices simply because they are part of one's home place. One thinks of Berry's defense of tobacco growing in his beloved Kentucky. To combat the questionable practices of our home places, it may be necessary to wander forth or to invite others in. We need to see the effects of our practices on others and also the effects of our place on visitors to understand how place has shaped us. How are visitors transformed by the place they visit? How are residents shaped by their place of residence?

Consider a place that is both a residing place for some and a temporary residence for those dwelling as wanderers—a vacation community. Little is orchestrated in such a place, and yet players fill typical roles year after year. In the small shore community where my family takes up summer residence, the hours just before dark yield typical scenes: young people playing volleyball on the beach, fantastic kites flying over the green space perpendicular to the beach, a few people still splashing about in the surf, older couples strolling on the boardwalk, an occasional bi-cyclist whooshing past illegally, kids crying because it's time to go home, a fisherman casting from the rock jetty, the last small plane of the day trailing an advertisement for a new place to eat, people walking their dogs on the grassy strip beside the boardwalk.

Every time of day has its well-cast scenes. Sunrise discloses joggers, fishermen, people practicing yoga or martial arts, people meditating or munching on doughnuts or bagels while waiting for the sun to come up, beachcombers looking for treasures cast up by the sea or left behind by careless visitors, surfers testing the currents, and people in cars who stop for a few minutes by the shore to settle their souls before going to work. Residents move to the rhythm of the tides. At low tide the beach is broader and the waves better for riding. High tide packs everyone in close to the boardwalk; there is no space; there are no good waves to ride; and beach blankets get soaked when people forget to pull them back against the incoming tide. Residents learn to do their daily work during high tide and head to the beach at low tide. Vacationers some-times learn this rhythm too late to make the most of their holiday.

Residents dread the sound of helicopters beating back and forth off shore. When that happens, people come out on their porches to watch. They know someone has been lost in the surf, and there's nothing they can do. Those so inclined may pray; others feel at least an aching mo-ment of compassion and remind themselves to watch the kids more closely and to check for riptides. Residents learn the fire signals. In a close-packed community of old houses, fire is a constant danger. Two blasts of the siren mean first aid. Three signal fire, and when this happens residents are again out on their porches, looking, listening, sniffing, testing the wind.

Thus, in countless different ways, the place shapes us. Our porches tie us closely to both the physical surroundings and our neighbors. Weather directs our activities. We switch from linear time to cyclic time, daily with the tides, weekly with rain and wind patterns, more deeply with the seasons. Spring brings homeowners out to paint, and plant, and repair winter damage to steps and porch railings. Early summer sees teenagers greeting one another, renewing friendships, and sharing the excitement of a long beautiful summer stretching ahead. Late summer sees the same kids subdued, wondering where the summer went, clus-tering quietly to say goodbye and to regret the shortening of day and season.

It has been argued that we carry place with us, and in some sense this is true. What happens if we know that we will never return to the beloved place and that there is no one with whom to share its visions? Rebecca Reynolds tells the story of an elderly Greek woman, Irene, who lived in a chronic care hospital. Irene, who could speak only Greek, had given up trying to communicate. Even her relatives could not arouse her interest. A visiting museum group changed her life dramatically.

On this day we came with an ocean program. Along with sand and shells, we brought indoors thick piles of seaweed. When Irene saw the seaweed being lifted up out of the buckets, she wheeled her chair over, her expression shifting profoundly.

Picking up handfuls of the kelp, Irene smelled its saltiness and began weeping. Slowly, haltingly, she began to speak. None of us understood her Greek, but we all understood her joy. Such beauty lit her face as she poured forth descriptions of the ocean and her childhood home![4]

When her family visited, they were amazed to hear Irene talk passionately about her childhood—the sea, the beaches, sailing vessels, and evening hospitality. Evoking memories of her childhood home restored some of Irene's habitual self.

Infused with the spirit of a place, we may live more fully in relation with both the physical place and its various inhabitants. Deprived of the place and its people, we may suffer a chronic homesickness very like a mortal wound. Casey describes the importance of the spirit of a place:

To get into the spirit of a place is to enter into what makes that place such a special spot, into what is concentrated there like a fully saturated color. But the spirit of a place is also expansive. Moving out, entering not just the area lying before and around me but entering myself and others as its witnesses or occupants, this genial spirit sweeps the binarism of Self and Other (yet another of the great modernist dichotomies) into the embracing folds, the literal im-plications, of implacement. Such a spirit, like the souls and feelings with which it naturally allies itself, submerges all the established metaphysical limits and many of the physical borders as well.[5]

In my small beach community, we all become residents, at least for a time, of *this place;* our residency is revealed in the greetings and the small talk of strangers. We are all part of a scene that is repeated year after year against a well-defined land- and seascape.

Place and Identity

Place has effects that, to some degree, shape us. Bachelard, in his analysis of poetry and space, advises the psychologist of imagination to do a "cosmic" reading of literature as well as a social one. With such a reading the psychologist "comes to realize that the cosmos molds mankind, that it can transform a man of the hills into a man of islands and rivers, and that the house remodels man."[6] I am not arguing for a strict determination of place. Its influence may be subtle. It may also be dramatic: the effects of homelessness go well beyond the discomfort caused by lack of shelter, and living in a shelter on which one can make no personal mark must also have undesirable effects. As we consider the effects of place on the developing self, we must look at both regional surroundings and the more intimate environment we call home.

Identity can be so closely related to place that displacement threatens survival. The Navajo experience cited in the last chapter has been widely documented in this regard. Place, for the Navajo, is alive; it is a Great Self, and "to move away means to disappear and never be seen again."[7] For the Apache, "wisdom sits in places," and the capacity to foresee trouble and avoid it involves both an intimate and historical knowledge of places.[8] The Apache custom of naming places for how they looked and what happened there on first encounter facilitates the wisdom that sits in places. Notice that encounter is fundamental in all of these accounts. We encounter the place, but the place also encounters us. We must play a certain partially scripted role in order for the place to continue to be the place first identified.

Although most of us do not tie our identities so closely and specifically to place as the Navajo or Apache, Casey suggests that "our own culture suffers from acute nostalgia."[9] We seem to long for a past time and, more than that, for the places that represent that time in our memory or fantasy. Literature is filled with such poignant nostalgia. Often the longing, as illustrated in Hood's poem, is for a childhood place and the feelings of security and wonder associated with that place. Casey quotes Sven Birkerts on this familiar longing.

No matter what pleas or adjustment I make, I cannot catch hold of the peculiar magic of those [childhood] places. . . . No effort of will can restore to me that perception, that view of the horizon not yet tainted by futurity—it runs through me sometimes, but I cannot summon it. And yet everything I would say about place depends on it, and everything I search for in myself involves some deep fantasy of its restoration. My best, truest—I cannot define my terms—self is vitally connected to a few square miles of land.[10]

Sometimes the longed-for place is a region, sometimes a garden, sometimes a town, sometimes a house. When I was a child (before adolescence), my family lived in a second-floor apartment owned by relatives who lived downstairs; my grandparents lived next door. I can still walk around both yards in my imagination, easily locating the lilac hedge, the walnut trees dripping with caterpillars, the row of hollyhocks covered with bees, the climbing roses, cherry trees, snowball bushes, rock garden, mock orange, and the beautiful line of maples along the street. I can remember almost nothing of the interior. Unlike Proust, I would be hard put to describe the bedroom I shared with my sister. In early adolescence, when my family moved to the Jersey shore, my attention and affection were transferred to a region. Again the inside of the house is insignificant in my recollections of place. I don't know why yards and gardens, and later region, were more important to me than interiors, but I know they have had important effects on me.

Although cases of psychological disorientation and even death as a result of displacement are well documented, the relation of place and identity is still not well understood. As urban and suburban places become more and more alike, will people, too, become more alike? Will it matter to people who grow up in a variety of such places where they live? Will people be content with virtual communities, and what sort of persons will "inhabit" such communities?

In recent decades the attention of policymakers in education has concentrated heavily on the problems of urban education. Little attention has been given to rural education, but such attention might contribute to our understanding of place and identity. Many rural dwellers are deeply attached to their land and its surroundings, but schools give almost no attention to place. Indeed, it is clear that current reform movements are, at least implicitly, aimed at establishing curricula, school structures, and pedagogies that ignore place and try to design education for one great world economy. This may be a very great mistake but, in the absence of comprehensive knowledge about the role of place and identity, we are not in a position to make definitive recommendations. More-general recommendations that schools should give more attention to place are reasonable, however, if only as experimental proposals from which we may learn more about the importance of place. Paul Theobald, for example, espouses both the cause of rural schools and the centrality of place in education.

First, rural schools ought to have a place in the educational landscape of this country. They have an indispensable role to play. Second, schools ought to attend more consciously to their physical place on earth and the social, political, and economic dynamics that surround it. Doing so could render the entire school experience more meaningful and, in the process, would contribute in a small, though not insignificant, way to a cultural healing desperately needed in American society.[11]

I suspect that Theobald is right, but we need to know much more about the ways in which place-sensitive education might contribute to an education that is meaningful. Theobald thinks that such education can contribute to the enhancement of community. In this he may well be right again, but it may also help to develop a fuller sense of personal identity. Along with this, education for place should encourage students to "wander forth" and come to an understanding of the love other people have for their towns, regions, and homes. It is conceivable that place-sensitive education could make valuable contributions not only to personal identity but also to peace education. It is hard to hate people who love their mountains, forests, fields, lakes, rocks, and sky. Somehow, that love, while directed at particular physical features of a particular landscape, is universal in healthy-minded people. It seems reasonable, then, to suggest that history and geography be filled out with stories, pictures, songs, and poems that depict how people actually relate to the regions in which they live. In literature, students should be encouraged to read novels set in places that interest them.

As we explore the function of place in the development of self, we recognize the centrality of encounter. It is unlikely that one would be shaped by mountains he or she has never encountered. This result is not impossible, however; it is conceivable that whole generations might be shaped by customs developed in one setting and transposed without reflection to another, and some people have been deeply affected by places entered only in fiction. We are influenced by encounters with cultural space as well as physical places. Further, this influence may be conscious or unconscious. A form of transitivity seems to be operating in the phenomena of encounter. Group A is directly shaped by its physical environment, emigrates to another environment, and yet socializes its young to the practices developed in the original place. In such cases later generations may not be able to connect what they do in any logical way to their surroundings. Practices become detached from physical imperatives. We can describe what happens here in terms of needs. The older generation infers a need, comparable to its own, in a younger generation. Its hope, conscious or unconscious, is that the younger generation will *feel* the need, that it will become for them too an expressed need. The end result, however, is often a social ambivalence, even bewilderment, and sometimes the result is alienation or vigorous rejection.

Education in "advanced" societies has long been characterized by the aim of transcending place, but there is a paradox in this aim. First, it is assumed that some identifiable universal truth underlies all knowledge and should guide all educational efforts; second, it is supposed that some group, a group necessarily "im-placed," has possession of this knowledge or the path to it. Therefore, although the underlying truth is said to be universal, some people must bring other people to see and appreciate it. This, of course, was the great conceit of colonialism — the refusal to acknowledge the accomplishments and values of even highly literate societies different from the dominant colonial powers.

One may ask, however, in just what way the traditional knowledge associated with western civilization is im-placed. Surely it is not tied to mountains and rock configurations in the way that Navajo culture is. Well-educated persons are part of it, *feel* part of it, in all areas of the western world. If its elements were ever tied tightly to a particular place, that connection is no longer obvious, and yet many astute thinkers insist that the connection still has its effects. We who have submitted to higher education in America are, inevitably, forever affected by ideas formed in highly elite and/or patriarchal societies — societies whose ideas were formed in response to physical situations very different from our own.[12]

Although we might, then, go at the study of im-placement historically, it is more useful for present purposes simply to acknowledge the pervasiveness and power of the western tradition and to continue the analysis of place and identity at another level. In particular, we have to account for the fact that many people living in societies where the western tradition is considered *the* culture nevertheless do not feel part of that tradition. Although it is clearly true that academics in, say, Berlin, London, New York, and Johannesburg share a culture that transcends place, it is equally true that hosts of people in those same cities do not share that culture in any but a nominal way. This situation suggests that we either have to abandon the thesis of place-identity connection or move the analysis to a more local level. We must ask what characterizes the local environments of people who ostensibly share the "western culture" that dominates both the economic and social worlds.

It is also necessary to ask what is meant by "unconscious influence." If the self is a relation consisting of encounters marked by meaning or affect, how can we acknowledge unconscious influence? The answer to this is that, as A. S. Neill once said, man's misfortune is that "like the dog, his character can be molded."[13] This conditioning requires encounter, however, and encounter is always accompanied by meaning of some sort. The meaning imputed by the subject undergoing conditioning may be silly in the eyes of the conditioner; it may be trivial and unreflective. Certainly, it is not necessary that the affect attached to an encounter be so profound as to trigger a search for sources and ultimate grounding. All that is required for an encounter to enter the relation we call a "self" is that it mean *something,* however superficial, trivial, or mistaken. Something is felt and noted even if it is then promptly forgotten. By "unconscious," then, I mean simply that the encounter is not followed by reflective thought and may even be dropped from easily retrievable memory. It has, nevertheless, had its effect.

This way of looking at the self is different from both the identification of self with disengaged reason and the search for self through historical and cultural phenomena. Taylor, for example, finds the sources of morality in "three large domains":

the original theistic grounding for these standards; a second one that centres on a naturalism of disengaged reason, which in our day takes scientistic forms; and a third family of views which finds its sources in Romantic expressivism or in one of the modernist successor visions.[14]

Taylor identifies these sources of morality in close connection with what he sees as the sources of the self. These are:

first, modern inwardness, the sense of ourselves as beings with inner depths, and the connected notion that we are "selves"; second, the affirmation of ordinary life which develops from the early modern period; third, the expressionist notion of nature as an inner moral source.[15]

Although it is certainly true that *conceptions* of the self have arisen and been revised through the sources identified by Taylor, individual selves cannot be described in such sweeping terms, and this is not just a matter of psychology. Beneath the great historically defined cultural domains lie other realities: home and family, geographic place, the possibilities of encounter. It is tempting to describe "modern life" and trace its sources in terms of "webs of interlocution" and "traditions," but there were selves as I am describing them well before a concept was carefully defined, and multitudes of selves have lived in severely limited webs of language, largely unaware of the sophisticated traditions described by, say, MacIntyre.[16] The early emphasis placed by male philosophers on public life has led to scholarly neglect of the original condition and all it contributes to the development of selves and morality. Thus the question remains: what if we studied the original condition carefully—philosophically—and attempted to apply what we learned there to the wider world instead of working in the other direction?

It can be argued, of course, that homes and families are situated in cultures and that what occurs there is a reflection of those cultures. The two great domains are obviously interactive, and I am not suggesting that we try to find the roots of theology, say, or the disengaged self in the acceptance or rejection of what happens in homes. I am claiming that a *self* cannot be adequately described in terms properly attached to eras and traditions. A *self* is, rather, a product of encounter and response. Indeed, one defining feature of modernism is the proliferation of possible encounters. In previous ages encounters were limited by the state of technology. This does not mean that people living in earlier times or those living in low-technology cultures today engage in more reflection—that is, more encounters with self. On the contrary, reflective encounters have often been limited by the struggle for survival. Moreover, ideologies dictated, and still dictate, what is thinkable.

The sort of reflection that contributes to critical evaluation today is blocked not by lack of leisure but by the proliferation of objects and possibilities and, of course, by deliberate manipulation. Sound bytes, flashing pictures that are mere miniseconds in duration, spectacle after spectacle—all these may rob the self not only of reflection but also of any vestige of unity. Jean Baudrillard puts it this way:

Tentacular, protuberant, excrescent, hypertelic: this is the fate of inertia in a saturated world. To deny its own end through hyperfinality—is this not also the process of cancer? The revenge of growth in excrescence. Revenge and denunciation of speed in inertia. Masses are also swept up in this gigantic process of inertia by acceleration. Mass is this excrescent process that hurls all growth to its doom. It is a circuit short-circuited by a monstrous finality.[17]

Too many encounters, too brief, may well be one source of the alienation and loss of community so widely recognized. If all sorts of encounters are available without community, why make the commitment that community requires? If constant stimulation is easily achieved, why develop creative responses? If one can hop on a plane and fly to a tropical paradise, why lovingly maintain the potential paradise in one's own backyard? What sort of self would be described if we asked our giant computer to gather and report clusters of related encounters? Would there be enough related clusters to describe a fairly unified, or even orderly, self?

The purpose of the last few paragraphs has been to reassert the primacy of encounter in the development of self. I still have to explore more fully the function of place in this development and, in doing this, I must avoid two errors. First, I do not want to claim that place is the only or even the greatest shaper of identity;[18] second, however, I do not want to abandon the topic before exploring the possibilities at a finer level than the geographical. The inclination to concentrate on the geographical is not an error for those who have deliberately set out to trace the "identities" of whole peoples or the sources of abstract selves. It would be an error for one who is interested in the development of actual, individual selves.

How does place affect the development of selves in present society? Clearly it is necessary to separate the effects of time and place. In exactly the same location one hundred years ago, my daily encounters would be very different from those I experience today. Indeed, we often refer to great technological differences in contemporary societies in terms of time. One group is "advanced," another "backward" or "behind the times." The clear implication is that the backward groups will catch up with time and instruction; they will "develop."

Even within a given society some things are affected as much by time as by place: mode of dress, hair styles, patterns of speech, sexual behavior, recreational activities, housing and other architectural designs. Most of the roses in my garden, for example, are modern creations, although there is at least one that could have been encountered by Julius Caesar. Technological changes create enormous changes in place. Plants that were once specific to a particular place are now spread over the world, and creatures that were curiosities or even pets in one place have become marauders and pests in another.

Still, an individual human being, even though clearly constrained by the time in which he or she lives, exists in place. At this time, large numbers of people live in places that are very much alike. Certain signs of the times appear everywhere. Does it matter for these people whether they live in a midwestern American city or a European city of roughly the same size? The dominant language will be different, of course, and the history taught in schools will have a different slant. But will there be the body-shaking difference illustrated in the case of the old Greek woman, Irene? Does it matter?

Academics who travel often are keenly aware of the apparent irrelevance of place; getting to a specific place *on time* is the main goal. It is a great advantage to travelers that airports are so similar in arrangement and that taxis, hotels, restaurants, and other public facilities and conveyances are sufficiently alike to promote easy negotiation. Occasionally, when I have become absorbed in my work while waiting at a gate for air transportation, I have looked up and experienced a moment of wondering where I am. Denver? Chicago? Washington? And, even before the answer comes, there is the important reassurance that *it doesn't matter*. The only thing that matters is that I am at the right gate—that the flight for which I am waiting is heading for the place I intend to reach.

The question arises as to how deeply we are affected by the irrelevance of geographical place, and I cannot answer that, although I am inclined to agree with Theobald, Casey, and others that the effects may be substantial. A question that interests me even more is what happens to people who *are* attached to place in an educational system that is designed to transcend place or that makes false or exaggerated claims connecting ideology to place. I will return to this important question in a later chapter when I argue that response to need is fundamental to social policy.

If geographic place has become irrelevant to the daily lives of many and is likely to become more so in the future, is there any sense of place that is central to the development of self? In his phenomenology of place Casey describes the room in which he is working as an extension of his own body.

Built places, then, are extensions of our bodies. They are not just places, as the Aristotelian model of place as a strict container implies, *in which* these bodies move and position themselves. Places built for residing are rather an enlargement of an already existing embodiment into an *entire life-world of dwelling*. Moreover, thanks to increasingly intimate relationships with their material structures, the longer we reside in places, the more bodylike they seem to be. As we feel more "at home" in dwelling places, they become places created in our own bodily image.[19]

The most fundamental place to study, then, is home. We started the analysis of encounters in the home with a discussion of bodies, and in the next chapter we will explore encounters with other selves. Here we need to say more about home as a place.

House and Home

Bachelard writes of the importance of home:

For our house is our corner of the world. As has often been said, it is our first universe, a real cosmos in every sense of the word. If we look at it intimately, the humblest dwelling has beauty. Authors of books on "the humble home" often mention this feature of the poetics of space. But this mention is much too succinct. Finding little to describe in the humble home, they spend little time there; so they describe it as it actually is, without really experiencing its primitiveness, a primitiveness which belongs to all, rich and poor alike, if they are willing to dream.[20]

Analysts would be right to describe a house "as it actually is." The real walls, colors, objects, and arrangements affect our dreams; they affect what we look for when we wander forth and what we seek when we return. Of course we are not doomed to endless conditioning. We are capable not only of adapting but also of making genuinely creative responses. We respond within parameters set by the possibilities of encounter. A child who has never encountered a book at home may nevertheless respond with joy when he encounters one in school, even though the chance of that happening is much reduced by the lack of encounter in his primitive, or primary, place. The encounters that concern us here are always accompanied by at least momentary affect. A child who grows up in a house where books are given pride of place, where adults look forward to reading and browsing, will more likely seek further encounters with books than will the child for whom they are merely inarticulate objects.

Inhabitants of a house try to make a place for themselves, even if that place is just a corner.[21] Children often stake out a temporary place for themselves by draping blankets and old sheets over chairs. The spot so enclosed becomes a "cave," "tent," or "shack." We express our interests and needs in these personalized corners. Children may be psychologically affected if there is no place that is an extension of their own bodies and selves, and this can happen in at least two ways. Clearly, children who are cramped into small places with many others lack such space. If they are rural dwellers, they may find (or make) a place for themselves outside. If they are city dwellers, the place sought may never be found; wherever they go, space is shared with others, and the only possibility for self-expression may be group identity. Stories abound of city children who *have* found corners in libraries, museums, or parks. In a second way, even well-to-do children may suffer from lack of their own place if they live in a house where every room is treated as a public space and no spot can be marked indelibly as theirs.

Contemporary life has produced mass dwelling places—huge developments of similar houses, similar streets, similar decor—and children leave these places to attend schools where place and all its associations are ignored. To make matters worse, many children are not allowed to wander forth on their own. Indeed, parents who permit such freedom are often regarded as careless. Something wonderful has been lost in the quest for safety. My husband and I both remember wandering outdoors as a special feature of late childhood. He spent hours in the ravine behind his house and on the lake, where he caught fish and turtles. I wandered freely about a small wooded pond and on the beach. As I think about that delight of childhood, I also think of much-loved stories. I reflect on Maria, who visited Mistress Masham's Repose to escape her cruel warders and wander forth on her own.[22] Her "found" place was not only a shelter for the imagination; it was the site in which she grew as a compassionate, moral person. Without the island, what would have happened to her dreams? Our children's lives may be over-protected as well as over-managed.

We encounter both human-made and natural objects in our houses and their surroundings: furniture, of course, but also flowers and trees, bugs, dust, sunbeams, creaky stairs, scary corners, dark spots, cool spots, special sounds. From the encounters of childhood, and the attitudes created by or forced on consciousness, a self develops. Noting how philosophy often misses the centrality of such primary experience, Bachelard remarks:

But our adult life is so dispossessed of the essential benefits, its anthropocosmic ties have become so slack, that we do not feel their first attachment in the universe of the house. There is no dearth of abstract, "world-conscious" philosophers who discover a universe by means of the dialectical game of the I and the non-I. In fact, they know the universe before they know the house, the far horizon before the resting-place; whereas the real beginnings of images . . . will give concrete evidence of the values of inhabited space, of the non-I that protects the I.[23]

From the perspective I am taking it is the things that are thought of as "non-I" that actually produce the "I" through encounter. Every object encountered holds the possibility of affecting the self, but usually encounters with objects are mediated by other selves. Is an object to be treasured or discarded? Studied or ignored? Given a unique place or replaced by a duplicate? It is not a matter of becoming thing-mad, of rampant acquisitiveness; rather, it is almost a contemplative exercise — to see things as individual, as quietly awaiting possibilities for beauty and service. Bachelard suggests that housework can be made into a creative activity:

The minute we apply a glimmer of consciousness to a mechanical gesture, or practice phenomenology while polishing a piece of old furniture, we see new impressions come into being beneath this familiar domestic duty. . . . How wonderful it is to really become once more the inventor of a mechanical action! And so, when a poet rubs a piece of furniture—even vicariously—when he puts a little fragrant wax on his table with the woolen cloth that lends warmth to everything it touches, he creates a new object; he increases the object's human dignity; he registers this object officially as a member of the human household.[24]

It is reasonable to ask what it means to encounter an object such as a piece of furniture—especially to encounter it phenomenologically. Phenomenologists try to disclose and describe what lies hidden under an object's surface manifestations. Sometimes they claim to uncover an object's "essence" through their investigations. If "essence" is taken to mean a structure or set of attributes that belong entirely to the object, this seems an error. Such attributes are the province of science. The possibilities uncovered by phenomenology are inextricably connected to human consciousness. Hence we might expect to find a whole array of possibilities for furniture or, as in Bachelard's account, for human interaction with furniture. It is not closer to the truth or essence to describe furniture polishing as Bachelard did, but it reveals something important about the possibilities for human consciousness. Such possibilities can be offered to others who may otherwise miss them entirely, and a change in conscious attitude can change a self.

If we were interested in metaphysics here, we would have to push back (perhaps fruitlessly) to the "things themselves," but if our interest is in human life and its improvement, then we will do better with a pragmatic attitude that asks about the consequences of describing an interaction as Bachelard has described it. Does it enrich life? Does it shape the attitude that consciousness might take in the next encounter? Does it arouse a fuller sense of cherishing and creativity?

Now and then children adopt an attitude of cherishing seemingly on their own. They collect pretty pebbles, dead but intact insects, shiny bits of ribbon. This can happen in old age, too. In the last years of her life, my mother collected pretty leaves. She made no attempt to identify them, or arrange them, or preserve them; she just picked them up and placed them on her dresser. She could no longer garden or even remember to water houseplants, but she could give a place to these pretty and plentiful objects. Usually, however, children must learn from others how to cherish the objects they encounter. If objects are valued only for their

monetary worth, few children will cherish them; such objects are re-
placeable with money. Cherishing is not taught by scolding and punishment but by example. After describing how new objects are created
from old by polishing, Bachelard remarks:

Objects that are cherished in this way really are born of an intimate light,
and they attain to a higher degree of reality than indifferent objects, or those
that are defined by geometric reality. For they produce a new reality of
being, and they take their place not only in an order but in a community of
order. From one object in a room to another, housewifely care weaves the
ties that unite a very ancient past to the new epoch.[25]

It may be this "community of order," extended to include all human
activity, that characterizes an adequate self. There probably is no such
thing as *wholeness* as it is usually conceived in philosophy; we are continually fractured, losing parts, picking up irrelevant pieces. And I have
expressed doubts about the reality (and even desirability) of autonomy.
But we can bring to our collections of things and thoughts a certain
order. We can look at the things with which we live with a loving eye.
Do they hold memories? Do they enhance one another? Should they be
moved? What have they to do with me or with those I love?

In the universe of the house we learn to cultivate things. Casey considers various meanings of the words *cultivate* and *cultivated*. We usually
take *cultivate* to mean "till," "work," or "plough." A cultivated field,
then, is one that has been worked. A cultivated person, Casey points
out, is "highly (perhaps over-) educated."[26] One who values more natural, ingenuous ways may use *cultivated* as a pejorative connoting "artificial," "snobbish," or "dishonest." Similarly, one who loves wilderness
and natural species may reject highly cultivated gardens and cultivars.
Nevertheless, cultivation extends into every form of learned activity. We
cultivate not only fields for crops and pastures but gardens for our
houses. We cultivate interests, talents, and manners in our children and
in our selves.

The most basic meaning of *cultivate,* says Casey, is "to care for."[27]
This is the meaning I find most useful. It is at home that we learn (or
fail to learn) to care for people, animals, plants, objects, and ideas.
Bachelard's poet polishing a piece of furniture is cultivating an appearance; he is caring for that furniture as he cultivates his own sense of
beauty and order. Children learn to care for things as they watch adults
exercise care and are invited to participate in care taking. Parents often
suppose that having a pet will teach a child responsibility, but if caring

for the pet is a chore unassociated with the delight described by Bachelard, care becomes synonymous with woes and burdens. In contrast, parents who themselves love pets and show their delight in feeding, grooming, and playing with them may lead their children to genuine caring. The difference in affect suggests a different slant on the words *responsibility* and *responsible*. Instead of the usual connotations of *responsible*—answerable, accountable, liable—we are interested in cultivating the ability to respond appropriately. We are interested in response-ability. The responsible person is not merely dutiful and dependable but capable of the response desired or needed. Thus as we cultivate things, we cultivate our selves—our response-ability—as well. Buck tells of her mother's love of beauty in things as well as in nature:

She could go drunk in a sunlit meadow on a spring day, laughing and sparkling and all but dancing. But she loved the beauty of clean, simple, steady things as well . . . a room made still and clean and fresh, . . . dishes newly washed and shining. I remember her saying that one of her pleasures in the austere times after the Civil War was that there were no new dishes to be bought and so every day they had to use the blue and white willow-pattern china and the thin crystal wine goblets that her grandparents had brought from Holland. Every day she chose to wash them, above every other household task, so that she might feel their delicacy in her hands. This remained to her a memory of beauty all the days of her life.[28]

It is not my intention to romanticize household tasks by citing examples of polishing furniture and washing dishes. Much housework is drudgery, but some of the drudgery has arisen from coercion, deprivation, and lack of appreciation. When a person is forced into a particular line of work, as almost all women were forced into housework, it is not surprising that the work should be resented and disliked. Now, with other choices open to women, it may be time for both women and men to reevaluate the tasks that, lovingly and competently done, contribute to the community of order established in the best homes—whether they are rich or poor.

Having excused myself from the accusation of romanticizing household tasks, I should answer a far more potent criticism. What of the children who have almost nothing material to cherish? It is odd, inaccurate, and surely unfeeling to suppose that all children live in homes with at least one heirloom, a few delicate dishes, or a private place to keep those treasures they pick up outside. That reality doesn't change the argument. Rather, the argument suggests strong reasons for changing the reality. It suggests, also, an education that will cherish but not romanticize the poor. Poor children, too, can learn to make evaluations, to poeticize their surroundings, and to resist gross consumerism in the interests of more genuine beauty. I think here of the accounts told with such power by Kozol—stories of impoverished children living in appalling places who nonetheless sing and see rainbows in chemically polluted rain puddles.[29]

No children should have to live in such places, and the claim that giving them a good education will help them leave these places is delusional because, while they live in squalor, many cannot take full advantage of a good schooling even if it is offered to them. It is the task, obviously, of the larger society to change the reality, the basic living conditions, of poor people, but it is the job of schooling to provide hope, to nurture talent, and to construct a place in which children can learn to see places as they might be. At its best, schooling might even provide a place to love and objects to cherish. Our encounters with objects, animate and inanimate, can be occasions of cultivation or of drudgery. At least part of the difference of judgment comes through our own attitudes. In this the existentialists are right, but our attitudes are themselves at least partly shaped by the people around us. We do not choose ourselves entirely, nor are we wholly and solely products of conditioning. If this is true, any form of adequate education should give much more attention to everyday encounters and the attitudes that might be developed in them and toward them.

Most of us learn care in homes. When this does not happen, the school must be a second home. As Casey puts it, the cultivation of built places "localizes caring."

We care about places as well as people, so much so that we can say that *caring belongs to places.* We care about places in many ways, but in building on them—*building with them,* indeed *building them*—they become the ongoing "stars of our life," that to which we turn when we travel and to which we return when we come back home.[30]

Before leaving this section, I want to say something about how the response-ability developed in the best homes is related to the satisfaction of needs. When adults set out to teach children responsibility in the traditional sense, they *infer* a need for children to internalize a sense of duty or obligation. This effort to shape responsible children may be conducted puritanically, and the children may be taught to feed or walk the dog because it is their duty to do so. Similarly, they may be forced to polish dishes or furniture because it is their job. Although reasonable coercion is sometimes indeed required to get the tasks done, in the best homes an inferred need to learn responsibility is transformed into an opportunity to learn how to respond to expressed needs. The dog expresses needs, children learn to respond to these needs, and both gain something in affection and companionship. As the relationship blossoms, parents may see that the child's deeper need (expressed a posteriori, as it were) is to reap the reciprocal rewards of response-ability. The need to see another respond—even an inanimate other—does not reveal itself as obviously as some expressed needs show themselves. It is inferred from what we observe when it is satisfied. Yet it is better classified as an expressed need than an inferred need because, once it is revealed, it is clear that it is inherent in every well-cared-for human being. The need to be cared for, the most basic expressed need, triggers a desire to care and to enjoy the satisfaction of fulfillment. The need to care, then, may be the fundamental need of a developing moral agent, and the happiest and most creative caretakers of people, property, or objects are those who act not from grim duty but from a recognized need to produce and cherish a special response.

It is reasonable to ask on what grounds one sort of home is to be regarded as better than the other; that is, why should we prefer the home that teaches its children how to respond and to enjoy the rewards of response-ability over one that emphasizes duty? One reason, already clear from the preceding discussion, is that children who learn that there is joy or at least positive affect in responding to expressed needs are likely to live happier lives. Much necessary work that seems like drudgery to others will not seem so to them. If one enjoys the glow of polished furniture, the sensory delight of well-cooked and attractively served meals, the vigorous growth of well-tended plants, the energy and affection of a pet whose needs are regularly met, the work involved in producing these results will fit more seamlessly with leisure activities. Play and work will not be sharply divided. The activities of people who respond to place and its objects in this way are hard to classify as "play" and "work" because elements of both pervade all that they do. There is the seriousness characteristic of work and the pleasure characteristic of play.

An ethicist may protest that we cannot base our preference entirely on the happiness of moral agents. The ethicist might ask which approach is more dependable. If a pet is ornery and hard to train, it still needs to be fed and exercised. If no positive response from the animal is forthcoming, will the response-oriented child just shrug off the necessary tasks? Wouldn't it be better to instill that deep sense of duty?

We have to do both, but the emphasis is rightly put on the response approach. A child whose development is guided by the reciprocity of response will be able to tolerate intervals in which a cared-for fails to respond. At such times we must behave "as if" the desired response might be produced. This is a situation in which the virtue sense of caring becomes very important. Deprived of the sustaining responses from the cared-for, a carer must turn inward and ask what she would do at her caring best. The danger in this reliance on the virtue sense of caring is that the carer may perform the necessary tasks in grim dutifulness, and her grimness may make it even harder to establish reciprocity. Clearly, this is a greater worry when the cared-for is another human being. I will return to this crucial problem when we discuss encounters with other selves in the next three chapters.

Can't we avoid the appearance of grim duty by insisting that one must do his duty cheerfully—that this in fact is part of one's duty? Such an insistence is almost surely a terrible mistake. If life's tasks take on an occasional grimness, if drudgery replaces joy, those around the sufferer need to see the distress and respond to it. A genuine expression of disaffection can be used by other caring agents to relieve the distress. Insisting that children do their work cheerfully can induce a phoniness that makes it more difficult to care for them. Worse, it may result in their concluding that feelings should not interfere with duty. People raised in this way are sometimes willing to do dreadful things to others in the name of duty and this, too, is a problem to which I will return.

Avoiding Provincialism

Wendell Berry says that we "cannot get good care in the use of the land by demanding it from public officials." Indeed, he insists, "If we want the land to be cared for, then we must have people living on and from the land who are able and willing to care for it."[31] This claim may be too strong. Children raised in loving connection with their homeplaces may well retain a dedication to the preservation of their national heritage, and as adults they may be effective in launching and maintaining conservation efforts even though they do not "live on the land." In another sense, however, Berry is clearly right; those who *do* live on and from the land must care for it.

There is speculation and some evidence, too, that human beings have a deep need for affiliation with nature.[32] It is one of those needs inferred by those of us who actually experience a connection to at least some natural places. What might be classified as an inferred need in children becomes an expressed need in most of those for whom an opportunity is provided. The need to experience living things in natural settings is, in this respect, comparable to the need to care. Children do not usually express such a need but, when they learn how to care, they cannot imagine living without caring for others. What was once a need inferred by wise adults becomes an expressed need.

As we consider social and educational programs that would promote love of place, we also have to ask whether such programs might lead to provincialism and a narrowing of opportunities for the children so educated. Should we educate for life in the mountains of Vermont, on the Jersey shore, on midwestern farmlands, on the range of Montana, and in Des Moines? Or should we educate for life in the universal western city? The trend today is to focus on the latter, and the trend in social policy is certainly away from the preservation of villages, face-to-face neighborhoods, and houses with yards and gardens. The question arises whether, in working against these trends, we risk raising ignorant and place-bound citizens.

Perhaps unsurprisingly, I am going to argue that the risk runs in almost exactly the opposite direction. The ignorant children and adults that we meet in some powerful novels with settings in Appalachia, Mississippi, and Oklahoma are not people educated narrowly for a particular place; they are simply uneducated. An education for place involves not only direct encounter with a natural setting and its inhabitants but also regional literature, poetry, music, art, history, religion, and crafts. Such an education has embedded in it the skills and concepts necessary for life beyond one's own region, but it does not deliberately sacrifice *this place* to a faceless "anywhere," nor does it sacrifice the here-and-now to a financial future.

Education for place—for appreciation of place—is beautifully illustrated in the *Foxfire* series.[33] Setting aside the scandal that surrounded its founder, we can still appreciate the power of the approach. In an Appalachian community in Georgia, a young teacher educated in Ivy League colleges discovered a way to connect with his students and to teach them English. He proposed that they publish a magazine. The students collected all sorts of stories—short stories, how-to-do-it stories, family stories, true stories, and legends—and they learned to write them up in ways that both preserved a culture and communicated it to a wider world. They collected art, music, recipes, and poetry; they talked to their grandparents and preserved local history; they raised money and contributed to community solidarity; they took pride in publicizing the region that they came to love more deeply; they learned the language and skills necessary for life beyond Rabun Gap. In the process they were educated in, by, and for the place in which they dwelled.

Now, of course, there is a danger that people will misunderstand (or willfully misinterpret) what is meant by "educating for place" and proclaim that "these kids" do not need Shakespeare, algebra, or molecular biology. We should remain open to the possibility that many children do *not* need much of what is offered in the traditional curricula for life "anywhere," but all children need poetry, story, and song. They need enough mathematics to understand what it means to live in a mathematicized world. They need the sort of biology that will help them to understand the life around them. The contemporary environmental movement is enormously rich in historical, scientific, and literary resources.[34] In addition, children's literature has always been filled with allusions to place. There is no reason, then, to fear that educating for place will result in provincialism. Provincialism is not a product of one sort of education; it is a product of miseducation.

There is a danger, however, that a standardized education for "anywhere" may result in an urban form of provincialism—one that gives central place to fast food, designer shoes, spectator sports, computer games, and television. Indeed, this way of life might properly be labeled the new provincialism, and it is rapidly becoming the new mode of colonization as well. Thus I would argue that an education for "anywhere" might easily deteriorate to an education for "nowhere"—that is, to an unhappy habituation to places and objects that have lost their uniqueness and their connection to natural life.

Wandering Forth

Encounter is fundamental in the construction of self. Walt Whitman understood this:

> There was a child went forth every day,
> And the first object he looked upon and received with
> wonder or pity or love or dread, that object he became,
> And that object became part of him for the day or a certain part of the
> day . . . or for many years or stretching cycles of years.[35]

The bodies, objects, selves, and ideas that a child encounters become part of the self. They can shape the self mindlessly or, if the child is reflective by nature or guided by a wise adult, they can be used as raw materials in a genuine construction process.

The encounters at home, together with the affects accompanying them, become the "stars of our life," guiding us toward a home place as we wander in the world. If we have grown up with a much-loved garden, the chances are that we will want a garden in our later life. If we have learned to enjoy a clean and orderly environment, we will probably not litter the streets and countryside. Public attention and laws also constrain us and have no doubt contributed to cleaner streets, but early encounters and their internalization are more powerful. Anyone who has canoed a small stream in a patch of urban wilderness knows that people no longer under the public eye will behave as the stars of their life guide them. The great modern tragedy is that so many people travel under a starless sky.

Perhaps the first step in wandering forth is learning to "welcome in." As children learn the rudiments of hospitality, they gain appreciation for the objects in their possession and also for the ways of strangers. Of course, they also learn forms of diplomacy that range from the standard rules of courtesy to gross hypocrisy. How welcome are guests in one's home? If guests are unmercifully "deconstructed" when they leave, children are likely to doubt the sincerity of those they encounter in other homes, but if guests are discussed lovingly (not sanctimoniously) and with good humor, children may learn that love endures beyond mild forms of exasperation. Guests are treasured for the attributes that contribute to the community of order (or, occasionally, the fun of disorder), and they are forgiven the odd foibles that rub the household's fur in the wrong direction. In homes children learn what is valued in residents and guests. In the poem "Silence," Marianne Moore says,

> My father used to say,
> "Superior people never make long visits,
> have to be shown Longfellow's grave
> or the glass flowers at Harvard . . . "

In Moore's house, silence and self-reliance were valued in guests. She concludes:

> Nor was he insincere in saying, "Make my house your inn."
> Inns are not residences.[36]

Children learn not only what is valued in residents and guests but what is expected when they move out into other homes. Sometimes the ways encountered in other homes differ dramatically from one's own, and a productive interaction begins. Are the other ways better? Are they shocking? Why do we choose the ways that are so familiar to us? Does it matter? Through reflection and conversation, we have opportunities to distinguish between gentle and gracious preferences and snobbishness. One is prepared well or poorly at home for life in the wider world.

Besides "welcoming in" and learning the ways of others through visits and role-play, there are intermediate places that prepare us for life in a larger world. Gardens are among these places. A garden may extend the beauty and orderliness of the house into the world or, as a tangle of weeds and rubbish, it may reflect the disorder and neglect within. Those who love gardens often think of them as places of serenity even when they require hard work. Gardens provide a bridge between built places and nature. They help us to "get away from it all" and, paradoxically, to get closer to both nature and the self we may be consciously trying to build. Possibly no part of the house and its property is more associated with the dreaming described by Bachelard. The dreaming may begin in winter with seed catalogs and extend well beyond the thriving plants of summer.

Gardens have, of course, been romanticized by poets and songwriters. Sometimes new gardeners become disillusioned when they find out (quickly) that gardening produces backaches, scratches, rashes, dirt under the fingernails, and variable results. But garden books written by real gardeners are realistic, and the charm of these accounts is often greater than that of poetry. Beyond romance and charm, gardens yield solid satisfaction—bodies better exercised and better nourished; minds stretched by reading and problem solving. For some, gardening provides convincing evidence that the soul exists; for many, gardening enhances relations with neighbors as the excess of summer produce is distributed.

Gardens connect not only houses and nature but also relatives and neighbors. Sharing produce, clumps of irises, cuttings, seeds, catalogs, and planting instructions, people come to share more richly in a *place*. A prime site of cultivation in the most basic sense, gardens also promote the cultivation of admirable habits, conversation, and shared experience. When my children were small, they loved to walk about our garden and those of their grandparents and be told the names of all the flowers, vegetables, and shrubs. It is sad to note that they never learned these things in school. In biology they learned the parts of the flower and a bit about taxonomies, but nothing about how to grow things, nothing about the needs or growth habits of various plants, and nothing about the long and lovely history of the association between human beings and plants.

In a rich community of relatives, friends, and neighbors, children learn not only about gardens but also about ways of life, and schools could play a much larger role in helping students to understand and appreciate both their own customs and those of others. Recall Zeldin's remark that playing the role of another is "in effect . . . an invitation to widen one's idea of what a home is."[37] Educating for home life, then, may well contribute to life beyond the home.

Historically, schooling—except for certain forms of all-female education that had both salutary and pernicious effects and salutary and pernicious purposes—has concentrated on public life, not on home life. As Bachelard said of philosophers, we educators too have acted as though life starts "out there" somewhere in a transcendent world of skills, information, and ideas. Providing the best education for our children is not just a matter of psychologizing subject matter, of starting with items of familiarity as Dewey recommended; rather, the best education recognizes that children should be educated *for* the centrality of home life, not merely *from* it. It makes it possible for children to move out and be at home in the world. To be at home in the world benefits both the wanderer and the world, for the wanderer feels safe and retains a sense of belonging, and the world is treated with the care characteristic of home.

In this chapter we have concentrated on the centrality of place in our lives: houses, rooms, and corners as extensions of our bodies; gardens as intermediate spaces between home and wilderness or city; regions as home places. It is clear that place becomes part of the developing self and, in the extreme, the self may even become inextricable from its physical place. Place does not *determine* the self, but it influences and shapes it.

Our encounters with the house and all its physical attributes and contents shape us. We learn the scope of our creativity as we bring out the best in old objects, create new scenes by moving things about, get ideas for modifications by observing things in a certain light. When we move out into the world, the habits of respect (or disrespect), of conservation (or profligacy), of cultivation (or carelessness), and of appreciative observation (or sightless neglect) go with us. The habit of response is learned at home, and it is directed at the animals, plants, and objects encountered there. As the capacity for response develops, a basic moral need — the need to care — is revealed and, with it, there is a move beyond duty to something deeper that may go by the same name but induces the great joy of reciprocity. The self that moves about in the greater world is guided by what it encountered at home.

However important objects and built places are in our lives, the most important entities in early life are other selves. Even in intellectual life, it is not so much objects and buildings that shape us as it is other intellects. We turn to that topic next.

CHAPTER 8

Attentive Love

The growing child encounters not only bodies, objects, and places but also other selves. Indeed, no self at all could develop without such encounters, and other selves are certainly involved in the child's encounters with bodies and places. In this chapter and the next two, other selves will be central to the discussion. In all three chapters I draw on the language of Ruddick to organize the analysis.[1] Ruddick identifies three great maternal interests: preserving the child's life, fostering growth, and shaping an acceptable child. Ruddick writes from the perspective of mothers (people who do the work of attentive love—usually but not always women), whereas I concentrate on the needs of the child and the effects of various practices on the child's life and growth. Although the foci are different, the accounts are largely complementary. Ruddick acknowledges that maternal interests are anchored in "demands";[2] my preference is to speak of needs and wants.

In this first chapter on other selves I look at the work of attentive love and the effects it should produce in children, particularly their growth. I should offer a reminder here. When I discuss "best homes" and "best practices," I will argue on pragmatic grounds; that is, I will always argue that some practices are better than others because they produce demonstrably better effects in societies that may be characterized as liberal democracies transformed by a public recognition of the importance of caring. More generally, however, consequences of universal importance will be the maintenance of caring relations and growth in the capacity to care.

Sheltered by Attentive Love

With newborns, the first job of attentive love is to assure them that they are heard and that help and comfort can be reliably summoned.[3] The response captured by the words "I am here" meets a basic expressed need of every infant. That response induces and helps to maintain the "expectation of good" held sacred by Weil, and its constancy provides the communion described earlier by Buber "in face of the lonely night which spreads beyond the window and threatens to invade."[4] The budding self is constituted in large part by encounters with the ones who say "I am here" and by those other encounters that they arrange in the child's interests.

The growing child knows implicitly that she will not be harmed by those who care for her, and she feels almost instinctively certain that they will protect her from external threats. Caregivers in the best homes want children to retain trust in the world, but they do not want to increase their children's vulnerability to harm. To these ends they control their children's encounters with real people and with the people portrayed in the media. All good homes try to keep children safe from harm, but the best homes also try both to reduce their children's fears and to maintain their faith in other human beings. This is delicate work, requiring great sensitivity and regular dialogue. Children should be encouraged to say "Good morning" or "Hi" to strangers who greet them but not to accept gifts, enter cars or strange houses, or accompany strangers on walks. Friendliness can be modeled, but the warnings have to be accomplished through conversation and moderated by the assurance that one can indeed expect good from most people.

Caregivers who forbid all exchanges with strangers may be caring more for themselves than their children. If "anything happens," they can assure themselves and the world that they warned the child "over and over again." It may be characteristic of the best homes that certain minimal risks are taken in the interest of mutual trust and growth. Caregivers in such homes envision a community of care and trust, and they hope that their children will eventually be partners in building that community. All good caregivers accept the responsibility to protect their children, but the best want to do it in such a way as to promote moral growth, and they remain sensitive to the balance described so well by Michael Slote between caring in our immediate circles and caring in the larger world.[5] Children raised by people whose caring extends beyond the inner circle without sacrificing the special quality of care that is rightly expected there learn that care is not a commodity to be selfishly hoarded.

There are subtle and important points here. In a culture that glorifies romantic love, people often suppose that concentrated, one-on-one care is the ideal. The phenomenological analysis of care may even contribute to this misunderstanding because it describes the engrossment or non-selective attention of carers in caring encounters. Caring is not infatuation; it is attention focused on receiving what is there in the Other so that a caring response can be generated. This "engrossment" is synonymous with nonselective attention, and this may be given to strangers who address us as well as to family members. It is a mark of caring even in brief encounters. In our intimate circles these encounters occur again and again, and they achieve a certain permanency in memory. Caring-for does not in itself connote the closeness or long-lasting concern associated with family life. It implies an appropriate response, and the appropriateness of response is largely determined by the needs of the cared-for. Children who are the center of single-minded, doting love are not necessarily strengthened by that love; they are not necessarily cared for. Indeed, it may well be that they become more dependent and vulnerable as a result. Children who are well cared for by adults whose caring extends in a balanced way into the wider world are likely to be both freer in their associations and more appreciative of the care they receive from these thoughtful people. There is nothing obsessive or threatening in genuine care.

Although attentive love is not obsessive, it is pleasure seeking. When what-is-there in the other is playfulness, anticipation, or affection, a carer responds with pleasure. In the best homes adults look forward to being with the children they care for. Their care does not deteriorate to "cares and burdens." Observing and admitting to the great pleasure that often accompanies the care of children does not commit us to a rosy and unrealistic picture of eternal bliss. There are moments and, yes, longer intervals in which children are not fun and their care is tiring.[6] Then we have to respond "as if"—as if both we and the children are at our best, and that response requires an effort. In the previous chapter, when I discussed the furniture polishing of Bachelard's poet, I noted that I did not intend to glorify ordinary housework, and here I do not want to glorify childcare. The greater danger is not that we will romanticize the tasks of everyday life but that we will fail to see the pleasure and joy that are actually there. Further, it seems obvious that, holding constant the details of care-giving activity, we would all prefer to be cared for by someone who enjoys our company rather than by someone who acts out of grim duty.

Sheltered by attentive love, people in the best homes are allowed to enjoy their bodies. This does not mean that children will not be taught to observe the conventions governing the ways in which we clothe, touch, and expose various parts of our bodies, and I'll say more on this in the next section. It does mean that carers in the best homes acknowledge bodily pleasures. Most children love to play in the bath, for example, and reasonable adults also luxuriate in a hot shower or steaming bubble bath. Similarly, most of us enjoy good food and drink and the bodily pleasure of eating things we like.

Admitting that bodily pleasure is important to us does not commit us to either philosophical or psychological hedonism. With Hume, we can agree that pleasure is highly valued and that we find agreeable people pleasurable,[7] but we need not name pleasure as the only good or as the sole human motivation. Pleasure is clearly not the only goal that motivates us, but we are often eager to seek it. If we are wise, as Epicurus advised, we sometimes accept a measure of temporary discomfort in order to achieve a more lasting pleasure, and when we are in pain or grief we console ourselves with the remembrance of past pleasures. I am arguing here, with Hume, that people who accept their own love of pleasure are more likely not only to live happy lives themselves but also to contribute to the pleasure of others.

It has been hard for people raised in Christian cultures to accept the goodness of bodily pleasure. Witold Rybczynski points out that even the word "comfort" as it relates to bodily enjoyment or contentment is relatively new in western language. Before the eighteenth century, "comfort" referred to consolation and, a bit later, "comfortable" connoted a tolerable level or quality of possession or income.[8] Even as people built homes for private use, comfort was not at first a criterion. A well-to-do man might well be more concerned with the impression his home (as an edifice) made on his neighbors than on the comfort of those who would dwell therein. The vastly more numerous poor did not have the resources to provide comfort for themselves, but it seems that they too did not think in terms of comfort or their right to it. Their comfort or consolation was a promise for something better in the next life. Centuries-long acceptance of the separation of body and soul surely had some influence on this attitude.

Today, in the shelter of attentive love, everyone—including children—should have a room or at least a corner of his or her own. The inviolability of this space encourages children to respect the space of others. Poetically, the idea of shelter moves easily from the image of loving arms to a picture of the house, and sometimes the house itself is described as having sheltering arms or wings. The image stretches, too, to include porches, gardens, neighboring woods or parks, and whole regions where one is sheltered. Bachelard says that

the house's virtues of protection become human virtues. The house acquires the physical and moral energy of a human body. . . . Such a house as this invites mankind to heroism of cosmic proportions. It is an instrument with which to confront the cosmos. And the metaphysical systems according to which man is "cast into the world" might meditate concretely upon the house that is cast into the hurricane. . . . Come what may the house helps us to say: I will be an inhabitant of the world, in spite of the world.[9]

Bachelard refers here to a physical house, but also more than that. One need not live all one's childhood in one sturdy, sheltering house. In his poetic analysis Bachelard refers to the house and everything in it. He writes of the house that is constructed in poetic memory; that house is a product of both physical place and the attentive love that one receives there. A child's special places should be places of comfort in both important senses — places of consolation and places of bodily comfort. As an extension of his or her body and spirit, a child's place can be one of merriment and serenity or one of fear and gloom.

Ms. A tells the story of her grandmother, who used to admonish children by saying, "Laugh before breakfast, cry before dinner." The children never figured out whether this was a prediction, a personal warning, or just the transmission of a superstition, but several reported stopping themselves from prebreakfast merriment well into adulthood. The fear that the gods will somehow take offense at signs of human pleasure seems to be widespread across many cultures and, almost certainly, it has reduced the total sum of pleasure in the world. We must question, however, whether the seriousness required for success in the world requires, in turn, a damper on pleasure. Should the best homes put a limit on pleasure? I'll consider this further in the next section.

As children grow, they express wants in addition to basic needs. In the shelter of attentive love they feel free to express these wants. Now, if pleasure is properly recognized as important in human life, should the wants of children be acknowledged as needs to whatever level parents can afford? Somehow, a positive answer to this question seems intuitively wrong, but what counsels against it? What stands between acceptance of the response "I am here" that must be given to every real need and rejection of the response "I will give you whatever you want"?

Growth

Most of us feel that it is not good to indulge a child's every whim, but if pleasure is an unqualified good, why do we feel this way? One obvious reason for rejecting a child's demands is that we simply cannot afford to meet all of them, and every child must learn something about the limits of time and money that govern all lives. Even if we could give a child everything she asks for, most of us would back off, insisting that such indulgence is not good for the child. This very familiar reaction is not entirely a puritan legacy. Reasonably, we fear that the child will eventually reap a smaller net amount of pleasure if every whim is indulged. Delayed gratification is taught, at least in part, in the service of pleasure itself.

Do we control pleasure, then, only for the sake of pleasure itself? As we think about this, we are likely to find ourselves agreeing with the ancient philosophers that something called "happiness," rather than pleasure, should be identified as the highest good. But, then, we face Aristotle's problem: how should we define happiness? Aristotle considered three possible ways of life that might be described as happy: the life of gratification (pleasure), the life of action (honor or virtue), and the life of study.[10] Few of us today would accept his eventual conclusion that contemplation and study constitute the life of happiness, and I will argue—along with Dewey—that it is probably a mistake to identify one greatest good.[11] Human beings recognize a great variety of goods and, as Aristotle himself pointed out, recognition can depend on circumstance: we are likely to identify health as the greatest good when we are ill and wealth when we are poverty-stricken. Still, happiness and pleasure are goods that we desire for themselves. Other goods may well be paramount at a given time, but we desire them because they serve one of these great intrinsic goods.

The best families, then, want happiness above all for their members, and it is for the sake of happiness that some pleasure is curtailed. This is a tricky business at best. Social policies, such as utilitarianism, that aim directly at happiness can cause considerable pain and confusion for several reasons. First, it is often hard to tell what effects the chosen means will actually have on happiness. Second, a particular group or individual may be hampered in pursuing a more immediately pressing goal or even deprived of it as policy opts directly for the happiness of the greatest number. Third, reasonable people differ on the meaning of *happiness*—this is the perennial problem. The best homes promote conversation that explores this meaning; they remain open to the possibility that the most powerful adults in the group should not decide for all the others exactly what constitutes happiness.

In remaining open to a variety of meanings and manifestations of happiness, we must cultivate sensitivity to a concomitant set of signs that children are growing in the capacity to experience happiness. Do they often exhibit pleasure and delight (as opposed to restlessness, boredom, or sulkiness)? Can they give sustained attention to activities that both challenge and please them? Are these activities likely to lead to further activities that will bring more mature challenges and pleasures? Are their pleasures well balanced between the solitary and the social? Do they show curiosity and appreciation for the life and objects around them? On the negative side, do they get pleasure from teasing and hurting? Are their pleasures exhibited in aimless running about and careless handling of objects? Are they never satisfied? Are their pleasures too narrowly concentrated?

Good homes promote the growth of their members. What do we mean by *growth*? Dewey said that the "cumulative movement of action toward a later result is what is meant by growth."[12] For Dewey, education and growth are very nearly one; neither has a goal beyond itself. The great mistake traditionally made, Dewey insisted, was to suppose that education or growth must lead to fixed goals beyond itself. If this were so, then education or growth would stop when these goals were achieved. Dewey wanted growth to be continuous: "Hence education means the enterprise of supplying the conditions which insure growth, or adequacy of life, irrespective of age."[13]

Many critics—even many sympathetic to Dewey's educational philosophy—have found his notion of growth inadequate, and I do, too, but I also believe there is something important in it. Dewey did not want to make final and definite pronouncements on what constitutes growth, but neither did he mean to suggest that, in the absence of definite criteria, there could be no real disagreement—that the concept was clear enough in itself to guide teachers and parents in every detail. It is worth quoting Dewey at length on this.

Realization that life is growth protects us from that so-called idealizing of childhood which in effect is nothing but lazy indulgence. Life is not to be identified with every superficial act and interest. Even though it is not always easy to tell whether what appears to be mere surface fooling is a sign of some nascent as yet untrained power, we must remember that manifestations are not to be accepted as ends in themselves. They are signs of possible growth. They are to be turned into means of development, of carrying power forward, not indulged or cultivated for their own sake. Excessive attention to surface phenomena (even in the way of rebuke as well as of encouragement) may lead to their fixation and thus to arrested development. What impulses are moving toward, not what they have been, is the important thing for parent and teacher.[14]

In the rest of this passage Dewey goes on to agree with Emerson that a proper respect for the child (or, by implication, for anyone) involves "immense claims on the time, the thought, and the life of the teacher." The lack of fixed ideals makes the teacher's job more challenging, not less so. Similarly, I will suggest that wise social policy must leave room for the judgment of those charged with helping, connecting, or guiding others. Policies aimed at eliminating judgment are bad policies.

We cannot expect, then, that Dewey will tell us exactly how to recognize growth when we see it. We have to work this out for ourselves, and we will make mistakes. Families that want their children to grow vary tremendously in what they see as growth. Some define it rigidly in terms of religious salvation; others define it just as rigidly in terms of educational outcomes. The care perspective rejects this rigidity, however beautiful its end is held to be, on the grounds that it weakens, destroys, or warps caring relations both in the present and future. The Pontifex family in Butler's *Way of All Flesh* is an example I used earlier. Even when a child comes to accept deliberately inflicted pain as caring, the pain and misery obvious to a thoughtful outsider indicate not only that the present relation is not one of caring but also that future relations will likely exhibit the same features and spell misery for future generations.

Rejecting rigidity is not enough, however. We clearly have to set limits and recognize preferences. Dewey shows how some choices, even though they are marked in the present by an increase in skill, cannot be counted as growth. Someone who gains greater skill as a burglar, for example, cannot be said to be growing, because his choice will almost certainly close down valuable possibilities for the future.[15] Most of us have little difficulty in deciding that we do not want our children to become criminals, prostitutes, beggars, or professional gamblers, but will we accept our child's choice to be a carpenter or beautician even though we can send him or her to a fine college? In what way is a home that will accept such a decision cheerfully better than one that will actively discourage it or deride it?

I argue here that the accepting home is better from both personal and public perspectives. From the personal perspective it is better for young people to know that their worth depends far more on attributes of character and personality than on occupational status. At school, too, students need to learn and come to believe that their worth does not depend on academic prowess. Children who grow up in families that can afford to provide the most prestigious academic experiences sometimes transmit the message that children must somehow prove themselves worthy of their parents' gift—even though the gift is not given in response to an expressed need and may even run counter to it.

From a public perspective our attitude toward the full range of honest work needs examination. Trying to atone for decades of educational neglect resulting from racism, educational policymakers are now insisting that all children must study the academic subjects once required of only the college bound. Most such authorities do not stop to ask whether the old college preparatory curriculum was *ever* the best, even for the college bound. In the name of equity, they simply insist that all children should now have the academic experience once reserved for a few. Well-intended thoughtlessness is exacerbated, then, by coercion. The coercion exercised here is of the "someday you'll thank me for this" sort, and in some cases the results may indeed be happy ones. Before using these happy cases as a justification for wholesale coercion, however, we should ask whether the same result might have been achieved without coercion. The fear is that unhappy cases will far outnumber happy ones and that adequately intelligent children will fail or do poorly because their own legitimate interests have never been engaged.

The personal and public perspectives are, of course, interdependent; each feeds the other. The message in schools today is that kids can become whatever they aspire to be and that their aspirations should be high. Regardless of talent, motivation, or genuine interest, they are urged to prepare for college. Notice that this is not so much a message of encouragement as it is one of coercion, even threat. I'll say much more about this problem in a later chapter on social policy, but here the argument centers on what happens at home. Imagine the following conversation:

Father: What do you mean, you don't want to go to college? Your
    mother and I have slaved to send you to good schools. We've

hired tutors to get you through math. We've given you music lessons so that you have something impressive to list under extra-curricular activities . . .

Son: I want to grow things. I . . .

Father: You want to grow things! You want to be a migrant worker? What?

Son: Dad, listen. I want to go to a community college that has a great two-year program in horticulture. It's a good business, and the one job I've always enjoyed around the house is gardening. I want to grow things, plan gardens . . .

Father: I don't understand where we went wrong—all that tutoring.

Son: "All that tutoring" was because I hated math, and I didn't like the music lessons either. I'd rather draw or paint.

Father: Yeah, I know, pretty pictures of flowers.

In a better home a child's expressed needs are taken seriously. As I admitted earlier, it is not always easy to distinguish needs from wants. We look for signs of stability (the want is expressed consistently over time), instrumentality (it is connected to worthwhile ends), reasonableness (it is within the family's means and the child is willing to work for it), intensity (it means much to the child), and harmlessness (it will do no obvious harm to either the child or others). If all these criteria are met, the best home will try to satisfy the expressed need. Notice here how important Dewey's warning on interests is: to evaluate the legitimacy of expressed needs takes time and care. We have to attend, and we have to allow our motive energy to flow toward the needs of the one addressing us.

My argument does not imply that children should be assessed early for aptitudes and then directed ("relegated") to specific occupations. This practice is just another, and worse, form of coercion. Rather, I am making a plea similar to the one made so elegantly by Walt Whitman in his "Song for Occupations."[16] In the most loving terms Whitman calls on people to recognize their own worth and the potential happiness that abides in everyday life. He sees something "remarkable" in every human being including himself, and he puts the question squarely:

Why what have you thought of yourself?
Is it you then that thought yourself less?

Is it you that thought the President greater than you? or the
rich better off than you? or the educated wiser than you?[17]

Then, in more than three solid pages of ringing song to the great variety
of occupations on which we are all dependent, Whitman celebrates ordinary, remarkable human beings. It is no wonder that Dewey called
Whitman "the seer of democracy."[18] It is this great affirmation of respect
and interdependence that parents should remember in guiding their children. Such respect in no way precludes inviting children to participate
in the "life of the mind" whether or not they choose an occupation that
requires mental accreditation.

The best homes provide a shelter for the imagination.[19] They are
concerned with growth along multiple lines. They do not discourage
the growth of mind and soul (however that is construed), but neither
do they separate mind and soul from everyday life or elevate them above
activities associated with mere bodies. Now and then educators have
had insight into the breadth of legitimate educational needs. In 1918
Clarence Kingsley produced a document called the Cardinal Principles
Report. In this short report seven aims of education were listed:
"1. Health. 2. Command of fundamental processes. 3. Worthy home-
membership. 4. Vocation. 5. Citizenship. 6. Worthy use of leisure.
7. Ethical character."[20] Although schools have found ways to ignore several of those categories ("anti-intellectual!"), the best homes cannot neglect any of them and may well want to extend the list. The child's
imagination is not confined to books but is sheltered in gardens, kitchens, playing fields, friendships, conversations, and explorations of the
living world around him.

I have devoted several paragraphs to the deceptively simple question
of whether the best homes should accept, even encourage, the decision
of a child to work with her or his hands, and I have argued that it is
important on both personal and public levels. Children from well-to-do
homes have often been pressed into college and occupations for which
they were unsuited and in which they were unhappy. Often the nature
of a child's discontent has gone undetected by both parents and child.
Prep schools, incubators for "tomorrow's leaders," have their fair share
of problems with dishonesty, alienation, drug and alcohol abuse, and
depression.[21] Not all of the problems can be traced to inappropriate
courses of study, but many of them result from a basic lack of honesty
on the part of parents and educators, who fail to talk with young people
about the power of the discipline exerted by the larger culture and by,
in particular, that part of the culture in which they are growing up.

Today, children from the opposite end of the economic spectrum suffer associated problems. Middle-school children in blighted urban centers often respond to questions about what they would like to be when they grow up with "doctor" or "lawyer." Their teachers have urged them to have high aspirations, and the uniformity of their answers reflects how well the society's hierarchical evaluations have been inculcated. And why shouldn't inner-city kids aspire to medicine or law? Such aspiration is to be applauded if it is realistic; that is, the aspiration should be encouraged if it is well informed. I am not suggesting that we judge solely on the basis of either academic aptitude or financial resources. I am noting that many youngsters have little or no sense of what is required to enter these professions. Their answers are practically equivalent to those of a three-year-old who wants to be a fireman. While well-intentioned but careless observers applaud the aspiration, no one is spending time with these youngsters to help them arrive at reasonable choices.

Further, in a misguided effort to prepare everyone for college, schools often provide academic courses that are below par. Students graduate from high school with credentials for college admission but no genuine preparation. As a result, many students—too many that are poor and members of a minority—drop out of college. Fewer students will experience this failure if they are well prepared to enter a field of study in which they have both interest and aptitude.

Understandably, minority parents and many sympathetic educators bristle at the thought that children should be encouraged to think about work that does not require four years of college. For too long minority children have been pushed into jobs seen as less desirable. My argument is that the world of work should be fully open to all children, that the dignity of honest work should be celebrated, and that children should be able to choose a line of work with pride—not fall into it by default. Children who struggle with academic subjects, dislike reading, and hate the bondage of schooling should not be coerced into preparing for college.

In doing the work of attentive love we remain open to and interested in the expressed needs of our children. However, some needs that might rise to the level of expression never do so because the child's encounters are limited or because, as Dewey pointed out, we take superficial expressions as indicative of something deeper. This observation underscores the difficulty of educating. Of course children should encounter books, ideas, and the possibilities that lead to traditionally prestigious work; they should also encounter tools, practical problems, repair jobs, cooking, serving, cleaning, and making things. The choices they make should be based on what interests them, what they are good at — not on what they have to settle for because they cannot meet the inferred needs we establish for them. Parents should act on inferred needs by providing a host of varied encounters for their children. One cannot choose intelligently if one has no real knowledge of alternatives. Both expressed needs and inferred needs are at least partially satisfied in encounters that are offered freely.

What makes it so hard to guide children (or, for that matter, adults) is that we are rarely sure whether we should accept or reject their expressed needs. It is certainly appropriate for adults to arrange a variety of encounters for children, and it is probably right for parents and teachers to use gentle coercion in exposing children to the ideas and practices that they themselves value. The great hope is that the needs we infer for our children will become expressed needs. Our children will come to *need* books, intellectual conversation, music, art, mathematics, skill at cooking, gardening, the companionship of animals, time for the sacred, and all the things we have come to love. Indeed, we would be poor guides and mentors if we did not leave open this possibility and extend repeated invitations. We must remember, however, that any such invitation may be rejected, and it may be right for a particular child that it be rejected.

The great message of this chapter is that the work of attentive love requires listening and responding. Parents and educators may have to use coercion occasionally, but its use always raises a question and induces a round of hard work in maintaining or restoring caring relations. Used wisely, coercion implies negotiation in the implementation of whatever is coerced. The message, "You must do *x*," should be followed by the sincere question, "How can we help you?" In the next chapter we consider how encounters with other selves shape a child's acceptability.

CHAPTER 9

Achieving Acceptability

Children in happy homes are sheltered by attentive love. Their health, safety, and growth are promoted by parents—other selves—who are there for them. Parents listen, respond appreciatively, and help their children make well-informed choices, although they cannot respond positively to every desire expressed by their children. Parents have a vision of the kind of person their child should become and, as Ruddick points out, the training required can be hard work for parents and children alike.[1]

Acceptability

There are needs that we properly infer for all children. I argued earlier that when these needs begin to be met they usually rise to the level of expression; that is, once a child learns to care for others, he or she shows a need to care. Indeed, some psychologists and anthropologists have argued that the universal need of infant creatures to be cared for triggers a corresponding care response in many organisms, and I have argued that this desire to respond is the foundation of morality in human beings.

The desire to respond with care, the need for affiliation, and the desire for acceptability are closely related. All are directed to the maintenance of relations, but affiliation and acceptability do not necessarily imply caring. One can do just enough to maintain a connection to others without really caring about their welfare, and some people purposely choose to associate with groups whose members will not make personal demands on them. Thus, a certain sociality is maintained, but caring encounters may occur infrequently and caring relations may not be sustained over time. Still, the desire for affiliation may contribute to participation in activities that present opportunities to learn how to care.

The desire for acceptability also invites encounters that may themselves be caring or may lead to relations of care, but the desire for acceptability, like the one for affiliation, is in itself free of norms. Rejected by adults or peers in the larger domain of acceptability, young people may seek acceptability in groups considered deviant by the main culture. This is a familiar and troubling phenomenon. An opposite sort of reaction may also occur. Some children so long for parental approval that they become docile and subservient. They blame themselves for every loss of acceptability even when sensitive outsiders suspect that the criteria for acceptability are too tightly drawn, perhaps warped.

The desire for acceptability is, in most people, broader and more dangerous than the one for affiliation. If basic needs for affiliation are met, we may not seek a wider domain of affiliation, but we may still need to be considered acceptable by a host of groups with which we do not seek affiliation. For example, people do not usually seek affiliations with fellow theatergoers or restaurant customers, yet we want to be considered acceptable to these groups. As we saw earlier, the desire to be acceptable is encouraged and exploited in disciplining the body. It is used, too, to reduce what might otherwise be reflective (mental, cognitive) activity to the level of habitual bodily behavior. Again, this powerful discipline is not always bad. A society depends on it for the smooth running of its ceremonies, routines, and scripts of all sorts. One of the most difficult of all human tasks is to evaluate the behaviors we are disciplined to accept and enact. Should we defy etiquette and talk with our mouth full? Scratch our armpits in public? Yell "Bullshit!" at a lying preacher? Walk out on a teacher who doesn't know what she's talking about? Dance when our bodies are itching to do so? Remain sitting when everyone around us rises for the national anthem? Agree publicly with our friends when we really disagree? Vote with the Democrats just because we are Democrats? Say "This stinks," and quit the execution party? Go on strike if we are teachers even though many citizens believe that striking is not acceptable behavior for teachers?

The job of ideal parents and educators is to help students make such evaluations. We cannot escape cultural discipline, and even evaluating it is a discipline of sorts. We can claim that by teaching people to evaluate their disciplined behavior we are teaching them to be autonomous, but I have already raised questions about the concept of autonomy. There is, of course, a nucleus of something true and valuable in it: it seems preferable to make choices without physical or emotional coercion in most cases, although at times we are grateful for such coercion; it seems preferable also to act on what we believe rather than the opinions of others, but doing so may be more a matter of courage than "autonomy." Berry says that autonomy "has nothing to do with the assumption of responsibilities or the renewal of connections. . . . There is, in practice, no such thing as autonomy. Practically, there is only a distinction between responsible and irresponsible dependence."[2]

Berry's assertion, perhaps too strongly put, is compatible with my earlier argument. When we are tempted to use the word "autonomy" we should think more deeply on exactly what we mean. The important case considered here involves a rejection of two extreme positions. In the first, adults use coercion to inculcate the values they associate with acceptability; in the second, adults encourage cynicism and the destruction (at least, at the level of thought) of their society's disciplinary structures. Both positions may properly be called irresponsible because they encourage a pernicious form of irresponsibility in the young—either an attitude of unreflective acceptance, or equally unreflective rejection of conventional norms.

The best families want their members to make distinctions between facilitative behaviors (most rules of etiquette), emotionally destructive behaviors that often go unquestioned, and behaviors that are to be morally approved or disapproved. Psychologists often speak of such parental guidance as "supportive of autonomy."[3] The sort of thinking supported by this guidance is rarely the sort that says merely, "Decide for yourself," and almost never, "Do as you please!" It usually sets boundaries within which choices can safely and acceptably be made. It makes distinctions: here are practices that should be outlawed or that *are* outlawed in this community; here are matters of fashion or custom that make life more pleasant and predictable for everyone; here are practices that "we" should challenge; here are wants that may fail to attain the status of needs; here are things we should revisit because I'm not sure myself; here are things you really can decide for yourself, but be careful.

In a recent newspaper column reviewing Cynthia Whitham's *The Answer Is No: Saying It and Sticking to It,* the reviewer quotes the author approvingly and summarizes her message this way: "The most important [way of setting limits] is saying no and sticking to it—no matter what. And forget trying to reason with your children, Whitham says. Reasoning only further frustrates the parent and sends the message to the child that there needs to be a good reason behind every decision."[4]

But, of course, this is exactly the message that good families want to send. Parents must sometimes say no and make no exceptions, but there is an especially good reason for this absolute response: "You might hurt yourself or someone else." In other situations the "no" may be conditional, temporary, or replaced by "We'll see," "Let's talk about it," or "Here are our choices." Parents don't lose control and authority by talking to their children and listening to them. The object is to teach children how to make crucial distinctions. When such a parent says that there are no options (because of potential harm), the child knows that this particular matter is one of great importance. He or she learns that good people avoid inflicting unnecessary pain and that they try to prevent others from doing so, that this is the reason that trumps all others.

The book mentioned above gives a reason for saying no and avoiding reasons and arguments: parents are tired and need peace. But one would hardly give this reason for neglecting one's occupational work or for doing it in an irresponsible way. It is one thing to request (even claim a right to) occasional "peace and quiet" as Ms. A did in our earlier example; it is quite another to neglect a central task of parenting to spare oneself the demanding work of care. Parents cannot responsibly purchase peace and quiet at the cost of sacrificing real dialogue with their children.

Desert

Listening to, reasoning with, and responding sensitively to children (or clients, patients, students, and the like) does not mean indulging them or granting every passing want. The best homes recognize a concept of positive desert. One should be able to earn certain privileges and rewards in a given community, and it is important for all citizens in a democratic society to make connections between their diligent performance of accepted duties and the positive consequences of such diligence.

Should we use the word *desert* in this connection? We do say things such as, "Joe deserves a night off; he's done dishes every night this week," "Mary deserves our trust," "Billy deserves a treat for being so brave at the dentist's." The sense here is that certain actions earn rewards for their agents. The relevant public, a family, notices the praiseworthy act and rewards it. In the larger world, too, a public gives prizes and recognition to those it deems especially worthy—to those who deserve them. Occasional use of such language is probably harmless, but its regular use invites counterclaims: Jack objects that he was not rewarded for services similar to Joe's, Ann also deserves trust, Jack suffered more than Billy, and so on. In the larger public arena the criteria for desert of prizes, rewards, and recognition are usually well publicized, but even here counterclaims are frequent.

Desert can be described in contractual terms. Rewards acquired under contract are deserved in the sense that all parties have agreed that if certain acts are performed, certain rewards will follow. It is legitimate, then, to say that someone has earned prescribed pay for a job defined by contract. For example, parents might establish a basic allowance for children (by age) that is earned by certain basic contributions to the family enterprise. These contributions might be minimal, and the allowance would be withheld only upon infractions that threaten the general welfare of the family. It is assumed under such a scheme that everyone deserves a certain minimal level of monetary reward for basic contributions. Beyond these, special contracts might be awarded for specific tasks not defined as basic. These special contracts are very like contracts in the adult world of business. The first sort of contract is more controversial in the larger social world (although I suggest something like it in chapter 12). The notion that everyone "deserves" a certain minimal monetary award assumes that membership in the family makes certain reasonable demands and gives certain assurances in return. Membership in a well-ordered society—and the good family may come as close to this as we are likely to see in actuality—brings with it legitimate expectations, and it may be better to speak in such terms than in terms of desert.[5]

The domain of legitimate expectations may properly be divided into two main parts. One set of expectations will always be met in the best home; this is the set that responds to basic expressed needs: food, shelter, clothing, medical care, protection from harm including all forms of deliberately inflicted pain, emotional support, and educational opportunities. One can expect these things from a good family without having to earn them. These goods may never properly be withheld. A second set of legitimate expectations comes closer to the idea of desert. Granting a basic allowance, particular nonbasic needs or wants, increasing independence, use of certain tools, instruments, or objects, and privileges that almost automatically accompany growing maturity can be grouped under legitimate expectations. This second set, however, must be earned in the sense that the recipient must maintain basic acceptability in the family. The rewards associated with this set may be withheld for egregious offenses. We would not assess a home as good if it did not meet these expectations under conditions of mutual compliance, but we would not condemn a home that withheld one or more of these wants or needs for good reasons—for example, when a child does not meet expectations for basic acceptability or when family circumstances create hardships that make it impossible to satisfy the usual expectations. This second level of legitimate expectations is contingent; its legitimacy is conditioned by available resources, competing demands, and the acceptability of those expressing needs or wants.

What is central in this discussion is the insistence that some things may never properly be withheld. Family members are always protected from the deliberate infliction of pain, and this means that the best home rejects the notion of negative desert. One does not deserve physical pain or emotional pain that is inflicted deliberately. Consider the experience suffered by Ingmar Bergman:

When he wet his bed, which he did chronically, he was forced to wear a red skirt for the entire day; minor infractions of family rules meant that the child was temporarily "frozen out," meaning that "no one spoke or replied to you"; serious misdemeanors were met with thrashings, which were carried out with a carpet beater in his father's study.[6]

Scarcely any argument has to be mounted today against such parental treatment. We have enough empirical evidence to convince us that the deliberate infliction of pain often breeds violent attitudes in the victims. This is not to say that children bear no responsibility for acts that precipitate painful responses. Parents cannot be required to be saints. Even very good parents sometimes slap a child, whack his bottom, or yank him uncomfortably. Contemporary American society is, perhaps, too hard on young mothers. On the one hand, they are held responsible for the behavior of their young children, and this responsibility is often unrelieved for long hours. On the other, they are castigated for slapping or spanking their children even when these events may be rare and the situation one of great provocation. Good parents feel bad about these lapses, but they use them to help the child understand why behavior that would never be deliberately chosen sometimes occurs. The following conversation might be typical:

Mother: I'm sorry I slapped you. I shouldn't have done that, but you made me awfully mad.

Bobby: You hurt me.

Mother: I know, honey, and I *am* sorry. I asked you three times to stop jumping on the sofa, and you just laughed at me. I'm a little hot and tired. Do you ever get that way?

Bobby: Sure. That's why I hit Nick yesterday. But I shouldn't have.

Mother: Right. In a way, Nick brought it on himself, but he still didn't *deserve* to be hit. Do you think you'll notice next time when I'm getting really mad?

Bobby: I better, and I hope Nick notices when *I'm* getting mad.

Ideally, the conversation should continue:

Mother: This doesn't excuse us, though, does it? I feel guilty for hitting you, and you feel guilty for hitting Nick. We've got to try harder not to do this.

Bobby: I guess.

As children grow older, parents are not so hard pressed to control them, and both have learned strategies that reduce occasions of minor violence.

The difference between deserving pain and bringing it on oneself is a crucial distinction to be learned in encounters with other selves. If one deserved pain, the one who inflicted it would be justified. When we reject the idea that pain is deserved, we must accept the fact that we are not justified in inflicting it. From the relational perspective, however, we must recognize our own role in bringing on pain. This may involve reckless behavior, provoking others, ignoring signs of growing anger, neglecting one's health, or repeated failures to reciprocate in caring. Indeed, most of us bring some of the pain we suffer on ourselves. It seems better to use this language than the language of desert.

Why is one language better than the other? As Rawls points out, it is notoriously difficult to determine fairly exactly what a person deserves, and this is as true for negative desert (one deserves something bad) as for positive desert (one deserves something good). But surely, one might argue, some people do deserve pain. You can't possibly argue this way outside the family setting, a critic might insist. But it is not a matter of adopting the best family practices wholesale and unmodified. It is a matter of sorting through existing and potential policies to see which might be improved by an extension of family practices. Because we cannot discard the notion of negative desert entirely does not mean that we cannot drop it from some social practices.

I agree with Rawls that desert is difficult to assess and, further, that the concept of negative desert has caused far more trouble than it is worth. Consider this century's most frequently used example. Surely Adolf Hitler deserved pain for his crimes, but how could a community ever inflict anything like the pain he deserved, if desert is measured by the pain one has caused? We can't kill one man six million times, and death by extraordinarily painful torture would disgust most of us. Further, we rarely accomplish anything positive by retribution. People speak of "closure." The criminal is dead, and the horrible episode is finished — yet horrors such as these seem to occur again and again. So I will argue for prevention, intervention, and a sort of restraint that does not permit the deliberate infliction of pain.

Before leaving this topic I want to defend my contention that the idea of negative desert has been more harmful than helpful in human affairs, and I have to defend it in the face of a widely shared intuition that pain is often deserved. The first arena to which we might look for documentation of my claim is religion. Here I extend the argument started in chapter 6. Christianity has — in both its theological traditions and ordinary pulpit preaching — promoted the idea that pain is deserved.[7] The notion of damnation, for example, is a horrendous one from a parental perspective. Can any loving parent imagine inflicting long-lasting pain on a child? Can anyone imagine inflicting (or suffering) eternal pain? A reasonable mind would have to protest that even Hitler should be given surcease after, say, six million years of suffering. And six million years do not make a scratch on eternity.

Many Christians have given up the old belief in Hell and damnation — they have found such beliefs inconsistent with a more basic belief in a loving God — but the legacy remains. It is not at all unusual for people to believe that they "must have done something" to deserve the pain they suffer,[8] and it is a major function of enlightened religious leaders to convince them that they do not deserve their pain. Further, many people — deeply influenced by their religious traditions — identify all sorts of small infractions with the desert of pain. Even the exhibition of happiness (laughter before breakfast) can warrant the infliction of pain (tears before dinner). It is not too strong to say that the legacy of belief in deserved pain has produced generations of inhibited and fearful people, and it may not be too strong to suggest that rebellion against this legacy has contributed to equally deplorable and more dangerous behavior. For example, if a person's only reason for refraining from murder is fear of punishment, and that person commits a murder despite this fear, he or she has even less reason not to commit additional murders. One could argue, in opposition, that the possibility of detection and an increased likelihood of painful punishment would remain deterrents, but this could be countered by arguing that a murderer, having once killed, would have a powerful incentive to murder others who might aid in his detection. My main point here is that the belief in negative desert has had negative effects on both social policy and individual lives.

Closely connected to the notion of negative desert is the glorification of pain. The major forms of monotheism glorify those who willingly suffer pain for the sake of others or for the cause of faith itself. The idea of negative desert lingers like a shadow. When the sufferer is clearly without sin, religious authorities may credit him or her with suffering for the sins of others. *Someone,* that is, deserves pain, and the saintly sufferer has taken on those pains to spare the guilty. In another scenario, penitents inflict pain on themselves, the body is subjected to deprivation, or the palate is "mortified" by eating something repulsive, and acts of personal compassion are enhanced by the suffering of carers. A relational view of caring abhors and fears this tendency because it distracts carers from the cared-fors and focuses attention on themselves.

In yet another variation on the embrace of what is naturally avoided by all normal animals, pain is often held to be "necessary." Why else would an all-good God permit so much of it? As we saw in chapter 6, C. S. Lewis, trying to make sense of his beloved wife's final suffering from cancer, decided that pain must be necessary. Belief in an all-good God and the reality of pain in the world require, Lewis thought, the conclusion that such pain is necessary in soul-making. Lewis's response is, of course, far too simplistic. There are other choices that have been offered and debated for years.[9] But his interpretation is widely accepted in a school of thought that often is called "soul-making." From this perspective souls are tested and shaped by suffering. In his classic work on theodicy John Hick rejects the tit-for-tat theory of desert and punishment, yet holds to the soul-making idea. The necessity of pain is shrouded in mystery, Hick says, but suggests both meaning and a promised greater good.[10]

When we move from possible explanations at the cosmic level to reflection on everyday life, the danger arises that we will interpret pain itself as having meaning. Hence, a sufferer is led to ask: what am I supposed to learn from this? Asking the question this way suggests again that the pain, if not actually deserved, has been inflicted for our own good. The best homes work hard to avoid this compounding of misery. A child may indeed bring pain upon himself, and as we saw in an earlier example, both parent and child may contribute to a minor incident of pain and violence. The lesson to be learned in such cases is clear, although it may have to occur repeatedly before it sinks in. The best parent does not suggest to the child that some grand scheme lies behind these occurrences or that the pain itself has meaning. Rather, one must reflect on such events and incorporate them into a larger scheme of meaning. One *constructs* meaning together with other selves; one does not "find" meaning that has been buried whole for a discoverer to dig out.

The idea of shared blame needs far more attention from both psychology and sociology. Too often observers seem to choose dichotomous positions: either the perpetrator or the victim receives full blame. Today, when a critic suggests that a victim might share the blame, he or she is accused of "blaming the victim." As Sharon Lamb has pointed out, however, the victim *is* sometimes partly responsible for his or her victimization.[11] In a carefully constructed argument, backed by convincing evidence, Lamb shows that many females have contributed to their own sexual abuse. This conclusion in no way excuses the perpetrators of such abuse; rather, it underscores the complexity of interactions among selves. Without excusing one party, the other party can be held responsible for her part in the offense. Learning is the objective in all discussions centered on the sharing of blame. Learning can lead to an understanding that may prevent future occurrences.

We have to be very careful here. I don't want to argue that wives bring battering on themselves. Husbands are not charged with the control of their wives as mothers are with their children. Where this legacy remains, it should be eliminated. Physical pain should not be deliberately inflicted, and no one deserves it, but women can learn strategies to avoid it, just as men can learn strategies to control their violent impulses. Sometimes the best strategy is to end the relationship.

Is there a contradiction here? Our present version of an ethic of care tells us that carers establish, maintain, and enhance caring relations. How can that description be compatible with severing a relationship? It is useful to make a distinction between "relation" and "relationship." *Relation,* as I have been using it, is a set of encounters, and a caring relation has the particular qualities described earlier. A relation in this sense may actually be improved by ending a formal relationship. Many divorced couples find it possible to talk civilly to one another, and some even become friends. Thus there is no contradiction at either the theoretical or practical level; ending a formal relationship may help to build a caring relation. An understanding of how we bring things on ourselves—without deserving them—should help us in future relations. Even if a relationship must be entirely abandoned, the web of caring may be strengthened by what we learn in analysis and reflection.

It is worth noting here that despite an even-handed treatment that emphasizes shared responsibility, prevention, and rehabilitative education, Lamb succumbs at the last to the tradition of negative desert. Citing P. J. Strawson, Jeffrie Murphy, and Lewis, she seems to endorse the notion that offenders deserve pain, that they have a human right to be punished. Her last words echo Lewis:

C. S. Lewis, in his essay "The Humanitarian Theory of Punishment," wrote that "to be punished, however severely, because we have deserved it, because we ought to have known better, is to be treated as a human person made in God's image." Perpetrators not only deserve blame but are *worthy* of it, in the fullest, most human sense of the word.[12]

How does one become *worthy* of blame and punishment? Simply by being sane under some definition? In what sense does this worthiness reflect God's image? What could one possibly mean in saying that a slayer of young children is "worthy of blame"? Such language takes its toll in nonsense, in debilitating guilt, in perennial excuses for revenge, and in destroying the complexity in human interactions. What do we gain by persisting in such talk?

Much of the pain that humans suffer is neither deserved nor brought upon ourselves, and good parents have to assure children of this. Neither is there meaning in the pain itself. It is a misery to be relieved, a suffering that needs consolation. In their most tender and loving aspects the traditional religions recognize this and try to respond accordingly, but they are perpetually caught in a web of contradiction, and the sufferer goes on wondering, "What did I do to deserve this?" Biography and fiction are replete with accounts of children who blame themselves for the loss of their parents or siblings.[13] This false guilt cannot be traced unerringly to a religious legacy (it may be a deep psychological flaw), but the religious tradition has done little to relieve it, and in many cases the tradition has exacerbated it.

Before turning to a classroom example to illustrate methods of positive discipline, I want to conclude my argument against negative desert with some cautionary words. The impulse to do something bad, something that hurts, to those who commit crimes or go too far in annoying us is strong in all of us. Everyday conversation is loaded with examples of the traditional attitude: "This will teach him!" "Some people only understand one language." "Let that be a lesson to you!" "Spare the rod and spoil the child." "You can't talk to some people." "Lock 'em up and throw away the key."

The violation of legitimate expectations (those associated with basic expressed needs) occurs frequently in homes, and we still regard such homes as good provided that the discipline is moderate: spankings that do not leave bruises, bed without supper occasionally, mild forms of public shaming for especially egregious infractions. I am suggesting that more nearly ideal homes reject methods associated with negative desert and use instead positive incentives. Reasons for my claim should be clear. Relations unburdened by negative desert put emphasis on mutual consideration, self-knowledge, and caring responses. They are less likely to breed fear, anger, unnecessary guilt, and the repression of creative and happy impulses.[14] If homes can use such methods successfully, can a whole society base its policymaking on a positive concept of desert? What are the promises and limits in such an approach?

Classroom examples may help in suggesting the promise of positive methods. Years ago, when I was a high school mathematics teacher, I was disturbed by what might be called "cumulative ignorance" and the failure accompanying it. Typically, when a unit test is given in mathematics, grades are assigned and, if many students do well, the class moves on to the next unit. What happens to students who fail a test? If the material is prerequisite to the next unit, they will probably fail that unit, too, and the unhappy process continues until the case is quite hopeless.

One traditional answer to this familiar dilemma has already been alluded to in Orwell's description of his primary school. Failing students should be beaten physically or emotionally until they apply themselves industriously (and successfully). But surely other approaches are possible. I reasoned this way: if the point of what I'm doing as a math teacher is to get students to learn math, then I should not permit them to continue in a state of unreadiness that will make it impossible for them to learn. I announced that any failed test could be retaken. "What will the grade be?" a student asked. "Whatever you get," I replied. "That's not fair," another said; "a person who gets a 95 on the second try isn't as good as one who gets a 90 on the first try." Despite my assurance that the second, third, and n^{th} tests would be different forms, not the very same test, and that he (who had a 90) could retake the test, too, he remained unconvinced of the "fairness" of my offer.

The objecting student and many others who take this position have implicitly accepted a notion of discipline very different from the one I was using. For me, discipline meant a concentrated and shared effort to master the material at hand; for them, discipline meant a system of external controls and rewards that would separate the proficient from the deficient, maintain a scarcity of good grades, and reward the "morally good" who were compliant, smart, and reasonably industrious. By the time they reach high school many students have already internalized the practices that go with their society's implicit disciplinary machinery. Although teachers constantly tell students that the purpose of teaching is student learning, students find it hard to believe this. More obvious purposes are to secure compliance, rank order students, punish noncompliance, penalize failure (even when students are in basic compliance), and encourage competition.[15] Allowing students to retake tests until they exhibit enough proficiency to tackle the next unit is a practice belonging to a different sense of "discipline."

This approach—retaking tests, rewriting papers—also aroused objections from colleagues. Their argument was that some kids deserve a second chance and some do not. They warned that students would not take their work seriously if a poor first grade could be discarded. This is an empirical claim, of course, but I have not found it to be true in my own practice. A few students will try the "wing and a prayer" method, but not many. Those who do slack off need a lesson in self-understanding, and that is more likely to be learned through dialogue than through punishment. The idea of negative desert is pervasive. It was assumed in this case that many students *deserve* their bad grades. My assumption was that grades are indicators of learning (and not always good ones) and that students could legitimately expect that I would work hard to help them learn. Penalizing them for failure would just induce greater anxiety, and of course it would contribute to the next round of failure.

Astute readers will have a question at this point. Were my students allowed to retake tests or were they coerced into doing so? The answer is that they were coerced. At the outset I invited, persuaded, and encouraged, but eventually I announced that students could not go on to the next chapter or unit until they had shown at least a minimal grasp of the present material. There are times—in family, school, or community life—when coercion is necessary. The coercion must be for the sake of the one coerced, and it should be followed by negotiation. The assurance, "I am here," must have positive reality. When we coerce, we must explain why we are using coercion, stand ready to help, and take measures to maintain or repair caring relations. And, of course, we must consider the possibility that we have made a mistake in choosing to coerce.

I'll give one more classroom example because the idea here is central to my overall argument. Periodically, high school faculties become upset by student tardiness to classes. A crackdown usually results in careful record keeping and prescribed penalties. The name of every tardy student is listed on a slip that is collected and recorded in a central office. I resisted this practice. I told my students that I would start on time and that I expected that they, too, would be present and ready for action. I suggested that we leave a few seats near the door for those who might be unavoidably late. Latecomers were to take seats quietly and wait for a break in procedures to ask their neighbors what they missed. This worked well. Kids responded with respect to my respect for them. It just did not seem reasonable to waste valuable instructional time on a bureaucratic procedure that reinforced a sense of discipline I wanted to resist.

An adult doing the work of attentive love is necessarily concerned with her own culture's sense of acceptability, but that adult may be influenced by more than one culture. A teacher in the United States cannot responsibly ignore the dominant culture—the one that determines who will succeed economically and how that success is achieved—but there is more than one way of acknowledging the dominant culture. Instead of enforcing its demands for compliance, a teacher may help students understand what is being done to them. She can talk about mutual respect instead of obedience. She can help them to understand the positive rewards for acceptable forms of behavior. In particular, in a liberal democratic society, a caring teacher will help students to acquire the skills and understandings necessary for full participation. At the same time she will encourage them to question the use of coercion and to challenge obvious hypocrisy. We do not have to speak in terms of autonomy, but as I noted earlier, we can speak more explicitly of what that term often captures.[16] In the two cases described I wanted students to take responsibility for their own learning and to feel that they had some control over it, and I wanted them to understand that following agreed-upon guidelines could be a mark of consideration and respect, not mere compliance.

What would I have done if these methods had not worked, and what do we mean when we say that they "haven't worked"? The best homes and schools are slow to decide that methods consonant with their ideals are not working. Their first efforts are directed to understanding. Infractions are treated with analysis and dialogue. We might have to say to a repeat offender, "You haven't earned the privilege of taking the test again," or "You haven't earned the respect that allows others to arrive late occasionally." Notice that such responses are still based on a positive concept of desert. Pressed by a student's bad behavior, we withhold something that would be a legitimate expectation under conditions of acceptability.

There may be cases when the concept of negative desert must be invoked. We will certainly meet such cases in our discussion of social policy. There a central question will be how far we can extend methods that depend, at least in part, on the intimate understanding characteristic of the best homes and small communities. We will encounter limits, but those limits will never force us to endorse the deliberate infliction of pain or the refusal of basic legitimate expectations such as food, shelter, and protection from physical harm.

It should be obvious that good families use positive methods with older as well as younger members. Uncle Jake is always granted a meal or a night's shelter, but a new loan is contingent on his record with previous loans. Grown children are assisted in buying homes provided they demonstrate their seriousness with substantial contributions of some sort. Elderly members are encouraged to maintain their cognitive abilities by being accorded the respect that accompanies our depending on them for various tasks, but they are not punished for lapses. In this last case acceptance is not a matter of deserving or earning, but the strategy is similar: the wise family arranges its affairs so that all members have incentives to remain acceptable to the family community and to satisfy their own individual needs.

We have not yet discussed *punishment*. Closely associated with negative desert, punishment has been considered necessary to maintain balance in families, communities, societies, and even the universe; thus, evil of any sort is balanced by the appropriate suffering of the guilty. Today most of us reject this notion. Instead of balance we see a never-ending accumulation of suffering. A better argument for punishment is deterrence. If punishment of the guilty reduces the likelihood that they or others will repeat the offense, then in fact the practice should reduce the amount of suffering in the world. Does punishment have this effect? The question has been debated for centuries, and the weight of evidence is against the efficacy of punishment as deterrent.

"Punishment," like other widely used terms we have discussed, has acquired several meanings. The basic meaning that we find in political, theological, and legal philosophy points to socially endorsed practices that deliver a hurt of some kind to a person who has earned that hurt.[17] We also speak of "punishing" journeys, contests, efforts, and struggles of all sorts, but here we mean simply that the odds are great and the effort painful. No desert is involved, unless those punished can be said to have incurred the wrath of the gods. In still another sense punishment refers directly to what the dominant do to subordinates to get their obedience. In animal studies the abusive behavior of males toward females is often called "punishment." As Michael Ruse points out, "There is an all-too-easy chain of inference from 'punishment in humans is good' to 'punishment is natural' to 'punishment includes beating up females for sexual ends,' and the reverse inference back again."[18]

The "reverse inference back again" is especially interesting. Because the infliction of pain in nonhuman groups acts to keep subordinates in line, it might be supposed that the same tactics will work among humans. And they might! But the fact that they work does not necessarily make them ethically justified. We have to know what they are working toward, what undesirable side effects often appear, and whether there are better ways to accomplish the ends we deem desirable. It is not enough to say, out of context, "they work."

The literature on child development provides overwhelming evidence that authoritarian methods—methods characterized by the use of power and threats of punishment—are largely ineffective in producing internalization of the desired standards.[19] It is also well documented that punishment is not used at all in many good homes. When it is used in good homes or schools it usually takes the form of temporary denial of some expectation that is contingently legitimate; that is, a child may be denied some expressed need that would be honored if he or she were in good standing. In such cases the children are not treated under rules of negative desert; rather, they are helped to understand that they have not met the requirements of positive desert.

Positive desert is not to be confused with bribery. In bribery we offer someone a reward for doing something that a) she should not do at all, b) she should do without reward as part of her regular duties, or c) we want for ourselves. In contrast, when we remind a child that he has not yet earned some benefit, we pledge support for the result *he* desires, not merely one that we want for ourselves. The behavior upon which the reward is contingent falls within the range of acceptability already established, and the desired result (a reward) also is recognized as within the second level of legitimate expectations.

Readers may wish that I would lay out specifically the kinds of expectation that lie in this range of "legitimate but not basic." I cannot do this. Every family, community, and school must do this for itself. I refer readers to the criteria I set out earlier. Using these, we must decide what expectations are legitimately contingent. I would add to those criteria that when a child's expressed need is used as a focus of social control, those in power must be sincere in their expressed support for the child's success; it must be possible for the child to earn the reward that is temporarily withheld.

Before ending this chapter I want to remind readers that the descriptions of adult guidance offered here are not free of culture, nor are they so intended. I have been exploring the practices of ideal families (and near-ideal families) in a liberal democracy modified by a theory of care. Empirical claims for the effectiveness of certain child-rearing practices are tied closely to the kind of society for which they are designed. There is no claim that they are best in a universal sense, and there certainly is no claim that "we" who belong to the dominant culture have nothing to learn from other cultures. The test for our recommendations is twofold. The first is universal; the second is specific to liberal societies:

1. Will what is recommended contribute to the establishment, maintenance, or enhancement of caring relations?
2. Will those in our care fare better in this society?

The primary test is the first. A positive answer to the second can be negated or severely weakened by a negative response to the first.

In this chapter we discussed the difficult task of shaping an acceptable child. We noted that the best homes not only guide children toward norms they should accept but also help children to understand why these norms have been established and how they function. In addition, the best homes encourage children to reflect on the norms and rules that govern their behavior. Consolation is offered when rules are oppressive and cannot be easily changed.

We discussed an important distinction between deserving pain and bringing pain on ourselves. No one, I argued, deserves the deliberate infliction of pain, but all of us—through carelessness, ignorance, or moral lapses—sometimes bring pain on ourselves. Under the best conditions we learn from these experiences. The best homes reject the notion of negative desert (the idea that one who has done wrong deserves pain) and use positive desert (an incentive for doing what is acceptable) instead. Carers do not inflict unnecessary pain but, rather, offer to remove it, relieve it, or offer consolation for it. In the next chapter we will concentrate on how children learn to care.

CHAPTER 10

Learning to Care

In caring for children, parents and teachers hope that they will grow strong physically, intellectually, and emotionally by learning to care about their bodies, intellectual objects, and themselves as feeling organisms. Parents and teachers also want children to develop the capacity to care for other human beings. How children become caring individuals through their encounters with other selves is the primary concern of this chapter. I begin with a discussion of interdependence that emphasizes the roles of both carer and cared-for. Next I consider ways in which to educate the caring response, and, finally, I return to Dewey's concept of growth—this time to analyze its weakness in the moral domain.

Interdependence

The caring relation, as I have defined it, requires a contribution from both carer and cared-for. Parents and teachers recognize the contribution of the cared-for, at least implicitly, when they express their own delight with responsive infants, children, and students. Indeed, caregivers at every level find their work more satisfying when the recipients of care respond positively in some way. A smile or cuddle from an infant, a look or nod of gratitude from an older child, a sigh of relief from an elderly patient—all contribute to the maintenance of caring relations. In classrooms, eager hands raised, suggested projects pursued, and expressed needs to read or question are the kinds of responses by which teachers judge their own effectiveness. Imagine what it would be like to face a classroom full of sullen, apathetic, or even hostile students. The teacher's first task would be to overcome the apathy and hostility.

An appreciation of interdependence is central in learning to care, and a first step in acquiring this appreciation is to have one's own contributions acknowledged. To say to a child, "It's so much fun doing this with you," or to a class, "You folks make the effort worthwhile," is an explicit acknowledgement of interdependence. Too often we fail to express an appreciation, yet we are quick to voice our disappointment when the cared-for does not respond. We recognize our interdependence by blaming the other person for failing to respond, but we merely take for granted the response when it occurs. This attitude is part of a long legacy from Aristotle and others who believed that love and appreciation are required *from* the less powerful *for* the more powerful. This attitude is revealed when we, as parents and teachers, think that our children and students should be responsive and appreciative because we are doing something for them.

A recognition of interdependence suggests the obvious need for appreciative response in both directions. The contribution of the cared-for to the caring relation should be discussed. Specific responses should be acknowledged, and the general phenomena should be discussed as well. How does someone feel when nothing she does seems right? How does a teacher feel when, day after day, she is treated as an outsider, someone not to be trusted? Why do we enjoy being with some people so much more than with others?

Appreciation of interdependence should be extended into the wider world. Children need to see that salespeople, service workers, and all other legitimate workers should be treated with courtesy and, when appropriate, with gratitude for their contributions. Notice that this need starts as an inferred need, one that some of us suppose is a need for everyone. Our hope is that it will become an expressed need and that our children will want to recognize their interdependence.

Possibly no aspect of interdependence is harder to recognize than our shared responsibility for injuries that are inflicted on us. Several examples of shared responsibility were considered in chapter 9. We noted that when we give up, or at least minimize, the notion of negative desert, we shift to an attitude of analysis. What might we have done to bring this on? What positive incentives might be offered to change the perpetrator's attitude?

Many people have no patience with this approach. They want an attitude that is "tough on crime," even the small crimes committed in ordinary homes. We take great risks when we use methods that deliberately inflict pain, for the reaction against pain is more often anger than remorse. If our objective is to reduce pain, not to balance it with pain to the perpetrator, then we would do better to think of consequences and engage in analysis. Especially at home, where children's infractions are likely to be less than criminal, we would do well to avoid the violence of inflicting pain. In his study of violent prisoners James Gilligan observes that "the use of violence as a means of resolving conflict between persons, groups, and nations is a strategy we learn first at home. All of our basic problem-solving, problem exacerbating, and problem-creating strategies, for living and dying, are learned first at home."[1]

Taking an attitude of analysis does not imply that victims of wrongs must submit to abuse and become martyrs. On the contrary, the purpose of analysis is to prevent further harm. Lamb recounts many cases in which women brought abuse on themselves.[2] This does not mean that they deserved their pain or that the perpetrators did not deserve blame. It means that other women, in a situation roughly similar, would have avoided the abuse by knowing how to handle the situation. The woman who invites abuse and the one who avoids it have very different histories of encounter. It is a problem for social analysis to study the pattern of encounters in various groups and what, if anything, society can do to improve these patterns. It is an individual's problem to analyze one's own encounters and exercise some control over them.

Consider an example. Ann, a college student, is invited by Jack to attend a fraternity party. Ann does not know Jack well, but she is attracted to him and would like to know him better. She has heard rumors that the "date-rape drug" often appears at this fraternity's parties. Should she take a chance, telling herself that she "can handle it"? It would be wiser for Ann to tell Jack that she would like to meet him in a different setting, that she's heard about the frat's reputation and would prefer to avoid the party. If Jack is a decent man, probably both will start the relationship with respect for each other.

Suppose Jack finds a way to drug Ann's drink in the alternative setting? Does Ann still share the responsibility? Of course not. Here is where we so often go wrong in establishing policies or trying to push a theoretical position too far. Jack is a bounder and bears full responsibility for his act. Even so, without agonizing over what she "did to deserve this," Ann might spend a little time in analyzing the situation. Were there signs that might have warned her about Jack's character? In the larger community the task of analysis is more extensive. What is it in Jack's background that has produced such behavior? What can education do to reduce the number of these occurrences?

The position taken here is one of moral interdependence, and it is very different from traditional moral theories. Kant, for example, insisted that it is "contradictory" for one person to take responsibility for another's moral perfection.[3] But care theory points out what we all know about human interactions: how good I can be depends at least in part on how you treat me. When someone consistently brings out the worst in me, I have to analyze the situation for what each of us contributes to a pattern of behavior I deplore. Both of us have responsibility for the relation that, in part, defines us as selves.

Discussion of those who bring out the worst in us points up another weakness in the traditional emphasis on autonomy. If I am autonomous, I should be able to resist pressures that push me in a direction I abhor. I can't always do this. Do we then say that although I have the capacity for autonomy, I don't always exercise it? That doesn't seem to get us very far. Perhaps I should say, instead, that the behavior I deplore in myself is entirely justified when interacting with this clod. My reactions *are* chosen, and I can defend them. This, too, seems an unhappy mistake for, in choosing this position, I choose to continue to build a self I do not admire. It's not that I am denying a "true" self; I have already rejected that idea. The self I build in encounter with others is as nearly a true self as we can find. With some reflection I can at least prevent the kinds of reaction I regret from becoming habitual. Better, I can experiment a bit to see whether changes in my behavior might induce changes in the other's behavior. I might try to strengthen the relation. Again, a conscientious person faced with this problem can go too far with analysis and effort. Sometimes avoidance is the answer. That, too, is a way of controlling encounter.

Another aspect of interdependence is revealed in the satisfaction of needs. In chapter 9 legitimate expectations were separated into two categories: those associated with basic needs and those associated with certain nonbasic wants. The legitimate expectation that basic needs will be met should never be violated, but other legitimate expectations may be contingent. Whether a family or other social group satisfies these expectations may depend on the standing and/or effort of the one expressing the need. For example, it may be legitimate for an adolescent in a given family to expect help in buying a car when she graduates from high school. The expectation derives its legitimacy from a family history:

perhaps older siblings have enjoyed such a benefit, and the family has the resources to provide it. Still, this expectation may be denied if the adolescent has fallen short of the concomitant expectations for acceptability. The best homes recognize that the satisfaction of some nonbasic needs is itself a basic need, but this does not commit them to satisfying each such need as it is expressed, nor does it preclude their establishing conditions for the fulfillment of particular needs.

Earlier I asked why we should not give a child everything he wants when our resources allow such munificence, and the answer seemed to be that we fear for the child's future happiness. A child who does not learn to delay gratification, to work for things he wants, and to reconsider and establish priorities is likely to be a disgruntled and deeply disappointed adult. A more practical answer would be that resources are rarely sufficient to meet the wants of every member of a social group. Children have to learn not only to prioritize their own wants but also to consider those of others. Family meetings at which wants are discussed might be very valuable. Has a want met the criteria for consideration as need? Are there other needs more pressing? What are the ways in which the need might be met? Faced with a pressing need expressed by one member, are others willing to delay satisfaction of their own? Does everyone understand that basic needs must be met first? The aim, again, is an understanding of how thoroughly interdependent we are.

Homes must also do something to avoid the kind of encounters that reduce our sense of interdependence. Homes are usually better than schools are in avoiding pernicious competition—the kinds of situations in which the success of some depends on the failure of others. Better homes do not induce competition by comparing siblings or encouraging competitive sports that undercut the spirit of cooperation and healthy growth. Some homes, good in many respects, foster a highly individualistic and competitive attitude as part of the "American way." Others, very few, reject competition almost entirely. Both positions may be held unreflectively. As part of their work in helping young people to understand the disciplinary power that conditions them, parents and teachers should urge students to analyze competition and its effects. Competitive events can be fun, and they can inspire greater individual effort. Elsewhere I have suggested three criteria by which a participant may judge the worth of competitive activities: Is the activity still fun? Am I getting better at doing this or at something to which these skills contribute? Can I take pleasure in the victories of my opponents?[4] To these criteria for individual judgment, I would now add two for the social groups that support competitive activities: Do the participants appreciate the interdependent nature of the activity? That is, do they understand that opponents are as much a part of the enterprise as teammates and, as such, are to be appreciated? Are the participants growing morally as well as physically, intellectually, or artistically?[5]

The best homes reject ruthlessness and greed at every level, but they do not necessarily reject competition entirely. We (members of industrial and postindustrial societies) live in a capitalistic culture, and capitalism, like liberalism, has both positive and negative moral features. Rather than condemn it verbally and continue to live by it because we feel powerless to eliminate it, we should find ways to modify it. In taking this approach we avoid hypocrisy, and we bring our reflective action into line with social reality. Instead of trying to stamp out the competitive spirit, we direct it, control it, study it, and balance it with an appreciation of cooperation that clearly establishes a priority of cooperation over competition.

Here again we see how an ethic of care shows important elements of an ethic of virtue. We are concerned to develop certain virtues in the recipients of our care because we *care for* them and want the best for them. We work to develop other virtues in them because we *care about* the whole web of care and want to maintain it. Thus we must ask how best to develop attitudes and habits that will enable our children to recognize and live by what is understood about moral interdependence, material interdependence, and social interdependence.

Educating the Response

A caring response is the centerpiece of an ethic of care, and the capacity for such response is developed in the best homes and schools.[6] Again, we notice a strong similarity between care ethics and virtue ethics. Both consider a wide array of virtues, not just moral virtues.[7] One reason for this is that moral virtue develops alongside other virtues and is not easily separated from them. Some virtues associated with social life—congeniality, civility, cultural sensitivity, patience—are not, strictly speaking, moral virtues, yet, as David Hume pointed out, they contribute substantially to moral life. Indeed, we might agree with Hume and try to avoid the word *virtue* entirely, preferring to speak of *qualities*.[8] But *virtue* is so widely used and so important in both traditional and current writing that I will continue to use it.

Other reasons for including virtues that are not universally accepted as *moral* virtues arise from the relational perspective. First, the great ethical aim of care ethics is to establish, maintain, and enhance caring relations. Virtues of the sort cited above play an important role in this work. Second, self and other are not so entirely separate in care ethics as they are in traditional ethics. Recognizing that the self is a relation, we find it hard to distinguish self-interest and other-interest. If what I do for another enhances the relation, I have done something for myself as well. This is not to say that the distinction disappears entirely. When a human being sacrifices his life for another, it would take an odd theoretical stretch to say that he has also contributed to his "self."[9] Similarly, it would be odd to say that someone who concentrates entirely on his own good is thereby contributing to the good of others through a relational self.

In the vast middle range of human interactions, much of what we do for others redounds to our own happiness, and at least some of what we do for ourselves contributes to the pleasure and well-being of others with whom we come in contact. The best homes, then, try to develop a wide range of admirable qualities in their members. In keeping with their emphasis on positive desert, they encourage recognition of the positive effects that accompany acts of care and the satisfactions that arise from the response of the cared-for. In addition to accepting and encouraging individual talents, even if they are not ones obviously associated with financial success, the best homes cultivate both aesthetic and moral sensibilities.

When we set out to cultivate admirable sentiments, we should be aware that no method or approach is foolproof. Philosophers have long sought methods by which to teach virtue or morality to the young and, of course, they have put a high priority on finding a theory that would be both comprehensive and empirically defensible. Socrates, for example, cannot decide whether virtue can be taught.[10] If it can be taught at all, he said, surely it must be taught by people who are themselves virtuous—those who have the knowledge we call virtue. But then, he asks, how is it that men we all recognize as virtuous (Themistocles is one example) have sons who are not virtuous? Socrates cannot even decide finally whether virtue is knowledge. We might argue in response that Socrates expects too much of any practical approach. Even if the underlying theory (if there is one) is consistent, the practice will fail occasionally. Our consolation has to lie in the fact that adults who try hard to be good themselves and who teach their children with care are more likely to produce good adults than will parents who are bad and/or treat their children cruelly.

Wanting to do a good job commits us to looking for strategies that may be helpful, but we know there are no guarantees. One such strategy, long used with mixed effects, is the use of stories. Some parents and educators, in the character-education tradition, choose stories for their inspirational power.[11] One difficulty with this approach is that the stories are often about heroes and, by definition, heroes are those who perform acts not expected of ordinary people. They can stand as models of perfection, but using them as such models risks an unfortunate response: I could never do that, so why try? Recall Orwell's comment that, as a child, he lived in a world where it was impossible to be good. Most of us today want to arrange the encounters of children in a way that will make it possible—even attractive—for them to be good.

We sometimes use stories to illustrate moral dilemmas. Instead of aiming at inspiration, we aim at enhanced thinking.[12] Children are encouraged to examine chains of events and decision points, to weigh values, to consider what they might do in a similar situation. One objection to this approach is that the stories are often too short, too lacking in affect, and too obviously contrived to have much impact. If we believe that moral people are regularly moved by good reasons, we might be attracted by this approach, but if we believe that people must *feel* something to be morally motivated, then we would have doubts.

There are moral education programs in schools today that use one or the other of these approaches and some that combine the two.[13] It is beyond the scope of this book to review them as carefully as they deserve. An obvious difficulty with any approach that sets out deliberately to teach morality or virtue is that it falls prey to the whole range of pedagogical difficulties. Has there ever in all the world's long history been a subject taught effectively to all children? Anything that we want everyone "to catch" must be a product of pervasive socialization, but then, of course, we encounter a problem discussed earlier: how far to go in encouraging the young to analyze and criticize their own conditioning. This is a problem that both better homes and better schools must tackle.

It would seem reasonable to work on every front for the development of caring and, at the same time, to encourage continual reflection on what it means and how to act on it. We can cultivate moral sentiments such as sympathy, concern, and joy in our relations directly by displaying them ourselves and by acknowledging acts that exhibit these sentiments.

Here again we walk a fine line between authenticity and a host of positions that are not so admirable; we don't want to play Pollyanna, nor do we want to produce a cadre of goody-two-shoes.

In schools moral sentiments can be cultivated in every subject. In music class, after listening to the Emperor Concerto or some other passionate piece by Beethoven, students might be invited to consider how Beethoven felt after he had been deprived of hearing the beautiful music he had created. A science class might be moved almost to tears by the story of Mary Somerville, a self-taught mathematician and scientist in nineteenth-century England. She produced fine scientific work, including a text that was used at Cambridge University, and she received many honors. Because she was a woman, however, she was deprived of the most basic privileges that would have been granted a man. David Noble observes: "Her book was used as a required text in a university in which she could not teach nor have her daughters study. Her bronze likeness was placed in the Royal Society's Great Hall, from which she herself was barred."[14] Toward the end of her long life, having overcome obstacles that many students today can hardly imagine, she declared that she had "intelligence, but no genius. . . . That spark from heaven is not granted to the sex, we are of the earth, earthy, whether higher powers may be allotted to us in another existence God knows, original genius in science at least is hopeless in this." Noble comments, "Her despair haunts us still."[15]

Teachers and parents who make an effort can find a host of stories that both arouse feelings of deep sympathy and also stimulate criticism. In addition, these stories make up a good part of what we call cultural literacy, and they are learned incidentally ("when they aren't trying to teach us," as Casaubon, Eco's character, said). No reasonable person would argue that all learning should be incidental, but it would be equally foolish to ignore the power of "untaught lessons."[16] If we are deeply concerned that our children grow up as people who care for others, we must provide opportunities for their development as carers within all learning contexts.

As we try to educate the caring response in every subject that we teach and in a myriad of everyday activities, we contribute to the construction of an ethical ideal. At the core of this ideal is a habitual self that is caring. Under ordinary circumstances a person educated as a carer will respond as a carer. He or she will not have to refer to a principle to decide where duty lies. Such a person will have to deliberate about exactly what to do, but the inclination to respond in some positive fashion will be strong. Even so, there will be times when — tired, fed-up, turned-off, or disgusted — one will resist caring. The inclination has fled. At these times one needs the ethical ideal that is built up in long practice as a carer. A carer learns to ask: What would I do if I felt better? If this person were less obnoxious? If I had time?[17] The answer may still not be as positive as it might be with a more deserving cared-for or at a more propitious moment, but it is guided by the capacity for caring already developed.

We cannot expect that children will build their ethical ideals without help. Neither can we expect that, at some magic age, they will become fully rational and capable of summoning the moral law that is supposedly within each of us. Nor can we suppose that rationality will bring a sense that every person should count as much as every other. Indeed, this utilitarian expectation flies in the face of universal legitimate expectations. If I cannot expect more from my mother than from any other woman, my life is diminished. Neither Kantianism nor utilitarianism is empty of insights, but they are both weak on moral motivation. We act morally because we are moved to do so and, in large part, this occurs because we have an ideal of caring that may be consulted. Further, this ideal is a reality; it exists as part of the self and requires only activation.

I do not mean to minimize the problem of "activation." Just as we reject a principle or rationalize our ordering of principles, just as we may find it impossible to summon a moral sentiment, we may reject the tug of our own ethical ideal. Still, there is no escape through logical reordering or rationalization when we do this; we cannot claim emotional incapacity. We have to confess, "I was not myself." Of course, ever afterward that regretted act *is* part of one's self.

When we fail to act in accordance with our own ethical ideal, we feel guilty, and this guilt is usually a healthy sign. We are trying to build a self that is consonant with that subset we call our ethical ideal, and every response that violates the ideal contributes to a different sort of self. Thus, under a healthy feeling of guilt, we try to make restitution, and we analyze the situation that gave rise to the undesirable response. Perhaps our response was justified, and we should not feel guilty. Perhaps the other party really was at fault, and even a saint would have been sorely tried. But something still nags at us. If we had been clearly wrong, the next step would be apology and restitution — but what do we do when we are quite sure that we were *not* wrong? If our focus is on justification, we should be finished with the incident. In the care perspective, however, our focus is not on justification. We may go through the same mental procedures, find ourselves innocent (or nearly so), and still have two problems. How do we maintain a caring relation and how do we behave in the future to preserve and enhance a caring self?

In some situations the best course of action is to control our encounters more tightly. If Mr. D consistently brings out the worst in us, we might try to avoid him. Notice that a lack of encounter does not automatically destroy a caring relation. The relation sits empty without encounter. If Mr. D addresses us, we have to respond, of course, and take responsibility for our response. But avoidance, if we can manage it, may give us time to gather our ethical strength and create new strategies for the next encounter.

I have spoken here of "healthy" guilt. When is guilt unhealthy? The direct answer is that guilt is unhealthy when it persists without justification, when we blame ourselves even though disinterested observers would find us innocent. It is not our being troubled that is unhealthy here; it is the focus of our concern that is wrong. When we have gone through the mental deliberations characteristic of a search for justification and found good reason for holding ourselves innocent, we can make one of two mistakes: We can go on blaming ourselves anyway, or we can conclude our examination without the crucial analysis of relations discussed above. Either course of action is unhealthy. The first is clearly a case of unhealthy guilt; the second is a form of inauthenticity that leaves something nagging at us that is at once rejected by rational argument but sporadically entertained by feeling. This, too, is unhealthy guilt. It should be replaced by practical analysis. Unfortunately, there are tragic events that force unhealthy guilt on innocent moral agents. The death of a child, for example, may cause this sort of tragic guilt in a parent.

Now the question arises whether we should encourage children to feel guilt for their trespasses. I think the answer is yes, but it is necessary to distinguish between guilt and shame. I will make no attempt here to defend a particular definition of shame, but *if* we define it as a form of public condemnation, one of dishonor or disgrace, then I would recommend against shaming children. Guilt, as I am using it, is an internal sense that I have wronged someone or transgressed against the beliefs I have agreed to uphold. It may be impossible, in some cases, to avoid a sense of shame when I encounter my own best self after an egregious offense; that is a matter to be worked out, perhaps with solicited help, by each moral agent. But we should avoid the deliberate infliction of shame in the public arena. Guilt, aided by caring analysis, may encourage restitution and a determination to do better next time. Shame is more likely to induce resentment, anger, and even denial.[18] Having rejected the notion of negative desert, we must also reject the idea that one deserves shame (in the public sense), because such shame is a form of pain.

Another reason for rejecting shame is that it has so often been used to maintain questionable forms of honor. Violating the code of one's group has been a cause of shame although, clearly, some codes should be violated. Men who have been reluctant to go to war have been shamed; teenagers who have refused to perform the mandates of a gang have been shamed; children who have insulted Aunt Hilda have been shamed; boys who have confessed to fear have been shamed. Shame is a powerful tool of control, and, sadly, it works best on the conscientious. Invoked too often, shame no longer shames—it maims.

James Gilligan, too, notes that shame is damaging to self-esteem and that, when experienced frequently, it tends to deaden feelings entirely. It leads to violence because, simultaneously, one is angry at others for the infliction of pain and one is unable to feel the pain of others. Gilligan says, simply and with persuasive evidence, that a shame-ethic leads to violence.[19] He is not enthusiastic about a guilt-ethic either, because the desire to do violence is then directed inward. An ethic of care wants to prevent harm to the self as well as to others, and therefore we have to differentiate between what I have called healthy guilt and unhealthy forms. To feel healthy guilt is to want to do better for both others and oneself.

Gilligan and I are in agreement, then, that there are pathologies of guilt, and some of them have been encouraged by religious traditions that glorify pain. I would not advise a child who has been hurt by another child to "turn the other cheek." This reaction is likely to bring out the worst, not the best, in an attacker. In a deep sense it is a declaration of our own moral superiority—that we are willing to bear the pain that properly belongs to the guilty. If we reject the notion that anyone deserves pain, we commit ourselves to its elimination or alleviation, not its displacement from guilty party to martyr.

The best homes want children to feel guilty when they hurt others and to understand that they must, if possible, set things right. Unproductive agonizing is not encouraged, but guilt does produce degrees of agony. We feel bad, and should feel bad, when our deliberate or negligent acts hurt others, and I am not suggesting that simple recognition and restitution should restore self-respect and emotional balance. Such a view would qualify as a "banking concept" of morality: do something bad, do something equally good, and the account is balanced. No—the agony has its place. Its function is not to inflict an appropriate amount of pain on the guilty, however, but to fuel a new commitment to do better. In a sense one can never make up entirely for a wrong to another. It becomes part of both selves, and no subsequent act can cancel it out. One must do something to set things right, but "things" will never be what they were before the guilty act. The self records and retains every encounter that affects the organism.

This way of looking at things casts some doubt on the value of forgiveness.[20] When forgiveness is a product of loving generosity, it may well contribute to the maintenance or reconstruction of caring relations. If it is construed as a duty, one on which one's own status (perhaps even salvation) depends, it may have undesirable effects. First, if the forgiveness comes through a channel other than the one wronged, it may block restitution and the effort required to rebuild a relation. Second, if a victim is unable to forgive, he or she suffers anew—this time from what may be unhealthy guilt. Third, if one goes through the motions of forgiving, perhaps to fulfill a religious duty, she may incur all the bad effects of inauthenticity—repressed guilt, anger, rationalization, and denial. Finally, although religious doctrine suggests that our sins can be "wiped out," this doctrine does not sit comfortably with a relational ethic. Sartre was more nearly right on this: what we do becomes part of us, and nothing can wipe out what has been done.

The best homes help children to understand that caring involves responding as positively as possible when addressed. Forgiving in the form of making up, going on from here, understanding what drove the other is a central task in caring. The expectation of forgiveness should not be allowed to support negligence and deliberate harm. Children should learn something about the concept of moral luck.[21] For example, suppose A and B both treat a baby roughly—shaking it too hard. Suppose, further that the baby shaken by A suffers great damage, but the one shaken by B shows no signs of damage; indeed, B may be the only one who knows how badly the baby was treated. Is B less culpable than A, or is it just moral luck that B's baby escaped injury? Discussions of moral luck should help children (and all of us) walk more gently in the world.

Another side of moral luck is revealed when we recognize that selves are unique and that they are built from encounters, not all of which are under the agent's control. We act, but we are also acted upon. In chapter 4 I raised a question about the legal doctrine of equal, impartial punishment for a given crime. I said that although it seems fair to threaten me with the same punishment as A if we both, say, torture cats, there is something troubling about the law—namely, that I, as I am now, could not commit such a crime. Recognizing this crucial difference in selves should lead us to ask how A became a self for whom such an act is possible. It may indeed be my moral luck that saved me from becoming an A-like self. It is not that A bears no responsibility for his acts—of course he does—but in this thoroughly interdependent framework, others share responsibility for the self A has become. This is another reason to walk gently in the world.

Before leaving this section we should return briefly to the theme of care and coercion. Even in the best homes coercion is sometimes necessary. A parent may have to insist that a child make restitution for an object deliberately damaged or appropriated without permission. As in all cases of coercion, the need for it signals a consequent need for dialogue and, perhaps, negotiation. The caring relation is almost always shaken by coercion, and follow-up is required. When we coerce restitution, we are not trying to balance the scales of good and evil; we are trying to educate the caring response. We should not coerce forgiveness, for all the reasons already discussed, but we might encourage something like it by acknowledging generous gestures when they occur, and we might good-humoredly chastise a child who harps too long on another's faults. Again, the aim is to educate the response, and that effort includes the cultivation of social virtues as well as the more obviously moral ones.

A Moral Sense of Growth

In chapter 8 I discussed Dewey's use of "growth" as a criterion for education, and I concluded that it was useful for many of the decisions we must make as parents and teachers. Guided by Dewey's idea of growth, we ask whether a proposed course of action will open desirable possibilities, maintain the desire to learn and, generally, contribute to a better condition for both the individual and the community. But a problem nags at us: what do we mean by "better," and how do we decide when conditions are indeed better?

In much of his writing Dewey concentrated on the method of deliberation and left criteria of judgment to separate discussion. In *Ethics,* for example, he describes deliberation as "dramatic rehearsal"[22] and, in many places, he makes it clear that the methods of science may be used equally well in morals.

Deliberation is actually an imaginative rehearsal of various courses of conduct. We give way, *in our mind,* to some impulse; we try, *in our mind,* some plan. Following its career through various steps, we find ourselves in imagination in the presence of the consequences that would follow; and as we then like and approve, or dislike and disapprove, these consequences, we find the original impulse or plan good or bad.[23]

Now we know that Dewey does not mean to suggest that one person's idiosyncratic approval or disapproval makes an act good or bad, but he does not pause in this particular discussion to warn that, of course, we must have sound criteria for making these judgments. If we read a lot of Dewey, we know that he means to apply "social" criteria, especially those associated with democratic life, but we are still left with an uneasy feeling. It is rather like the feeling we get on reading about liberalism's "thin theory" of the good.[24] We know there is more to it than that — but what, exactly?

Dewey explores the possibility that Aristotle's "good man" may serve as a reliable judge, and he acknowledges that people often refer their moral dilemmas to "some other person in whose goodness they believe."[25] They ask what this model person would do or what he would think of them were they to do what they contemplate. In the end, Dewey says, "this method cannot supply the standard of their own judgment." It can, however, help "emancipate judgment from selfish partialities, and it facilitates a freer and more flexible play of imagination in construing and appreciating the situation."[26]

The worry here is, as it has been from the days of Aristotle, that children may pick the wrong exemplars. What, then, makes an exemplar a good or right one? I have argued that a moral agent must consult her own ethical ideal when the impulse to care does not present itself spontaneously. She must also consult it for criteria of judgment as she deliberates on what to do. It is this best self that must decide on what one approves or disapproves. It is the task of parents and teachers to help in the construction of an ethical ideal, and they do this mainly by cultivating the caring response. Of course, they do this in part by serving as models, but they do not pretend to be perfect models. They encourage thoughtful criticism, and they understand that children will construct their own ideals, at least in part, in opposition to those exhibited by exemplars. The ideals of both parents and children are under continuous construction.

We may agree with Dewey that Kant's separation of moral and empirical selves is a great mistake and that the separation of feeling from reason makes the Kantian ethic impossible to apply in any strict sense.

We may agree that the "happiness" by which utilitarians would have us judge our acts is too vague when applied to individuals and too easily subject to abuse (the sacrifice of a few for the good of many) and that the moral rules established by a society or culture must be used in educating the young, but should always remain open to review and change. Further, we may agree that the method of deliberation may be used effectively (up to a point) in moral problems as well as scientific, although an important difference between these two types of problems must be noted. In science the test of our success is whether our predictions are fulfilled, whether our ends are accomplished. In morals we must ask whether we should aim for certain ends at all. For this task we need moral criteria.

Moral criteria arise in the human condition. We need not manufacture principles that precede us in the world or lie beyond us in some transcendent realm. All normal human beings avoid pain and dread its extremes. From that widely accepted fact about human beings, we cannot derive (in a strict logical syllogism) a rule that says we should not inflict pain. Our capacity to reason is not limited to such rigid logic, however. It is fundamentally rational to abstain from inflicting pain and to alleviate it when we perceive it in another. That every human being desires a positive response (defined in a multiplicity of ways) suggests strongly that we should respond to others as positively as the situation and our capacities allow. The need for care should trigger a corresponding desire to care. That most human beings prefer the company of people who display the personal and social qualities described by Hume suggests again that we should try to cultivate these qualities—always checking their exercise against the fundamental response of caring. They have an honored place in the ethical ideal.

We might wish that Dewey had more consistently and explicitly built on the Humean concept of sympathy with which he closely agreed.[27] At the end of his chapter on reason in moral life he claims that sympathy is "the general principle of moral knowledge" and that it "furnishes the most reliable and efficacious *intellectual* standpoint." He concludes this way: "It supplies the tool, *par excellence,* for analyzing and resolving complex cases. . . . [I]t is the *fusion* of the sympathetic impulses with others that is needed; what we now add is that in this fusion, sympathy supplies the *pou sto* [a place to stand on] for an effective, broad, and objective survey of desires, projects, resolves, and deeds."[28]

It appears here that Dewey was so averse to anything that smacked of "foundations" that he resorted to the Greek *pou sto* rather than say straight out that we require a place to stand on. Caring supplies that foundation. It is a foundation without prescribed dimensions, open to the use of a wide variety of materials, subject to correction in the exchange characteristic of interdependence, and necessarily enhanced by a superstructure of intellectual, emotional, and spiritual qualities. Moral growth, in the care perspective, requires the education of the caring response.

In this chapter we discussed how children learn to care. We put great emphasis on moral interdependence—our shared responsibility for the moral strength or weakness of each member of our society. In "educating the response," caring parents and teachers provide the conditions in which it is possible and attractive for children to respond as carers to others. We show them how to care. Children educated in this way gradually build an ethical ideal, a dependable caring self. A society composed of people capable of caring—people who habitually draw on a well-established ideal—will move toward social policies consonant with an ethic of care. We explore that possibility and what it involves in part III.

Part Three

TOWARD A CARING SOCIETY

Interlude

In part II we established a foundation for social policy making by starting at home. We saw that all homes present certain features and encounters. All provide shelter, support certain attitudes about places, objects, and bodies, introduce the young to other selves and ways of interacting, and train the young to some standard of acceptability. Ideal homes universally provide protection as well as shelter, offer an adequate supply of material resources, encourage growth, have at least one adult who does the work of attentive love, and educate for a form of acceptability that is simultaneously adapted to and critical of the cultural standards in which the home is located.

In the western liberal societies to which my analyses are confined, each of these features can be described in more detail. Ideal or best homes in these settings are continually under construction. No ideal is permanent or, even at a given time, fixed beyond question. The one fixed element — and this is perhaps universal — is that every member of such a home can count on the response "I am here" when he or she calls.

I have suggested that ideal homes recognize and encourage a healthy attitude to the body and its pleasures, to places as extensions of the body, to living things and our natural surroundings, to material objects, buildings, and the like, and to the reasons that all of these things are important to us.

All good homes resist cruelty, but for the best homes every act of coercion raises a question. Many acts of coercion are artifacts of power and expedience, not of responsibility toward the cared-for. There are times when, because we *are* responsible, we must use coercion. When it is used in the best homes, it is followed by negotiation. The person in control helps the one who is controlled to understand why coercion is necessary, and she negotiates conditions that make the use of force more palatable and more profitable. The aim is always to shift more control to the one who is more dependent, but there is no denial of interdependence. Responsibility trumps autonomy.

Again, all good homes put an emphasis on shifting the locus of control from the stronger and more mature to the weaker or less mature, but the best homes retain and promote the idea of shared responsibility. They do not divide the world either into those who stand on their own feet and those who must lean a bit on others, or into the entirely good and the thoroughly evil. Such homes make an important distinction between negative desert and bringing unwelcome things on ourselves, and they reject negative desert almost entirely. No one in an ideal home deserves the deliberate infliction of pain. When one person hurts another, the conversations and decisions that follow are aimed at restitution, at understanding what happened, how each party might have behaved differently, and how similar future events might be prevented. Healthy guilt is encouraged; unhealthy guilt and shame are minimized.

Growth is encouraged in all good homes, but the best homes have more flexible ideals. Most middle-class parents want their children to achieve a level of financial success compatible with contemporary standards for the reasonably well-to-do. This understandable desire often leads to coercion that is unhealthy for both the children who are coerced and for the society in which they will live. Why should skilled tradespeople be less highly valued than members of a profession? The argument I have offered has little to do with markets and salaries. It focuses on self-esteem, job satisfaction, and social appreciation. A society that does not value all of its competent workers is a sick society, one mired in self-deception. Thus the home that denigrates a young person's well-informed choice of occupation injures both child and society.

The ideal home is continually negotiating between expressed and inferred needs. Children do have impulses that need restraint; they do sometimes misunderstand what is in their own best interest. Some children should be urged strongly to engage more fully with academic work; some should be praised for following a different path. As Dewey rightly pointed out, teaching and parenting are hard, time-consuming work. There are no recipes.

Perhaps the greatest difference between homes that are "just good" and the best homes is the emphasis in the latter on understanding how we are all conditioned. The best homes do not flout social etiquette and rules of behavior, but they discuss—often with humor, sometimes with dismay—why it is usually best to know and follow these rules. They leave open the possibility that some rules should be broken and that some should be changed. They do not try to internalize the stern father as a conscience but to educate the caring response.

The ideal home in a liberal, democratic society does not reject all of the liberal tradition—it would be foolish and hypocritical to throw away hard-earned rights and a tradition of open discourse—but it rejects the individualism and emphasis on autonomy that characterize liberalism. The caring home also modifies the liberal attitude towards coercion. It is willing to use coercion, even on adults, if the move is necessary for the good of those coerced, but it is far less inclined to use coercion on children than are most homes in liberal societies. Starting at home, we see that liberalism is itself a product of a certain mode of upbringing. The improvement offered here is an approach that puts a realistic emphasis on interdependence, on understanding and appreciating an inevitable heteronomy, and on learning to care.

Nothing I've said should be interpreted to mean that material resources are unimportant—that, for example, the poor should learn how to raise children properly and all would go well for them. On the contrary, material well-being is of fundamental importance. Neither should there be complaints that my descriptions are dismissive of minority cultures because they are culture bound. Those recommendations that are frankly culture bound are offered as best bets—as ways of enabling children to function well in a liberal society modified by an ethic of care. It would be irresponsible to say that all ways are equally facilitative and to hide what we've learned under the hypocritical guise of respect for other ways. I'll say much more about this in the chapter on education.

As we move to a discussion of social policy the question will be how far we can take the ways of ideal homes into policies that will work in the larger world. We are not seeking a perfect plan or theory that can be set down without change upon a social arena, but we hope that what works at home may help us to do better in the world.

CHAPTER 11

Developing Social Policy

Having laid out a description of life in ideal or best homes, one might be tempted to write a utopian tract on social theory. My point is not to describe a perfect society, however, only one that might be better. To attempt a wholesale transfer of life in ideal homes to the wider world would be, in effect, to imagine a utopia, and the description would encourage both snorts of disbelief and the sort of wary dread produced by behaviorist and socialist utopias.[1] There is no such danger here. In describing best homes I left room for mistakes and shortcomings—losses of temper, shared blame, acts of coercion not strictly necessary, doubts about the importance of inferred needs and the good of expressed needs. Further, to attempt a wholesale transfer would be to destroy the special nature of homes. The world at large, even the small community, is not a home. Nevertheless, some of the attitudes acquired in homes—ways of responding, of controlling encounters, of coming to understand—may profitably be tried out in the larger world.

Our questions now concern what part of life in ideal homes can be transferred to the wider world, and how what has been learned there may guide social policy. This chapter concentrates on a general approach to social policy; it includes examples, but not in great detail. In some cases I suggest possibilities at a somewhat abstract level. Specifics should be filled out by those who work in particular fields, but my hope is that the suggestions made here will clearly proceed from what has been established in part II.

Chapter 12 will consider an expressed need—the need for a home—and its denial—homelessness—in considerable detail. Chapter 13 will attempt a similar analysis of an inferred need—social acceptability—and its denial—deviance—in some detail (not every form of deviance can be considered). Finally, in chapter 14, I will consider the changes that must be made in education if our society is to be transformed in the direction of caring.

The Basic Attitude

The basic attitude, one captured by the response "I am here," arises in the original condition. There we learn to feel secure or insecure, able to control events to a certain degree or unable to do so, willing to share both joys and burdens or selfishly protect our own good fortune. Gradually, we gain (or fail to gain) the capacity to respond to others, "I am here."

Social policy guided by the basic attitude would reject any principle or rule that makes it impossible for people in responsible positions to respond with care to those who plead for care or obviously need it. Lisbeth Schorr makes the important point that people in social services often complain that the system itself gets in the way of their best efforts. She says, too, that "in their responsiveness and willingness to hang in there, effective programs are more like families than bureaucracies."[2] This means that professionals must be trained to a high level of competence and trusted with a wide range of decisions. Social workers should be able to tinker, within limits, with amounts, deadlines, eligibility requirements, and the like. There should be no mandatory sentencing laws that effectively remove judgment from judges. (Even to say "take judgment out of the hands of judges" is a verbal absurdity.) Schools should not adopt zero tolerance rules and, if they already have them, they should abolish them. It is one thing to say that "we" will not tolerate certain kinds of behavior; it is quite another to insist on uniform penalties for infractions that cannot easily be categorized. If, for example, a child accidentally brings a sharp instrument to school (by, say, mistakenly picking up his mother's lunch box, which contains a paring knife), that child should not be subject to a penalty designed to reduce the threat of violence. Educators, like judges, need to exercise judgment.

Rigid rules are often justified in the name of impartiality: the same rules and the same penalties apply to everyone. At the practical level the administration of justice in the United States is not impartial, and that is one strong argument against capital punishment. But so long as impartiality is held as the ideal, we will continue to tinker with rules and penalties in the hope that reality can be made congruent with the theoretical ideal. Even at the theoretical level there is something obviously wrong with most applications of impartiality. Events that are similar on the surface involve very different selves and, thus, are really different events. Further, the penalties fixed before the fact assume not only that no one should perform certain acts but also that all persons are equally likely to perform them. This may be true for some small offenses—parking briefly in a loading zone, exceeding the speed limit a bit, failing to renew the dog's license on time—but it is not true for the great offenses against social order. There is a story to be told about the construction of selves who commit horrendous crimes, and this story should be taken into account both in the treatment of the criminal and in programs of prevention. Of course there must be broad guidelines specifying the seriousness of various offenses and describing a range of penalties for infractions, but within those broad guidelines each offender must be treated as a unique self. Professional discretion coupled with cycles of coercion and negotiation are necessary in both law and social work.

The clear danger in granting judgmental discretion to professionals is abuse of individual professional power, but the prevention of abuse through the removal of judgment institutionalizes abuse and leaves the whole system open to a charge of absurdity. The utopian answer to the possibility of abuse is to deny that, in the proposed utopian scheme, it will happen—"that never happens here." In a utopia guided by care theory, members of the caring professions would simply be immune to abuses of power. In actual life, however, provision must be made to curb both error and abuse, and one answer to the problem is the establishment of review boards or informal counseling groups. Judicial decisions are routinely open to appeal, but the process could be made more efficient and more instructive. Small groups of professionals in every occupation might be organized to monitor one another's work, make suggestions for reconsideration, and mediate disputes with clients. In teaching, for example, a teacher's grading might well be reviewed by two or three other teachers who might also make suggestions for remediation. Students, too, should be able to request a review when they are dissatisfied with a grade. Review boards should be regularly constituted in all the caring professions. These boards should provide protection for clients and both support and education for those making judgments.[3] A strong system of review boards, immediately accessible in the arena of decision making should, in addition to increasing fairness, reduce litigation and increase the general feeling that agencies and institutions are responsive.

We have not made use of review boards in education. Instead, distrusting the judgment of individual teachers, we have put greater emphasis on high-stakes testing in deciding whether students should be promoted, graduated, or awarded various credentials. This move has weakened the integrity of teaching, damaged student-teacher relationships, encouraged dishonesty, and opened the system to mockery when large-scale errors are uncovered.[4] It would be far better to rely on teacher judgment strongly backed by the evaluative review of a competent professional board.

The basic attitude, "I am here," should be encouraged by flexible guidelines and backed by peer support. To pursue the problems of applying the basic attitude to social policy, it seems reasonable to start as we did in the original condition, with a consideration of bodies, those complete physical mental organisms of encounter that give rise to selves.

Protection of Bodies

Plans for socialized or nationalized medicine are no longer confined to utopian tracts. Working models are in evidence all over the postindustrial world. Sooner or later the United States will follow. What stands in the way? Besides economic issues, two attitudes remain strong in the United States. First, there is a lasting dread of communism and everything it represents. People seem unable to sort out and adapt ideas according to their current worth. Instead they choose ideological positions and stay close to partylike lines. This is a problem for education writ large. Second, there is an unquestioning acceptance of competition. In moderation, competition makes us inventive and prosperous, but in its extreme version—in the "We're number one!" version—it makes us obnoxious, paternalistic, and shortsighted. Many Americans fail to see that people in other parts of the world compete successfully without insisting on being first and that these other people find our incessant bragging unattractive.

The "top of the heap" attitude also makes our generosity paternalistic instead of genuinely cooperative, and because this attitude blocks deep critical thinking, many of us really believe that we are "number one" in areas where we simply are not. It isn't unusual to hear someone proclaim that we have the best medical system in the world, but this is untrue if we measure its effectiveness by the widely accepted standards of, for example, infant mortality, life expectancy, and adolescent motherhood. We do have one of the world's most technologically sophisticated medical systems. If you have an exotic problem, this is the place to come, but if you are poor or troubled, you might get better everyday care in any of several other nations.

Our failure to provide universal medical coverage is, at least in part, an issue of caring. An ethic of care is based on needs. Carers listen and respond as positively as resources and moral evaluation will allow. At present, the care we provide is almost always in the spirit of charity, not in the recognition of interdependence. Edward Bellamy, in his very popular utopian novel of 1888, had some interesting words on this. Dr. Leete, his speaker from the year 2000, patiently corrects a young guest from the nineteenth century. Leete insists that in the society of 2000, members of the "incapable class" are not considered objects of charity. When his guest protests that they are, after all, incapable of self-support, Leete answers this way:

"Who is capable of self-support? . . . There is no such thing in a civilized society as self-support. In a state of society so barbarous as not even to know family cooperation, each individual may possibly support himself, though even then for a part of his life only; but from the moment that men begin to live together, and constitute even the rudest of society, self-support becomes impossible."[5]

I agree with Bellamy that every society is marked by the interdependence of its citizens, but I disagree that this mutual dependency is based on our deciding to live together. Our interdependence is part of the original condition and in no way a product of some social contract. We would not be "men" at all if we did not have one another to call upon.[6] Culture and individual prosperity sometimes lead us to believe that we are independent, but the reality is obvious to anyone who thinks deeply on it. This is surely an understanding produced in the best homes, and it can be used effectively in making social policy. The idea, entirely compatible with liberal economics, is to shift the balance of control to individuals where this is possible, but to recognize that all of us remain interdependent both economically and morally. We must logically reject the independent-dependent dichotomy.

Care of bodies—whole organisms—requires more thoughtful consideration in education, too. Debate often arises over a distinction between early childhood education and childcare, but every form of childcare provides encounters of some sort, and these can be educative or miseducative. To suppose that childcare can be responsibly provided without considering education is a mistake. A different sort of mistake is made by those who argue that we must feed inner city children in schools so that they can learn. The mistake here is in elevating cognitive outcomes over physical ones. We should feed hungry children because they are hungry,' because that is the need to which a caring society should respond. In the same vein, there are those who demand proof that certain early childhood programs "work," but they seem interested only in academic gains and threaten to cut off funding if such evidence is not forthcoming. A caring society wants for all its children what the best homes provide for their own.[8] This means that no child should be deprived of basic legitimate expectations and that every child should be given opportunities to satisfy legitimate contingent expectations. It does not mean that every child should study the same curriculum, meet one preestablished standard, or prepare for college. On the contrary, every morally acceptable talent and interest should be respected and encouraged.

In today's world any ethical discussion of bodies must include abortion and euthanasia. A complete treatment will not be undertaken here, but I should at least indicate how thinking from the perspective of care should proceed. First, an ethic of care as it has been developed here leaves matters open for responsible decision making, and *responsible* is interpreted in terms of exercising the capacity and competence to respond to needs. In making decisions about either abortion or euthanasia, we must consider needs throughout the web of care, but we must also carefully identify the greatest needs and the consequences that may follow from meeting them. Care ethicists may differ not only on their practical decisions but, possibly, even on the ultimate reasons they offer. For example, some may develop an ethic of care from a religious base, and God may appear in their reasoning.[9] The ethic of care developed here does not involve a god at all, but depends entirely on the basic relatedness of human life. God may or may not be a reality, but deity in any form need not be invoked in ethical life.

Why should a care ethicist allow abortion? Our answer is not given in terms of rights. We may believe that such a right should be granted under law, but we do not believe that any right "exists" before it is granted. Instead, we consider needs. The pregnant woman's needs are primary because it is she who must bear both the bodily burden and the burden to self. The decision should not be made lightly, and it should be well informed; it should be made early—before the fetus has developed the capacity to respond with its own characteristic human needs. If review and counseling boards are in place, the recommendation that a decision be well informed should not conflict with the general rule that it should also be made early. Any young woman who resists counseling—"I just want to get it over with!"—should be gently coerced to accept the counseling. The purpose is not to make her feel guilty about whatever decision she makes; on the contrary, the purpose is to help her make a decision she can accept as responsible.

Is there no one else in the web of care whose needs must be considered? Religious ethicists will likely identify the fetus as the one to bear the greatest burden. If abortion is chosen, it will not live to become a self. There is no denying this, and we should not pussyfoot about, using euphemisms. But what is killed is not a self. The fetus has had no encounters with other selves and objects in the world; it has not experienced the affects that are induced by these encounters. When we consider the astonishing prolificness of nature—all the animal embryos that do not come to full life, the seeds that do not germinate, the seedlings that die, the eggs that are never fertilized—we are filled with awe, but we don't seem to be troubled by an ethical issue. A woman who aborts a preresponsive fetus is eliminating a potential life, but, for that matter, a woman who lives a life of celibacy or of carefully controlled contraception is eliminating a host of potential lives. When an interested man is involved in the decision, his needs, too, should be considered, but cases in which the man desperately wants the child and the woman does not are probably rare. Similarly, there may be potential grandparents whose interests should be considered in making a well-informed decision. Full consideration of these interests might change the decision, but they should not be allowed to dictate it.

The complete dependency of the fetus on its mother-host underscores the relational nature of all human life and of ethical life in particular. If a woman wants the fetus as a child, if she cherishes it, an encounter of a sort already exists, but it is a one-way encounter: the mother has encounters, mostly in imagination and anticipation, and these encounters will influence the baby when it is born. If the woman does not want a child, the fetus has no status as a pre-self. Other individuals cannot say, "Well, *we* want it!" because to insist on its continued existence would override and ignore the expressed needs of the woman. Unrelated people who make this claim do not want the unique individual that the fetus will become. They are responding either to a principle, not to an individual, or to a personal need. In the latter case it is clear that no woman has a responsibility to bear a child for another. When a fetus is viable, the picture changes because others can now respond directly to the infant's needs.

This ethic of care leaves us uncertain as to final rules of action. It instructs us to respond to any organism in pain by relieving the pain and to respond to a human self by considering its needs and meeting them if possible. It does not pronounce once and for all that abortion is right or that abortion is wrong. It *suffers with* as it judges. If, after receiving the help that is required to make a well-informed decision, a young woman says, "I want to get rid of it!" a carer's response has to be, "I will help you." A carer would give the same response to one who decides to see the pregnancy through. It is part of what is meant when we say, "I am here."

Suppose, now, that an infant is born with enormous handicaps. Should we allow infanticide? I think an ethic of care can responsibly say, "yes, sometimes." Our reasons would be somewhat different from those of Peter Singer, who offers a utilitarian rationale for allowing parents to make this decision.[10] First, we would not argue from a calculation of the greater happiness that might be produced by the birth of a later, normal child. Our basic argument is that a society should not insist that one or two people (or a family) should bear long-time suffering in the name of a principle—the alleged sanctity of life. It is easy to mouth such principles, and it may be a matter of justifiable pride for medical technology to keep babies alive despite handicaps and deformities, but it is another matter entirely to hand over such an infant to its parents. If there is no possibility that an infant can develop the responses characteristic of normal human life, it would be a compassionate and caring move to kill the infant mercifully and allow the parents to get on with their lives.

Now, obviously, I am not saying that parents should be allowed to kill any newborn they don't want. I have already pled the case for a near-term fetus. As carers, we must respond to the expressed needs of the infant, but we are concerned with both current and future needs. The immediate needs of a normal infant are food, warmth, cuddling, and mild stimulation. Satisfying these needs contributes to the child's growth and to parental satisfaction through the infant's response. If the

child cannot grow and, especially, if it is in pain, then the merciful move
is to end its struggle for life. It is not only the infant who must be
considered here. There are parents who may be sentenced to a lifetime
of suffering, siblings who do not receive enough of their parents' attention as a result, and a whole circle of intimates who may be affected.

Several recent news stories and responses have dramatized the plight
of parents struggling to care for severely handicapped children. The help
that is said to be available to parents in this situation often requires still
more effort on their part. In addition to caring for their child, they are
often expected to join "help" groups, attend meetings, and give aid and
support to other sufferers. Further, the suffering of parents is often mis-
read as the children get older. The children suffer more, and what little
hope the parents might have had now fades entirely. One letter writer,
responding in sympathy to the story of parents who had left their child
at a hospital, wrote, "I have traded my freedom to be the primary care-
taker of my daughter. In the nine years since her birth, my husband and
I have never been away alone together."[11]

Safeguards should, of course, be instituted. A medical team, not just
one physician, should supply the prognosis of hopelessness, and the
parents—not the state—should make the decision. Parents who for religious reasons want the child to be kept alive should be respected. So,
too, should those who can't face the prospect of caring for a badly handicapped child or who see no point in doing so.

There will be debate on which conditions are so hopeless that infanticide should be allowed. Here Singer and I may differ again. I would
not name either hemophilia or Down syndrome as hopeless conditions
unless they were complicated by other conditions that would make the
construction of a human self impossible or would visit predictably in-
tolerable pain on the child. Indeed, I would be slow to name any one
condition that should evoke a decision to end life, although there are
some conditions that will spontaneously end life in a short time. Every
case must be considered in its fullness and specificity, and that means
considering the capacity and convictions of the parents. The test I would
use is this: if an infant can never become a self—if it will not be able to
communicate or in any recognizable way respond to human care—then
it is probably best for everyone if that life is not continued. The body,
after all, is the means of meaningful encounter, of making a self. If
meaningful human encounter is impossible, then mere life may be ter-
minated, and the unfortunate parents of the infant should not be made
to feel guilty.

It is worth noting here that although both Singer's utilitarian view and my care perspective allow killing a severely handicapped infant, there are important differences. Following the utilitarian argument to its logical conclusion, parents should feel *obliged* to terminate the child's life in order to secure the best possible ratio of happiness over pain. No such conclusion follows from the care view. Because we are primarily concerned with the needs of those suffering, we can support parents in either decision.

The case of incompetent, permanently damaged adults is similar in the problems it presents. The case must, of course, be medically hopeless and the patient permanently unresponsive. Now the family must be the concern of carers. Are they ready to let go? Will the patient's death release them from great stress and suffering? The needs of those actually suffering are the needs that must be met, and either decision—for continued mere life or death—must be supported.

The case for voluntary euthanasia is somewhat easier, but again, it is a decision requiring a team effort. The primary decision maker is the patient; medical staff give professional information and advice; family, too, contribute to the debate.[12] A stable, well-informed decision to die, when death is inevitable from the sufferer's condition, should be respected. Any other response bypasses the patient and addresses itself to a rule or principle.

All of these cases are complex and difficult, and—by discussing them in this abbreviated form—I do not mean to suggest that I have solved problems that involve great suffering, mental agonies, and real tragedy. I only intend to describe an approach—one that makes it possible for human beings working together to care for one another and reach responsible decisions.

The approach can be illustrated also in considering the problem of battered women. In chapters 9 and 10 I discussed shared blame and the important distinction between bringing pain on ourselves and deserving it. I noted that our society expects mothers to control their young children and that sometimes, predictably, tired mothers slap or spank their unruly children and then feel guilty about it. The guilt is appropriate, but it should not be aggravated by shame. Restitution is best made through an analysis of shared responsibility; both mother and child learn how to avoid violent reactions in the future. The case of battered women is very different. A husband or male partner is no longer expected to control his wife, and he has many alternatives (for example, leaving the house to cool off) that a young mother does not have. Therefore even a slap or a yank inflicted on an adult woman is a clear abuse and, because it demonstrates that one party is dominant and the other subordinate, it inflicts great emotional pain. Anything beyond a slap—any act that leaves bruises or other physical damage—cannot be allowed or excused whether the victim is a child or an adult.

Should social policy, then, endorse shared blame or responsibility when a male partner batters a woman (or, rarely, when a woman batters her male partner)? Is any such approach a case of blaming the victim? In a very interesting study of informal adjudication—Navajo Peace-making—Donna Coker debates these issues.[13] I agree with Coker that there are risks in openly analyzing cases of battering. The introduction of discussion may convey the false impression that the batterer's acts may be justified. Appropriately conducted sessions must make it clear at the outset that violence is not condoned—there must be no insistence on forgiveness—but it should be possible for the battered woman, both families (if they can be involved), and close friends to analyze their contributions to the problem and how they might help to prevent future occurrences. A procedure that involves a significant number of participants is hard for people in an individualistic culture to entertain. Coker is careful to point out that we need to use caution in borrowing from other cultures because the ways of one may not fit the ways of another.[14] Although this is true, we should not forego opportunities to learn from one another. Whether it comes from Navajo culture, African culture,[15] or a middle-class ethic of care, the idea of moral interdependence and shared blame is worth exploring.

One of the most obvious ways that women share responsibility for their own battering is by staying with their batterers. I said earlier that maintaining a caring relation does not require maintaining a formal relationship. It does not require one to continue living with a violent partner. That means that women must have alternatives—places where they and their children will be safe and where they can learn how to support themselves. This much is commonly accepted even when resources are inadequate to act on accepted knowledge. Resources must be increased.

More needs to be done. The relation must be transformed to one of nonviolence and, optimally, to one of care. Even if the relation remains empty—no encounters—for a considerable period of time, the aim should be for each party to understand his or her role in battering or allowing the battering to continue. The only lasting protection a woman has is for her batterer to feel genuinely guilty and give up the practice of battering. Too, it is *his* only hope for future, amicable relations. Further, her understanding of her own role should help the woman form new, healthier relations. For a real transformation to take place, members of the couple's inner circle will have to work with sympathetic, well-trained professionals. Again, we have to overcome our fear and distaste for intervening in the "private" lives of others. We intervene not just in the liberal spirit to keep a man from harming a woman, but in the spirit of care to save the woman from herself and the man from himself.

The process I have outlined has much in common with liberal philosophy. It emphasizes process rather than fixed goods. Its one exception—the insistence on caring relations as fundamentally good—makes all the difference because it allows us to intervene to prevent harms to self as well as harms to others. It does not pronounce abortion or euthanasia good or bad in any final or fixed sense; instead, it asks about their effect on caring relations. It favors policies that allow choices, but those choices are collaborative[16] and they are not anchored in rights. This is not to say that care ethicists do not ever use the language of rights. I have already acknowledged that we often do. But rights have a way of becoming entrenched and inflexible. As a result, debates on abortion and euthanasia often deteriorate to a conflict of rights. The modification made by an ethic of care directs us to consider needs. In doing so we must face up to the built-in conflict between expressed needs and inferred needs. This both broadens and deepens the practical debate and, in the most successful cases, leads to mutual understanding and a sense that the participants have done the best thing for all involved.

Because care theory is based on needs and responses, it is also experience-based in the sense that we must listen to what others are going through in order to respond as carers. Susan Behuniak argues that jurisprudence should be transformed to allow the inclusion of particular persons' experience.[17] She argues for an integration of care and justice in the context of abortion and physician-assisted suicide cases. Although I agree that a caring response to the plight of particular persons in their particular experience should be possible in law, I suspect that the transformation alluded to by Behuniak would go far beyond an "integration" of care and justice. Justice as a body of doctrine and practical guidance would itself be radically transformed if it were acknowledged that it arises from the "caring-about" that is firmly anchored in "caring-for."

Because we are discussing social policy and bodies, it would be reasonable to discuss capital punishment here, but I will defer that until the section on desert and moral interdependence. Similarly, I will put off discussion of homelessness for the next chapter. Here I do want to say a little about place and social policy.

Places

In the earlier chapter on places I suggested that the biophilia hypothesis might be correct. It may well be that most of us need to feel a connection with nature. There are exceptions, of course. Some individuals (Sartre seems to have been one) dislike the natural world and find greenery distasteful. Some groups, historically deprived of stable home places, show little attachment to natural places. Gerald Gamm notes that the Jews of Boston were not "territorial" in the way characteristic of Catholics: their place of worship was not necessarily connected to a residential neighborhood.[18] Yet it was the long separation from land and agriculture in the diaspora that led many Jews to establish agriculture as the main function of the kibbutz in Israel. Thus, although the longing can be missing in particular individuals and suppressed for centuries in groups, it seems to arise in most human beings.

It may not be enough to preserve large pieces of wilderness, although this should certainly be done for the sake of the plants and creatures that live there. It may not be enough to provide large parks in urban centers. If people need a connection to nature, then accessibility is all-important. Many small parks, neighborhood garden plots, fountains, and container plants should be provided. Small parks are easier to supervise, too, and can be used more safely by neighborhood children. Housing and zoning boards should be interested not only in how *much* open space is preserved but also in the number, quality, and placement of these spaces.

Schools are beginning to add gardens and greenhouses to their facilities, and I have seen some urban schools—where lack of space prevents such additions—fill their windowsills with plants. At home, at school, and in the community, children should be encouraged to make a connection to nature and to take responsibility for natural places. Thoughtful environmentalists know that care of the larger world starts with care of one's local space. Writing on a sound forest economy, Berry emphasizes local education. "[B]oth at home and in school, it would want its children to acquire a competent knowledge of local geography, ecology, history, natural history, and of local songs and stories. And it would want a system of apprenticeships, constantly preparing young people to carry on the local work in the best way."[19]

Peter Kahn points out that it is not enough "to provide urban children with good environmental education. We must also provide urban children with a good environment."[20] I would go further and say that good environmental education is probably impossible without a good environment. This means that not only schools but also homes, streets, neighborhoods, and commercial establishments should be planned to maintain and encourage a connection to nature.[21]

As we discuss social policy with respect to places, we must consider the bodies that will occupy those places. After World War II developers planned large residential communities, and they were asked to build schools that would accommodate the large number of children who would live in these new communities. Now perhaps it is time for builders to consider living arrangements for older citizens in their own communities. Why couldn't apartment buildings have whole floors or sections set aside for the elderly relations of families who will live there? In rural areas, why not subsidize small prefabricated homes that can be added easily to ample existing properties? Instead of moving steadily to "homes" and neighborhoods restricted to the elderly, it seems reasonable to use more imagination to find ways to keep the elderly in their home communities or to integrate them into the communities of their children. When we separate the elderly from their families and their friends, we lose both models of care and opportunities for younger people to care.

Even prisons should provide ways for inmates to connect with nature. It has long been a practice to allow "trustees" to work on prison farms. The practice in itself is evidence that we believe a connection to nature is highly valued by most people. We could consider forms of nature therapy. No person should be entirely deprived of connection to the natural world and, where such connection threatens security, a system of incentives could be established so that convicts have something definite and attractive (other than eventual freedom) to work toward. Again, some imagination is required, but even more, thinking along these lines requires a fundamental shift in attitude.

Desert and Moral Interdependence

We have seen that the best homes have almost no use for the concept of negative desert; they do not establish rigid rules and fixed penalties for infractions because every human encounter has unique features that must be taken into account. Expectations are both high and reasonable. Adults, in agreement, expect children to be present at dinner, to come home at agreed upon hours, to do the work assigned to them, to treat family members and guests with civility, and to respond with care to needs that they are competent to meet. In turn, all family members know that expectations associated with basic needs for food, shelter, clothing, medical care, and protection will never be denied. All members know, too, that some legitimate nonbasic expectations are contingent and may be withheld if a member fails to satisfy the basic requirements of acceptability.

No adequate social policy can ignore the bodily health and safety of its citizens. No good home would allow one of its members to live in misery because "he deserves it." Instead, it finds ways to reward the behaviors and attitudes it espouses. By providing care—doing the work of attentive love—it helps to teach care. Can a society use a similar approach in caring for its citizens?

A society based on what is done in the best homes will certainly reject social Darwinism. It could not argue that the poor deserve their poverty because they are naturally less fit. It could not declare that because infant mortality among some groups is nature's way of eliminating the weak we should accept this and thereby discourage the reproduction of "bad strains."[22] Instead, we are committed to meeting the needs of all human beings capable of expressing needs.

The United States lags behind many other countries in providing health care for all its people. We are even more backward in our retention and defense of capital punishment, and many of us are willing to execute even juvenile offenders. We join just five other countries in having executed young offenders in the last decade, and some legislators in this country are arguing to make the age of eligibility for the death penalty even lower.[23] The most persuasive argument for the death penalty is deterrence but, as Kotlowitz points out, the very young are least likely to be deterred by the threat of the death penalty, and there is considerable evidence that the death penalty is not effective as a deterrent.[24]

If deterrence is not a good argument, how about retribution? Do some people deserve to die? I used to think so, but even then I argued against capital punishment because I believed that the rest of us do not deserve to live in a society marked by state violence. Now I would argue that no one deserves to die. The cruelty and suffering that inevitably accompany the death penalty are avoidable only by abolishing it. No rule should be so fixed that we cannot respond to another's cry for help. It is incongruous to respond to someone who wants to live with "I am here" and "I am going to kill you."

Recall Orwell's comment on "the unspeakable wrongness of cutting short a life when it is in full tide."[25] Any chance a criminal might have to redeem himself in the world of humanity is ended. Given the obviousness of this end to all possibilities, one wonders why so many American Christians defend capital punishment. This is a dilemma explored by William McFeely.[26] He notes that lynching and an increased interest in religion appeared together in the 1890s, and he looks to the historian Donald Matthews for a possible reason. Matthews suggested that torture and death are central metaphors of the Christian religion and that perhaps only death can atone for perceived sins. Where, then, do the other central metaphors in Christianity—those of love and forgiveness—fit in? The correlation remains baffling. One would suppose that Christians would insist on giving every person a chance to redeem himself—at least as far as this is possible—in this world. Perhaps once again it is the otherworldly focus that stands in the way. Some Christians welcome confession, conversion, and the promise of divine forgiveness and remain staunch supporters of executions. They might argue that only God knows whether remorse and conversion are genuine, but the horror is that the perpetrator—hopeless and filled with a terror that he dare not admit—may not know himself whether his remorse is genuine.

Albert Camus argued persuasively that executions should be public.[27] People should see what their government has been allowed to do. Camus's own father permanently rejected his initial endorsement of capital punishment after witnessing an execution by guillotine. In 1957, disgusted that France, England, and Spain were the only nations in Europe outside the iron curtain to retain the death penalty, Camus argued that the practice of execution must be discussed—that "when silence or tricks of language contribute to maintaining an abuse that must be reformed or a suffering that can be relieved, then there is no other solution but to speak out and show the obscenity hidden under the verbal cloak."[28] He believed that witnessing an execution, hearing a head fall, would cause people to repudiate the death penalty.

Camus considered reforming capital punishment—that is, killing by lethal injection or even allowing the condemned person to do it himself in Socratic style. This, he said, would bring "a little decency" to a "sordid and obscene exhibition."[29] He suggested this, however, only as a compromise prompted by despair. We in the western world reject public executions, and we recoil in horror at accounts of people burned at the stake, gutted, torn into fours, decapitated, pressed, crucified, and otherwise tortured to death. We are aesthetically displeased when electrocution causes nosebleeds or minor fires and disgusted at stories of people choking on cyanide fumes. Thus governments have tried to find more and more fastidious ways of killing condemned criminals. The executions practiced in the United States are purportedly painless. This compromise has apparently made it easier to kill, and because the end itself is supposedly without pain, we can more easily ignore the months and years of psychological suffering that precede the final moment.

Both Camus and McFeely (and Orwell) argue that proximity to a condemned person and/or attendance at an execution should produce moral loathing of the death penalty. Reviewing McFeely's book, Russell Baker notes that, as a journalist, he was saved from observing an execution when a colleague took the duty for him. "He saw three men dropped through the trap and was sick for days."[30] This underscores the argument I made earlier—that if some criminals do deserve to die, the rest of us do not deserve what Camus calls the "weight of filthy images."[31]

A larger question remains: does anyone deserve to be deliberately killed? I would not argue, as Darrow did, that what people do is solely a result of conditioning and genetic accident and that criminals bear no responsibility for their acts.[32] I *would* argue that prior conditions, the encounters on which selves are built, have much to do with the acts that are performed at any time. It is not a matter of sole blame or no blame. It is a matter of holding a self largely responsible, partly responsible, or barely responsible; further, responsibility is rightly shared among individuals and by communities and whole cultures. Thus offenders have not earned the kind of rewards they might legitimately expect in a condition of acceptability, but a caring society cannot deprive them of legitimate expectations that are unconditional. Further, restitution should be our main aim. A murderer cannot restore the life of one he has murdered, but he can spend his own life preserving and enhancing other lives.[33]

When we reject capital punishment, are we forgetting the victims? This is an accusation often leveled at those opposing executions. The death of the perpetrator is said to bring closure and a sense that justice has been done for the victim's survivors. "Now it is finished," is a common reaction. Does an execution finish anything but the life of the perpetrator? Some of those who must participate are haunted for years.

Some of those who should be deterred are actually attracted by the possibility of being killed by a society they hate.[34] And all of us should be disgusted by people demonstrating enthusiastically outside prisons where executions are taking place: "Now he's going to burn, now he's going to fry, now he's going to shake, now he's going to die."[35] What sort of self accumulates and exudes such hatred?

The basic approach of an ethic of care, learned in the best homes, is one of response to the needs of the cared-for. It is captured in the response "I am here." An expressed need cannot always be met. Sometimes resources are lacking, and sometimes the need is only contingently legitimate. Sometimes, also, needs conflict. We cannot responsibly allow a murderer his freedom simply because he expresses a need for it, but we can allow his life to continue so that he can earn the satisfaction of some other needs. Expressed needs and inferred needs often clash. When we feel justified in using coercion to satisfy an inferred need, we must follow up with negotiation that makes the need more plausible and more likely to become an expressed need.

The caring approach implies shared responsibility. Behind every good or evil act, there is always a story. Some selves are clearly incapable of certain acts. How did they get that way? What encounters contributed to the present state? What interventions contributed to the good? Which to the bad? What did the cared-for do to sustain caring relations? How can child-rearing practices enhance the possibility that caring relations will develop more widely?

In the next chapter we will consider an expressed need—the need for a home—and its denial—homelessness—in considerable detail.

CHAPTER 12

Homes and Homelessness

In this chapter we consider how social policy should address a fundamental constellation of expressed needs. The constellation or related set
might itself be considered a basic expressed need, and I'll refer to it here
as the need for a home. We'll look first at the needs of the homeless
generally, and then, in a separate section, at the needs of the homeless
who are mentally ill. Finally, I'll suggest ways in which social policy
might better meet the housing needs of the working poor. Notice that
housing isn't exactly the word we want here. The need is for something
deeper, more basic, than mere shelter. But just as there is no word for
the one-who-needs that is nearly as dignified as *rights-bearer,* there is no
single word that applies to one who longs for a home or fears losing
what she has. *Homeowner* and *householder* are words of pride. What shall
we call one who longs for or needs a home?

The Needs of the Homeless

Social policy with respect to the homeless in America today concentrates
mainly on preserving life: it is directed at providing nighttime shelter
to prevent freezing and enough food to prevent starvation. Increasing
numbers of people have become specialists in dealing with the homeless.
Certainly these good people are not part of a conspiracy to maintain
homelessness; rather, as the availability of services grows, more and
more people are found to have a need for the services offered. Many

cities and charitable agencies have launched campaigns to increase the number of beds and shelters and to provide more soup kitchens. These measures are better than letting people freeze or starve in the streets, but they are clearly inadequate. The homeless need homes, not halfway measures that actually contribute to their continued homelessness.

We saw earlier that a home provides not only shelter and food but also a place from which, and in which, one claims an identity. The house—or a room, or a corner—becomes an extension of one's body. A human organism interacts with the building, the objects it contains, and its setting. In an ideal home every inhabitant beyond infancy has some control over doors—those physical objects and psychic symbols that close out the world, let others in, and allow ingress or egress for the individual controlling the door. There is a place to store one's belongings and cherished objects. There are people who respond to an individual's needs and who will make claims on that individual to respond to theirs. The home is created and maintained to promote the growth of all its members. It is a place of some stability and, for better or worse, it is a place where members can be found by the world and where they will be missed if they wander off.

A social policy driven by care theory will make finding homes for those now homeless its first priority. Its second priority will be establishing policies that ensure that those who have a tenuous hold on their dwelling places do not lose them. While this effort is being pressed, emergency services will, of course, be provided, but it should be emphasized that such services are like army field hospitals: they prevent death, but they do not provide a long-term cure or rehabilitation.

Sharon Quint, in a book that tells the wonderful story of a school principal who works with social agencies to find homes for her students, inadvertently underscores my point by quoting Joseph Johnson Jr., Texas's first State Coordinator for the Education of Homeless Children.

As America's public schools confront an increasing population of homeless students who present increasingly complex needs, schools have a choice. On the one hand, school staff can contend that they cannot or should not expand their services to address the needs of homeless children and youth. Perhaps other social service agencies should assume these responsibilities. Perhaps parents should be expected to do more. Perhaps the resources simply are insufficient. Perhaps the school cannot handle any more responsibilities. On the other hand, school staff can contend that they truly can make a difference. Perhaps the resources can be found. Perhaps it is primarily a change in attitude that is required. Perhaps school staff can insure that today's homeless children will not be tomorrow's homeless parents. Perhaps there truly is not a choice.[1]

Why, in a nation as prosperous as ours, should there be a "State Coordinator for the Education of Homeless Children"? Establishing such an office with such a title is chillingly Kafkaesque. Why not an office charged with finding homes for every family with children? When Johnson suggests, with the best intentions, that school staff "can insure that today's homeless children will not be tomorrow's homeless parents," he pulls the heartstrings of people who are highly susceptible to such calls. Educators, for the most part, are people who want to make a difference in the lives of children; that's why most enter the profession.[2] So they will try. A society that will not face its worst social problems — poverty, crime, and general misery — speaks romantically of the wonders education can accomplish. But schools cannot solve society's massive social problems and, as I will argue in the last chapter, they are not even allowed to teach those things that might help relieve social problems. Moreover, our objective should not be ensuring that homeless children today will not be homeless parents tomorrow. Our objective should be that there are no homeless children today.

The homeless need homes. This should become a working mantra of sorts. The homeless need an address so that they can register to vote, give appropriate information on medical forms, receive the benefits to which they are entitled, receive information, and be counted in the census. In even a minimally satisfactory housing situation there should be an information center on the site where people actually live. For example, small private bedrooms might be clustered around an open space containing reading material and computers. Recognizing that the gap between haves and have-nots will be increased by access to information technology, Nicholas Negroponte proposed that each homeless person should be given a laptop computer![3] The foolishness of this suggestion leaves one speechless. When the basic problem of finding homes has been solved, the technical problem of providing access to information technology can be reasonably attacked.[4]

The temptation is to throw the problem back at schools. Critics might argue (and I have) that it is silly to give computers to people who do not know how to use them and have no place to plug them in. Even if schools had the opportunity to effectively teach everyone how to use computers, would that solve the problem of homelessness? Homeless children (suffering the massive disadvantages of homelessness) would be least likely to learn and would have no place to practice without standing in line and, without the sort of advice and encouragement available in the best homes, would use the computer as many do television—as a source of entertainment. One can envision a crazy sort of dystopia in which homeless people (who have not sold their computers for temporary shelter, clothing, food, drugs, or alcohol) sit on the streets playing computer games. We are not going to eliminate homelessness by either technology or education, although both may contribute to better lives once homes are provided.

An address is crucial not only for the formalities of citizenship in contemporary society but also for dignity and self-respect. An answer to the question, "Where do you live?" is accompanied by pride, embarrassment, contentment, ambivalence, apology, or humiliation. When I say, "I live at 3 Webb Avenue," I am saying at least that part of my identity can be found there. We interact with our addresses. We encounter daily the places we have made our own, and we encounter others through the identity established there. There is an element of stability in having a permanent address even if one is away at school, in the service, or living abroad. That stability should not be regarded as rigid; it may be a temporary stability that will give way to a desirable move to yet another form of stability.

People in a home or homelike setting establish conditions under which all inhabitants can grow. The first address for a recently homeless person may meet only what I referred to earlier as basic legitimate expectations. Other expressed needs must be earned. The best home provides encounters that point its members upward, inspire hopes and dreams, and make it reasonable to suppose that at least some of these may be reached. Thus a basic question for policy makers is this: how can we house people so that their basic expressed needs are met? And then: how can we make it possible for people to earn the fulfillment of other expressed needs? In asking these questions, and seeking answers to them, we have to analyze basic needs and reject hasty answers.

It is common, for example, to list food, shelter, safety, and medical care as basic needs. Consider the importance of an integrating or unifying response to these needs. In good homes all of these needs are provided or planned for under one roof. One does not find nighttime shelter in one place, breakfast in another, dinner in still another. As we think about the unity of homes, we discover other basic needs: privacy, a place to keep one's possessions, a place to receive visitors. These are all basic needs that most of us take for granted.

What sort of arrangement might meet all of these needs? One can envision a building appointed for single men or women: small private bedrooms, a common dining hall, bathrooms conveniently located for each block of bedrooms, a library and information center staffed by volunteers or by residents who have already acquired the requisite knowledge. No one would be forced to move out, but strong incentives would be provided for "moving on." Everyone would do some kind of work to maintain the community. Some might work outside and pay a small rent until they could move into a situation more nearly self-supporting.

Questions of coercion arise at every level. Should we coerce people to use this housing? The answer must be yes, if they cannot provide for themselves; that is, a caring community is justified in saying, "You may not sleep on the street." When an objection is raised, we must listen, like a caring parent or teacher. Then a process of negotiation follows. The possible arrangement described above (for illustrative purposes) is offered as a response to objections that have been made repeatedly by the homeless: shelters are unclean and unsafe, there is no place to keep one's belongings, one has to leave every morning, there is no privacy. These complaints must be taken seriously and addressed. When we decide that coercion is necessary, negotiation and remediation are the next steps.

Should inhabitants of these houses be allowed free ingress and egress? Of course. The rooms to which they are assigned and all of the public space constitute their home. They, like any homeowner or renter, should be free to come and go as they please. They should be encouraged to tell a person in charge where they will be if an absence will be lengthier than a day or two, and they should understand that their rooms may be reassigned if they disappear for, say, a month. But they should not be prisoners.

No rules, then? Of course, there must be rules—or, better, guidelines—and I cannot possibly anticipate all that might be necessary. Excessive noise, abusive language, and rank filth would all have to be controlled. Huge collections of combustible materials would be forbidden; halls and doors would have to be free for passage in case of fire. Rules of this sort apply to people living anywhere.

Should inhabitants work or somehow pay their way? A "yes" answer to this implies another act of coercion, but I think it is necessary. Any home that supports the growth of its members will help them to understand that they must contribute something to their own support.

When we say, "You must work," we should be prepared to hear what the new worker might like to do. Just as members of a family have some choice of jobs, so should the formerly homeless. If a person has no immediately employable skills outside the homeplace, then she must select a job that needs doing inside. A panel of advisors, together with a professional social worker, should keep track of what needs doing and which jobs are thought desirable and which repugnant. It is entirely conceivable that a new member will be confronted with a job list that offers little choice. When that happens, the officer in charge might announce "good news and bad news." The bad news is that Mr. Smith has to clean bathrooms; the good news is that he may get a slightly larger room or a bit higher allowance for doing work that others find unattractive.

I do not want to go too far in suggesting specific arrangements and specific responses to predictable problems. What I hope to show is that an approach based on response to need is feasible and that it should not be permissive. It makes use of positive incentives (and not all should be material incentives), and it tries not to invoke the concept of negative desert. Indeed, it should be an occasion of mourning when we have to concede that someone deserves to be deprived of a want that might easily be met if he would shape up.

Illustrative suggestions are useful not only in concrete planning but also in testing our thinking and the grounds on which it rests. We might note, for example, that there are abandoned military camps all over the country and that these might be used to house and retrain the homeless. Indeed, we saw just how quickly such camps could be made ready when they were utilized to shelter refugees from Kosovo. Yet our own homeless live on the streets. Why would some of us be more receptive to the use of military camps than to the form of housing previously described? Why would some reject the use of military camps? To some, it might be more acceptable to collect the homeless in barracks-style camps than in places affording private sleeping quarters. Underlying this preference may be the belief that the homeless simply do not deserve a homelike setting. Further, discipline could be better enforced in camps designed for the military, and it is often believed that discipline is what these unfortunate people need most. Those who oppose the use of military camps may equate those settings with concentration camps and shudder at the thought. Both groups may be wrong. If we agree that privacy, control over one's own movements, a certain unity of life afforded by homelike settings, and access to growth-inducing encounters are essential—that these are basic needs—then we can organize any available facilities with these needs in mind. It is wasteful to allow military structures to sit idle.

The setting should not predetermine forms of encounter—that is, the coercion characteristic of military life should have no place in camps converted to civilian use—but can this be avoided? In discussing the new environmental studies building at Oberlin College, David Orr points out the link between the building and the activities that take place within it.

The curriculum embedded in any building instructs as fully and effectively as any course taught in it. The extravagant use of energy in buildings, for example, teaches students that energy is cheap and can be wasted. Windowless rooms, or those with windows that do not open, teach that nature is to be held at arm's length.[5]

We saw in an earlier chapter that our physical and biological surroundings do affect us strongly, and so we have to ask what lessons will be learned from the forms of housing provided. Will the housing we provide convey the message that a compassionate society will keep its poor alive but remind them constantly of their low status and the generosity of others? Or will it show that even economically minimal housing can be made beautiful? If we want to teach the second lesson, then the encounters provided must set the stage, and the inhabitants themselves must be encouraged to continue the effort.

We are talking about a problem that goes to the very heart of social policy. Inner city schools, for example, often teach the lesson that education is a way out of the inner city or barrio. They also often teach students to fear and scorn the sort of lives led by their parents and adult relatives. Every hope offered involves a rejection of present life. A care perspective counsels positive response to present expressed needs. Make the present setting more livable now—safer, healthier, more attractive, more educative. Provide incentives to continue the work both for individual mobility and for community improvement. The attitude that accepts present misery and holds out hope for a better future life for those who conform is all too familiar in traditional religion. A better way is to respond to basic expressed needs now, to illustrate by our actions that certain inferred needs should become expressed needs, and to stand ready both to help and to yield control as progress is made.[6]

Before leaving this section I want to discuss a particular case. John (not his real name) is a thirty-five-year-old black man who has been homeless for years. He has family in the area, but they will not take him in. He is hard to get along with, talks back to police officers, and often gets into minor squabbles on the street. He typically spends two or three months of the year in jail and emerges somewhat healthier. Many homeless people are no doubt tempted to commit some minor offense so that they will be housed and fed during the worst winter weather. The communities in John's area, however, charge a stiff fee for their "room and board" in jail, and John owes such money plus fines to three or four local jails. There is now a strong disincentive for breaking the law in order to be housed. In John's case there is no real evidence that he deliberately breaks the law to get into jail. He says that he hates being jailed and complains bitterly about the "racial discrimination" that lands him there regularly. He has been jailed several times for trespassing in order to use a restroom. This is another excruciatingly embarrassing and sometimes physically painful problem for the homeless. If one has to be a customer in order to use the restroom, where will he or she get the money to qualify as a customer? Many of the stories John tells about harassment (from both merchants and police) are convincing. More than that, they are outrageous. Picture yourself on the street with a bellyache or bursting bladder. What would you do?

John is on supplementary social insurance (SSI); he has had a recognized disability since early childhood. He can read a little, but he has a hard time reading letters from social agencies and lawyers. An older couple who frequently employ him to do odd jobs help him with these communications. He picks up his mail at a relative's house, but the relative will have nothing else to do with him, and it is obvious that he often misses communications. He has no permanent address. His employers say that he is a willing worker and can work hard for about four hours in a day. Then he is literally gray with fatigue. He is willing to work when his SSI is gone, typically after one or two weeks. His employers have tried to convince him that he needs a permanent address. They have (more than once) set him up in a room, supplied him with linens and a clock radio, and provided groceries. After a short time he leaves for the street. He says the other boarders are dirty, crazy, and dishonest. He can't stand sharing a bathroom with dirty people. This is a point to which caring professionals should listen; they should not brush aside such complaints with "beggars can't be choosers." John *is* personally clean, and he greatly appreciates the use of his employers' bathroom and laundry facilities. He needs a room and bath of his own, and he is willing to work for that accommodation. Instead of one check per month—which is immediately spent on a motel room, fines, and gambling—John needs a home, even if he is coerced into living there. Coercion, as I have argued, should be followed by negotiation. If such living arrangements met John's needs, he might not have to be coerced to live there. He will, however, always need someone to manage his money. A conservatorship could be minimal if housing were guaranteed.

John is neither retarded nor mentally ill, but he is not academically bright, and his personality is dysfunctional. He will never be able to hold a full-time job. He can't resist gambling when he has a few dollars. He smokes and drinks moderately. The public assistance he receives is not enough to live on, and if it were increased he would still go through it in a week or two. He does not take his employers' possessions without asking. Although his employers trust him anywhere in the house, bicycles and tools that they lend him disappear. John says they are stolen, but, almost certainly, many of them are sold for spending money. John, like many other homeless people, needs a guaranteed home first and then a special program of negotiated care.

The Mentally Ill Homeless

Many of today's homeless are mentally ill. Estimates range from 40 percent to 60 percent.[7] With these people, the first coercion—one that forbids sleeping on the streets—must be followed by another—treatment of the illness. Here again we run into a conflict of goods. The liberal tradition puts tremendous emphasis on freedom or liberty. Under some versions neither society nor small community is justified in intervening in adult lives to prevent harm to themselves. The mentally ill, then, should be permitted their illness; under a different construal, they should be permitted their choice of a different way of being in the world.[8]

Are we justified in coercing people into treatment? Care theory does not hold so sharp a line against coercion as does classical liberalism. If real harm is evident, caring directs us to intervene. Even with this drastic decision to coerce—to force treatment—there is room for negotiation. A patient should be encouraged to evaluate various treatments, to say why she prefers one to another, to assess her own ability to function under various conditions.

Perspectives on the mentally ill, like so many others that we have considered, are often unduly polarized. On the one extreme are those who are quick to label the excitable mentally ill "raving maniacs"; on the other are those who romanticize them and suggest rather strongly that the mentally ill are more sane (and have a better senses of fun) than those deemed normal.[9] A reasonable position recognizes the misery and shame that accompany mental illness but still insists on listening to those so labeled and taking their complaints seriously. Often patients have good reasons for refusing certain medications, and it seems perverse— even contradictory—to ignore their evaluations in the interest of restoring them to a condition in which their evaluations will find credence.[10] Further, the love and trust offered by those who listen may well have strong therapeutic effects.[11]

Clearly, it would be much easier to reach the mentally ill if they were not homeless, as Judge Robert Coates notes.

Laws concerning involuntary civil commitment need to be amended. The right of seriously mentally ill individuals to refuse treatment must be balanced against the duty of society to help people whose conditions are so grave as to require that help and treatment be imposed. Of course, the person deserves the maximum possible respect. Mandatory outpatient treatment should be considered before involuntary commitment. . . . But . . . such proposals for changing the law will do no good . . . unless and until there is a large influx of the funding needed for the community mental health treatment system originally envisioned by the proponents of deinstitutionalization. A street is not a home.[12]

Mandatory housing might preclude the necessity for mandatory treatment for at least some patients. With outpatient-style treatment available mainly on-site, patients might have a chance to form relations of trust with the staff appointed to care for them. Coates also emphasizes the need for care and trust, and he is right in recognizing the need for increased funding. Perhaps an even greater need is for the wiser use of available funds. Planning is required. Where, in the complex of suggested housing, will the mentally ill be placed? Under what circumstances will their status fall under conservatorship? How will shifts in status be handled?

Most observers agree that the move to deinstitutionalize the mentally ill was made without adequate planning. Many involved in it were well intentioned, and their arguments fell into the classical liberal line— liberty and freedom of choice for all but the most demonstrably incapacitated. But these good intentions were also used by politicians wanting to spend money in other ways and by property developers who coveted the land on which some mental hospitals stood. The idea of outpatient treatment is promising, but its success depends on the willingness and diligence of patients in keeping appointments, taking medications, and reporting their condition honestly. These are tasks that, by definition, many of the mentally ill cannot perform. The result to date has been a proliferation of group homes, sometimes poorly supervised, squabbles at the community level over where these homes will be located (the NIMBY—"not in my backyard"—phenomenon), a dramatic increase in the number of the homeless, and a general loss of control over the whole situation.

Should we reestablish institutions? Once again we run into the common habit of dichotomizing the issue. One side, envisioning the "snake pits" of earlier times, recoils in horror at the thought. They are joined by people who value freedom above all else. It is not unusual to hear protests against moving people off the streets, and these protests are often made in the name of human dignity. The other side responds heatedly that there is no dignity in sleeping on the street, raving to oneself on the corner, begging for money, and wasting one's life. People in this condition, they argue, should be institutionalized.

Both sides make important points, but neither extreme is defensible. We must be willing to provide necessary funding, of course. Before money is appropriated there must be a plan that lays out what we want to accomplish, and the plan must be open enough to respond to careful experimentation. Even before a plan is developed there must be discussion along the lines suggested by Berlin. Human goods, Berlin said, come into conflict. Indeed, "to admit that some of our ideals may in principle make the fulfillment of others impossible is to say that the notion of total human fulfillment is a formal contradiction, or metaphysical chimaera."[13] If, by coercion of the mentally ill, we produce for them a better life than they might have had, the loss of freedom is to that degree justified. If their lives are not improved—and here we have to listen to their evaluation of their own experience—then, as Berlin would put it, the loss of freedom is absolute.[14]

A defensible plan, then, will avoid extremes. The mentally ill will not be left alone in the name of freedom, nor will they be incarcerated in what is claimed to be their best interests. The plan will lay out the goods that should be preserved or sought. It will employ coercion sparingly and always with consideration of these questions: Is the stated end a good that all rational people seek? Is there any other way, one that is less coercive, to achieve it? What can we do to make the coercion tolerable? What do those coerced suggest? We engage in negotiation.

The sort of housing plan I have suggested (but only to get practical thinking started) is, in a sense, institutional. We should not be afraid of the word or the idea.[15] After all, colleges are institutions, and we seem eager to enroll our children in them. All institutions need to examine their patterns of coercion. We need to study carefully those patterns that have desirable effects and those that do not. How large should housing complexes be? Should inhabitants have a choice of urban or more rural settings? (Many old military camps are somewhat isolated and in quite lovely natural surroundings.) Should the mentally ill be housed with the mentally well? Should families be entirely separated from singles? Might it be facilitative to place the elderly near families and encourage mutual support? Should there be recreational facilities, as well as information centers, on-site? Another important question concerns how these new institutions should be staffed. The staff will be there to help, to guide, to educate. They are not hotel clerks, security guards, bouncers, or deans of students. An effective staff will certainly include both full-time and part-time professionals. It should also include adequately prepared volunteers and some of the inhabitants.

Today many of the mentally ill are housed in group homes where, on the positive side, they may enjoy freedom and some companionship. But there is often great reliance on medication, and a frequent public complaint is that the house supervisors are not conscientious in ensuring that patients take their medicines. However, even within the field of psychiatric medicine there is some concern about the use and overuse of psychoactive drugs. Patients may be right about the effects of which they complain. Moreover, residents in group homes located in ordinary neighborhoods may feel stigmatized. They are no longer segregated by lock and key, but they are segregated nonetheless.[16] Small, residential institutions might be better for many patients. When I envision one of these new institutions I see something like Hull House with an expanded facility for housing.[17] Whether anything like this is feasible should be part of the study that guides planning. No doubt there have been and currently are promising programs in many parts of the world, and all should be studied in light of the criteria we establish for homelike settings.

In all of our planning the objective should be to use as little coercion as possible and to provide incentives for those coerced to achieve greater levels of independence. For example, there could be degrees of supervision ranging from partner-type arrangements that would provide mutual support to conservatorship. Even when a person has been assigned to a conservator who will make legal decisions for her, that person must have access to a review panel that can assist, admonish, or even replace the conservator. Finally, there should be an honest effort to remove the stigma of dependence. In the long run, although none of us is fully independent, almost all of us can exercise some degree of independence, if only in the kind of everyday choices most of us take for granted.

The Near-Homeless

Many of the homeless are mentally ill; many others are drug-dependent, alcoholic, and/or have poor job records. We might, with good reason, say that many in the second set have brought homelessness on themselves. Even so, I have argued, they do not deserve the pain that accompanies homelessness, and a program initiated by coercion and followed by negotiation is recommended. An increasing number of the homeless, however, are victims of poverty and misfortune. These are people who have worked, who have owned or rented houses, who have raised or are in the process of raising children. These are people struggling at the edges of financial ruin. One major catastrophe or a series of minor problems can force them into real poverty and homelessness. Can something be done to prevent the slide from being near-homeless to becoming homeless?

If we examine the stories told by people who have lost the battle to keep a roof over their heads, we find significant similarities. A local newspaper recently ran a feature about a married couple that had lost their home. The husband was hospitalized, and the wife could no longer hold a job because of heart problems, lack of transportation, needing to be at her husband's side, and the demands placed on her to care for young grandchildren. At the time the story was written, she (together with a daughter and infant granddaughter) was housed one night at a time in various rooms funded by social agencies, churches, and individual charity. Her belongings were heaped in plastic garbage bags. Let's call this woman Ms. A.

As Ms. A tells her story, we hear something familiar — the enormous difficulties people have in working through the formalities imposed by social agencies. This is rarely the fault of social workers, who, for the most part, are also frustrated by the system.[18] By the time deserving people qualify formally for disability aid, they may be hopelessly in debt. They encounter other problems. If they receive disability checks, they no longer qualify for food stamps. If they feel well enough to do some work and are lucky enough to find work compatible with their abilities, they may lose all or part of the assistance. They encounter a long waiting list for subsidized housing. If they are lucky enough to find shelter they can afford on their own (and this is always "barely"), they may be evicted for overcrowding. Ms. A experienced this when she tried to care for two young grandsons. These children are now in foster care.

Next there is the hassle of qualifying for Medicaid. People who have worked — the husband in this case worked for twenty years — and were once covered by insurance now have to prove that they have neither insurance nor resources to pay for medical care. By the time that it becomes obvious that the problem is large, such families have already lost everything. At the same time, spouses and other close relatives who are waiting in line and filling out forms in order to procure aid are losing their hold on jobs because of time lost to the Medicaid system, lack of reliable transportation, worry, and plain fatigue.

If we follow the trail of these families step by step, we begin to understand their confusion, fear, and feeling of helplessness. One has to try to find a place to rent but, without a home, how does one make telephone calls? The answer sounds simple, but it isn't. Everything must be done standing up at a phone booth, sometimes in the cold, often in a noisy place. Change — money — is necessary, and one can rarely get change without buying something. If the relevant party cannot be reached, the call still costs something, and there is no way to receive a callback. Mail is not easily forwarded, and one can use general delivery for only a short time. Meanwhile sick family members await a visit, children have to get to school, school memos have to be signed and returned, children have to be fed, and one needs to be decently dressed to appear at school or a job interview.

Families who lose their homes and become dependent on public assistance also experience humiliation. In many cases there is no wicked public servant who deliberately shames the homeless. But, as their stories are told, details of family history are disclosed. There may be a child out of wedlock. Never mind that affluent young couples may live together for years without marrying and that many babies are born to single mothers who do not need public assistance. *This* story becomes part of the record. Someone in the immediate family may be in prison, often for a drug offense. Again, in a more affluent family the sentence — and even the conviction — might have been avoided. Teenagers may be truant or may already have dropped out. Alcohol may be a problem. All of these details, closely guarded secrets in financially secure homes, become part of a record that strengthens a stereotype. It is what we come to expect of "people like these." The emotional pain for those to whom many of these things have happened in rapid sequence must be excruciating.

Without meaning to do so, schools often add to the pain and humiliation of such families. We are fond these days of saying that "poor children can learn as well as rich children." What we mean, of course, is that a child's capacity for learning should not be judged by his socioeconomic status. But it is ridiculous and unfair to suppose that teachers' efforts can compensate for the monumental difficulties in some children's lives.[19] Something has to be done to change the conditions in which these children live.

Where might a caring community intervene in the downward spiral described above? Here, again, I want to emphasize a way of thinking more than a concrete solution, but I will do so through a possible example. Suppose families could apply for substantial help before foreclosure or eviction. A social worker or financial advisor might help them to evaluate their needs for a period of, say, five years. Job prospects would be assessed. Medical costs would be figured in. Then the agency would grant a loan that should keep the family afloat through the period of emergency. If their living arrangements have been clearly beyond their means for some time, a move might be recommended or, in rare cases, even coerced. If the record shows that they have managed until the current emergency, then the effort should be directed at maintaining continuity.

How and when will such families pay back the loan? In the best families incentives are offered instead of penalties. The same approach could be tried with public assistance. For every year of financial stability—no new calls on public assistance—part of the loan might be forgiven. Under such a plan families would have a real incentive to follow a plan cooperatively formulated. For those families that fall into deeper trouble, a stricter conservatorship might be imposed. Their money, including debt repayment, might be managed by a publicly appointed conservator. Again, every plan should include an incentive to move toward greater control of their own affairs. The important point is this: whether a family deserves the full reward of the initial incentive or fails miserably to meet its part of the bargain, no family would become homeless. At worst, it would take up residence in the semi-institutional arrangement described earlier.

A social policy of this sort should be accompanied by a transformation of economic policies with respect to low-wage workers. Government could supply supplements directly to workers, or it could subsidize employers who hire many low-wage workers. The idea under the latter plan is that full employment of low-wage workers could, by creating a shortage, drive up their wages.[20] Caring as a general approach directs us to work toward a society in which no person or family working full-time at an honest job will live in poverty.

The suggestions I have made here for incentives and forgivable loans have been tried in some international programs.[21] Most incentives require repayment, and I am not arguing against repayment. The differences between rich and poor are growing, however, making the odds of climbing away from the brink formidable, and policies that include incentives may make the difference. The combination of incentive and cooperative, expert advice may relieve the fear that accompanies near-homelessness and extend a realistically founded hope.

Before leaving this discussion I want to emphasize the importance of planning and designing homes and homelike institutions. In addition to the functions of housing listed by Bauhaus architects,[22] we must look at the features of *homes*. Although Meyer and others list "gardening" as one activity that might influence the design of a house, they did not dig beneath this interest (one that might be considered idiosyncratic) to a more basic one rooted in biophilia. One might suppose, then, that if housing meets functional needs, it meets fully human needs. This may not be the case. There may be a need for both beauty and connection to nature, a need that goes too often unrecognized. "Everyone has a garden inside them," said Gailard Seamon. "But you have to find your garden. Some people never do. Life doesn't offer it to them."[23]

In examining the problems of homelessness and near-homelessness we have uncovered a feature of "home" that remained somewhat hidden in the earlier analysis—its function in integrating basic human needs. All of the characteristics identified earlier remain important: shelter, food, control over coming in and going out, a place to keep belongings, physical and emotional protection, promotion of growth, persuasive direction toward acceptability, someone to listen and respond, place-based identity, shared control, connection to the natural world, and acceptance of the goodness of pleasure. If we consider all of these, we are swept up by a sense of awe. A *home* holds the promise of so much. Indeed, we may now insist that the need for a home is in itself a basic expressed need, and therefore a legitimate expectation that should never be violated. When our society awakes to this, we may develop policies that recognize a *right*. Having a home may then be construed as a right.

We have discussed the problems of the homeless and near-homeless, and we have given special attention to the problems of the homeless who are mentally ill. Throughout the discussion illustrative solutions were offered to the most difficult problems. Perhaps the most important point in this chapter is the recognition of the home as fundamental to one's identity. Even if all the other separate basic needs of a human being were somehow to be met, there would remain the need for that place — that extension of the self — we call home.

The analysis of homes has been offered as an illustration of how social policy might be designed to respond to certain expressed needs. Societies are also interested, however, in satisfying inferred needs — needs that a normative group identifies for its members. Among these is the need to conform to laws and certain social rules or customs. When people refuse to comply with these norms we say that they are "deviant." How should we shape social policy to handle deviance?

CHAPTER 13

Deviance

Deviance is always judged relative to a set of accepted norms. Parents, teachers, correction officers, and therapists often try to prevent deviance and, when it has occurred, to restore deviants to acceptability. The felt or imposed duty to prevent and correct deviance is taken so seriously that we infer needs in those for whom we have responsibility. Thus, a child *needs* to address authorities respectfully, a drug user *needs* to quit, a loafer *needs* to work, a sinner *needs* to find God, and so on.

Difficulties arise when we must judge how serious certain acts of deviance are and whether it is important to insist on conformity. I said earlier that the best homes help their members to understand the social pressures under which we all live. In this process we come to view some forms of deviance as heroic, some as harmless, some as humorous or eccentric, some as annoying, some as dangerous, and some as both dangerous and despicable. Instead of accepting the norms of our groups as given, it would seem both reasonable and liberating to ask questions about them, discuss them, and evaluate them.[1]

In this chapter, after a brief discussion of changing conceptions of deviance, I will concentrate on the problem of drugs. I hope to show that both the libertarian insistence on drugs as property that cannot lawfully be confiscated from individuals and the law-driven concern that now imprisons thousands of our citizens are wrong. Finally, I will say a bit on the treatment of criminal deviance from the perspective of an ethic of care.

Changing Conceptions of Deviance

Norms change. Today most of us find Victorian norms for dress, women's comportment, and public language somewhat humorous. We can hardly imagine a day when "nice" women did not read newspapers (or read only those parts that their husbands had already read and approved), when an exposed female leg ("limb") was nearly scandalous, and when a gentleman could be easily distinguished from other men by his dress. It is also hard to imagine living in a time or place where failure to attend religious services could merit punishment and/or public condemnation. But the era when women were thought to be not quite nice if they smoked, and neighborhood taverns had "ladies entrances" and permitted only escorted women to enter, was not that long ago. Audiences, even at mid-twentieth century, were shocked by profanity in films, and mild profanity in schools was likely to bring punishment.

Norms guide our activities in every part of life, and most of us simply take them for granted. From the moment of birth, arbitrary norms treat girls and boys differently—baby girls get pink blankets and booties, baby boys blue. Girls are expected to behave according to one set of norms, boys to another. Only in the last decades of the twentieth century were these norms seriously questioned. Even today, the labels "tomboy" and "sissy" have not entirely disappeared from our vocabulary, and it is important to consider the value that we put on these judgments. It is far more acceptable for a girl to dress and to behave like a boy than it is for a boy to behave like a girl. Thus, "tomboy" is no longer entirely pejorative, but "sissy" is still very hurtful. Women wear pantsuits regularly in professional life, but we are astonished and thrown off balance when a man wears a skirt, and there are no skirt-suits designed especially for men. A pipe- or cigar-smoking woman is still something of an anomaly, and so is a man who shaves his legs. All of the norms applying separately to males and females have come under question in recent decades. Some seem innocent—mere customs. Others, such as the exclusion of women from prestigious occupations, have been strongly challenged.

Even those that seem innocent on the surface require some analysis. For example, it seems a trivial matter that men wear pants and women skirts. However, when we observe that it is now acceptable for women to wear pants but not for men to wear skirts, we see something else operating. The male model still establishes the dominant norm. In the matter of dress we may agree readily with the preference for pants because the male form of dress permits more freedom of action and is usually more comfortable. Acceding to the male norm in other matters may be a mistake. Should women be more aggressive? Should they serve in combat units of the military? Should they learn to interrupt and demand a greater share of talk-time in conversations? Should they abandon the occupations traditionally associated with women?

This last points up an important issue in the analysis of changing conceptions of deviance. It seems clearly desirable that women are no longer considered deviant — "unnatural women"[2] — when they enter traditionally male fields. But are young men encouraged to enter the professions typically associated with women? Are these occupations to assume a universally low status — a status not desirable for bright people of either sex? If the latter is the case, we have to ask whether it is desirable that the male occupational model set the standard. Should only second-rate people commit themselves to the helping professions? All over the country today, bright young women are being counseled into high-status professions.[3] Some are even told, straight-out, "You are too smart to be a teacher!" And many young women are choosing against themselves; that is, they are choosing not the fields they love but those that will reward them with money and status. These issues are of central importance in education and should be discussed openly and thoroughly.

The best homes and schools help young people analyze the norms that govern their behavior. Many young people think that certain forms of dress, speech, and music are signs of individuality. These forms clearly separate the young from adults, but, of course, from an adult perspective, the kids all look alike and seem easy prey to weird norms. Why wear visor caps backwards when visors were designed to protect the eyes from direct sunlight? Why wear pants with crotches that fall below the knees when trousers were designed to enhance mobility? The answer is that people of every age want to be accepted in certain highly valued groups, and this desire for acceptance often outweighs common sense.

Most of us find it harder to question norms than simply to follow them, and even those who deviate sharply from society's dominant norms usually find groups whose norms they follow unreflectively. Consider how difficult it is to convince some minority adolescents that they are working against themselves when they actively resist their teachers and classroom success. Black teenagers who study and participate actively in class are accused of "acting white" or "sucking up" to the teacher, and Hispanic boys are accused of a failure of masculinity. Working-class boys of all races face a similar accusation.[4] In reaction, teachers—following teacherly norms—scold, punish, and ignore or, alternatively, talk loftily about high wages for academic success, great expectations for all, and the delights of intrinsic motivation. Neither course of action gets at the root of the problem, which is understanding the norms by which we are all disciplined. Indeed, most teachers have never been encouraged to reflect on the norms that govern their own lives, and so they are not in a position to help students to do so.

Many norms are facilitative, and their acceptance helps things to run smoothly. People who regularly violate trivial norms in the facilitative category are boors and nuisances. We prefer to avoid them. Some facilitative norms are nontrivial. Traffic laws, for example, are both facilitative and protective. Violation can risk life and safety, and we regard the worst violations as morally reprehensible. Driving at high speed through a school zone or leaving the scene of an accident that caused injury would fall into this category. Good parents want their children to conform to most facilitative norms but, in addition, the best parents want their children to make judgments on the grounds of the likely harm inflicted by violation of a norm. The boor comes under a form of aesthetic judgment, but the reckless driver is judged morally.

Deviance may be deplored and reinforced at the same time. For example, the parents of a reckless boy may warn him to be more careful and yet, within his hearing, brag about his "fearlessness." A teacher who scolds or mocks the "class clown" may habitually turn to him for comic relief. A child who is fussed over in minor illness may find the sick role a comfortable one to play regularly. In a similar way, mental patients may find it more rewarding to embrace their illness than to get well.[5] In all of these cases people cast as helpers actually contribute to the maintenance of deviance.

Every society has an obligation to examine its own norms and modes of enforcement in light of a central question: What harm or good does this norm (or mode of enforcement) offer? Sometimes, when the time is right, the question is easy to answer, and we wonder why our predecessors had difficulty with it. It seems utterly right, for example, to eliminate prison for honest debtors, even though we want to encourage a norm of paying debts. It seems right, also, to eliminate norms that require certain religious beliefs of office-holders or teachers, but such norms may operate informally even when they have been formally abolished. In the past half-century we have begun to question norms of patriotism, sexuality, marriage, religious affiliation, and gender. Many welcome these changes, arguing that great harms were done by enforcing or even tacitly endorsing such norms. Others trace present observable harms to the rejection of these same norms. Answering the question on harm or good requires open and patient analysis, willingness to acknowledge uncongenial points that are well grounded in evidence, and tolerance of ambiguity.

In parenting, one of the most difficult decisions to make is whether to encourage or discourage deviance from whatever norm a family has established for education and career preparation. I argued strongly in chapter 8 that adolescents should not be coerced into college preparation or prestigious careers, and I argued on the basis that such coercion harms both the child who is coerced and the society that demeans many necessary occupations. Still, since so much is at stake—given society's present values—parents understandably worry over what position to take. Should the child of professional parents be allowed to deviate and enter a trade? Notice that we would not hesitate to give a positive answer if the question were whether the child of tradespeople should be allowed to deviate and enter a profession. As in my earlier example of male and female norms, these questions expose the dominance of a professional norm, and we have to ask what harm may be done as a result of maintaining it.

Among the hardest questions to answer are those that involve criminal deviance. We have to ask first whether a given form of deviance should be regarded as criminal, and here we must address the harm issue squarely. Second we must decide what, if anything, should be done with the deviant. If we decide that a particular form of deviance is so harmful that it is justifiably labeled criminal, will our treatment of deviance make things better or worse? This is the sort of difficult analysis we face in considering what to do about the drug problem, and I turn to that next.

Drugs and Deviance

Citizens of the United States are clearly worried about the "drug problem," but they are just as clearly divided on what to do about it. We have been at war against drugs for several decades, and the costs are staggering. A recent report listed the following figures:

In 1993 . . . , Americans spent an estimated $49 billion on illegal drugs. . . . Federal, state, and local governments collectively spend about $30 billion a

year to reduce illegal drug use and trafficking and deal with their consequences. The annual social cost of illicit drug use is $67 billion, mostly from
the consequences of drug-related crime. Each year over one million persons
are arrested on drug-related charges.[6]

In the same report it is claimed that "over 20,000 of our citizens die
every year because of illicit drugs."[7] But to keep things in perspective,
an Associated Press article reported that as many as 90,000 hospitalized
patients die annually because of medical mistakes.[8] One cannot conclude
from these figures that it is safer to indulge in illicit drugs than to enter
a hospital as a patient, but one might reasonably suggest that the reform
of medicine is at least as important a problem as the control of drugs.

Many thoughtful observers today recommend that the war on drugs
be called off.[9] I think an ethic of care has to make this recommendation
also, but we must exercise caution in making it. First, we cannot make
it on libertarian grounds—that drugs are private property and should
not be confiscated by government.[10] Because we are primarily concerned
with needs and harms, we might well reject such an argument when it
is applied to, for example, handguns or child pornography. Thus our
question has to center on the harm done by drug use and the good or
harm done by criminalizing drug activity.

Care ethicists cannot brush aside lightly the harm that drug usage
often induces, but we have to separate the harm actually done by taking
drugs from the harm that is done by labeling such use as criminal deviance. We know from countless biographies that the use of alcohol has
had both facilitative and debilitative effects on creativity. Many highly
productive adults use alcohol in moderation, and some even use more
than moderate amounts without descending to drunkenness or losing
their creative powers. Can the same be said of drug use?

The answer to this is unclear. We first need to specify which drug is
at question. We do not have as many frank accounts of drug use as of
alcohol, possibly because drug use is illicit. We know that the great
mathematician Paul Erdös regularly took amphetamines, and that his
productivity fell off when he briefly abstained.[11] On the opposite side
of things, we know also that many drug users claim unusual insights
while under the influence of drugs, yet produce nothing whatever to
substantiate their claims. The weight of evidence seems to be against
drug use, but one must acknowledge that studies are handicapped by
the preponderance of reports on people who are dysfunctional drug
users. We do not have good information on people who use drugs moderately. Moreover, in accounts of those whose "lives are ruined" by

drugs, we seldom know why they started to use them. If drugs are used to excess by those already anxious, troubled, or deviant in other ways, we might do better to address the underlying problems than to blame drugs.

Recognizing the difficulty in establishing clear lines of cause and effect should not lead us to deny that drug use exacerbates existing problems. Its promise as an escape or as a means of enhancing productivity is rarely fulfilled, and lives in trouble can descend rapidly to ruination. The caution to be observed here is that we should not decide that homeless cocaine-takers are homeless *because* of cocaine use. Causality may well run in the opposite direction.

On balance, a reasonable society probably wants to encourage its citizens to live as free of drugs as possible. This seems to be a desirable norm, yet it is violated repeatedly and dramatically by a continuous stream of advertisements for all sorts of drugs that consumers should "ask your doctor about." Even if we were sincere about a drug-free norm, we would have to ask serious questions about how to encourage compliance, and this we have not done.

The harm done by the war on drugs almost certainly exceeds the harm done by drug use. We can grant that if marijuana and various forms of cocaine were made legal, consumption would increase. Alcohol consumption increased when prohibition was lifted. But increased consumption, however undesirable it may be, is not necessarily a sign of increased harm. That is a separate and crucial question. The net tally of harms might be greatly reduced by largely eliminating the black market that has been created by the war on drugs. Steven Wisotsky lists three great interests that are jeopardized by the black market:

1. the social interest in avoiding or minimizing the aggrandizement of governmental enforcement powers at the expense of individual rights;
2. the social interest in avoiding the secondary crimes committed as a necessary adjunct of cocaine trafficking and money laundering; and
3. the social interest in avoiding subversion of basic social, political, and economic institutions.[12]

Consider, first, the growth of governmental activity that violates (or threatens to violate) individual rights. Wisotsky lists illegal (trumped-up) searches and seizures, withholding bail, publishing the names of those accused (but neither tried nor convicted) of possessing drugs, excessive sentences, forfeiture of property, application of criminal forfeiture to the fees of defense counsel, and intrusion into the client-lawyer relationship.[13] All of these violations should be appalling to a rights-oriented society.

I said earlier that care ethicists need not avoid the powerful language of rights, but we should remain aware that rights arise from expressed needs and the power to grant or to seize these needs. When a right is well established, it makes sense to use rights-language. Our presumption is that a well-established right is the outcome of a hard-earned process originating in an expressed need. To overturn or modify such a right should require a rigorous argument that reveals the right as less weighty than the harms induced by granting it. In no case should a well-established right be arbitrarily or prejudiciously suspended. This great gift of liberalism should be appreciated even by those of us who differ on other of its aspects. Why is rights-language not invoked more often and more effectively in drug cases?

One reason is, as noted, that rights are called into question when harms and needs seem to outweigh them. If drugs are terribly harmful and the need of society for protection has become great, people begin to question whether those who pose such an enormous threat should enjoy even well-established rights. In a sense this phenomenon reinforces my initial description of rights. In times of danger, rights talk reverts to its original venue in needs and harms. Hence, although it is entirely appropriate to attack governmental incursions that violate individual rights, we might want to go beyond rights to find deeper arguments grounded in needs and harms. After all, if the harm really is great enough, we might want to argue for the elimination or at least the reinterpretation of a right. Many of us feel this way, for example, about the right to bear arms. Thus, a care ethicist cannot argue, as Szasz does, that drugs are property and people have a right to them.[14]

A care ethicist might still defend the rights of those accused of drug crimes against the governmental violations described by Wisotsky. The question here would be whether the harm done by recognizing a given right outweighs the harm done by suspending it. In most of the violations listed above, it would be hard to argue this way. One might do so successfully on the matter of pretrial and posttrial detention (denial of bail), but this rationale would be overturned by consideration of Wisotsky's third interest, (3). If we were to permit violations of the right to bail (without convincing evidence that a given offender really is likely to flee), we would undermine the trust we have in our system of justice. This lapse of trust would, in turn, weaken the whole web of care.

Therefore, even if care theorists cannot reach a firm conclusion on the basis of fears expressed in (1), they can do so when these are combined with the interests in (3).

From the care perspective the most important reasons for abandoning this war on drugs are found in (2) and (3). The increase in collateral crime and corruption is demonstrable. Further, as more and more people have been imprisoned for drug offenses, the prison business has grown and threatens to be self-perpetuating, and the drug trade itself flourishes within prisons. Profits and temptation go hand in hand, and it is difficult for people in hard and low-paying jobs to resist pervasive temptation. Recall the earlier account of Orwell's childhood in which he became convinced that he lived in a world where it was impossible for him to be good. We have come a long way since then in making schools more humane, but we have not done much to change the general living conditions of many in our society. Most law enforcement officers would not commit murder or torture for money because these acts are almost universally judged to be morally wrong. It is not nearly so clear to most people that buying, selling, or using drugs is morally wrong. Without a firm and widely acknowledged moral consensus, temptation can become overwhelming. It becomes very difficult, in such a world, to be good, and it is not unusual for law enforcement officers to give way.

The terrible cost of domestic crime is exacerbated by international crime and corruption.[15] When drug trafficking is excused in the name of some great national or international good (overturning a Communist regime or overthrowing a dictator), it becomes still harder for otherwise law-abiding people to evaluate drug dealing as an unambiguous moral evil. If it is not such an evil, then the slide from pseudo-patriotic motives to one of personal gain is well oiled. As more and more incidents of government involvement are disclosed, citizens lose respect for their government and trust in its institutions.[16]

Among the most reprehensible methods used by law enforcement agencies in the drug war is the practice of paying informers or drastically reducing the penalties of those who are willing to give evidence against others. Suppose A and B are demonstrably guilty of the same drug-related offense. A goes tight-lipped to prison, whereas B "rats" on a number of colleagues and goes free. We cannot, even in a burst of foolish optimism, suppose that B has given evidence for some newly found civic reasons. Indeed, if we set aside the morality of the original offense, we would find A more morally respectable than B. And pity the poor "runner" or other bit player who has no one to expose. Should government, an institution that should provide a moral example, promote such behavior? Again, it seems clear that the whole web of care becomes tangled and torn by such activity.

One possible alternative to the drug war is to return the control of all narcotics to medical professionals.[17] In the early part of the twentieth century legislation removed the responsibility for certain drugs (those that provide "gratification of a diseased appetite")[18] from medicine and conferred it on law enforcement agencies. Control of illicit drugs in the United States has passed from the Treasury Department to the Justice Department and, within Justice, to a variety of agencies. It has not rested in the hands of the surgeon general or the Food and Drug Administration, where at least the misclassification of various drugs, especially cocaine, might be avoided.[19] A move to give responsibility to the medical profession would, in effect, decriminalize drug use.

This possibility should be discussed thoroughly. Although it represents a possible approach to the drug problem, it presents problems of its own. One has difficulty imagining a nation that does not even support universal health insurance financing drugs that "gratify a diseased appetite." Unless clinics that supplied drugs were publicly supported, poor addicts would still have problems in purchasing drugs. Further, physicians would rightly be reluctant to write prescriptions for the recreational use of drugs, and so the market demand might not be much reduced. Indeed, we might find ourselves in a position where physicians, instead of law enforcement officers, fall prey to corruption.

The best solution, hard as it is to entertain, is probably the legalization of marijuana and cocaine and, perhaps, heroin. This step should not be taken without careful study, but it should at least be given a fair hearing. We need not deny the negative effects of any of these substances in calling for consideration of legalization. Too often, moves to prohibit or to permit are made without a careful study of historical conditions. We learned through horrible experience that the prohibition of alcoholic beverages was a mistake, but that does not mean that Carrie Nation and the Women's Christian Temperance Union were entirely wrong. At the time of their greatest activity, many families lived in misery aggravated by alcohol. Here we have to be careful in fixing the blame for misery *on* alcohol. Rather, it seems that widespread low wages, overwork, and loss of family-centered enterprises engendered misery, and that misery often led to alcohol consumption as a means of relief. Unfortunately, the means of relief made life even more miserable. In raising questions about the causal chain, we should not deny the role played by alcohol in making matters worse.

In a thematic investigation conducted by one of Paulo Freire's colleagues, tenement residents singled out an obvious drunk (in a picture of men talking on a street corner) as "the only one who is productive and useful to his country . . . the souse who is returning home after working all day for low wages and who is worried about his family because he can't take care of their needs. He is the only worker. He is a decent worker and a souse like us."[20]

The men who responded this way recognized the futility of alcohol as a means of escape, but they also understood both the decent motivation and the awful frustration of men in that hopeless situation. As Freire notes, sermonizing on the evils of alcohol would have had little effect on these men. Prohibiting alcohol might very well give them an opportunity, albeit an illegal one, to overcome the desperate poverty in which they labor. An ethic of care counsels alcohol education, but the greater priority is doing something about the social problems that lead to excessive use of alcohol.

A similar story might be told of drug use. In the late nineteenth and twentieth centuries the use of cocaine and heroin was widespread. So was social misery. Those who wanted to stop the ravages of drugs were not totally misguided, but, again, they interpreted effects as causes. In support of their faulty inferences, we would have to admit that these "effects" did, in turn, become causes that worsened the original miseries.[21] A caring society would go after these causes and would educate its citizens honestly about not only their condition but also its own role in producing that condition.

Thus, at this point—and my thinking is tentative, open to argument—I would consider allowing some drugs (probably the three mentioned) to be sold by licensed stores in just the way alcoholic beverages are sold. I would launch a massive and totally honest educational campaign on the demonstrated evils of drugs, the purported benefits, and the few actual benefits.

Then what? Then we might have to increase penalties for criminal negligence (negligence under the influence) to reinforce the norm that choice and responsibility go together. Instead of exercising lenience when people commit illegal acts under the influence, we would make the penalties greater—just as we do with DUI cases. For those who commit no offenses and retain their capacity to function in professional and personal life, there would be no penalty. For those who show signs of slipping into incapacity, there would be help. Of greatest importance here would be the realistic educational campaign that should help people understand themselves—why the temptation arises, when indulging it is most dangerous, the likely effects on different personality types, where to get help before yielding to temptation, and how to get help if things go too far.

At the present time our educational programs are heavily laden with propaganda. Trying to encourage abstinence (which is a good but difficult choice), we lie to our students about alcohol, sex, and drugs, and then we wonder why they ignore us when we tell them about the real dangers attending all three. The most effective education is based on relations of care and trust, and such relations require honesty and openness. We need not tell them that famous people used various drugs with positive effects, but we can tell them that claims have been made by respectable people and that the truth of such claims is still unclear. We should of course tell them about negative effects, but we should avoid the gross exaggerations that have characterized certain cycles of drug education in the past.[22]

When we face honestly the cycles of enthusiasm and recrimination that have characterized American attitudes toward drug use, we see that those attitudes have been affected by racial biases. David Musto comments on the development of these attitudes:

Americans had quickly associated smoking opium with Chinese immigrants who arrived after the Civil War to work on railroad construction. This association was one of the earliest examples of a powerful theme in the American perception of drugs: linkage between a drug and a feared or rejected group within society. Cocaine would be similarly linked with blacks and marijuana with Mexicans in the first third of the twentieth century.[23]

If Chinese immigrants were using opium heavily, they were also doing some of the heaviest and most grueling work on the railroads, and *if* Mexicans were using marijuana, they were also doing backbreaking work in the fields. Crack use among blacks can also be traced to forms of social misery. Prejudiced attitudes extend beyond race to the poor in general. For example, James Q. Wilson makes the odd comment that "regular heroin use incapacitates many users, especially poor ones, for any productive work or social responsibility."[24] If it is the drug itself that is addicting and debilitating, why should it differentially affect the poor?

No reasonable society would jump to legalize drugs without careful study, and as such studies are conducted and reported, those of us who now lean toward legalization might change our minds. Few of us would argue that drugs are a good thing to use nonmedicinally (as Freud initially argued for cocaine), but it seems obvious that prohibiting their sale and use has created more harm than drug use itself. As we move toward the possibility of legalization, we should prepare carefully for a likely increase in both harmless consumption and abuse. We should not risk the disastrous effects that resulted from summarily closing mental hospitals.

Wilson and others are right to express alarm and dismay about "crack babies" — babies born with terrible handicaps as a result of their mothers' abuse of cocaine. There are many such babies now, and as they reach school age they pose a special problem for teachers. Certainly something should be done to reduce the number of such tragedies, but it is not at all clear that the legalization of cocaine would produce a larger number. Women who persist in habits that endanger their unborn children have problems that run deeper than the drug problem at the surface. They need extensive help, and society may be justified in using some coercion to prevent harm to themselves and to their children.

When adequate and respectful prenatal care is universally available, it should be possible to identify pregnant women who use cocaine or alcohol. In extreme cases confinement in the sort of homelike environment described earlier might be justified. Again, women should be free to come and go in this environment unless that freedom results in continued use of the damaging drug. Even then — when a woman effectively loses control of her own door — the setting should not be prison but a supportive and educative homelike place that is designed to promote health and growth. In this approach drug taking is not criminalized, but coercion is used to prevent demonstrable harm.

Dare we use coercion on noncriminal adults? On this, the liberal tradition responds with a clear "no." Moreover, it would not criminalize behaviors that harm only the self. It makes a sharp distinction between what we can do to criminals and what we can do to noncriminal adults. But must an act be criminal before we can use coercion to prevent or control it? John Braithwaite and Philip Pettit remark that

the two major attacks on the liberal position come from legal moralism and legal paternalism respectively. Legal moralism would allow that an activity may be criminalized just because it is immoral or is at least regarded as immoral in the community at large. Legal paternalism would allow that an activity may be criminalized because it is likely to cause harm to the agent herself. The legal moralist questions the harm restriction in the harm-to-others constraint; the legal paternalist questions the restriction to others.[25]

Both of these opponents of the liberal position can find good reasons to support the criminalization of drug abuse. Legal moralism can even support the criminalization of drug *use;* from this perspective drug use is immoral. Legal paternalists would have to convince us that such use is always harmful or establish guidelines for the point at which use becomes abuse.

I am arguing, from the care perspective, that a society should be able to use some forms of coercion without labeling those coerced as criminals. After all, we force children—even adolescents—to go to school, and we do this because we infer a need for all children to be educated. We make serious mistakes when we do not follow this coercion with age-appropriate negotiation. Children should have much more say about their own education, but some element of coercion seems unavoidable. Similarly, in the adult world, we have established seat-belt and helmet laws, and although a minority still rail against the loss of freedom, most of us recognize the laws as lifesavers. With adults new forms of coercion must be constrained by effective protections. If a woman protests her confinement, there must be a review board to which she can turn. If she is clearly no longer at risk of hurting her child and wants to be left alone, she should be free to go her own way. If a homeless man is ready to find his own address, of course he should be supported in doing this. In every case coercion should be avoided if possible and should always followed by the sort of negotiation aimed at shifting the balance of control to the one coerced. This is among the most powerful attitudes we learn at home.

It can be argued that, in addition to sliding into questionable forms of paternalism, programs of the type suggested here are just too expensive. If, however, the prison population were reduced by 25 to 50 percent and funds for enforcement were unnecessary, money should become available for constructive treatments. Further, law enforcement personnel, freed from the sleazy and violent tactics often used in drug enforcement, might focus on activities that are more supportive and educative. The parallel here is the retraining of military personnel for peacekeeping rather than war making.

Criminal Deviance

Some forms of criminal deviance can be eliminated simply by removing them from the criminal category. Selling contraceptives was once a criminal act in some states. Abortion, homosexual activity, and interracial marriage were all criminal offenses. We could name many more. When activities are removed from the criminal category, part of the population rejoices and another part despairs, fearing the moral degeneration of the nation. The hardest cases, however, are those in which the majority of us agree on a social or moral norm but disagree on criminalization. From a care perspective we would certainly prefer that people abstain from the use of potentially harmful drugs; we would educate toward this end, but we would not criminalize drug use.

On a simpler level, many classroom and school-ground offenses can be eliminated by not labeling them offenses. In chapter 9 I used tardiness as an example. A teacher may well retain a norm for punctuality and yet not treat occasional tardiness as an act to be punished or even commented on. Chewing gum, talking, and eating in class are other examples. There are limits in these cases. If tardiness becomes chronic, chewing unsightly, eating too messy, or talking too loud or inappropriate, teachers have to engage in some coercion. The incentive for students not to violate the norm flagrantly is to avoid this coercion and to feel part of a group that conforms to certain norms for the comfort and benefit of all.

There are offenses that cannot be so easily eliminated. Offenses against persons and property, for example, are usually regarded as crimes, and they must be handled by a system of criminal justice. Care theory cannot argue against this, but the care approach can make some suggestions on how to treat criminals. The concept of negative desert cannot be entirely avoided here. People who deliberately harm others deserve a response that they would prefer to avoid. When events of this sort (but not criminal) happen at home, we usually respond by suspending or removing some privilege that would otherwise fall into the domain of legitimate expectations. A girl who has hit her brother may be restricted to her room until she cools off. A boy who frequently flouts the house norms on work or civil speech may have to postpone some activity or purchase that would otherwise have been granted forthwith. In adult society harming another often results, properly, in the loss of freedom, which, under conditions of minimal acceptability, is rightly regarded as a legitimate expectation.

We cannot transpose the entire structure of best homes on the society at large. Members of the larger community do not live together in the way that families do. Because we live with Sue and Jack, we usually know when Sue has cooled off and when Jack is meeting our norms for acceptability. We do not, and cannot, know in the same way when a given criminal is "ready to behave." Moreover, offenses in society are typically much greater in the harm they cause, and we properly expect a higher level of responsibility from rational adults. Thus, our question here has to be, what insight can we achieve by "starting at home"?

The most obvious recommendation, to be discussed more fully in the last chapter, is to make homes better. Children raised in the best homes, as described earlier, are unlikely to become wards of the criminal justice system. There are no guarantees, of course, but the single most important factor in both success in school and acceptability in society is the home. In preventing crime, then, we would do better to invest in the improvement of homes and schools than in prisons and law enforcement.

What should we do with the criminals we do have? We learned, starting at home, that positive incentives are usually more powerful than negative ones. Further, positive incentives invite people to belong and to expect something good to come as a result of their striving for acceptability. "Time off for good behavior" is a positive incentive. There are many other possibilities. Prisoners could earn privacy, for example. Not every prisoner is going to forge weapons or concoct some evil scheme behind a closed toilet door. They could be allowed greater freedom to move about in a given area. They could be allowed more possessions. Most prisons today operate on a system of negative incentives or disincentives. Inmates are easily moved into worse conditions—even "permanent lock-down"—but they have little to hope for by way of better conditions.[26]

In considering a system of positive incentives we should think about those features of homes that are valued so highly. Besides food, clothing, and shelter, a home provides protection from bodily harm, humiliation, and the threat of harm. A prison is not a home, but it should certainly provide such protection. Indeed, in doing so it might give some inmates their first glimpse of life without fear. A home provides privacy and companionship, and a system of positive incentives—well advertised—should offer a reasonable increase in both for acceptable prisoners. Homes promote the growth of their members; prisons should expand their educational efforts instead of closing them down.

Prisoners, by definition, are not free to come and go as they please, but it seems wrong to confine them in places that shut out sunlight and the natural environment entirely. To prevent escape and internal violence, prisons have incorporated features that tend to destroy the human spirit. It is obvious that not all prisoners can be trusted with garden implements, that weapons can be concealed in planters, that ambushes can be set up behind closed doors, that bodies can find ways to get out of windows wide enough to accommodate them. Contemporary prison designers and managers know a great deal about both the deviant activities likely to occur and a wide range of negative responses to these activities. What we still know far too little about is the kind of positive responses that might restore the desire to belong. It is not my purpose to offer specific details on crime and the handling of criminals — I am neither a criminologist nor a legal theorist. The purpose of a reasonable criminal justice system should be to protect the innocent, including victims, and if possible to restore those convicted of crimes to complete and healthy citizenship. If this purpose is accepted, then the notions of restitution and reintegration become central.[27]

When crimes are committed against property, it surely makes sense to require restitution, and often restitution plus compensation could replace imprisonment. Braithwaite and Pettit suggest, in addition, reprobation. This goes almost without saying; that is, a just society will, of course, express its public disapproval of acts forbidden under the criminal code. Requiring confession, statements of remorse and/or apology, and a plan for restitution seems reasonable so long as it stops short of using shame as a form of punishment. As we saw earlier, shame tends to focus a deviant's attention and sympathy on himself. Our purpose should be to keep his attention on the one he has wronged and, if possible, on how to set things right. Supervision is required to be sure that restitution is made, but the costs for supervision should be considerably less than those of imprisonment. Further, the victim gains something tangible, not just revenge, and the deviant's family will not be made to suffer as acutely as it often does when one of its members is imprisoned.

Reintegration is clearly central from a care perspective. The whole process is one of finding not just the least restrictive environment compatible with the interests of both deviant and society but, better, finding the most supportive environment for both. Its first move is not to remove people from their communities by labeling them as deviants or criminals unless this step is necessary to prevent demonstrable (not just vaguely potential) harm to themselves or others. Next, it would use forms of restitution, service, and reeducation to keep people in the community even as they are firmly reproved for their unlawful acts. When it is necessary to imprison deviants, thoughtful plans should be made for their reintegration on release. Finally, when there is no hope of release or the term of imprisonment is lengthy, there should be a system of positive incentives aimed at integrating prisoners into the community of prisoners closest to a respectable society. In this last case, although freedom may never be granted, there may be mutually beneficial exchanges between this better group of captives and the larger society. A crucial lesson learned at home is that it pays to create a world in which it is not only possible but also attractive to be good.

Society infers a need for its children to follow certain social rules and for its adult citizens to obey those norms written into law. In this chapter we have emphasized the importance of helping children to think about these rules and laws and to find well-considered reasons for accepting or rejecting them. Public response to the drug problem in the United States was used as a powerful example of the sort of conflict that can arise when the legal enforcement of norms does more harm than the deviance it aims to correct. I recommended that the war on drugs be abandoned because it threatens to destroy the web of care and trust on which we all depend. I also suggested ways in which the concept of positive desert might be used in the reintegration of those who are convicted of serious crimes.

In every chapter of this book I have argued that encounter and its accompanying affects are central to the development of a fully human, caring self. I have discussed, too, the importance of educating the caring response. The next (and last) chapter concentrates on the vital tasks of education.

CHAPTER 14

The Centrality of Education

Education may be thought of as a constellation of encounters, both planned and unplanned, that promote growth through the acquisition of knowledge, skills, understanding, and appreciation. The home is clearly a primary site of education, and what we have discussed about the best homes may help us to think more deeply about schooling. A full discussion of the aims of education, its conduct and content, will be pursued in a separate volume. Here the discussion will serve both as summary and prolegomenon.

We will look first at what the best homes do by way of educating. Then we will explore how a caring society might ensure that all children live in at least adequate homes. Finally, I will make a specific recommendation for social policy: that schools should educate not only for public life but also for home and private life. This last is an admittedly radical suggestion. I am not talking about an occasional course that might be labeled "home economics" or "child development." Rather, I am suggesting a curriculum that gives serious and pervasive attention to the development of young adults who will be capable of establishing better homes. Both contemporary liberals and conservatives are likely to oppose such a recommendation—liberals on the grounds that government (through public schools) should not intervene in private lives, conservatives on the similar grounds that families and religious institutions should control this area of education.

Best Homes as Educative

The best homes provide not only food, shelter, clothing, and protection but also attentive love; that is, at least one adult in the home listens to the needs expressed there and responds in a way that maintains caring relations. The way of relating characterized by attentive love is educative. Because it is attentive it sets the stage for children to explore more or less freely, to learn things that they really want to learn, and to understand why they must become at least minimally competent in some things they would prefer to avoid. With good-humored help in this last category, children sometimes adopt inferred needs as their own expressed needs.

The best homes prevent physical harms as far as possible, and they also minimize psychological harms. Children are neither beaten nor shamed. They are certainly not ignored or allowed to follow any whim that arises, and they are, infrequently, coerced. When coercion is used, it is explained and followed by negotiation. Adults in the best homes recognize the tension between expressed needs and inferred needs, and they regularly evaluate, reconsider, and negotiate both sets of needs.

The best homes approve of pleasure, and many pleasurable activities are shared. These activities may well be educative, but they are not always chosen with a specific learning objective in mind. They are chosen for the quality of experience expected. All kinds of learning may occur, and parents may guide and deepen the learning experience, but the children's expressed needs are always considered. They provide starting points, turning points, and end points. An activity may be encouraged for a while even when it has ceased to be pleasurable; that is, parents may push a child to persist because they spot a talent, see mastery on the horizon, or feel quite sure pleasure will return. But they do not use fear to motivate and, if fear arises, they address this first before resuming the planned activities.

Bertrand Russell wanted education to eliminate or reduce fear, not to aggravate it.

An education designed to eliminate fear is by no means difficult to create. It is only necessary to treat a child with kindness, to put him in an environment where initiative is possible without disastrous results, and to save him from contact with adults who have irrational terrors, whether of the dark, of mice, or of social revolution. A child must also not be subject to severe punishment, or to threats, or to grave and excessive reproof.[1]

The task is not quite so easy as Russell makes it sound, and in some ways it is more difficult today than it was in Russell's time. Children today, through technology, have many more encounters with strangers, and these encounters are harder to control. Fear is spread through the media, and it is not easy to tell when a particular fear is irrational. A school shooting two thousand miles away seems close because we see the images of grief directly and because this dreadful thing happened *in school*, a place that by its very familiarity seems close to all of us. Many parents today say that they cannot let their children play unsupervised outside. Kids can't wander about neighborhoods as they once could. This caution is inspired by fear.

Is this fear irrational? In many communities, if not most, it probably is irrational; that is, if people thought critically about the issue, their fear would be considerably reduced. Most neighborhoods are quite safe, and it is an educational loss that children are no longer permitted to explore nearby lanes, woods, and streams. How many children today are allowed to answer the question, "Where have you been?" with "Out!" Because parents see potential disasters in every unsupervised activity, it is not easy to establish environments "where initiative is possible." The best homes, assessing risks realistically and finding them small, allow their children some freedom to roam about outdoors.

The greater real danger probably arises in the privacy of homes. Children hear and see things on television and the Internet that would never be heard or seen in actual good homes. How can these encounters be controlled? There are electronic devices that can be used, but parents have to know what should be blocked, and there is no effective way to screen out undesirable lyrics that may appear on radio or on purchased CDs. Dependence on mechanical, recipelike quick fixes leads to frustration.

The way of attentive love suggests listening to and talking with children—living with them instead of guiding their lives by remote control. Some families get rid of their television sets and limit time on the computer. There is no one solution that will fit all families. The essential move seems to be one emphasized earlier: to help children (and ourselves) to understand the conditioning, the disciplinary powers, under which we all live. This is a fundamental task for any educational institution.

Parents monitor and limit television time to prevent harm, not to foreclose pleasure. We do not usually regard it as a waste of time when a child lies face down in the summer grass watching bugs and just "feeling the earth go round," nor do we make such a judgment when children build snowmen or lie down to make snow angels. Reasonably, we have to admit that a given child might "get more" from a well-chosen television program than from making a snowman. Why, then, choose bug watching and snowmen over television? Many good parents make this kind of choice unreflectively: "It's good for them to get outside." "They need some exercise." Beneath these platitudes, at a subconscious level, biophilia may be operating. Nostalgia may also affect our decisions on what to encourage. We remember our own pleasure in certain outdoor activities and want our children to experience them.

The best parents know, at least implicitly, that encounters build selves, and so they exercise some control over what their children encounter. Knowing that they cannot entirely eliminate undesirable encounters, they encourage their children to talk about these encounters, and, without watching them every minute or scheduling every hour, they provide opportunities for their children to have educative encounters. Educative encounters do not necessarily imply lessons. Indeed, many lessons are miseducative; that is, they turn the child away from the subject at hand and cause a breach in the relation between carer and cared-for. An educative encounter is marked by pleasure or satisfaction with the experience itself, and it leads to further experience—not necessarily of the exact same kind but of experiences thought to be somehow similar. A child who enjoys an afternoon or evening at the symphony might look forward to more musical experiences, but she may equally well be more open to theater, opera, or other cultural encounters suggested by her parents. The child who finds the evening at the symphony boring may still gain satisfaction from it if she is allowed to express her opinion and her parents say, "Okay, next time you get to choose." Similarly, an encounter with challenging material or a skill that is hard to master may yield little pleasure but some satisfaction. Parents provide support when children engage in such activities, but they avoid coercion, and they do what they can to enhance the quality of experience, perhaps reviving a pleasurable element.

This constant movement back and forth between expressed needs and inferred needs characterizes the home that takes its educative function seriously. Now and then an expressed need may be indulged even though the parents disapprove of it. Perhaps the whole family will watch a deplorably violent movie, but then there will be discussion. The hope, of course, is to move a child closer to the opinion his parents hold of such entertainment, and parents should be honest about this. The time together need not be spoiled by moralizing. Both children and parents express their opinions freely and question one another. This is a way of cultivating aesthetic and moral judgment without imposing it in an authoritarian way. Do we never say "This is disgusting" or "This is wrong!"? Of course we do. But when adults in the best homes make such pronouncements, children are likely to listen. They know that these statements are serious, that they are made from a deep sense of commitment. A violent movie may prompt a parent to say simply, "That's too much blood and gore for me," or "There wasn't much of a story there, was there?" Another sort of performance may bring outright condemnation: "Using that kind of language about women is wrong. Please get rid of that CD."

The fundamental aim of education is to help children grow in desirable ways. This is best accomplished by modeling, dialogue, practice, and confirmation.[2] Modeling is very powerful, and it appears as a component in almost every form of moral education. To be effective it must be genuine; that is, an exemplar must not consciously exhibit one form of behavior and then—caught off-guard—act in a way that contradicts what he or she has modeled. Even when modeling is entirely genuine, it does not always have a positive effect in a particular domain of study. A top-notch mathematician modeling mathematical thinking consistently, for example, will not necessarily inspire either her children or students to follow her ways. It may be, however, that something deeper than mathematical thinking—some positive attitude or approach to intellectual affairs—will be awakened in students. Modeling may be more effective in the moral domain than in the intellectual because its very authenticity is morally significant.

Dialogue is essential to education. In a true dialogue participants engage in mutual exploration, a search for meaning, or the solution of some problem. The teacher or leader does not have the answer at the outset, and the eventual outcome is uncertain. In the best homes dialogue often addresses the tension between expressed and inferred needs. What is the best thing to do? Johnny wants to do X. Father is not sure that this is a good course of action, at least at this time. Why not Y first? In a true dialogue both parties are open to discussion.

Ordinary conversation plays an important role, too. As we saw earlier, many of the things we learn at home or school are learned incidentally in ordinary conversation. This underscores the necessity of living with our children, delighting in their companionship, and sharing our interests with them. It underscores the centrality of attentive love. When the moment is right, we tell stories, recite lines of poetry, quote Abraham Lincoln, prepare an Italian meal, point out something wonderful in a piece of music, pose a mathematical puzzle, comment on world affairs, raise a question about how some gadget works, invite conjectures on why a pet is out of sorts . . . The possibilities are endless. We share, offer, invite, and try not to impose.

Clearly, however, not everything can be learned incidentally. My contention is that we rely far too little on incidental learning, but no reasonable person will claim that all education can proceed in this way. When a child becomes interested in some topic or in mastering some skill, direct instruction and practice are usually necessary and often welcome. When children are told honestly what can be expected as a result of practice, they often work diligently toward mastery of routines. Again, the idea is to use positive incentives in the form of culminating activities, not as rewards. To be able to play an admired piece of music may be incentive enough to keep a child at piano practice. Mathematics students will often slog willingly through manipulative exercises if they believe an important and interesting theorem requires these skills. Readers could offer many like examples. Parents and teachers have to remain sensitive to the rise and fall of interests in their students. This is yet another way of balancing expressed and inferred needs. If children cease to believe us when we tell them that there will be (or could be) a payoff for their deferring their own wants, then our work as educators becomes harder.

Guiding practice toward something worthwhile is part of educating for discrimination. We want children to distinguish between the important and the trivial, and their learning to do this depends on our talking to them, giving them honest reasons for the practice we require or strongly suggest. Too often we fail to give reasons ("just do it") or we put uniform weight on everything we require them to do. My math students were sometimes surprised when I suggested that they complete enough easy exercises "to get the idea." If you can do the harder ones, I told them, skip the easy ones. In the same vein, it may be a mistake to push children to do uniformly well in all subjects. What of their real interests? We should not want to destroy burning interests by turning the whole curriculum (at home or school) into a standard set of tasks— demanding that all be done well. The very best students often learn to do an adequate job on requirements and save their best efforts for their central interest.

The last element in the model described here is confirmation. When we see a realistic possibility of a better self or a better performance about to emerge, we confirm the child in this image. This truly beautiful gesture, confirmation, can be used in a range of situations. If a child is struggling with a math problem or a musical passage, we can say, "You've almost got it!" instead of "This part is still wrong." In moral education we attribute the best possible motive consonant with reality for the child's acts. This is not a mere strategy or technique and cannot be used in the absence of some knowledge of the child. The motive attributed to anyone's act must be consonant with reality in the sense that it really is the sort of motive we have come to expect of this person. Confirming a person avoids shame and leads upward toward a vision of a better self.

The purpose of this brief discussion of educative homes is to impress on the reader the great importance of the education that goes on in homes. One of the few things we know with virtual certainty from educational research is that there is no single factor more important in a child's success than the home. Sometimes we locate this importance in the socioeconomic status of the home, sometimes in the educational status of the parents, sometimes in parental attitudes toward schooling, and sometimes in the methods parents use to educate their children. All are important.

For present purposes, discussion of the home as primary educator leads to two major recommendations for social policy: first, that every child should live in a home that has at least adequate material resources and attentive love; and, second, that schools should include education for home life in their curriculum. A third recommendation—that schools should, as nearly as possible, use the sort of methods found in best homes to educate—I will defer for another volume.

A Home for Every Child

I have already discussed homelessness and ways to eliminate that condition. We have the resources. We now need the will to move ahead, the imagination to design flexible plans, and the patience to revise them as we put them into action. The more rigid the plan, the less likely it is to work. Then, of course, people will say that "we tried that, and it didn't work." The appropriate response to this defeatism is that we will never have tried hard enough until homelessness is eliminated.

Sometimes, however, although a family is housed, the home provided is not adequate from an educational perspective. In many cases there is little we can do; the parents in question need parent education and may be unwilling to accept it. In other difficult cases children are moved about among relations, and there is no stability in their lives.[3] In still others a single parent may be working so many hours that he or she simply cannot cope with the demands of parenting. And sometimes, although the family is well meaning, the local school is so bad that we would have to call it miseducative. Then, understandably, parents who are unable to perform the educative function themselves give up. They and their children are beaten by a society that should extend a helping hand. There is no voice responding, "I am here."

Carole Boston Weatherford has suggested a revival of boarding schools for some inner city students.[4] This is a radical suggestion, but Weatherford points out that traditionally black colleges once provided such services quite effectively. Moreover, we have learned from the disastrous residential programs for Native Americans how not to conduct boarding schools for minority children. I think her idea is important and should be tried experimentally. Again, in addition to existing college campuses, abandoned and underutilized military camps could be used. The children in these schools would be enrolled on a voluntary basis.

I want to suggest an alternative that might be less expensive and would do more to build up a healthy home environment. In talking with school principals I have learned that some parents just can't get their children to school, help with homework, supervise playtime, and do all the things we expect of good parents. Sometimes a single mother is a drug or alcohol addict; she wants to do right by her child but fails again and again. Sometimes the mother is a prostitute and knows that her home is an unsavory place, especially when she works at home. Sometimes the mother is just exhausted. If there were a school-operated boarding home near the school, many of these mothers would voluntarily enroll their children. The children would check in on Sunday night and return to their parents on Friday afternoon. Under this plan children would not be taken away from parents who love them, but they would learn something about how good homes function. Parents who are able to do so could also attend homemaking and parenting courses provided in the boarding house.

These homes would not be dismal institutions. They would model the best practices of home life, and—since they would be under the school's supervision—they would be able to provide continuity between home and school life. All of the legitimate expectations children have in the best homes should be met in these school-homes: snacks, help with homework, good meals, the right to have friends visit, lots of books and games, perhaps a resident pet or two. The place should be safe, orderly, and attractive. It should be educative. Children would not be "inmates," and only those children in danger of being removed entirely from their families would be coerced into enrolling. All of the others would be voluntary.

Additional benefits of this plan would include the improvement of at least a few housing units near the school. Districts could buy or rent properties and increase or decrease their occupancy depending on need. Volunteers, including teenagers, could help with painting, yard work, and a host of home-related tasks. Everyone involved would learn more about what it takes to establish and maintain an attractive home. A further benefit would be the likely number of families saved from dissolution. A plan of this sort gives parents who are foundering a fighting chance to rehabilitate themselves or to get on their feet financially. With the school's active help, other social services could concentrate on the problems of adult family members. This, too, represents an auxiliary benefit: schools and social agencies might work more effectively together.

"Boarding" or "lodging" children in homes near schools so that they can be "day students" has a long history,[5] but in the past parents usually had to pay the bill. However, it was not uncommon for rural American teenagers in the early twentieth century to trade work for lodging with reputable townspeople.[6] These people were usually highly respectable (guarding the virtue of their female lodgers), and sometimes they acted as mentors, greatly expanding the education of their charges. There were also the Dickensian characters who overworked their young lodgers and humiliated them. Every system has a potential for abuse, but the remedy for abuse is careful supervision and responsible revision and renewal. Only if the treatment does more harm than the original ailment (as in the war on drugs) should the treatment be given up.

A combination of privately funded residential schools and publicly funded weekday boarding homes should be tried and carefully evaluated. The latter might help to strengthen the public schools by protecting and motivating some of the schools' more difficult pupils, thus improving the academic environment for all students. In contrast, current plans for providing a better education for poor students often tend to undermine the public schools. Voucher plans, ostensibly offered to aid poor families whose children are trapped in failing schools, purport to strengthen public schools by increasing competition. The idea is that consumer demand and satisfaction should act to squeeze out inadequate schools and increase support for those doing a good job. The fallacies here are several.

First, education should be regarded as a public good, not a consumer good. Families supplied with vouchers will never be able to buy the kind of education that upper-middle-class parents can afford, any more than they can purchase comparable houses, cars, or medical services. Second, shutting down a school that is failing because of market forces—because, with the help of vouchers, parents have moved their children to another school—is not the same as closing a corner bakery or gas station. Children's daily lives are involved. Continuity in education is important. Where do parents turn when it is announced that their child's school is closing? They have to find another and disrupt the child's friendship patterns, relationships with teachers, and place-centered attachment. If voucher enthusiasts insist that this will rarely happen, how can they argue at the same time that *market forces* will improve education? Market forces will inevitably induce entrepreneurs to get into the business, and a significant number will fail. One of the enormous strengths of the local school is that, to borrow from Robert Frost, "When you have to go there, they have to take you in."[7] Our task is to make the schools better so that children are not made to suffer when they "have to go there."

Finally, without arguing the constitutionality of using vouchers for education in religious schools, we have to recognize that some religious institutions would deprive girls of the knowledge and choices guaranteed by a liberal-democratic society. It can be argued, of course, that what "we" see as deprivation is part of God's loving plan for family life. We are pledged to allow this as religious instruction, but we cannot endorse it as part of public education. A child may choose this way of life in her maturity, but the public school stands as a guardian of her right to make this choice or some other.

Educating for Private Life

There has always been strong resistance in America to teaching home-related topics and skills in public schools. Indeed, one objection to some of progressive education's recommendations was its intrusive (and perhaps superfluous) attempts to teach everyday skills. Household skills, parenting, home nursing, and the like were not part of traditional male liberal education. When young women were educated separately, they studied such topics; they were explicitly prepared for private life if they were educated at all.[8] In contrast, young men were prepared for public life, and the pattern that emerged in their education became the foundation of liberal education. When girls were admitted to the schooling once reserved for boys, it seemed a great victory. To suggest, then, that all children should be exposed to an education once meant only for girls seemed, and still seems to some, an outrageous, "anti-intellectual" move.

The liberal legacy is itself involved here. Traditional liberalism has been strongly resistant to any intervention in private life. As we saw earlier, only harm to others warranted intervention, and a man's home was his castle. This policy of nonintervention did not, however, apply to women and children. They were not regarded as fully rational, independent persons. Teaching girls how to manage homes and raise children was regarded as appropriate training for the roles they were expected to play, not as an intrusion into private life. When suggestions are made today that all children should learn something (a lot, I would say) about household management, child rearing, and a host of topics related to home life, the response is likely to be, "Oh, no. Those are topics for the home to teach," or "I don't want someone else teaching those things to my child." Yet, in a time not long ago, it was entirely acceptable to school girls in these matters.

Few girls were being prepared for college at that time, and even at mid-twentieth century those girls who did attend college rarely went on to full-time employment outside the home. The liberal education that was widely touted as nonoccupational nevertheless seemed to prepare young men for almost any field—a broad education appropriate for public and professional life. The same education finally granted to women seemed to prepare them for work only as teachers or secretaries. In this we have one of the great educational contradictions of all time: a form of education that does not prepare anyone for a particular occupation, yet prepares a whole class of people for almost anything they want to do. It is not surprising that, because liberal education no longer has quite the exclusionary effects it once had, it is no longer so attractive. Instead of questioning the whole pattern, most feminists have accepted the male model and have objected only to the inequality.

An honest objection that can be raised against education for home life is that it might do little to prepare students for college. After all, that was, traditionally, not its purpose. Indeed, its purpose was antithetical to college preparation, and for this reason many prominent women educators also opposed it.[9] Now the question arises how the schools could possibly manage to perform both tasks well. One response to this is to back off a bit and ask just what role the school actually plays in preparing students for college. It clearly provides the credentials and many of the bits of information and particular skills required, but it is the start at home that makes the school's success possible, and many of the specific requirements of colleges are both arbitrary and artificial. Thus, by withholding the knowledge needed for success in life construed more broadly, we are ensuring that some families and their children will never succeed.

We talk the opposite line of course. We promote the notion that we are giving children a chance at life's goods by forcing them all to take algebra and geometry, when in fact relatively few will actually use what they learn in these subjects. Consider that, in contrast, all of us establish homes, and most of us become parents. Success cannot be defined, either, in just occupational or financial terms.[10] If this were a utopian tract, which it is not, we would have to explore and describe a totally new and properly balanced curriculum.

It is entirely possible and highly desirable to transform the existing curriculum from the inside of each discipline. This still gives priority of name and place to the traditional male curriculum, but it is probably the only practical way to begin. We begin by asking what it is that all children need to lead lives that are both productive and deeply satisfying. Educators have, from time to time, considered this question seriously. In 1918, for example, the Cardinal Principles report suggested seven major aims for education: health, command of fundamental processes, worthy home membership, vocation, citizenship, worthy use of leisure, and ethical character.[11] The writers were not suggesting, of course, that these aims become the titles of courses, but that every subject taught in schools should contribute significantly to one or more (preferably more) of the aims. A subject too narrowly constructed to achieve one aim might fail even at that because life is not easily broken up into discrete categories.

Notice how far we have moved from this reasonable approach to curriculum building. With the present emphasis on higher test scores for familiar, traditional subjects, we have all but discarded several of these important aims. Thinking deeply on the matter, we might want to expand the aims by adding something on aesthetic appreciation and spirituality. We would surely not want to eliminate any of the seven.

In what follows I will give suggestions for illustrative purposes. The idea is to show that what we learn about and care about at home can be creatively and profitably extended to schools. Consider, first, an example at the level of secondary school English. Not long ago I talked to a group of sophomores at a so-called Abbott district school in New Jersey. This school is in one of the thirty poorest districts in the state, and under a recent ruling of the state's supreme court, they are eligible for extra funds. So far it isn't clear that extra funds will strengthen a dull curriculum. These tenth graders spent almost an entire semester reading (and, presumably, discussing) Hawthorne's *The Scarlet Letter*. They hated it, struggled with the vocabulary and, as nearly as I could tell from listening to them, completed the unit with even greater contempt for literature, reading, and school learning in general. Why force these kids to read *The Scarlet Letter*? The answer given was that it is part of the time-honored academic curriculum and that kids "like these" have been too long deprived of such material.

This is a wonderful example of caring-as-virtue undermining caring-as-relation. The kids do not feel cared for, and I doubt that they will ever look back on this experience and say, "I'm so glad I was forced to read *The Scarlet Letter*." The experience was miseducative for almost all of them, but the teacher and school feel justified because they are "being fair" to everyone.

Suppose, instead, the class had been asked to do a study of children's fairy tales. This would provide an opportunity for some to revisit much-loved stories from their childhood and an equally important opportunity for others to read the stories for the first time. Now, is this just a paternalistic way of saying that "these kids" can only read children's stories? Certainly not. It could be a challenging and relevant unit for any high school student. The stories could be combined with accessible psychological studies — Bruno Bettelheim's *Uses of Enchantment*, for example — that discuss the pros and cons of various themes in fairy tales. Students might be invited to compare the stories in their original form (quite cruel and gory) with various modified forms. Consider, for example, the version of "Snow White" in which the end of the wicked queen is described thus: "But iron slippers were heated over the fire and were soon brought in with tongs and put before her. And she had to step into the red-hot shoes and dance until she fell down dead."[12] This ending offers good questions for discussion. Should small children hear this version? Why or why not? Is Bettelheim right that mothers should never be cast as witches nor fathers as ogres? What is the rationale for this warning?

Students might also compare movie versions with written texts. They might spend time on the illustrations in different versions and be invited to make evaluations of them. Some might want to study Caldecott Medal winners and try their own hands at children's illustrations. Such a project might encourage cooperation between art and literature teachers. It should certainly encourage the discovery of talent and the sort of discussion that should lead to finer discrimination.

Students could be asked to locate on available maps the places in which the fairy tales and fables were written or to which they refer. They could learn that there is a fairy tale road that is popular with tourists in Germany, and they should be able to locate Denmark, the home of Hans Christian Andersen. Can they find Greece, where Aesop's fables originated? When did these writers live? It should be obvious that an enormous amount of incidental learning can be acquired as students revisit the literature of childhood. The study could hardly be called nonintellectual.

The main purpose of rereading and analyzing children's literature is to enrich the personal lives of students and the families they will some day establish. Connections can be made to myths and to Jungian psychology, hence to gender studies and further explorations of the various differences that have been ascribed to males and females. The cultural-intellectual possibilities are rich.

Time should be spent, too, discussing how parents read to children. Students would learn that as parents and their children spend time together looking at illustrations, wise parents encourage children not only to name the various objects and creatures that appear but to count them. "How many birdies?" The classroom discussion could center on the development of numeracy. How can we tell when children are ready to count and begin some simple arithmetic processes? Why is a sense of one-to-one correspondence so fundamental? What kinds of games and activities will help children to develop a sense of cardinality—of two-ness, three-ness, and so on? Here is an opportunity to cooperate with a mathematics teacher but, more important, it is an opportunity for adolescents to learn something valuable about how to work with younger siblings and, eventually, with their own children.

Much of what I am discussing here (and of the huge amount of material that *could* be discussed here) belongs to the domain of early childhood education. Why should the material learned by preservice professionals be confined to professional training? It is demonstrably more valuable in the hands of parents who will use it around the clock and continuously over several years. It is material that should be part of every child's preparation for parenthood.

What, then, of *The Scarlet Letter*? Suppose there are questions about it on some required test. While we are rereading fairy tales and fables, teaching adolescents some psychology, helping them to learn something about cognitive development, and sharing information on mathematics and geography, the test demands that they identify Hester Prynne, Arthur Dimmesdale, and Roger Chillingworth. We might respond to this mentality, which tests trivia and piles it in ever-greater loads on our children, with Susan Ohanian's recent "to hell with it."[13] I think she is right to express exasperation and to plead for a change in educational policy that is, in essence, a major reflection of social policy.

As long as these tests threaten our children with high stakes, however, we have to respond with help. One reasonable move is to prepare single sheets on each of the novels and other literary works about which students will be asked and tell them to memorize the facts for the test. Of course, material learned in this way will decay rapidly, but the effects of a whole semester of slogging through *The Scarlet Letter* are no better with respect to retention and far worse for most students with respect to any appreciation of the place of literature in a full personal life, a desire to read, or an ability to use what is learned in family life. If one truly believes that no child should be deprived of *The Scarlet Letter*, there is another solution. Small book clubs could be established in each class. In addition to the whole-class study of fairy tales (for example), small groups could choose a book from an approved list of great classics and study it together. The groups could report to the class so that everyone could become at least familiar with the themes and characters. The literature read in this way might be deservedly appreciated, and so it, too, would contribute to the richness of personal life and not merely to passing a test.

Just as we properly ask now what a given course may contribute to important competencies in reading, writing, speaking, the exercise of citizenship, the use of technology, appreciation of the arts, and occupational preparation, we should ask what it may contribute to a full personal life and, especially, to parenting and home life. In addition, a continuing course (every year of secondary school) in home and parenting would be useful. This course would treat more intensively and systematically the topics central to family life and would include sex education, pregnancy, birth, motherhood and fatherhood, child development, home design and aesthetics, the care of nonhuman living things, nutrition, meal planning and cooking, care of those with special needs (including the elderly), home repair and safety, budgeting and consumer knowledge, moral education, exercise and recreation. Competent, creative educators will find ways to connect most of these topics to both the existing disciplines and to individual lives.

A dilemma arises out of the recommendation for a "continuing course" in home and parenting. Should this be a required course? Another act of coercion? I have already argued that although we often fail to intervene in the lives of adults even when they are demonstrably harming themselves, we are too quick to coerce children. But if the course is not required, many students who have their eyes narrowly focused on advanced placement courses and entrance to elite colleges will not take it. It will be labeled "Mickey Mouse"—an easy course for kids who can't take the rigors of tough courses. These conscientious (and, one might say less approvingly, grade-grubbing) students badly need education for private life; they need it for themselves, their families, and their enlightenment as citizens.

If it is required, however, we can be quite sure that it will be subjected not only to a flood of predictable complaints but also to the usual academic rigors—prescribed courses of study, tests, and grades. Further, there will be constant pressure to construct the course in a way that favors those who typically do well in academic courses. This tendency is real and powerful. We have seen it in art, for example, where some educators have tried (with considerable success) to deemphasize studio art—which attracts the artistically talented—and emphasize instead art history and criticism which, predictably, appeal more to the academically talented. If we add to this worry the question of whether the new course will qualify for college entrance credit, we greatly increase the loading in favor of preparation for college, not for a full and happy personal life.

We could answer the worries of parents who fear that the new course might distract their children from "real" academic studies by giving each year of the course an official label. One year might be divided between mathematics and economics, and the subject matter would be budgeting, consumer education, and the like. Another would be a science course devoted to nutrition, home nursing, sex education, birth . . . and so on. The problem is by now a familiar one. The traditional disciplines still control our efforts. Topics and issues that should be treated holistically—as they arise and must be handled in real life—are fragmented and narrowly constrained. Dare we talk about values in sex education if sex education is part of *science*? If the new course were not required, the solution explored above would be no solution at all because the course would be construed as an alternative to "real" science, mathematics, social studies, and so forth.

I cannot suggest an easy solution to this dilemma. The sensible way is probably to move slowly and persistently. Insist that topics central to private life be incorporated in all courses. Add one course at a time to home and parenting. Start with child development and call it psychology to give it respectability. The heart aches. We women have won tremendous victories in, finally, entering the realm of male-controlled public life, but much of the victory has come at the expense of denigrating our own traditional contributions. Were these contributions negligible? Were these occupations and ways of being so unimportant that no one needs to pursue them now? Or is it possible to start with what is learned in better homes and rebuild both education and the wider social world?

Dare we teach for private life? I think we must. A caring society will be sure that all its people have at least adequate housing, material resources, and medical care. Beyond satisfying basic legitimate needs, it must ask how it can best encourage the kind of encounters that will support the development of competent, caring, fully alive, and interesting people. Our present emphasis on academic learning for all is a misguided effort at doing this. We suppose that by giving all children a formal opportunity (that is, by coercing them) to learn the subjects once reserved for the privileged, we are thereby giving them all a chance at the good life. We skip over the essential starting place when we fail to recognize the home as first and primary educator.

It is not only those who cling to a form of classical liberalism who object to educating for private life. Some multiculturalists object on the grounds that, in so doing, we will inevitably favor one way of life over another. Albeit with good intentions, we will convey the notion that some cultural patterns are deficient. We have to answer this objection with sensitivity and honesty. Some ways of child rearing *are* deficient, but they are not necessarily associated with particular "cultures" if we mean by "culture" a race-based or ethnicity-based set of customs. And some ways that are associated with specific cultures may indeed be deficient if we mean by deficient "not likely to produce the best outcomes" in a society dominated by a different culture.

What is needed here is not a fearful, undiscriminating, and basically dishonest respect for anything and everything found in "an other" culture, but an honest and generous sharing, a recognition of interdependence and the possibility of learning from one another. Jane Addams, sometimes criticized today as an "assimilationist," was actually a strong advocate of maintaining the original cultures of immigrants. She wanted "to build a bridge between European and American experiences in such wise as to give them both more meaning and a sense of relation."[14] This is the attitude we need today.

When people are hurting their own chances for success and happiness we have to muster the courage to intervene. Intervention need not imply coercion. We can make an offer of help and accept its rejection. We can even back off and admit that the ends we seek are nonessential and, in some cases, ill-advised. But sometimes we have enough evidence to suggest that the needs we infer for others really are crucial. Then we can at least insist that people be exposed to the crucial possibilities. We cannot consider seriously that which we never encounter. In education we do this now with a poorly justified insistence on algebra and geometry for all, but we give poor and minority students little reason for accepting our coercion. We tell them that they will gain entrance to college, that they will get better jobs, even that they will use this material "some day," but we do not introduce them to ways of life that might help to make sense of all this. We are not honest about the fundamental differences in family life that make it possible to suffer nonsense and sometimes to bring sense to it all for the very sake of a cherished way of life.

I am certainly not arguing that only poor and minority children need preparation for home life. I have already insisted that all children do. Those from homes that approximate what I have called "best homes" need to know that people differ on parenting practices, and all socially acceptable practices should be discussed. With time at a premium in most homes, schools must supplement and reinforce the educational efforts of homes.

Parenting need not be taught in a dogmatic fashion. We should avoid indoctrination where we can. Most of the psychology we would teach children should be presented as "the best we have today" or the "prevailing position," not as absolute truth, and opposing positions should be discussed. Yet our efforts should not be restricted to theory, technical vocabulary, and the opinions of particular experts presented for memorization. There should be a substantial provision for practice—for "how to do it." Practice, too, should be open to responsible experimentation and revision. Like care theory itself, education for parenting remains deliberately incomplete—open to what is learned in caring relations.

We would be foolish indeed to reject the hard-won rights that liberalism has brought us. Much of what has been learned in public life can be usefully applied to private life. The reverse is also true, however, and its consideration is long overdue.

Jean Bethke Elshtain has remarked that "the activation of a female participatory capability must begin with her immediate concerns, go on to give a robust account of them, and then bring these concerns to a transformed vision of the political community."[1] I have suggested here that women's concerns go well beyond interests in their own advancement in public life. They have roots in an underappreciated tradition, particularly in the fundamental and complex enterprise of establishing and maintaining a home that can support the growth of all its members. Although we cannot simply transpose the caring characteristic of home life onto social and political life, we can take what is learned—starting at home—and use it to build a public ethic of care. As Grace Clement has said, construed rightly, "The public ethic of care supports rather than undermines its corresponding private ethic of care."[2] The response of carer to cared-for in either domain is a reassuring "I am here."

I have tried to show that an ethics of care in the public domain shares a tension characteristic of natural caring. We must attend to both expressed and inferred needs, using coercion rarely but with great sensitivity. We do not stand by and allow people to harm themselves, but we are spare in our definition of harms and we do not define our caring in terms of our own favorite virtues. We aim to establish, maintain, and enhance caring relations. Wherever possible, we avoid the notion of negative desert. Admitting nevertheless that we often "bring things on ourselves," we try to learn and to teach how this happens, and we offer positive incentives in the form of realized expectations for behavior that promotes the mutual good. An ethic of care, private and public, works to create a world in which it is both possible and attractive to be good.

NOTES

Introduction

1. See, for example, Grace Clement, *Care, Autonomy, and Justice* (Boulder: Westview Press, 1996); Ann Diller, "An Ethics of Care Takes on Pluralism," in *The Gender Question in Education,* ed. Ann Diller, Barbara Houston, Kathryn Pauly Morgan, and Maryann Ayim (Boulder: Westview Press, 1991), 161–169; Nancy Fraser, "Social Justice in the Age of Identity Politics: Redistribution, Recognition, and Participation," Tanner Lecture on Human Values, Stanford University, 1996; Virginia Held, *Feminist Morality* (Chicago: University of Chicago Press, 1993); Joan Tronto, *Moral Boundaries: A Political Argument for an Ethic of Care* (New York: Routledge, 1993); Margaret Urban Walker, *Moral Understandings* (New York: Routledge, 1998). In addition, some writers have examined extensively the relation between care and moral excellence. See, for example, Jeffrey Blustein, *Care and Commitment* (New York: Oxford University Press, 1991); Lawrence Blum, *Moral Perception and Particularity* (Cambridge: Cambridge University Press, 1994); Michael Slote, "The Justice of Caring," *Social Philosophy and Policy* 15, no. 1 (1998): 171–195; also Michael Slote, "Caring versus the Philosophers," in *Philosophy of Education 1999,* ed. Randall Curren (Urbana: Philosophy of Education Society, 2000), 25–35.

2. See Lorraine Code, *What Can She Know? Feminist Theory and the Construction of Knowledge* (Ithaca: Cornell University Press, 1991).

3. See Isaiah Berlin, *Four Essays on Liberty* (Oxford: Oxford University Press, 1969).

4. See, again, Code, *What Can She Know?* Also Sara Ruddick, *Maternal Thinking: Towards a Politics of Peace* (Boston: Beacon Press, 1989).

5. See Nel Noddings, *Caring: A Feminine Approach to Ethics and Moral Education* (Berkeley: University of California Press, 1984).

Chapter 1. Caring

1. Milton Mayeroff, *On Caring* (New York: Harper & Row, 1971), 1.

2. See Jacques Derrida, "'Genesis and Structure' and Phenomenology," in *Writing and Difference,* trans. and ed. Alan Bass (Chicago: University of Chicago Press, 1978), 154–168; also Jean-Paul Sartre, *Being and Nothingness,* trans. Hazel E. Barnes (New York: Washington Square Press, 1956), 9–24.

3. For a discussion of such situations, see Noddings, *Caring.*

4. Webster's New Universal Dictionary, 1979. For a history of "empathy," see Susan Verducci, "A Conceptual History of Empathy and the Questions It Raises for Moral Education," *Educational Theory* 50 (2000): 63–80.

5. Ibid.

6. Ibid.

7. The primacy of the cared-for is similar conceptually to Levinas's primacy of the other. We are morally obligated even before meeting a particular other. See Emmanuel Levinas, "Ethics as First Philosophy," in *The Levinas Reader,* ed. Seán Hand (Oxford: Blackwell, 1989), 75–87. There is an important difference of emphasis, however, in that—from the care perspective—"I" may be (indeed must be at the start) the cared-for. "I" am not always and only the responding moral agent.

8. Simone Weil, *Simone Weil Reader,* ed. George A. Panichas (Mt. Kisco, N.Y.: Moyer Bell Limited, 1977), 51.

9. Ibid.

10. Quoted in H. J. Blackham, *Six Existentialist Thinkers* (New York: Harper & Row, 1959), 80.

11. Ibid.

12. Martin Buber, *I and Thou,* trans. Walter Kaufman (New York: Charles Scribner's Sons, 1970), 59.

13. Martin Buber, *The Way of Response,* ed. Nahum N. Glatzer (New York: Schocken Books, 1996), 17–18.

14. Buber, *I and Thou,* 58.

15. Sara Ruddick, "Maternal Thinking," *Feminist Studies* 6, no. 2 (1980): 342–367.

16. Noddings, *Caring,* 112.

17. Susan Okin, "Reason and Feeling in Thinking about Justice," *Ethics* 99, no. 2 (1989): 230.

18. See Charles Dickens, *Bleak House,* 2 vols. (New York: Peter Fenelon Collier, n.d.).

19. See the discussion in Held, *Feminist Morality.*

20. Okin, "Reason and Feeling," 231.

21. See John Rawls, *Political Liberalism* (New York: Columbia University Press, 1993).

22. David Hume, *An Enquiry Concerning the Principles of Morals* (Indianapolis: Hackett, 1983), 15.

23. John Rawls, *A Theory of Justice* (Cambridge: Harvard University Press, 1971), 490.

24. Urie Bronfenbrenner, "Who Needs Parent Education?" *Teachers College Record* 74 (1978): 774.

25. Umberto Eco, *Foucault's Pendulum,* trans. William Weaver (San Diego: Harcourt Brace Jovanovich, 1989), 49.

26. See Philip W. Jackson, *Untaught Lessons* (New York: Teachers College Press, 1992).

27. Martin Buber, *Between Man and Man* (New York: Macmillan, 1965), 88.

28. Ibid., 98.

29. See Charles Taylor, *Philosophy and the Human Sciences,* Philosophical Papers 2 (Cambridge: Cambridge University Press, 1985).

30. See Richard A. Seltzer, Jody Newman, and Melissa Voorhees Leighton, *Sex as a Political Variable: Women as Candidates and Voters in U.S. Elections* (Boulder: Lynne Reinner, 1997); Sue Tolleson Rinehart, *Gender Consciousness and Politics* (New York: Routledge, 1992).

31. P. D. James, *A Taste for Death* (London: Sphere Books, 1986), 431.

32. For a history of women's role in caring, see Susan Reverby, *Ordered to Care* (Cambridge: Cambridge University Press, 1987); for a discussion of attitudes remaining today, see Nel Noddings, "Moral Obligation or Moral Support," in *Bringing the Hospital Home,* ed. John Arras (Baltimore: Johns Hopkins University Press, 1995).

33. See Kari Waerness, "The Rationality of Caring," in *Caregiving,* ed. Suzanne Gordon, Patricia Benner, and Nel Noddings (Philadelphia: University of Pennsylvania Press, 1996), 231–255.

34. See Noddings, *Caring,* ch. 5.

35. See Rawls, *A Theory of Justice.*

Chapter 2. Harm and Care

1. John Stuart Mill, *"On Liberty" and "Utilitarianism"* (New York: Bantam Books, 1993), 12.

2. See, for example, James Fitzjames Stephen, "The Doctrine of Liberty in Its Applications to Morals," in *Morality, Harm, and the Law,* ed. Gerald Dworkin (Boulder: Westview Press), 26–35; see also Isaiah Berlin, "Two Concepts of Liberty," in *Liberalism and Its Critics,* ed. Michael Sandel (New York: New York University Press, 1984), 15–36.

3. *Prosser and Keeton on the Law of Torts,* ed. W. Page Keeton (St. Paul: West, 1984), 375.

4. Mary Ann Glendon, *Rights Talk* (New York: Free Press, 1991), 79.

5. John D. Caputo, *Against Ethics* (Bloomington: Indiana University Press, 1993).

6. Glendon, *Rights Talk,* 77.

7. Held, *Feminist Morality,* 207.

8. Alasdair MacIntyre, *After Virtue* (Notre Dame: University of Notre Dame Press, 1981), 69.

9. Plato, *The Great Dialogues,* book 1, *Republic,* trans. B. Jowett (Roslyn, N.Y.: Walter J. Black, 1942).

10. George Orwell, *The Orwell Reader* (New York: Harcourt, Brace, 1956), 11.

11. Ibid., 13.

12. Quoted in Michael Walzer, *Just and Unjust Wars* (New York: Basic Books, 1977), 140.

13. Caputo, *Against Ethics,* 6.

14. Samuel Butler, *The Way of All Flesh* (Garden City, N.Y.: Doubleday, 1944), 30–31.

15. Ibid., 97.

16. Ibid., 287.

17. See Alice Miller, *For Your Own Good,* trans. Hildegarde and Hunter Hannun (New York: Farrar, Straus, Giroux, 1983). My use of her work is illustrative. I, like many others, have reservations about the strength of her argument.

18. Butler, *Way of All Flesh,* 241.

19. See Orwell's essay, "Such, Such Were the Joys," in *The Orwell Reader,* 419–456.

20. Ibid., 431.

21. Ibid., 423.

22. See "Symposium on Caring," in *Hypatia* 5, no. 1 (1990): 101–126.

23. See Tronto, *Moral Boundaries.*

24. Jane Roland Martin has also argued along these lines. See Jane Roland Martin, *Reclaiming a Conversation* (New Haven: Yale University Press, 1985); also, Jane Roland Martin, *The Schoolhome: Rethinking Schools for Changing Families* (Cambridge: Harvard University Press, 1992).

25. See Nel Noddings, "On the Alleged Parochialism of Caring," *Newsletter on Feminism,* 1991, 96–99. The *Newsletter* is published by the American Philosophical Association.

26. See Robin K. Berson, *Marching to a Different Drummer: Unrecognized Heroes of American History* (Westport, Conn.: Greenwood Press, 1994).

27. Ibid., 83.

28. Michael Slote's very interesting argument for "balance" in the distribution of one's care will be useful here. See Slote, "Caring versus the Philosophers."

29. Orwell, *Reader,* 249.

30. Edith Wyschogrod, *Saints and Postmodernism: Revising Moral Philosophy* (Chicago: University of Chicago Press, 1990), 49.

31. The quote from Emmanual Levinas appears in Jacques Derrida, *Writing and Difference,* trans. Alan Bass (Chicago: University of Chicago Press, 1978), 100.

32. Diana Koos Gentry, *Enduring Women* (College Station: Texas A & M University, 1988), 156–157.

33. See Carol Gilligan, *In a Different Voice* (Cambridge: Harvard University Press, 1982).

34. Wyschogrod, *Saints and Postmodernism,* 52.

Chapter 3. Needs

1. See Nancy Fraser, *Unruly Practices: Power, Discourse, and Gender in Contemporary Social Theory* (Minneapolis: University of Minnesota Press, 1989).

2. See Glendon, *Rights Talk.*

3. Many more details will be added to support this claim, but several such works should be mentioned here: Fraser, *Unruly Practices;* Held, *Feminist Morality;* Alison M. Jaggar, *Feminist Politics and Human Nature* (Totowa, N.J.: Rowman & Allanheld, 1983); Okin, "Reason and Feeling"; Ruddick, *Maternal Thinking;* Tronto, *Moral Boundaries;* Iris Marion Young, "Impartiality and the Civic Public," in *Feminism as Critique,* ed. Seyla Benhabib and Drucilla Cornell (Minneapolis: University of Minnesota Press, 1987), 56–76; also, Iris Marion Young, *Justice and the Politics of Difference* (Princeton: Princeton University Press, 1990).

4. See David Braybrooke, *Meeting Needs* (Princeton: Princeton University Press, 1987).

5. See Sissela Bok, *Lying: Moral Choice in Public and Private Life* (New York: Vintage Books, 1979).

6. See, among others, Derek Parfit, *Reasons and Persons* (Oxford: Clarendon Press, 1984); and Larry Temkin, "Harmful Goods, Harmless Bads," in *Value, Welfare, and Morality,* ed. R. G. Frey and Christopher W. Morris (Cambridge: Cambridge University Press, 1993), 290–324.

7. See Abraham Maslow, *Motivation and Personality* (New York: Harper & Row, 1970).

8. Jaggar, *Feminist Politics,* 42.

9. Tronto, *Moral Boundaries,* 138.

10. Ibid.

11. See Ruddick, *Maternal Thinking.*

12. Berlin, "Two Concepts of Liberty," in *Four Essays on Liberty* (Oxford: Oxford University Press, 1969), 118–172.

13. Ibid., 133.

14. Held, *Feminist Morality,* 211.

Chapter 4. Why Liberalism Is Inadequate

1. For a recent account of the merits of phronesis over the formalism of liberalism, see Joseph Dunne, *Back to the Rough Ground* (Notre Dame: University of Notre Dame Press, 1993).

2. See Dewey's still eloquent reminder of this in John Dewey, *Liberalism and Social Action* (New York: G. P. Putnam's Sons, 1935); also in John Dewey, *The Later Works,* vol. 11, *1935–1937,* ed. Jo Ann Boydston (Carbondale: Southern Illinois University Press, 1987).

3. See John Locke, *Two Treatises of Government,* ed. Peter Laslett (Cambridge: Cambridge University Press, 1960; originally published in 1690).

4. See Jean-Jacques Rousseau, *Political Writings,* 2 vols., ed. C. A. Vaughan (Cambridge: Cambridge University Press, 1915).

5. See, for example, Giovanni Gentile, *Genesis and Structure of Society,* trans. H. S. Harris (Urbana: University of Illinois Press, 1960); also Carl Schmitt, *Vital Realities* (New York: Macmillan, 1932); and Carl Schmitt, *Political Theology,* trans. George Schwab (Cambridge: MIT Press, 1985).

6. See Rawls, *A Theory of Justice.*

7. See, for example, Michael Sandel, *Liberalism and the Limits of Justice* (Cambridge: Cambridge University Press, 1982).

8. See MacIntyre, *After Virtue;* also Charles Taylor, *Sources of the Self* (Cambridge: Harvard University Press, 1989).

9. See the account in Alasdair MacIntyre, *Whose Justice? Which Rationality?* (Notre Dame: University of Notre Dame Press, 1988).

10. Taylor, *Sources of the Self.*

11. The quotation appears in David Rasmussen, ed., *Universalism vs. Communitarianism: Contemporary Debates in Ethics* (Cambridge: MIT Press, 1990), 6. In recent public discussion, Rawls has also discussed the culture-boundness of his own conception of justice.

12. See critiques of this universalizing tendency in Richard J. Bernstein, *The New Constellation* (Cambridge: MIT Press, 1992); Derrida, *Writing and Difference,* especially the essay "Violence and Metaphysics"; Michel Foucault, *The Foucault Reader,* ed. Paul Rabinow (New York: Pantheon Books, 1984); and Levinas, *Reader.*

13. John Dewey, *The Public and Its Problems* (Chicago: Henry Holt, 1927), 158.

14. Glendon, *Rights Talk,* 109.

15. *Mozert v. Hawkins County Bd. of Education,* 827F. 2d 1058 (6th Cir. 1987).

16. William Galston, "Two Concepts of Liberalism," *Ethics* 105, no. 3 (1995): 525.

17. Ibid., 529.

18. See Rawls, *Political Liberalism,* 154; see also Stephen Macedo, "Liberal Civic Education and Religious Fundamentalism: The Case of God v. John Rawls?" *Ethics* 105, no. 3 (1995): 473.

19. The quotation is used in Berlin, *Four Essays on Liberty,* 172. Although Berlin doesn't mention the writer, it is Joseph Schumpeter. See the brief discussion in Sandel, ed., *Liberalism and Its Critics,* 8.

20. For a comprehensive description of what happened to the communities involved, see Stephen Bates, *Battleground: One Mother's Crusade, the Religious Right, and the Struggle for Our Classrooms* (New York: Poseidon Press, 1993).

21. See Mary Catherine Bateson, *Composing a Life* (New York: Plume, 1990).

22. Gaston Bachelard, *The Politics of Space,* trans. Maria Jolas (New York: Orion Press, 1964), 7.

23. Ibid.

24. Weil, *Reader,* 315.

25. Berlin, *Four Essays on Liberty,* 121–122.

26. See especially section III, "Of Individuality, as One of the Elements of Well-Being," in Mill, *"On Liberty" and "Utilitarianism,"* 64.

27. Ibid., 68. Several liberal theorists today make the point about liberal virtues explicitly. See, for example, William Galston, *Liberal Purposes* (Cambridge: Cambridge University Press, 1991); Stephen Macedo, *Liberal Virtues* (Oxford: Clarendon, 1990); and Iris Marion Young, "Mothers, Citizenship, and Independence: A Critique of Pure Family Values," *Ethics* 105, no. 3 (1995): 535–556.

28. Mill, *"On Liberty" and "Utilitarianism,"* 87.

29. See Fareed Zakaria, "The Rise of Illiberal Democracy," *Foreign Affairs,* Nov./Dec. 1997, 22–43.

30. See the discussion in Zakaria, ibid.; also Robert D. Kaplan, "Was Democracy Just a Moment?" *Atlantic Monthly,* Dec. 1997, 55–80. See also a persuasive argument on the need for cultivating liberal rationality in Charles Taylor, "Atomism," in *Communitarianism and Individualism,* ed. Shlomo Avineri and Avner de-Shalit (Oxford: Oxford University Press, 1992), 29–50.

31. See Alan Ryan, *John Dewey and the High Tide of American Liberalism* (New York: W. W. Norton, 1995); Robert B. Westbrook, *John Dewey and American Democracy* (Ithaca: Cornell University Press, 1991).

32. John Dewey, *Democracy and Education* (New York: Macmillan, 1916), 87.

33. Mill was ambivalent on this. He clearly advocated government's responsibility to coerce parents to educate their children, but he feared that state-run schools would be dull and discourage originality. See Mill, *"On Liberty" and "Utilitarianism,"* 121–124.

34. For a powerful argument on including the traditional interests of women in the school curriculum, see the work of Jane Roland Martin: "Excluding Women from the Educational Realm," *Harvard Educational Review* 52, no. 2 (1982): 133–148; "Bringing Women into Educational Thought," *Educational Theory* 34, no. 4 (1984): 341–354; *Reclaiming a Conversation;* and *The Schoolhome.*

35. See Hannah Arendt, *The Human Condition* (Chicago: University of Chicago Press, 1958). See also the worry expressed even earlier by John Dewey in his chapter on the eclipse of the public in *The Public and Its Problems.* See, too, contemporary concerns in Robert Bellah, Richard Madsen, William M. Sullivan, Ann Swidler, and Steven M. Tipton, *Habits of the Heart* (Berkeley: University of California Press, 1985).

36. Arendt, *Human Condition,* 52.

37. On the domination of spectacle in our lives see Jean Baudrillard, *Fatal Strategies,* trans. Philip Beitchmen and W. G. J. Niesluchowski, ed. Jim Fleming (New York: Semiotext(c), 1990).

38. See Rawls, *Political Liberalism,* for what might be involved in comprehensive liberalism.

39. See Berlin's comments on pluralism of goods in *Four Essays on Liberty,* 167–172.

40. See the fascinating discussion of Darrow's behaviorist views in Kevin Tierney, *Darrow: A Biography* (New York: Thomas Y. Crowell, 1979).

41. Jonathan Kozol, *Savage Inequalities* (New York: Crown, 1991).

42. For a view that says exactly this, see Mortimer J. Adler, *The Paideia Proposal* (New York: Macmillan, 1982); for one that makes some allowances within a common core curriculum, see E. D. Hirsch, *Cultural Literacy: What Every American Needs to Know* (Boston: Houghton Mifflin, 1987).

Chapter 5. A Relational Self

1. Rawls, *A Theory of Justice,* 565.

2. Bateson, *Composing a Life,* 16–17.

3. Okin, "Reason and Feeling," 248.

4. See Immanuel Kant, "Perpetual Peace," in *Kant on History,* ed. Lewis White Beck (Indianapolis: Bobbs-Merrill, 1963).

5. Taylor, *Sources of the Self,* 36.

6. Socialized individuality is recognized by, for example, Isaiah Berlin. See *Four Essays On Liberty.*

7. MacIntyre, *After Virtue,* 33.

8. See ibid.

9. Martin Heidegger, "Letter on Humanism," in *Basic Writings,* ed. David Farrell Krell (New York: Harper & Row, 1977), 228.

10. See Amy Mullin, "Selves, Diverse and Divided: Can Feminists Have Diversity without Multiplicity?" *Hypatia* 10, no. 4 (1995): 1–31. Mullin names Friedrich Nietzsche, William James, George Herbert Mead, John Stuart Mill, Donna Haraway, and Chantal Mouffe as representative of this position. For a powerful description of multiple selves in a colonial situation, see Pradeep Ajit Dhillon, *Multiple Identities* (Frankfurt am Main: Peter Lang, 1994).

11. Diana T. Meyers, *Self, Society, and Personal Choice* (New York: Columbia University Press, 1989), 65.

12. See Baudrillard, *Fatal Strategies.*

13. Both Emmanuel Levinas and Martin Buber take this position. See Levinas, *Reader,* for a discussion of both his and Buber's views.

14. See Walter J. Freeman, *Societies of Brains* (Hillsdale, N.J.: Lawrence Erlbaum, 1995).

15. Theodor Adorno, quoted in Bernstein, *The New Constellation,* 81.

16. Hannah Arendt in a letter to Karl Jaspers. Quoted in Alan Ryan, "Dangerous Liaison," review of Hannah Arendt and Martin Heidegger, *New York Review of Books,* 11 Jan. 1996, 22–26.

17. See Jacques Hadamard, *The Psychology of Invention in the Mathematical Field* (New York: Dover, 1954).

18. Meyers, *Self, Society, and Personal Choice,* 7.

19. See Carol Shields, *The Stone Diaries* (New York: Penguin Books, 1995).

20. See Miller, *For Your Own Good.*

21. The latest biographies suggest that Orwell did not entirely escape the sadistic legacy of his school days. It is said that he exhibited a sadistic streak of his own with women. See Jeffrey Meyers, *Orwell: Wintry Conscience of a Generation* (New York: Norton, 2000).

22. See Baudrillard, *Fatal Strategies*.

23. See Sandel, *Liberalism and the Limits of Justice*.

24. See Immanuel Kant, *Grounding for the Metaphysics of Morals,* trans. James W. Ellington (Indianapolis: Hackett, 1981; originally published in 1785).

25. Alasdair MacIntyre shows quite convincingly how the categorical imperative as stated by Kant might be used, without logical inconsistency, in this way. See MacIntyre, *After Virtue*.

26. Marcel Proust, *Remembrance of Things Past,* vol. 1, *Swann's Way,* trans. C.K. Scott Moncrief and Terence Kilmartin (New York: Random House, 1981), 208.

27. Meyers, *Self, Society, and Personal Choice*.

28. From Walt Whitman, "Song of Myself," in *Complete Poetry and Selected Prose* (New York: Library of America, 1982), 87.

29. Meyers, *Self, Society, and Personal Choice*, 35.

30. See John Dewey, *A Common Faith* (New Haven: Yale University Press).

Interlude

1. See Peter Nathanielsz, *Life in the Womb* (New York: Promethean Press, 1999).

2. Ruddick, *Maternal Thinking*, 87.

3. Theodore Zeldin, *An Intimate History of Humanity* (New York: Harper Collins, 1994), 393.

4. There are many sources that document this feminist claim. See, for example, Eva Feder Kittay and Diana T. Meyers, eds., *Women and Moral Theory* (Totowa, N.J.: Rowman & Littlefield, 1987). See also Mary Ann Oakley, *Elizabeth Cady Stanton* (Old Westbury, N.Y.: The Feminist Press, 1972).

5. Anne Morrow Lindbergh, *Gift from the Sea* (New York: Random House, 1955), 124–125.

6. Edward S. Casey, *The Fate of Place* (Berkeley: University of California Press, 1997), xiv.

7. Bernhard Schlink, *The Reader,* trans. Carol Brown Janeway (New York: Vintage International, 1997), 141.

Chapter 6. Bodies

1. Pearl S. Buck, *The Exile* (New York: Triangle Books, 1936), 134–135.

2. Ibid., 135.

3. Adrienne Rich, *Of Woman Born* (New York: W.W. Norton, 1976), 36.

4. Ibid.

5. Shields, *The Stone Diaries,* 260.

6. Ibid., 261.

7. Pearl S. Buck, *Fighting Angel* (New York: John Day, 1936), 298–299.

8. Doris Lessing, *The Diaries of Jane Somers* (New York: Vintage Books, 1984), 235.

9. See accounts in Mary Daly, *Pure Lust* (Boston: Beacon Press, 1984); also

Simone de Beauvoir, *The Second Sex,* trans. H. M. Parshley (New York: Bantam Books, 1961).

10. Ruddick, *Maternal Thinking,* 214.

11. Weil, *Reader,* 315.

12. See Lectures VI and VII, "The Sick Soul," in William James, *The Varieties of Religious Experience* (New York: Mentor 1958; originally published in 1902).

13. Weil, *Reader,* 317.

14. For an elaboration on the centrality of the word and the face-to-face, see Levinas, *Reader.*

15. See, again, Butler, *The Way of All Flesh.*

16. Ruddick, *Maternal Thinking,* 42.

17. See Michel Foucault, *Discipline and Punish: The Birth of the Prison,* trans. Alan Sheridan (New York: Vintage Books, 1977).

18. Jill Paton Walsh, *Knowledge of Angels* (New York: Bantam Books, 1995), 172–173.

19. See, for example, the account of Schiller's *Letters on the Aesthetic Education of Man* in Bernard Yack, *The Longing for Total Revolution* (Berkeley: University of California Press, 1992).

20. Zeldin, *An Intimate History of Humanity,* 94.

21. Jim Lee, *Jim Lee's Cookbook* (New York: Harper & Row, 1968), 267–268.

22. See the discussion in Edward S. Casey, *Getting Back into Place* (Bloomington: Indiana University Press, 1993).

23. Psychologists once believed that infants were born with two innate fears: of loud noises and of falling. The current prevailing view is that all emotion (as it is now defined) has a cognitive element. "Fear" of falling in infants is now described as a precursor to the actual emotion of fear. See L. Alan Sroufe, *Emotional Development: The Organization of Emotional Life in the Early Years* (Cambridge: Cambridge University Press, 1996).

24. See descriptions of sensory-motor development in Jean Piaget, *Genetic Epistemology* (New York: Columbia University Press, 1970); and Jean Piaget, *Biology and Knowledge* (Chicago: University of Chicago Press, 1971).

25. Casey, *Getting Back into Place,* 35.

26. Ernest Becker, *Escape from Evil* (New York: Free Press, 1975), 1.

27. C. S. Lewis, *The Problem of Pain* (New York: Macmillan, 1962), 115–116.

28. C. S. Lewis, *A Grief Observed* (Toronto: Bantam Books, 1976), 50.

29. Augustine, "On Free Will," in *Augustine: Earlier Writings,* ed. John H. S. Burleigh (Philadelphia: Westminster Press, 1953), 3.9.26.

30. See G. W. Leibniz, *Theodicy,* trans. E. M. Huggard (New Haven: Yale University Press, 1952).

Chapter 7. Places, Homes, and Objects

1. See Casey, *Getting Back into Place.*

2. These are the first two lines of Robert Browning, "Home-Thoughts from Abroad," in *English Poetry,* vol. 11 (New York: P. F. Collier, 1910), 1110.

3. This is the first stanza of Thomas Hood, "I Remember, I Remember," in *Immortal Poems of the English Language,* ed. Oscar Williams (New York: Pocket Books, 1975), 346.

4. Rebecca A. Reynolds, *Bring Me the Ocean* (Acton, Mass.: Vander Wyk & Burnham, 1995), xi.

5. Casey, *Getting Back into Place,* 314.

6. Bachelard, *The Poetics of Space,* 47.

7. Pauline Whitesinger, a Navajo, is quoted in Casey, *Getting Back into Place,* 37.

8. See Keith Basso, *Wisdom Sits in Places* (Albuquerque: University of New Mexico Press, 1996).

9. Casey, *Getting Back into Place,* 37.

10. The Birkerts's quote is in ibid.

11. Paul Theobald, *Teaching the Commons* (Boulder: Westview Press, 1997), 1.

12. See the comments on this heritage in Caputo, *Against Ethics.*

13. See A. S. Neill, *Summerhill* (New York: Hart, 1960), 100.

14. Taylor, *Sources of the Self,* 495.

15. Ibid., x.

16. See MacIntyre, *Whose Justice? Which Rationality?*

17. Baudrillard, *Fatal Strategies,* 13.

18. Historians have sometimes made such claims. See, for example, Henry Nash Smith, *Virgin Land: The American West as Symbol and Myth* (Cambridge: Harvard University Press, 1971).

19. Casey, *Getting Back into Place,* 120.

20. Bachelard, *Poetics of Space,* 4.

21. Bachelard, ibid., for example, devotes a whole chapter to corners.

22. See T. H. White, *Mistress Masham's Repose* (New York: G. P. Putnam's Sons, 1946).

23. Bachelard, *Poetics of Space,* 4–5.

24. Ibid., 67.

25. Ibid., 68.

26. Casey, *Getting Back into Place,* 173.

27. Ibid.

28. Buck, *The Exile,* 65.

29. See Kozol, *Savage Inequalities;* also Jonathan Kozol, *Amazing Grace* (New York: Harper, 1996).

30. Casey, *Getting Back into Place,* 175–176. The expression "stars of our life" is from Merleau-Ponti.

31. Wendell Berry, *Another Turn of the Crank* (Washington, D.C.: Counterpoint, 1995), 55.

32. The "biophilia hypothesis" as advanced by Edward O. Wilson has roots in sociobiology, but other perspectives put greater emphasis on development and culture. See Edward O. Wilson, *Biophilia* (Cambridge: MIT Press, 1999).

33. See Eliot Wigginton, ed., *The Foxfire Book* (Garden City, N.Y.: Anchor

Books, 1972); also Eliot Wigginton, *Sometimes a Shining Moment: The Foxfire Experience* (Garden City, N.Y.: Anchor Books, 1986).

34. In addition to the works already cited, see Annie Dillard, *Pilgrim at Tinker Creek* (New York: Harper & Row, 1974); George Perkins Marsh, *Man and Nature,* ed. David Lowenthal (Cambridge: Harvard University Press, 1974; originally published in 1864); Gary Paul Nabhan and Stephen Trimble, *The Geography of Childhood* (Boston: Beacon Press, 1994); Robert Michael Pyle, *The Thunder Tree* (Boston: Houghton Mifflin, 1993); Scott Russell Sanders, *Staying Put: Making a Home in a Restless World* (Boston: Beacon Press, 1993); Gary Snyder, *The Practice of the Wild* (San Francisco: North Point Press, 1990). People living and loving their own regions must gather their own material. As a resident of the Jersey shore, my favorites include Henry Charlton Beck, *Forgotten Towns of Southern New Jersey* (New Brunswick, N.J.: Rutgers University Press, 1961); Henry Charlton Beck, *The Jersey Midlands* (New Brunswick, N.J.: Rutgers University Press, 1962); Rachel Carson, *The Edge of the Sea* (Boston: Houghton Mifflin, 1955); John McPhee, *The Pine Barrens* (New York: Noonday Press, 1988); David J. Seibold and Charles J. Adams III, *Shipwrecks and Legends 'Round Cape May* (Reading: Exeter House, 1987); David J. Seibold and Charles J. Adams III, *Cape May Ghost Stories,* 1988 (Reading: Exeter House, 1987); Frank R. Stockton, *Stories of New Jersey* (New Brunswick, N.J.: Rutgers University Press, 1961). In addition to local stories, seashore residents are likely to collect sea stories and poetry from all over the world. Thus education for a particular place expands to encompass much of the world.

35. Walt Whitman, "A Child Went Forth," from *Leaves of Grass,* in *Complete Poetry and Collected Prose* (New York: Library of America, 1982), 138.

36. The lines are from Marianne Moore, "Silence," in *Complete Poems* (New York: Macmillan/Viking, 1967), 91.

37. Zeldin, *An Intimate History of Humanity,* 393.

Chapter 8. Attentive Love

1. See Ruddick, *Maternal Thinking.*

2. Ibid., 17–23.

3. Many experts on infant–maternal relations support this position. The classic is, of course, Benjamin Spock, *Dr. Spock's Baby and Child Care,* 7th ed. (New York: Pocket Books, 1998). The connection between responsive parenting styles and both cognitive development and general well-being is also well-documented. See Diana Baumrind, "Current Patterns of Parental Authority," *Developmental Psychology Monographs* 4, no. 1 (1971): entire issue; Diana Baumrind, "The Development of Instrumental Competence through Socialization," in *Minnesota Symposium on Child Psychology,* ed. A. Pick (Minneapolis: University of Minnesota Press, 1973); Diana Baumrind, "Raising Competent Children," in *Child Development Today and Tomorrow,* ed. William Damon (San Francisco: Jossey-Bass, 1989), 349–378. The willingness of adults to respond and of infants to call forth the response is discussed also by James Q. Wilson, *The Moral Sense* (New York, Free Press, 1993).

4. Buber, *Between Man and Man,* ch. 1; Weil, *Reader,* ch. 6.

5. See Slote, "Caring versus the Philosophers," 25–35; also Michael Slote, "Caring in the Balance," in *Norms and Values,* ed. Joram G. Haber and Mark S. Halfon (Lanham, Md.: Rowman & Littlefield, 1998), 27–36.

6. Again, many references attest to the difficulties. Ruddick, *Maternal Thinking,* is especially eloquent on this.

7. See Hume, *An Enquiry.*

8. See Witold Rybczynski, *Home: A Short History of an Idea* (New York: Viking, 1986).

9. Bachelard, *The Poetics of Space,* 46–47.

10. See Aristotle, *Nicomachean Ethics,* trans. Terence Irwin (Indianapolis: Hackett, 1985).

11. See the discussion of utilitarianism in John Dewey, *Human Nature and Conduct* (New York: Modern Library, 1930).

12. Dewey, *Democracy and Education,* 41.

13. Ibid., 51.

14. Ibid., 51–52.

15. Dewey uses this example in *Experience and Education* (New York: Collier Books, 1963), 36.

16. Walt Whitman, "A Song for Occupations," in *Complete Poetry and Collected Prose* (New York: Library of America, 1982), 89–99.

17. Ibid., 90.

18. Dewey, *The Public and Its Problems,* 184.

19. See Bachelard, *Poetics of Space.*

20. See Herbert Kliebard, *The Struggle for the American Curriculum* (New York: Routledge, 1995), 98, or the original National Education Association, *Cardinal Principles of Secondary Education: A Report of the Commission on the Reorganization of Secondary Education* (Washington, DC: U.S. Government Printing Office, 1918), 10–11. The report was largely the work of Clarence Kingsley, a mathematics teacher.

21. See, for example, Louis Crozier, ed., *Casualties of Privilege* (Washington, D.C.: Avocus, 1991).

Chapter 9. Achieving Acceptability

1. Ruddick, *Maternal Thinking,* ch. 5.

2. Wendell Berry, *The Unsettling of America* (San Francisco: Sierra Club, 1977), 111.

3. See, for example, W. S. Grolnick and R. M. Ryan, "Parent Styles Associated with Children's Self-Regulation and Competence in Schools," *Journal of Educational Psychology* 81, no. 2 (1989): 143–154; also, W. S. Grolnick, R. M. Ryan, and E. L. Deci, "Inner Resources for School Achievement: Motivational Mediators of Children's Perceptions of Their Parents," *Journal of Educational Psychology* 83, no. 4 (1991): 508–517. See, also, Baumrind, "Current Patterns of Parental Authority"; Baumrind, "The Development of Instrumental Competence through Socialization"; and Baumrind, "Raising Competent Children."

4. Angela Potter, "Say No and Stick with It," *Asbury Park Press,* 15 July 1991, D1. The book reviewed is Cynthia Whitham, *"The Answer Is No! Saying It and Sticking to It* (New York: Perspective, 1999).

5. See Rawls, *A Theory of Justice.*

6. John Lahr, "The Demon-Lover," *The New Yorker,* 31 May 1999, 70.

7. Theology is loaded with such references. See the discussion in John Hick, *Evil and the God of Love* (New York: Harper & Row, 1977), esp. 172–176. See also Nel Noddings, *Women and Evil* (Berkeley: University of California Press, 1989). Paul Ricoeur has said that literal interpretation of the Adamic myth coupled with later Augustinian notions of original sin has done incalculable harm to human beings. See Paul Ricoeur, *The Symbolism of Evil* (Boston: Beacon Press, 1967), 239.

8. See the discussion in Harold Kushner, *When Bad Things Happen to Good People* (New York: Schocken Books, 1981).

9. For a more sophisticated discussion, see David Ray Griffin, *Evil Revisited* (Albany: State University of New York Press, 1991); also, Hick, *Evil and the God of Love.*

10. Ibid.

11. See Sharon Lamb, *The Trouble with Blame* (Cambridge: Harvard University Press, 1996).

12. Ibid., 186.

13. For a moving account of one child's suffering and blaming herself, see Francine Cournos, *City of One* (New York: Norton, 1999).

14. There are many references to support this position. See, for example, Mark Lepper, "Intrinsic and Extrinsic Motivation in Children: Detrimental Effects of Superfluous Social Controls," in *Aspects of the Development of Competence,* ed. W. Andrew Collins (Hillsdale, N.J.: Lawrence Erlbaum, 1981), 155–214.

15. See Alfie Kohn, *No Contest: The Case against Competition* (Boston: Houghton Mifflin, 1992); also Alfie Kohn, *Punished by Rewards: The Trouble with Gold Stars, Incentive Plans, As, Praise, and Other Bribes* (Boston: Houghton Mifflin, 1993).

16. Here I wish to remind readers of Diana Meyers's very useful emphasis on reflection, analysis, and commitment. Although I find the concept of autonomy too confused to be useful, Meyers's criteria remain useful in themselves. See her *Self, Society, and Personal Choice.*

17. The traditional principle is *lex talionis,* "an eye for an eye, a tooth for a tooth." The classic treatise is Hugo Grotius, *De Jure Belli ac Pacis* (Oxford: Oxford University Press, 1925; originally published in 1625).

18. Michael Ruse, *Mystery of Mysteries: Is Evolution a Social Construction?* (Cambridge: Harvard University Press, 1999), 212, see also 201–202 and 212–213.

19. See, for example, Diana Baumrind, *Child Maltreatment and Optimal Caregiving in Social Contexts* (New York: Garland, 1995).

Chapter 10. Learning to Care

1. James Gilligan, *Violence* (New York: G. P. Putnam's Sons, 1992), 5.

2. See Lamb, *The Trouble with Blame.*

3. See Immanuel Kant, *The Metaphysics of Morals,* part II: *The Doctrine of Virtue* (New York: Harper & Row, 1964), 44–45.

4. See Noddings, *Women and Evil;* on the generally pernicious effects of competition in schools, see Kohn, *No Contest.*

5. On the positive effects of participation in sports and healthy competition, see Ronald M. Jeziorski, *The Importance of School Sports in American Education and Socialization* (Lanham, Md.: University Press of America, 1994).

6. Many books are now available to help schools with this task. See, for example, Robin K. Berson, *Young Heroes in World History* (Westport, Conn.: Greenwood Press, 1999); Ruth Charney, *Teaching Children to Care* (Greenfield, Minn.: Northeast Foundation for Children, 1992); Jonathan Cohen, ed., *Educating Minds and Hearts* (New York: Teachers College Press, 1999); John Graham, *It's Up to Us* (Langley, Wash.: Giraffe Project, 1999). See also a series of books on social and emotional development available through the Developmental Studies Center in Oakland, California.

7. See Michael Slote, *From Morality to Virtue* (New York: Oxford University Press, 1992).

8. See Hume, *An Enquiry Concerning the Principles of Morals,* esp. 98–99.

9. But see the literature on process theology. Here the self is sometimes construed as a permanent record in the mind of God and, hence, in that sense immortal. The self as relation, as I have described it, may also survive the death of the organism but only so long as living persons can remember or a written record preserve it. One might also sacrifice one's life for honor or prestige, thus enhancing the self. On process philosophy and theology, see David Ray Griffin, *God, Power, and Evil: A Process Theodicy* (Philadelphia: Westminster Press, 1976); Charles Hartshorne, *Man's Vision of God* (Chicago: Willett, Clark, 1941); Charles Hartshorne, *The Divine Relativity* (New Haven: Yale University Press, 1948); Alfred North Whitehead, *Process and Reality* (New York: Free Press, 1967).

10. Recall Socrates's ambivalence about the nature of virtue in the *Meno.* Is virtue knowledge? Is it a gift from the gods? Can it be taught?

11. See, for example, William Bennett, ed., *The Book of Virtues* (New York: Simon & Schuster, 1993). Most character education programs use stories. Some go beyond mere inspiration and encourage critical thinking, however, and some of these use great literature to provide moral lessons. See, for example, Susan Resneck Parr, *The Moral of the Story* (New York: Teachers College Press, 1982); also, Matthew Lipman, *Thinking in Education* (Cambridge: Cambridge University Press, 1991). The best include stories that involve ordinary people in dilemmas not easily solved.

12. The best known program in moral reasoning is found in the work of Lawrence Kohlberg, *The Philosophy of Moral Development* (New York: Harper & Row, 1981).

13. See the teachers' manuals available from the Developmental Studies Center; also the Heartwood Program in Pittsburgh, Pennsylvania.

14. David Noble, *A World without Women* (Oxford: Oxford University Press, 1992), 280.

15. Ibid, 281.

16. See Philip W. Jackson, *Untaught Lessons* (New York: Teachers College Press, 1992).

17. See Noddings, *Caring,* esp. ch. 5, "Construction of the Ideal."

18. Bernard Williams makes the important point that, in the primitive conceptions of shame and guilt, shame is somewhat narcissistic—turning attention to the one shamed—whereas guilt maintains a focus on the victim and his or her anger. See Bernard Williams, *Shame and Necessity* (Berkeley: University of California Press, 1993).

19. Gilligan, *Violence,* 235. Shame is discussed at length throughout *Violence.* Like Williams, Gilligan argues that shame diminishes the self. In doing so, shame generates violence. If shame becomes guilt, the violence is directed at self. Even other-directed violence may have self-destruction as its motive.

20. See my discussion in *Women and Evil,* 210–214.

21. See Thomas Nagel, "Moral Luck," in *Mortal Questions* (Cambridge: Cambridge University Press, 1979), 24–38; Slote, *From Morality to Virtue;* Bernard Williams, "Moral Luck," in *Moral Luck: Philosophical Papers 1973–1980* (Cambridge: Cambridge University Press, 1981), 20–39.

22. See John Dewey and James Tufts, *Ethics,* vol. 5 of *The Middle Works, 1899–1924* (Carbondale: Southern Illinois University Press, 1978). *Ethics* (1908) was written in collaboration with Tufts. Dewey wrote part II, in which the description of deliberation as dramatic rehearsal appears. He discusses deliberation and imaginative rehearsal again in *Human Nature and Conduct* (New York: Modern Library, 1930).

23. Dewey and Tufts, *Ethics,* 293.

24. See Rawls, *A Theory of Justice.*

25. Dewey and Tufts, *Ethics,* 294.

26. Ibid.

27. See Dewey's Foreword to the Modern Library edition of *Human Nature and Conduct.*

28. Dewey and Tufts, *Ethics,* 303.

Chapter 11. Developing Social Policy

1. Criticisms of B. F. Skinner's *Walden Two* (New York: Macmillan, 1948) included comments such as "a slur upon a name, a corruption of an impulse," "alluring in a sinister way, and appalling, too"—both from the back cover of the paperback edition. Criticism of Edward Bellamy's *Looking Backward* (New York: New American Library, 1960) is discussed (but without much of the passion) by Erich Fromm in his Foreword to the volume.

2. Lisbeth B. Schorr, *Common Purpose: Strengthening Families and Neighborhoods to Rebuild America* (New York: Anchor Books, 1997), 6.

3. A suggestion along these lines is made by Richard A. Posner, *The Problematics of Moral and Legal Theory* (Cambridge: Harvard University Press, 1999).

4. See Linda McNeil, *Contradictions of School Reform* (New York: Routledge, 2000).

5. Bellamy, *Looking Backward*, 98.

6. This debt to the Other preexists our particular obligations to those we actually encounter. See Levinas, "Ethics as First Philosophy."

7. See the Symposium on Kozol's *Savage Inequalities* in *Educational Theory* 43, no. 1 (1993): 1–70.

8. This is a paraphrase from a well known comment of John Dewey's in *The School and Society* (Chicago: University of Chicago Press, 1902), 3. It is often misunderstood, however, to mean that all children should have exactly the same education, identical resources, and same treatments. Dewey clearly did not mean this. He believed that the best parents want for each child what *that* child needs.

9. Strictly speaking, these writers are not care ethicists because human needs and care are not fundamental for them. Their theory of care is God-based. See, for example, Morton T. Kelsey, *Caring: How Can We Love One Another?* (New York: Paulist Press, 1981). See, also, Donald P. McNeill, Douglas A. Morrison, and Henri J. M. Nouwen, *Compassion* (New York: Doubleday, 1983); also William F. Lynch, *Images of Hope* (Notre Dame: University of Notre Dame Press, 1974).

10. See Peter Singer, *Practical Ethics* (Cambridge: Cambridge University Press, 1993); also, Peter Singer, *Rethinking Life and Death* (Melbourne: Text Publishing, 1994). For a sense of the pain and suffering of families, see also Renée R. Anspach, *Deciding Who Lives* (Berkeley: University of California Press, 1993); Helga Kuhse, *Caring: Nurses, Women, and Ethics* (Oxford: Blackwell, 1997); Robert M. Veatch, *Case Studies in Medical Ethics* (Cambridge: Harvard University Press, 1977).

11. The original story appeared in *Newsweek*, "A Family's Breakdown," 10 Jan. 2000. The quotation is from a letter by Elizabeth Levine Wandelmaier, *Newsweek*, 31 Jan. 2000, 15. For a study that documents the suffering of such families, see Ann Hallum, "The Impact on Parents in Caring for an Adult-Age Severely Disabled Child," Ph.D. dissertation, Stanford University, 1989.

12. For an excellent discussion of nurses' attitudes on meeting the expressed needs of sufferers, see Kuhse, *Caring*.

13. See Donna Coker, "Enhancing Autonomy for Battered Women: Lessons from Navajo Peacemaking," *UCLA Law Review* 47, no. 1 (1999): entire issue. Coker uses the word "autonomy" but makes it clear (p. 10) that she is not using it in the classical liberal sense. Because the Navajo culture is a "partnership society," autonomy in that context is more nearly like "full partnership." This is compatible with care ethics.

14. Ibid.

15. For an interesting comparison of African morality and Carol Gilligan's

approach to an ethic of care, see Sandra Harding, "The Curious Coincidence of Feminine and African Moralities," in *Women and Moral Theory,* ed. Eva Feder Kittay and Diana T. Meyers (Totowa, N.J.: Rowman & Littlefield, 1987), 296–315.

16. See Coker, "Enhancing Autonomy for Battered Women."

17. See Susan M. Behuniak, *A Caring Jurisprudence* (Lanham, Md.: Rowman & Littlefield, 1999).

18. See Gerald Gamm, *Urban Exodus* (Cambridge: Harvard University Press, 1999).

19. Berry, *Another Turn of the Crank,* 40.

20. Peter Kahn, *The Human Relationship with Nature* (Cambridge: MIT Press, 1999), 225.

21. See Stephen R. Kellert, *The Value of Life* (Washington, D.C.: Island Press, 1996); also Stephen R. Kellert, *Kinship to Mastery: Biophilia in Human Evolution and Development* (Washington, D.C.: Island Press, 1997).

22. For a history of such thinking in the United States, see Steven Selden, *Inheriting Shame: The Story of Eugenics and Racism in America* (New York: Teachers College Press, 1999).

23. See Alex Kotlowitz, "The Execution of Youth," *The New Yorker,* 17 Jan. 2000, 23–24.

24. On the inefficacy of capital punishment as a deterrent, see Albert Camus, "Reflections on the Guillotine," in *Resistance, Rebellion, and Death* (New York: Alfred A. Knopf, 1969), 173–234; see also literature available from Amnesty International. The best evidence for its lack of deterrent value is that countries and states that have abandoned capital punishment do not record an increase in the number of murders.

25. Orwell, *Reader,* 11.

26. See William McFeely, *Proximity to Death* (New York: Norton, 1999).

27. See Camus, "Reflections on the Guillotine."

28. Ibid., 177.

29. Ibid., 233.

30. Russell Baker, "Cruel and Unusual," *New York Review of Books,* 20 Jan. 2000, 13. On the effects of proximity, in particular of getting to know the condemned prisoner, see Helen Prejean, *Dead Man Walking* (New York: Vintage Books, 1996).

31. Camus, "Reflections on the Guillotine," 234.

32. See Tierney, *Darrow.*

33. Apparently, Nathan Leopold, one of the young men whose life was spared by the eloquence of Darrow despite his confessions of guilt for a horrible murder, is evidence for such a possibility. He spent many of his prison years as a hospital assistant.

34. See the argument in Gilligan, *Violence.*

35. Quoted in Baker, "Cruel and Unusual," 13.

Chapter 12. Homes and Homelessness

1. Quoted in Sharon Quint, *Schooling Homeless Children* (New York: Teachers College Press, 1994), 132. The paragraph from Johnson may be found in Joseph Johnson, "Educational Support Services for Homeless Children and Youth," in *Educating Homeless Children and Adolescents,* ed. J. Strong (Newbury Park, Calif.: Sage, 1992), 175. Quint's account is compatible with the approach I suggest; that is, the principal's first priority is to find homes for her homeless students.

2. Year after year this has been the main reason cited by candidates applying for the teacher preparation program at Stanford University School of Education.

3. Negroponte's proposal is discussed in Leo Marx, "Information Technology in Historical Perspective," in *High Technology and Low-Income Communities,* ed. Donald A. Schön, Bish Sanyal, and William J. Mitchell (Cambridge: MIT Press, 1999), 134. See also Nicholas Negroponte, *Being Digital* (Cambridge: MIT Press, 1995).

4. See the other articles in Donald A. Schön, Bish Sanyal, and William J. Mitchell, eds., *High Technology and Low-Income Communities* (Cambridge: MIT Press, 1999).

5. Orr is quoted in Zoe Ingalls, "Notes from Academe," *The Chronicle of Higher Education,* 21 Jan. 2000, B2.

6. This way of thinking, one that gives real-world meaning to terms such as *resurrection, redemption,* and *salvation* is illustrated in liberation theology. In a powerful feminist contribution to liberation theology, see Sharon D. Welch, *Communities of Resistance and Solidarity* (Maryknoll, N.Y.: Orbis Books, 1985). The theme is extended in contemporary ecofeminism. See, for example, Carol J. Adams, ed., *Ecofeminism and the Sacred* (New York: Continuum, 1993).

7. See Robert C. Coates, *A Street Is Not a Home* (Buffalo, N.Y.: Prometheus, 1990).

8. A leading exponent of the view that much mental illness is socially constructed is Thomas Szasz, *The Meaning of Mind* (Westport, Conn.: Praeger, 1996).

9. Dorothea Dix fought a successful battle in several states to overturn attitudes toward "raving maniacs" and secure humane treatment for the mentally ill. See David L. Lightner, *Asylum, Prison, and Poorhouse: The Writings and Reform Work of Dorothea Dix in Illinois* (Carbondale: Southern Illinois University Press, 1999). A popular romanticized view appears in Ken Kesey, *One Flew Over the Cuckoo's Nest* (New York: New American Library, 1984).

10. See Thomas J. Scheff, *Being Mentally Ill* (New York: Aldine De Gruyter, 1999).

11. Scheff argues that much mental illness is rooted in unhappy social relations and that most "flare-ups" of symptoms can be traced to "events in the patients' social environment," ibid., 13.

12. Coates, *A Street Is Not a Home,* 187.

13. Berlin, *Four Essays on Liberty,* 167–168.

14. Berlin uses this language in urging us to face up to the sacrifices made on one good to achieve another; see, for example, ibid., 125.

15. Humanitarians in the nineteenth century worked tirelessly to establish decent institutions for the mentally ill, and these new hospitals or asylums were for the most part a big improvement over previous cruelty and neglect. See Lightner, *Asylum, Prison, and Poorhouse;* also, Nancy Tomes, *The Art of Asylum-Keeping* (Philadelphia: University of Pennsylvania Press, 1994).

16. See Scheff, *Being Mentally Ill.*

17. For a plan of the Hull House buildings, see Linda Kerber, *Toward an Intellectual History of Women* (Chapel Hill: University of North Carolina Press, 1997), 194; see also, Jane Addams, *Twenty Years at Hull House* (New York: Macmillan, 1910).

18. See Schorr, *Common Purpose.*

19. See the account of thirty-four children in Robert V. Bullough, Jr., *Life on the Other Side of the Teacher's Desk: Stories of Children at Risk* (New York: Teachers College Press, 2000).

20. See Edmund S. Phelps, *Rewarding Work* (Cambridge: Harvard University Press, 1997).

21. Organizations such as FINCA (Foundation for International Community Assistance) extend loans to poor women who use them to start small businesses.

22. See Karsten Harries, *The Ethical Function of Architecture* (Cambridge: MIT Press, 1998).

23. Gailard Seamon in the *New York Times,* 17 Nov. 1991. Quoted in Casey, *Getting Back into Place,* 172.

Chapter 13. Deviance

1. This is a continuing theme in the important work of Maxine Greene. See, for example, Maxine Greene, *The Dialectic of Freedom* (New York: Teachers College Press, 1988).

2. See the account of what women scientists faced in the late nineteenth and early-to-middle twentieth centuries in Margaret W. Rossiter, *Women Scientists in America* (Baltimore: Johns Hopkins University Press, 1982).

3. On the pervasive philosophical neglect of activities traditionally associated with women, see Martin, *Reclaiming a Conversation.*

4. On the plight of Hispanic youth in Anglo-oriented schools, see Angela Valenzuela, *Subtractive Schooling* (Albany: State University of New York Press, 1999); on the way working-class boys contribute to their own continued status in the working class, see Paul Willis, *Learning to Labor* (Farnborough, England: Saxon House, 1977).

5. See Scheff, *Being Mentally Ill.*

6. See "The National Drug-Control Strategy," in Jeffrey A. Schaler, ed., *Drugs: Should We Legalize, Decriminalize, or Deregulate?* (Amherst, N.Y.: Prometheus Books, 1998), 32–33.

7. Ibid., 32.

8. The figure appeared in an Associated Press report, *Asbury Park Press,* 23 February 2000, 1.

9. See Steven Wisotsky, *Beyond the War on Drugs* (Buffalo: Prometheus Books, 1990); see also chapters in Schaler, *Drugs,* especially those in part V.

10. Thomas Szasz is one of the best known supporters of the view that drugs should be regarded as private property. See Thomas Szasz, "Drugs as Property: The Right We Rejected," in *Drugs: Should We Legalize, Decriminalize, or Deregulate?,* ed. Jeffrey A. Schaler (Amherst, N.Y.: Prometheus Books, 1998), 181–208.

11. See Paul Hoffman, *The Man Who Loved Only Numbers* (New York: Hyperion, 1998). Hoffman points out that Erdös published more pages of mathematics than any mathematician in history except for Leonard Euler and remained highly productive into old age.

12. Wisotsky, *Beyond the War on Drugs,* 117.

13. Ibid.

14. See Szasz, "Drugs as Property."

15. See Peter Dale Scott and Jonathan Marshall, *Cocaine Politics: Drugs, Armies, and the CIA in Central America* (Berkeley: University of California Press, 1991).

16. Ibid.

17. This suggestion is often made. See, for example, John Braithwaite and Philip Pettit, *Not Just Deserts: A Republican Theory of Criminal Justice* (Oxford: Clarendon Press, 1990). Also see the worries expressed by Scheff in *Being Mentally Ill* and Szasz in "Drugs as Property."

18. See the useful chronology of the drug war provided by Wisotsky, *Beyond the War on Drugs,* 249–256.

19. Ibid., 67–68.

20. Paulo Freire, *Pedagogy of the Oppressed,* trans. Myra Bergman Ramos (New York: Herder & Herder, 1970), 111.

21. Some excellent fiction describes these conditions and the downward spiral of poverty, hopelessness, and drugs. See, for example, the Victorian novels of Anne Perry; and also Caleb Carr, *The Alienist* (New York: Random House, 1994).

22. See David Musto, "Opium, Cocaine, and Marijuana in American History," in *Drugs: Should We Legalize, Decriminalize, or Deregulate?,* ed. Jeffrey A. Schaler (Amherst, NY: Prometheus Books, 1998), 17–28.

23. Ibid., 19.

24. James Q. Wilson, "Against the Legalization of Drugs," in *Drugs: Should We Legalize, Decriminalize, or Deregulate?,* ed. Jeffrey A. Schaler (Amherst, NY: Prometheus Books, 1998), 19.

25. Braithwaite and Pettit, *Not Just Deserts,* 93.

26. On the conditions of prison and prisoners, consult the valuable work of The Women's International League for Peace and Freedom (WILPF) and, of course, Amnesty International.

27. See Braithwaite and Pettit, *Not Just Deserts.*

Chapter 14. The Centrality of Education

1. Bertrand Russell, "Has Religion Made Useful Contributions to Civilization?" in *Why I Am Not a Christian* (New York: Simon and Schuster, 1957), 46.

2. For the use of these components in moral education, see Noddings, *Caring;* and, also, Nel Noddings, *The Challenge to Care in Schools* (New York: Teachers College Press, 1992).

3. See Robert V. Bullough, Jr., *Life On the Other Side of the Teacher's Desk: Stories of Children at Risk* (New York: Teachers College Press, 2000).

4. Carole Boston Weatherford, "An Overnight Solution," *Education Week,* 8 March 2000, 60.

5. See Philippe Ariès, *Centuries of Childhood,* trans. Robert Baldick (New York: Vintage Books, 1962).

6. For vivid accounts of the experience of such lodgers, see the novels of Gene Stratton Porter; also several of those by Willa Cather.

7. The line refers to *home.* It appears in Robert Frost, "The Death of the Hired Man," in *Complete Poems* (New York: Henry Holt, 1949), 53.

8. There are many sources describing the education of girls in eighteenth- and nineteenth-century America. See, for example, Kerber, *Toward an Intellectual History of Women;* Kliebard, *The Struggle for the American Curriculum;* David Tyack and Elisabeth Hansot, *Learning Together: A History of Coeducation in American Public Schools* (New Haven: Yale University Press and Russell Sage Foundation, 1990).

9. See, for example, Barbara M. Cross, ed., *The Educated Woman in America: Selected Writings of Catherine Beecher, Margaret Fuller, and M. Carey Thomas* (New York: Teachers College Press, 1965). Note, especially, the essays of Thomas.

10. On women's views of success, see Gilligan, *In a Different Voice;* see also Bateson, *Composing a Life.*

11. See Kliebard, *Struggle for the American Curriculum,* 98. For the original document, see National Education Association, *Cardinal Principles of Secondary Education.*

12. *Grimms' Fairy Tales,* trans. Mrs. Edgar Lucas, illus. Arthur Rackham (London: Folio Society, 1996), 170.

13. Susan Ohanian, "Goals 2000: What's in a Name?" *Phi Delta Kappan* 81 (2000): 345.

14. Jane Addams, "Immigrants and Their Children," in *Jane Addams on Education,* ed. Ellen Condliffe Lagemann (New York: Teachers College Press, 1985), 162–163.

Concluding Remarks

1. Jean Bethke Elshtain, *Public Men, Private Women* (Princeton: Princeton University Press, 1981), 348.

2. Clement, *Care, Autonomy, and Justice,* 101.

SELECTED BIBLIOGRAPHY

Adams, Carol J., ed. *Ecofeminism and the Saved*. New York: Continuum, 1993.

Addams, Jane. "Immigrants and Their Children." In *Jane Addams on Education*, edited by Ellen Condliffe Lagemann. New York: Teachers College Press, 1985.

————. *Twenty Years at Hull House*. New York: Macmillan, 1910.

Adler, Mortimer J. *The Paideia Proposal*. New York: Macmillan, 1982.

Anspach, Renée R. *Deciding Who Lives*. Berkeley: University of California Press, 1993.

Arendt, Hannah. *The Human Condition*. Chicago: University of Chicago Press, 1958.

Ariès, Phillipe. *Centuries of Childhood*. Translated by Robert Baldick. New York: Vintage Books, 1962.

Aristotle. *Nicomachean Ethics*. Translated by Terence Irwin. Indianapolis: Hackett, 1985.

Augustine. "On Free Will." In *Augustine: Earlier Writings,* edited by John H. S. Burleigh. Philadelphia: Westminster Press, 1953.

Avineri, Shlomo, and Avner de-Shalit, eds. *Communitarianism and Individualism*. Oxford: Oxford University Press, 1992.

Bachelard, Gaston. *The Poetics of Space*. Translated by Maria Jolas. New York: Orion Press, 1964.

Baker, Russell. "Cruel and Unusual." *New York Review of Books,* 20 Jan. 2000, 13.

Basso, Keith. *Wisdom Sits in Places*. Albuquerque: University of New Mexico Press, 1996.

Bates, Stephen. *Battleground: One Mother's Crusade, the Religious Right, and the Struggle for Our Classrooms*. New York: Poseidon Press, 1993.

Bateson, Mary Catherine. *Composing a Life*. New York: Plume, 1990.

Baudrillard, Jean. *Fatal Strategies*. Translated by Philip Beitchman and W. G. J. Niesluchowski. Edited by Jim Fleming. New York: Semiotext(e), 1990.

Baumrind, Diana. *Child Maltreatment and Optimal Caregiving in Social Contexts*. New York: Garland, 1995.

———. "Current Patterns of Parental Authority." *Developmental Psychology Monographs* 4, no. 1 (1971): entire issue.

———. "The Development of Instrumental Competence through Socialization." In *Minnesota Symposium on Child Psychology,* edited by A. Pick. Minneapolis: University of Minnesota Press, 1973.

———. "Raising Competent Children." In *Child Development Today and Tomorrow,* edited by William Damon. San Francisco: Jossey-Bass, 1989.

Beck, Henry Charlton. *Forgotten Towns of Southern New Jersey*. New Brunswick, N.J.: Rutgers University Press, 1961.

———. *The Jersey Midlands*. New Brunswick, N.J.: Rutgers University Press, 1962.

Becker, Ernest. *Escape from Evil*. New York: Free Press, 1975.

Behuniak, Susan M. *A Caring Jurisprudence*. Lanham, Md.: Rowman & Littlefield, 1999.

Bellah, Robert N., Richard Madsen, William M. Sullivan, Ann Swidler, and Steven M. Tipton. *Habits of the Heart*. Berkeley: University of California Press, 1985.

Bellamy, Edward. *Looking Backward*. New York: New American Library, 1960.

Bennett, William, ed. *The Book of Virtues*. New York: Simon & Schuster, 1993.

Berlin, Isaiah. *Four Essays on Liberty*. Oxford: Oxford University Press, 1969.

———. "Two Concepts of Liberty." In *Liberalism and Its Critics,* edited by Michael Sandel. New York: New York University Press, 1984.

Bernstein, Richard J. *The New Constellation*. Cambridge: MIT Press, 1992.

Berry, Wendell. *Another Turn of the Crank*. Washington, D.C.: Counterpoint, 1995.

———. *The Unsettling of America*. San Francisco: Sierra Club, 1977.

Berson, Robin K. *Marching to a Different Drummer: Unrecognized Heroes of American History*. Westport, Conn.: Greenwood Press, 1994.

———. *Young Heroes in World History*. Westport, Conn.: Greenwood, 1999.

Blackham, H. J. *Six Existentialist Thinkers*. New York: Harper & Row, 1959.

Blum, Lawrence. *Moral Perception and Particularity*. Cambridge: Cambridge University Press, 1994.

Blustein, Jeffrey. *Care and Commitment*. Oxford: Oxford University Press, 1991.

Bok, Sissela. *Lying: Moral Choice in Public and Private Life*. New York: Vintage Books, 1979.

Braithwaite, John, and Philip Pettit. *Not Just Deserts: A Republican Theory of Criminal Justice*. Oxford: Clarendon Press, 1990.

Braybrooke, David. *Meeting Needs*. Princeton: Princeton University Press, 1987.

Buber, Martin. *Between Man and Man*. New York: Macmillan, 1965.

———. *I and Thou*. Translated by Walter Kaufman. New York: Charles Scribner's Sons, 1970.

———. *The Way of Response*. Edited by Nahum N. Glatzer. New York: Schocken Books, 1996.

Buck, Pearl S. *The Exile*. New York: Triangle, 1936.

———. *Fighting Angel*. New York: John Day, 1936.

Bullough, Robert V., Jr. *Life on the Other Side of the Teacher's Desk: Stories of Children at Risk*. New York: Teachers College Press, 2000.

Butler, Samuel. *The Way of All Flesh*. Garden City, N.Y.: Doubleday, 1944.

Camus, Albert. "Reflections on the Guillotine." In *Resistance, Rebellion, and Death*. New York: Alfred A. Knopf, 1969.

Caputo, John D. *Against Ethics*. Bloomington: Indiana University Press, 1993.

Carr, Caleb. *The Alienist*. New York: Random House, 1994.

Carson, Rachel. *The Edge of the Sea*. Boston: Houghton Mifflin, 1955.

Casey, Edward S. *The Fate of Place*. Berkeley: University of California Press, 1997.

———. *Getting Back into Place*. Bloomington: Indiana University Press, 1993.

Charney, Ruth. *Teaching Children to Care*. Greenfield, Minn.: Northeast Foundation for Children, 1992.

Clement, Grace. *Care, Autonomy, and Justice*. Boulder: Westview Press, 1996.

Coates, Robert C. *A Street Is Not a Home*. Buffalo, N.Y.: Prometheus, 1990.

Code, Lorraine. *What Can She Know? Feminist Theory and the Construction of Knowledge*. Ithaca. Cornell University Press, 1991.

Cohen, Jonathan, ed. *Educating Minds and Hearts*. New York: Teachers College Press, 1999.

Coker, Donna. "Enhancing Autonomy for Battered Women: Lessons from Navajo Peacemaking." *UCLA Law Review* 47, no. 1 (1999): entire issue.

Cournos, Francine. *City of One*. New York: Norton, 1999.

Cross, Barbara M., ed. *The Educated Woman in America: Selected Writings of Catherine Beecher, Margaret Fuller, and M. Carey Thomas*. New York: Teachers College Press, 1965.

Crozier, Louis, ed. *Casualties of Privilege*. Washington, D.C.: Avocus, 1991.

Daly, Mary. *Pure Lust*. Boston: Beacon Press, 1984.

Damon, William, ed. *Child Development Today and Tomorrow*. San Francisco: Jossey-Bass, 1989.

de Beauvoir, Simone. *The Second Sex*. Translated by H. M. Parshley. New York: Bantam Books, 1961.

Derrida, Jacques. "'Genesis and Structure' and Phenomenology." In *Writing and Difference*, translated and edited by Alan Bass. Chicago: University of Chicago Press, 1978.

Dewey, John. *A Common Faith*. New Haven: Yale University Press, 1934.

———. *Democracy and Education*. New York: Macmillan, 1916.

———. *Experience and Education*. New York: Collier Books, 1963.

———. *Human Nature and Conduct*. New York: Modern Library, 1930.

———. *The Later Works,* vol. 11, *1935–1937.* Edited by Jo Ann Boydston. Carbondale: Southern Illinois University Press, 1987.

———. *Liberalism and Social Action.* New York: G. P. Putnam's Sons, 1935.

———. *The Public and Its Problems.* New York: Henry Holt, 1927.

———. *The School and Society.* Chicago: University of Chicago Press, 1902.

Dewey, John, and James Tufts. *Ethics,* vol. 5 of *The Middle Works, 1899–1924.* Carbondale: Southern Illinois University Press, 1978. Originally 1908.

Dhillon, Pradeep Ajit. *Multiple Identities.* Frankfurt am Main: Peter Lang, 1994.

Dickens, Charles. *Bleak House.* 2 vols. New York: Peter Fenelon Collier, n.d.

Dillard, Annie. *Pilgrim at Tinker Creek.* New York: Harper & Row, 1974.

Diller, Ann. "An Ethics of Care Takes on Pluralism." In *The Gender Question in Education,* edited by Ann Diller, Barbara Houston, Kathryn Pauly Morgan, and Maryann Ayim. Boulder: Westview Press, 1991.

Dunne, Joseph. *Back to the Rough Ground.* Notre Dame: University of Notre Dame Press, 1993.

Eco, Umberto. *Foucault's Pendulum.* Translated by William Weaver. San Diego: Harcourt Brace Jovanovich, 1989.

Elshtain, Jean Bethke. *Public Man, Private Woman.* Princeton: Princeton University Press, 1981.

Foucault, Michel. *Discipline and Punish: The Birth of the Prison.* Translated by Alan Sheridan. New York: Vintage, 1977.

———. *The Foucault Reader.* Edited by Paul Rabinow. New York: Pantheon Books, 1984.

Fraser, Nancy. "Social Justice in the Age of Identity Politics: Redistribution, Recognition, and Participation." Tanner Lecture on Human Values, Stanford University, 1996.

———. *Unruly Practices: Power, Discourse and Gender in Contemporary Social Theory.* Minneapolis: University of Minnesota Press, 1989.

Freeman, Walter J. *Societies of Brains.* Hillsdale, N.J.: Lawrence Erlbaum, 1995.

Freire, Paulo. *Pedagogy of the Oppressed.* Translated by Myra Bergman Ramos. New York: Herder & Herder, 1970.

Frey, Robert G., and Christopher W. Morris, eds. *Value, Welfare, and Morality.* Cambridge: Cambridge University Press, 1993.

Frost, Robert. "The Death of the Hired Man." In *Complete Poems.* New York: Henry Holt, 1949.

Galston, William. *Liberal Purposes.* Cambridge: Cambridge University Press, 1991.

———. "Two Concepts of Liberalism." *Ethics* 105, no. 3 (1995): 516–534.

Gamm, Gerald. *Urban Exodus.* Cambridge: Harvard University Press, 1999.

Gentile, Giovanni. *Genesis and Structure of Society.* Translated by H. S. Harris. Urbana: University of Illinois Press, 1960.

Gentry, Diane Koos. *Enduring Women.* College Station: Texas A & M University Press, 1988.

Gilligan, Carol. *In a Different Voice.* Cambridge: Harvard University Press, 1982.

Gilligan, James. *Violence*. New York: G. P. Putnam's Sons, 1992.

Glendon, Mary Ann. *Rights Talk*. New York: Free Press, 1991.

Gordon, Suzanne, Patricia Benner, and Nel Noddings, eds. *Caregiving*. Philadelphia: University of Pennsylvania Press, 1996.

Graham, John. *It's Up to Us*. Langley, Wash.: Giraffe Project, 1999.

Greene, Maxine. *The Dialectic of Freedom*. New York: Teachers College Press, 1988.

Griffin, David Ray. *Evil Revisited*. Albany: State University of New York Press, 1991.

———. *God, Power, and Evil: A Process Theodicy*. Philadelphia: Westminster Press, 1976.

Grimms' Fairy Tales. Translated by Mrs. Edgar Lucas. Illustrated by Arthur Rackham. London: Folio Society, 1996.

Grolnick, W. S., and R. M. Ryan. "Parent Styles Associated with Children's Self-Regulation and Competence in Schools." *Journal of Educational Psychology* 81, no. 2 (1989): 143–154.

Grolnick, W. S., R. M. Ryan, and E. L. Deci. "Inner Resources for School Achievement: Motivational Mediators of Children's Perceptions of Their Parents." *Journal of Educational Psychology* 83, no. 4 (1991): 508–517.

Grotius, Hugo. *De Jure Belli ac Pacis*. Oxford: Oxford University Press, 1925. Originally 1625.

Hadamard, Jacques. *The Psychology of Invention in the Mathematical Field*. New York: Dover, 1954.

Hallum, Ann. "The Impact on Parents in Caring for an Adult-Age Severely Disabled Child." Ph.D. dissertation, Stanford University, 1989.

Harding, Sandra. "The Curious Coincidence of Feminine and African Moralities." In *Women and Moral Theory*, edited by Eva Feder Kittay and Diana T. Meyers. Totowa, N.J.: Rowman & Littlefield, 1987.

Harries, Karsten. *The Ethical Function of Architecture*. Cambridge: MIT Press, 1998.

Hartshorne, Charles. *The Divine Relativity*. New Haven: Yale University Press, 1948.

———. *Man's Vision of God*. Chicago: Willett Clark, 1941.

Heidegger, Martin. "Letter on Humanism." In *Basic Writings*, edited by David Farrell Krell. New York: Harper & Row, 1977.

Held, Virginia. *Feminist Morality*. Chicago: University of Chicago Press, 1993.

Hick, John. *Evil and the God of Love*. New York: Macmillan, 1966.

Hirsch, E. D. *Cultural Literacy: What Every American Needs to Know*. Boston: Houghton Mifflin, 1987.

Hoffman, Paul. *The Man Who Loved Only Numbers*. New York: Hyperion, 1998.

Hume, David. *An Enquiry Concerning the Principles of Morals*. Indianapolis: Hackett, 1983.

Ingalls, Zoe. "Notes from Academe." *The Chronicle of Higher Education*, 21 Jan. 2000, B2.

Jackson, Philip W. *Untaught Lessons*. New York: Teachers College Press, 1992.

Jaggar, Alison M. *Feminist Politics and Human Nature.* Totowa, N.J.: Rowman & Allanheld, 1983.

James, P. D. *A Taste for Death.* London: Sphere Books, 1986.

James, William. *The Varieties of Religious Experience.* New York: Mentor, 1958. Originally 1902.

Jeziorski, Ronald. *The Importance of School Sports in American Education and Socialization.* Lanham, Md.: University Press of America, 1994.

Johnson, Joseph. "Educational Support Services for Homeless Children and Youth." In *Educating Homeless Children and Adolescents,* edited by J. Strong. Newbury Park, Calif.: Sage, 1992.

Kahn, Peter. *The Human Relationship with Nature.* Cambridge: MIT Press, 1999.

Kant, Immanuel. *Grounding for the Metaphysics of Morals.* Indianapolis: Hackett, 1981. First published in 1785.

———. *The Metaphysics of Morals,* part II: *The Doctrine of Virtue.* New York: Harper & Row, 1964.

———. "Perpetual Peace." In *Kant on History,* edited by Lewis White Beck. Indianapolis: Bobbs-Merrill, 1963.

Kaplan, Robert D. "Was Democracy Just a Moment?" *Atlantic Monthly,* Dec. 1997, 55–80.

Kellert, Stephen R. *Kinship to Mastery: Biophilia in Human Evolution and Development.* Washington, D.C.: Island Press, 1997.

———. *The Value of Life.* Washington, D.C.: Island Press, 1996.

Kelsey, Morton T. *Caring: How Can We Love One Another?* New York: Paulist Press, 1981.

Kerber, Linda. *Toward an Intellectual History of Women.* Chapel Hill: University of North Carolina Press, 1997.

Kesey, Ken. *One Flew Over the Cuckoo's Nest.* New York: New American Library, 1984.

Kittay, Eva Feder, and Diana T. Meyers, eds. *Women and Moral Theory.* Totowa, N.J.: Rowman & Littlefield, 1987.

Kliebard, Herbert. *The Struggle for the American Curriculum.* New York: Routledge, 1995.

Kohlberg, Lawrence. *The Philosophy of Moral Development,* vol. 1. San Francisco: Harper & Row, 1981.

Kohn, Alfie. *No Contest: The Case Against Competition.* Boston: Houghton Mifflin, 1992.

———. *Punished by Rewards: The Trouble with Gold Stars, Incentive Plans, As, Praise, and Other Bribes.* Boston: Houghton Mifflin, 1993.

Kotlowitz, Alex. "The Execution of Youth." *The New Yorker,* 17 Jan. 2000, 23–24.

Kozol, Jonathan. *Amazing Grace.* New York: Harper, 1996.

———. *Savage Inequalities.* New York: Crown, 1991.

Kuhse, Helga. *Caring: Nurses, Women, and Ethics.* Oxford: Blackwell, 1997.

Kushner, Harold. *When Bad Things Happen to Good People.* New York: Schocken Books, 1981.

Lahr, John. "The Demon-Lover." *The New Yorker,* 31 May 1999, 70.

Lamb, Sharon. *The Trouble with Blame.* Cambridge: Harvard University Press, 1996.

Lee, Jim. *Jim Lee's Cookbook.* New York: Harper & Row, 1968.

Leibniz, G. W. *Theodicy.* Translated by E. M. Huggard. New Haven: Yale University Press, 1952.

Lepper, Mark. "Intrinsic and Extrinsic Motivation in Children: Detrimental Effects of Superfluous Social Controls." In *Aspects of the Development of Competence,* edited by W. Andrew Collins. Hillsdale, N.J.: Lawrence Erlbaum, 1981.

Lessing, Doris. *The Diaries of Jane Somers.* New York: Vintage Books, 1984.

Levinas, Emmanuel. *The Levinas Reader.* Edited by Seán Hand. Oxford: Blackwell, 1989.

Lewis, C. S. *A Grief Observed.* Toronto: Bantam, 1976.

———. *The Problem of Pain.* New York: Macmillan, 1962.

Lightner, David L. *Asylum, Prison, and Poorhouse: The Writings and Reform Work of Dorothea Dix in Illinois.* Carbondale: Southern Illinois Press, 1999.

Lindbergh, Anne Morrow. *Gift from the Sea.* New York: Random House, 1955.

Lipman, Matthew. *Thinking in Education.* Cambridge: Cambridge University Press, 1991.

Locke, John. *Two Treatises of Government.* Edited by Peter Laslett. Cambridge: Cambridge University Press, 1960.

Lynch, William F. *Images of Hope.* Notre Dame: University of Notre Dame Press, 1974.

Macedo, Stephen. "Liberal Civic Education and Religious Fundamentalism: The Case of God v. John Rawls?" *Ethics* 105, no. 3 (1995): 473.

———. *Liberal Virtues.* Oxford: Clarendon Press, 1990.

MacIntyre, Alasdair. *After Virtue.* Notre Dame: University of Notre Dame Press, 1981.

———. *Whose Justice? Which Rationality?* Notre Dame: Notre Dame University Press, 1988.

Marsh, George Perkins. *Man and Nature.* Edited by David Lowenthal. Cambridge: Harvard University Press, 1974. Originally 1864.

Martin, Jane Roland. "Bringing Women into Educational Thought." *Educational Theory* 34, no. 4 (1984): 341–354.

———. "Excluding Women from the Educational Realm." *Harvard Educational Review* 52, no. 2 (1982): 133–148.

———. *Reclaiming a Conversation.* New Haven: Yale University Press, 1985.

———. *The Schoolhome: Rethinking Schools for Changing Families.* Cambridge: Harvard University Press, 1992.

Marx, Leo. "Information Technology in Historical Perspective." In *High Technology and Low-Income Communities,* edited by Donald A. Schön, Bish Sanyal, and William J. Mitchell. Cambridge: MIT Press, 1999.

Maslow, Abraham. *Motivation and Personality.* New York: Harper & Row, 1970.

Mayeroff, Milton. *On Caring*. New York: Harper & Row, 1971.

McFeely, William. *Proximity to Death*. New York: Norton, 1999.

McNeil, Linda. *Contradictions of Reform*. New York: Routledge, 2000.

McNeill, Donald P., Douglas A. Morrison, and Henri J. M. Nouwen. *Compassion*. New York: Doubleday, 1983.

McPhee, John. *The Pine Barrens*. New York: Noonday Press, 1988.

Meyers, Diana T. *Self, Society, and Personal Choice*. New York: Columbia University Press, 1989.

Meyers, Jeffrey. *Orwell: Wintry Conscience of a Generation*. New York: Norton, 2000.

Mill, John Stuart. "On Liberty." In *Morality, Harm, and the Law,* edited by Gerald Dworkin. Boulder: Westview Press.

———. *"On Liberty" and "Utilitarianism."* New York: Bantam Books, 1993. Originally 1859.

Miller, Alice. *For Your Own Good*. Translated by Hildegarde and Hunter Hannun. New York: Farrar, Strauss, Giroux, 1983.

Moore, Marianne. "Silence." In *Complete Poems*. New York: Macmillan/Viking, 1967.

Mullin, Amy. "Selves, Diverse and Divided: Can Feminists Have Diversity without Multiplicity?" *Hypatia* 10, no. 4 (1995): 1–31.

Musto, David. "Opium, Cocaine, and Marijuana in American History." In *Drugs: Should We Legalize, Decriminalize, or Deregulate?,* edited by Jeffrey A. Schaler. Amherst, N.Y.: Prometheus Books, 1998.

Nabhan, Gary Paul, and Stephen Trimble. *The Geography of Childhood*. Boston: Beacon Press, 1994.

Nagel, Thomas. "Moral Luck." In *Mortal Questions*. Cambridge: Cambridge University Press, 1979.

Nathanielsz, Peter. *Life in the Womb*. New York: Promethean Press, 1999.

National Education Association. *Cardinal Principles of Secondary Education: A Report of the Commission on the Reorganization of Secondary Education*. Washington, DC: U.S. Government Printing Office, 1918.

Negroponte, Nicholas. *Being Digital*. Cambridge: MIT Press, 1995.

Neill, A. S. *Summerhill*. New York: Hart, 1960.

Noble, David. *A World without Women*. Oxford: Oxford University Press, 1992.

Noddings, Nel. *Caring: A Feminine Approach to Ethics and Moral Education*. Berkeley: University of California Press, 1984.

———. *The Challenge to Care in Schools*. New York: Teachers College Press, 1992.

———. "Moral Obligation or Moral Support." In *Bringing the Hospital Home,* edited by John Arras. Baltimore: Johns Hopkins University Press, 1995.

———. "On the Alleged Parochialism of Caring." *Newsletter on Feminism,* 1991, 96–99.

———. *Women and Evil*. Berkeley: University of California Press, 1989.

Oakley, Mary Ann. *Elizabeth Cady Stanton*. Old Westbury, N.Y.: The Feminist Press, 1972.

Okin, Susan. "Reason and Feeling in Thinking about Justice." *Ethics* 99, no. 2 (1989): 229–249.

Orwell, George. *The Orwell Reader.* New York: Harcourt, Brace, 1956.

Parfit, Derek. *Reasons and Persons.* Oxford: Clarendon Press, 1984.

Parr, Susan Resneck. *The Moral of the Story.* New York: Teachers College Press, 1982.

Phelps, Edmund S. *Rewarding Work.* Cambridge: Harvard University Press, 1997.

Piaget, Jean. *Biology and Knowledge.* Chicago: University of Chicago Press, 1971.

———. *Genetic Epistemology.* New York: Columbia University Press, 1970.

Plato. *The Great Dialogues.* Translated by B. Jowett. Roslyn, N.Y.: Walter J. Black, 1942.

Posner, Richard A. *The Problematics of Moral and Legal Theory.* Cambridge: Harvard University Press, 1999.

Potter, Angela. "Say No and Stick with It." *Asbury Park Press,* 15 July 1991, D1.

Prejean, Helen. *Dead Man Walking.* New York: Vintage Books, 1996.

Proust, Marcel. *Remembrance of Things Past,* vol. 1, *Swann's Way.* Translated by C. K. Scott Moncrieff and Terence Kilmartin. New York: Random House, 1981.

Pyle, Robert Michael. *The Thunder Tree.* Boston: Houghton Mifflin, 1993.

Quint, Sharon. *Schooling Homeless Children.* New York: Teachers College Press, 1994.

Rasmussen, David, ed. *Universalism vs. Communitarianism: Contemporary Debates in Ethics.* Cambridge: MIT Press, 1990.

Rawls, John. *Political Liberalism.* New York: Columbia University Press, 1993.

———. *A Theory of Justice.* Cambridge: Harvard University Press, 1971.

Reverby, Susan. *Ordered to Care.* Cambridge: Cambridge University Press, 1987.

Reynolds, Rebecca A. *Bring Me the Ocean.* Acton, Mass.: Vanderwyk & Burnham, 1995.

Rich, Adrienne. *Of Woman Born.* New York: W. W. Norton, 1976.

Ricoeur, Paul. *The Symbolism of Evil.* Boston: Beacon Press, 1969.

Rinehart, Sue Tolleson. *Gender Consciousness and Politics.* New York: Routledge, 1992.

Rossiter, Margaret W. *Women Scientists in America.* Baltimore: Johns Hopkins University Press, 1982.

Rousseau, Jean-Jacques. *Political Writings.* 2 vols. Edited by C. A. Vaughan. Cambridge: Cambridge University Press, 1915.

Ruddick, Sara. "Maternal Thinking." *Feminist Studies* 6, no. 2 (1980): 342–367.

———. *Maternal Thinking: Toward a Politics of Peace.* Boston: Beacon Press, 1989.

Ruse, Michael. *Mystery of Mysteries: Is Evolution a Social Construction?* Cambridge: Harvard University Press, 1999.

Russell, Bertrand. "Has Religion Made Useful Contributions to Civilization?" In *Why I Am Not a Christian.* New York: Simon and Schuster, 1957.

Ryan, Alan. "Dangerous Liaison." Review of Hannah Arendt and Martin Heidegger. *New York Review of Books,* 11 Jan. 1996, 22–26.

———. *John Dewey and the High Tide of American Liberalism.* New York: W. W. Norton, 1995.

Rybczynski, Witold. *Home: A Short History of an Idea.* New York: Viking, 1986.

Sandel, Michael. *Liberalism and the Limits of Justice.* Cambridge: Cambridge University Press, 1982.

Sanders, Scott Russell. *Staying Put: Making a Home in a Restless World.* Boston: Beacon Press, 1993.

Sartre, Jean-Paul. *Being and Nothingness.* Translated by Hazel E. Barnes. New York: Washington Square Press, 1956.

Schaler, Jeffrey A., ed. *Drugs: Should We Legalize, Decriminalize, or Deregulate?* Amherst, N.Y.: Prometheus Books, 1998.

Scheff, Thomas J. *Being Mentally Ill.* New York: Aldine De Gruyter, 1999.

Schlink, Bernhard. *The Reader.* Translated by Carol Brown Janeway. New York: Vintage International, 1997.

Schmitt, Carl. *Political Theology.* Translated by George Schwab. Cambridge: MIT Press, 1985.

———. *Vital Realities.* New York: Macmillan, 1932.

Schön, Donald A., Bish Sanyal, and William J. Mitchell, eds. *High Technology and Low Income Communities.* Cambridge: MIT Press, 1999.

Schorr, Lisbeth B. *Common Purpose: Strengthening Families and Neighborhoods to Rebuild America.* New York: Anchor Books, 1997.

Scott, Peter Dale, and Jonathan Marshall. *Cocaine Politics: Drugs, Armies, and the CIA in Central America.* Berkeley: University of California Press, 1991.

Seibold, David J., and Charles J. Adams III. *Cape May Ghost Stories.* Reading: Exeter House, 1988.

———. *Shipwrecks and Legends 'Round Cape May.* Reading: Exeter House, 1987.

Selden, Steven. *Inheriting Shame: The Story of Eugenics and Racism in America.* New York: Teachers College Press, 1999.

Seltzer, Richard A., Jody Newman, and Melissa Voorhees Leighton. *Sex as a Political Variable: Women as Candidates and Voters in U.S. Elections.* Boulder: Lynne Reinner, 1997.

Shields, Carol. *The Stone Diaries.* New York: Penguin Books, 1995.

Singer, Peter. *Practical Ethics.* Cambridge: Cambridge University Press, 1993.

———. *Rethinking Life and Death.* Melbourne: Text Publishing, 1994.

Skinner, B. F. *Walden Two.* New York: Macmillan, 1948.

Slote, Michael. "Caring in the Balance." In *Norms and Values,* edited by Joram G. Haber and Mark S. Halfon. Lanham, Md.: Rowman & Littlefield, 1998.

———. "Caring versus the Philosophers." In *Philosophy of Education 1999,* edited by Randall Curren, 25–35. Urbana: Philosophy of Education Society, 2000.

————. *From Morality to Virtue*. New York: Oxford University Press, 1992.

————. "The Justice of Caring." *Social Philosophy and Policy* 15, no. 1 (1998): 171–195.

————. *Morals from Virtues*. Oxford: Oxford University Press, 2000.

Smith, Henry Nash. *Virgin Land: The American West as Symbol and Myth*. Cambridge: Harvard University Press, 1971.

Snyder, Gary. *The Practice of the Wild*. San Francisco: North Point Press, 1990.

Spock, Benjamin. *Dr. Spock's Baby and Child Care*. 7th ed. New York: Pocket Books, 1998.

Sroufe, L. Alan. *Emotional Development: The Organization of Emotional Life in the Early Years*. Cambridge: Cambridge University Press, 1996.

Stephen, James Fitzjames. "The Doctrine of Liberty in Its Applications to Morals." In *Morality, Harm, and the Law*, edited by Gerald Dworkin. Boulder: Westview Press, 1994.

Stockton, Frank R. *Stories of New Jersey*. New Brunswick, N.J.: Rutgers University Press, 1961.

Szasz, Thomas. "Drugs as Property: The Right We Rejected." In *Drugs: Should We Legalize, Decriminalize, or Deregulate?*, edited by Jeffrey A. Schaler. Amherst, N.Y.: Prometheus Books, 1998.

————. *The Meaning of Mind*. Westport, Conn.: Praeger, 1996.

Taylor, Charles. "Atomism." In *Communitarianism and Individualism*, edited by Shlomo Avineri and Avner de-Shalit. Oxford: Oxford University Press, 1992.

————. *Philosophy and the Human Sciences*. Philosophical Papers 2. Cambridge: Cambridge University Press, 1985.

————. *Sources of the Self*. Cambridge: Harvard University Press, 1989.

Temkin, Larry. "Harmful Goods, Harmless Bads." In *Value, Welfare, and Morality*, edited by R. G. Frey and Christopher W. Morris. Cambridge: Cambridge University Press, 1993.

Theobald, Paul. *Teaching the Commons*. Boulder: Westview Press, 1997.

Tierney, Kevin. *Darrow: A Biography*. New York: Thomas Y. Crowell, 1979.

Tomes, Nancy. *The Art of Asylum-Keeping*. Philadelphia: University of Pennsylvania Press, 1994.

Tronto, Joan. *Moral Boundaries: A Political Argument for an Ethic of Care*. New York: Routledge, 1993.

Tyack, David, and Elisabeth Hansot. *Learning Together: A History of Coeducation in American Public Schools*. New Haven: Yale University Press and Russell Sage Foundation, 1990.

Valenzuela, Angela. *Subtractive Schooling*. Albany: State University of New York Press, 1999.

Veatch, Robert M. *Case Studies in Medical Ethics*. Cambridge: Harvard University Press, 1977.

Verducci, Susan. "A Conceptual History of Empathy and the Questions It Raises for Moral Education." *Educational Theory* 50 (2000): 63–80.

Waerness, Kari. "The Rationality of Caring." In *Caregiving*, edited by Suzanne Gordon, Patricia Benner, and Nel Noddings. Philadelphia: University of Pennsylvania Press, 1996.

Walker, Margaret Urban. *Moral Understandings*. New York: Routledge, 1998.

Walsh, Jill Paton. *Knowledge of Angels*. New York: Bantam Books, 1995.

Walzer, Michael. *Just and Unjust Wars*. New York: Basic Books, 1977.

Weatherford, Carole Boston. "An Overnight Solution." *Education Week*, 8 March 2000, 60.

Weil, Simone. *Simone Weil Reader*. Edited by George A. Panichas. Mt. Kisco, N.Y.: Moyer Bell Limited, 1977.

Welch, Sharon D. *Communities of Resistance and Solidarity*. Maryknoll, N.Y.: Orbis Books, 1985.

Westbrook, Robert. *John Dewey and American Democracy*. Ithaca: Cornell University Press, 1991.

White, T. H. *Mistress Masham's Repose*. New York: G. P. Putnam's Sons, 1946.

Whitehead, Alfred North. *Process and Reality*. New York: Free Press, 1967. Originally 1929.

Whitman, Walt. "A Child Went Forth." From *Leaves of Grass*. In *Complete Poetry and Collected Prose*. New York: Library of America, 1982.

———. "A Song for Occupations." In *Complete Poetry and Collected Prose*. New York: Library of America, 1982.

———. "Song of Myself." In *Complete Poetry and Collected Prose*. New York: Library of America, 1982.

Wigginton, Eliot, ed. *The Foxfire Book*. Garden City, N.Y.: Anchor Books, 1972.

———. *Sometimes A Shining Moment: The Foxfire Experience*. Garden City, N.Y.: Anchor Books, 1986.

Williams, Bernard. "Moral Luck." In *Moral Luck: Philosophical Papers 1973–1980*. Cambridge: Cambridge University Press, 1981.

———. *Shame and Necessity*. Berkeley: University of California Press, 1993.

Willis, Paul. *Learning to Labor*. Farnborough, England: Saxon House, 1977.

Wilson, Edward O. *Biophilia*. Cambridge: MIT Press, 1999.

Wilson, James Q. "Against the Legalization of Drugs." In *Drugs: Should We Legalize, Decriminalize, or Deregulate?*, edited by Jeffrey A. Schaler. Amherst, NY: Prometheus Books, 1998.

———. *The Moral Sense*. New York, Free Press, 1993.

Wisotsky, Steven. *Beyond the War on Drugs*. Buffalo: Prometheus Books, 1990.

Wyschogrod, Edith. *Saints and Postmodernism: Revisioning Moral Philosophy*. Chicago: University of Chicago Press, 1990.

Yack, Bernard. *The Longing for Total Revolution*. Berkeley: University of California Press, 1992.

Young, Iris Marion. "Impartiality and the Civic Public." In *Feminism as Critique*, edited by Seyla Benhabib and Drucilla Cornell. Minneapolis: University of Minnesota Press, 1987.

———. *Justice and the Politics of Difference*. Princeton: Princeton University Press, 1990.

———. "Mothers, Citizenship, and Independence: A Critique of Pure Family Values." *Ethics* 105, no. 3 (1995): 535–556.

Zakaria, Fareed. "The Rise of Illiberal Democracy." *Foreign Affairs,* Nov./Dec. 1997, 22–43.

Zeldin, Theodore. *An Intimate History of Humanity*. New York: Harper Collins, 1994.

INDEX

Clement, Grace, 301
Coates, Robert, 257
Coercion, 80, 202, 227, 229, 252–53, 256–59, 277–78, 284
Coherence, 113–14
Coker, Donna, 240
Comfort, 179
Communitarians, 71, 73, 82
Community, 72–74, 159, 174; of order, 165
Competition, 211, 233
Confirmation, 288
Conservatorship, 262
Control, 134–38, 194, 198
Cooper, Anna Julia, 47–48
Critical thinking, 76, 83, 227, 229, 234, 265, 267. *See also* Discipline; Power

Darrow, Clarence, 88, 246
Democracy, 82
Desert, 66, 192–206, 243–47; negative, 194, 196, 201, 203, 208, 279; positive, 203, 204, 205, 206, 213, 280–81. *See also* Pain; Punishment
Deviance, 265–82; changing conceptions of, 266–69; criminal, 279–82
Dewey, John, 2, 73–74, 76, 82, 136, 174, 181–83, 220–22
Dialogue, 287
Diaries of Jane Somers (Lessing), 130
Dickens, Charles, 23, 136
Discipline, 190, 191, 201
Diversity, 75
Drugs, 265, 269–79; and care ethics, 270, 272–73
Duty, 168

Eco, Umberto, 25, 215
Education, 82–84, 181–88, 200–202, 283–300; character, 214; of children, 85, 89, 235; for domestic life, 84, 292–300; and drugs, 276; of homeless, 249, 262; on norms, 267–68; for place, 170–71, 242; of response, 212–20; review boards, 233; rural, 155–56; and vocation, 183–86. *See also* Encounter
Elshtain, Jean Bethke, 301
Empathy, 13–14
Encounter, 3, 12, 21, 49–52, 61, 69, 79, 97–103, 109, 116, 126, 142, 283; and other selves, 176, 177, 211; and place, 156, 157, 172, 174; and self, 157, 159, 160, 210,

286; and spectacle, 159. *See also* Caring; Education
Engrossment, 14; and attention, 19
Equality, 70, 85, 86–89; dilemmas of, 86–89; moral, 86–87; and sameness, 88
Erdös, Paul, 270
Euthanasia, 239

Feminist theory, 57
Fighting Angel (Buck), 127, 130
Flett, Mrs. (*Stone Diaries*), 105, 108, 129, 146
Forgiveness, 219
Foucault, Michel, 137–38
Foxfire, 170
Fraser, Nancy, 54
Freedom, 70, 80, 81, 84, 85. *See also* Liberty
Freire, Paulo, 275
Fundamentalism, 74–77

Galston, William, 75
Gardens, 173–74
Gentry, Diana Koos, 50
Gilligan, James, 209, 218
Glendon, Mary Ann, 34, 74
Goffman, Erving, 95
Growth, 122, 181–88, 207, 228; moral, 220–23
Guilt, 216–18
Gutmann, Amy, 2

Habermas, Jürgen, 73
Hadamard, Jacques, 101
Happiness, 181, 182, 222
Harm, 32–52; legally protected, 33–39. *See also* Caring: pathologies of
Heidegger, Martin, 78, 96, 101, 125, 150
Heine, Heinrich, 93
Held, Virginia, 35, 67–68
Hick, John, 197
Hitler, Adolf, 196
Home, 248–64; as basic need, 248–52; features of, 263; and homelessness, 248–64, 289; and near-homeless, 260–64; and parenting, 300; and school, 290–91
Hood, Thomas, 151
Houses, 161, 162, 174, 180, 248; and housework, 164, 166. *See also* Bachelard, Gaston
Hull House, 259
Hume, David, 24, 179, 212, 222

Compositor: Binghamton Valley Composition, LLC
Text: 10/13 Galliard
Display: Walbaum, Copperplate Condensed, Galliard
Printer and binder: Haddon Craftsmen